THE
THREE
STOOGES
Scrapbook

Moe performs the "telling time" routine for Ted Healy as Larry and Curly look on.

Larry, Moe and Curly-Joe on stage during one of their tours.

THE THREE STOOGES Scrapbook

by

Jeff Lenburg

Joan Howard Maurer

Greg Lenburg

A Citadel Press Book
Published by Carol Publishing Group

A Citadel Press Book
Published by Carol Publishing Group
Citadel Press is a registered trademark of Carol Communications, Inc.

Editorial, sales and distribution, rights and permissions inquiries
should be addressed to Carol Publishing Group, 120 Enterprise Avenue,
Secaucus, N.J. 07094

In Canada: Canadian Manda Group, One Atlantic Avenue, Suite 105,
Toronto, Ontario M6K 3E7

Carol Publishing Group books may be purchased in bulk at special
discounts for sales promotions, fund-raising, or educational purposes.
Special editions can be created to specifications. For details, contact
Special Sales Department, Carol Publishing Group, 120 Enterprise Avenue,
Secaucus, N.J. 07094

Designed by Angelica Design Group Ltd.

Manufactured in the United States of America
ISBN 0-8065-0946-5

25 24 23 22 21 20 19 18 17 16

Library of Congress Cataloging-in-Publication Data

Lenburg, Jeff.
The Three Stooges scrapbook.

Filmography: p. 225
1. Three Stooges films—Miscellanea.
I. Maurer, Joan Howard. II. Lenburg, Greg.
III. Title.
PN1995.9.T5L4 1982 791.43'028'0922 82–12906

To the *Six* Stooges:

Moe Howard
Larry Fine
Jerome "Curly" Howard
Shemp Howard
Joe Besser
and *Joe DeRita*

Three cheers to you *all* for providing us and the
world with over 50 years of memorable antics.

Curly makes a brief gag appearance after his stroke in *Hold That Lion.* (1947). His bit was re-used in
Booty and the Beast (1953).

Acknowledgments

THE AUTHORS WISH to acknowledge the following people who offered us their invaluable assistance in order to make this book an accurate history.

First, we recognize the Stooges themselves, their families, and their many friends: Moe and Helen Howard, Larry Fine, Joe and Ernie Besser, Joe and Jean DeRita, Joe Baker, Charles and Julie Barton, Harold Bell, Edward Bernds, Joey Bishop, Lou Breslow, Dick Brown, Elaine Diamond, Mike Douglas, Morris Feinberg, Jim Hawthorne, Marie Howard, Paul Howard, Joe Kubert, Charles Lamont, Irma Leveton, Jeffrey Scott Maurer, Michael Maurer, Norman Maurer, Ken Murray, Leon Robb, M.D., Dolly Sallin, Clarice and Harry Seiden, Emil and Edith Sitka, Elwood Ullman and Jules White.

Likewise, the authors extend a special tip of the hat to the many dedicated individuals, corporations and facilities that gave us their unselfish cooperation and support; Dorothy Allard, Shirley Fain, Roger Mayer and Herbert S. Nusbaum of Metro-Goldwyn-Mayer, Sal Amico, Martin E. Appel and Ed Foote of WPIX-TV in New York, Dennis Aubrey of Meadowlane Productions, Sarah Baisley, William Hanna and John Michaeli of Hanna-Barbera Productions, Theodore J. Bass of the Department of Treasury (U.S. Savings Bond Division), Ira Steven Behr, Tom Bertino, Ann Best of Don Fedderson Productions, Eddie Brandt and Mike Hawks of Eddie Brandt's Saturday Matinee, Larry D. Bullion of the Three Stooges Deli, Bill Cappello, Ken Carberry and Patricia Gray of KPWR-TV in Bakersfield, John Cawley, Jr., Charles Christ, Sal Cincotta, David Collins, Jill Coplan of National Telefilm Associates, Gordon Cordoza, Mary Corliss of the Museum of Modern Art Film/Still Archives, Chris Costello, Cottage Hospital and its staff, Steve Cox, Charles M. Crane of Williamson-Dickie Apparel Mfg., Carol Cullen and Sam Gill of the Academy of Motion Pictures, Arts and Sciences and Margaret Herrick Library, Gary Deeb, Linda S. Downey of *World of Yesterday*, Glenn Dyckoff of Columbia Pictures' Merchandising Division, Ruth Engelhardt and Susan Shay of the William Morris Agency, Nisan Eventoff and Milt Larsen of the Variety Arts Museum, John Ewaniuk, Maxine Fleckner of the Wisconsin Center for Film and Theater Research, Ira Friedman of the Official Three Stooges Fan Club, Bob Frischman, Tom Hatten, David Hayes, Link Hullar, Rick Ingersol of ICPR, Larry Jensen, George Karamidas of ABC-TV, Bernard Klotz of Carry Case Mfg., Barry Kluger, Kenneth A. Knox, Dave and Joe Koenig, Cleve Landesberg of 20th Century-Fox Television, Mike, Nanci and Bobby Lefebvre, Catherine and John L. Lenburg, John Lenburg, Mark Lipschutz, Los Angeles Hall of Records and its staff, Mark Lyons, Ron Maloney, Leonard Maltin (*The Great Movie Shorts*), Marilyn Miller, Helen Molletta, Motion Picture and Television Hospital, Country Home and Lodge, New York Hall of Records and its staff, Maria Peters of United Artists, Robert Precht, Ron Holder and Marty Silverstein of Sullivan Productions, Lee Prusinski, Julie Radin of NBC-TV Program Research, Ralph Schiller, Zvi Shoubin of WPHL-TV in Philadelphia, Charlotte Shurman, Spencer and Zelda Skretvedt, Glenn Sonnenberg, Ray Strait, Frank Thompson, Omer Tomlinson, Brian Tracy, Brent Walker, Joe Wallison, Thomas J. Watson of CBS-TV, Jerry Weisfeldt of TV Cinema Sales Corp., Greg Wilkin and Jordan Young for excerpts from his Paul "Mousie" Garner interview.

And, saving the best for last, a very *special* thank you to: our agent Dominick Abel for suggesting the idea; author Randy Skretvedt, a true friend and dedicated historian in every sense of the word; and our editor Allan J. Wilson and publisher Lyle Stuart for making this book a reality.

Contents

Foreword 8

Preface 9

Ted Healy 13

Moe Howard 19

Larry Fine 27

Curly Howard 33

Shemp Howard 41

Joe Besser 47

Joe DeRita 53

1. Historical Overview 57

2. Three Stooges Merchandise 101

3. Comic Book Stooges 115

4. Three Stooges on TV 151

5. Three Stooges on Record 179

6. Three Stooges Impersonators 195

7. A Growing Cult 217

Filmography 227

Larry, Moe and Curly.

Foreword

THE HIGHEST HONOR any comedian can be paid is either to win an Academy Award or to have a book written about him.

Well, I have neither won any awards nor had a book written about me. But I am happy to report that three nice people have not only taken the time to get my association with the Three Stooges straightened out but have documented all the wonderful aspects of their careers as well, putting it all down in this book.

I always get mail from fans asking when I first met the Stooges. Well, here is the answer. I recall my first encounter with the Stooges when I was playing in a Broadway show for J.J. Shubert called *The Passing Show of 1932*. Ted Healy's Stooges during this period were Moe, Larry and Shemp and I never dreamed, at the time of our meeting, that our paths would ever cross again.

When Healy got into an argument with Shubert and left, taking Moe and Larry with him, Shemp stayed on with the show. Needing a Stooge replacement, Moe sent for his kid brother Curly to take Shemp's place in the act. Although I never got to know him personally, I felt that Curly was the greatest comedian in show business and a truly wonderful man.

Later, when we were both working at Columbia, Shemp and I became good friends and my wife Ernie and I would often visit him and his wife Gertrude. It was ironic that when Shemp died, in 1955, that I would replace him.

I played my own character in the Stooges comedies and hope to this day that fans appreciated what I did. I always tried to do the best job possible even though, I will admit, the Three Stooges' slapstick wasn't my cup of tea. I never tried to imitate Curly, nor did Shemp. We knew that Curly was a comedian in his own right and we thought we would carry out the third Stooge role the best way we knew how. My only regret is not having been with the Stooges longer, since it was a lot of fun. But fate stepped in when my wife Ernie

became ill and Moe and Larry hired Joe DeRita to take my place.

To me, the Three Stooges are a team that deserve as much recognition as Abbott and Costello and Laurel and Hardy. I swell with pride every time I tell people that I was a member of the Stooges. And adults and children continue to recognize me to this day, in such places as supermarkets and restaurants, even though I am now just voicing Saturday Morning cartoons. I know that if it wasn't for my brief association with the Three Stooges, maybe I would not be recognized today.

Therefore, I am grateful that three beautiful people—Jeff and Greg Lenburg and Joan Maurer—have written this book. It finally gives the Stooges the recognition they have long deserved. I also know that Jeff, Greg and Joan made sure that every fan's request for information was heard by covering such interesting sections of the Stooges' careers as comic books, television, merchandise and record albums. They even compiled a comically hilarious section on Three Stooges impersonators and sniffed out all the technical credits and summaries of every Three Stooges film, television appearance and even solo film appearances by Ted Healy, Shemp Howard, Moe Howard, Curly Howard, Joe DeRita and yours truly.

I know that Jeff and Greg have been collecting information about the Stooges for more than ten years, the same amount of time that I have known them. I consider them family, and know that they have made a conscientious effort to give the fans everything they want.

Of course, Moe's daughter, Joan, who is married to artist-producer Norman Maurer, has my blessings on anything she may want to do. I had great respect for her father, Moe, and know that she is as thoughtful and professional as he was.

So three cheers for those three musketeers of comedy—for without the Three Stooges, the word slapstick would be without a complete definition.

Joe Besser

Preface

THE THREE STOOGES SCRAPBOOK is an official, authorized book on the history of the Three Stooges comedy team and on all aspects of their career.

No amount of time has been spared to separate fact from fiction regarding the Stooges' history and to correct the many erroneous accounts that have appeared in other publications. Most of the data contained herein took over ten years to research and compile. Contracts, scripts, films, letters, tape recordings and other rare materials culled from personal family collections, have been reviewed to help paint an accurate picture of the Three Stooges' monumental career.

In addition, exclusive interviews were conducted over a period of years with Moe Howard, Larry Fine, Joe Besser and Joe DeRita—and with such co-workers as Edward Bernds, Jules White, Elwood Ullman, Norman Maurer, Charles Lamont, Lou Breslow, Emil Sitka and many others.

And, for the insatiable Stooges fan, *The Three Stooges Scrapbook* features the most comprehensive filmography ever compiled, which includes the Stooges' appearances as a team as well as its members' solo film appearances. Detailed summaries, production sidelights and production footnotes highlight each Stooge film listed; technical credits and a complete cast of characters are also included.

The Three Stooges Scrapbook also provides, for the very first time, the history of Stooges merchandise, a review of the team's countless television appearances, an extensive overview of the trio's record album career, and the illustrious history of Three Stooges comic books....And this book would not be complete without giving each of the Stooges his own intimate, biographical sketch.

For fun and laughter, *The Three Stooges Scrapbook* also takes a close look at Three Stooges impersonators. Even the comical antics of Stooges fans are recounted in a chapter on the growing cult of Stooges-enthusiasts and their attempts to glorify their three comic heroes.

It's a review of Three Stooges trivia, history, illustrations and comedy n'yuk-n'yuks at their best.

Moe, in drag, as Joe Besser's screen sister, Birdie, on the set of *Hoofs and Goofs* (1957).

The Three Stooges mugging as they watch Moe's daughter, Joan, reading a Spanish fan magazine.

THE THREE STOOGES Scrapbook

Ted Healy

TED HEALY, the Stooges' original straight man, was born Charles Earnest Lee Nash on October 1, 1896, in Kaufman, Texas. He was educated at Holy Innocents School in nearby Houston and completed his high school education at De LaSalle Institute in New York, where his family had moved in 1908.

According to Moe Howard, young Ted never intended to go on the stage; he had his heart set on being a businessman in Texas. It took Ted over ten years to realize that he wasn't cut out for business life and he finally tried the theatre.

Healy worked hard at polishing his skills as a comedian, coming up with an act as a single in blackface, comprised of imitations and burlesque jokes. The act was entirely impromptu because Ted was unable to memorize his lines. His graphic impersonations of such film luminaries as Ed Wynn, Eddie Cantor and Al Jolson, which he performed at local amateur shows, sparked considerable audience interest, but though the audiences appreciated his talent, he made little headway toward a stable career. He finally abandoned his amateur act and decided to become a full-fledged, professional performer. It was then he changed his name to Ted Healy.

Healy's comically crushed hat, an integral part of his wardrobe, received as many good reviews as his act. A critic for a Baltimore newspaper wrote: "Healy is remembered for the dilapidated hat he always wears, and about which there is much speculation as to whether it is always the same one. Many, as a matter of fact, hang on the wall of his dressing room. Healy's one of the most informal of comedians. His naturalness makes for his success."

Healy became a Broadway star and continued with his solo act through the pre-World War I years. Then, in 1922, he teamed up with a dancer-singer named Betty Brown, whom he later married. They were divorced ten years later in 1932.

Ted wrote all the comedy sketches for the act. Their first performance at a Keith Theatre in Jersey City was a smash success and they were signed to a 46-week contract by the Keith Circuit. Healy's slick-talk and quick-wit made him the highest paid vaudevillian of his day, earning as much as $8,500 a week. Throughout his career, Healy found that it took a particular blend of physical, slapstick comedy for him to induce audience laughter, and he realized he would need "stooges" to take the brunt of his comedy shtick. In 1922, he brought his boyhood pal Moe Howard into his act. Later, Moe, on stage with Ted, heard his brother Shemp's unmistakable laugh coming from the audience; he had Healy call him up on stage, and what resulted was a completely ad-libbed, wild, slapstick performance that had the theatre vibrating with laughter.

In a newspaper interview, Healy once explained the purpose in having stooges: "They're handy guys to have around. If a star's too busy to give an interview, he can send his stooge. And a stooge is a swell alibi. If a star's wife or girl friend says she saw him in Sardi's—a swank Hollywood restaurant—with another doll, he can always say, 'It must've been my stooge.'

"And then a stooge always comes in handy when you feel like throwing something at somebody. Whenever I'm in doubt or feel mixed up, I always hit the nearest stooge. Makes me feel better. Nothing like it. Hollywood's tired of 'yes-men.' That's why the stooge is coming into his own. A stooge is a 'guess-man.' You can never guess what he's going to do next."

With Moe and Shemp, his new Stooges, continuing to fracture audiences, Healy added a third Stooge in 1925—and thus a violinist named Larry Fine started on a long and successful career.

With his trio of Stooges, Healy appeared in a string of Broadway shows, including, *A Night in Spain* and *A Night in Venice*. (Moe Howard did not appear in *A Night in Spain*, nor did Larry. Moe left the team for a year to pursue a career in real estate and Larry had just married Mabel Haney.) Ted Healy and His Stooges made their first screen appearance in the classic 1930's comedy feature *Soup to Nuts*, for 20th Century-Fox. This film was followed by a series of comedies for Metro-Goldwyn-Mayer.

After Larry, Moe and Curly left his act in 1934, Healy appeared in a succession of films for 20th Century-Fox, Warner Brothers and MGM. He was forty-one and under contract to MGM at the time of his death on December 21, 1937. His untimely passing occurred only a few hours after preview audiences had acclaimed his work in the Warner Brothers film *Hollywood Hotel* (1937).

A cloud of mystery still hangs over the cause of Healy's demise. Newspaper accounts attributed his passing to serious head injuries sustained in a nightclub brawl while celebrating the birth of his first child, a son. Conflicting reports stated that the comedian died of a heart attack at his Los Angeles home. Apparently his physician, Dr. Wyant LeMont, refused to claim a heart seizure as the cause and refused to sign the death certificate. Despite his sizable salary, Healy died penniless. In fact, MGM's staff members got together a fund to pay for his burial. Moe later mentioned that comedian Brian Foy of the Eddie Foy family footed a great part of the bill for Healy's funeral.

Two days before his death, Healy visited Moe's wife, Helen, at their Hollywood apartment with the news that Betty (Hickman), his second wife, was expecting. Excited at the prospect of his first child, he told Moe's wife, "I'll make him the richest kid in the world." Moe later related in an interview that Ted had always wanted children and that it was ironic that the birth of his first child came the night of his death. Moe recalled, "He was nuts about kids. He used to visit

Moe and Ted Healy enjoy happier moments during a hunting trip.

Ted relaxes on the set at MGM.

The KING of STOOGES

TED HEALY

Presenting
A NEW EDITION OF
NEW YORKER NITES
Featuring
HOWARD FINE and HOWARD
BONNIE BONNELL   DORRIS ROCHE
BETTY GRABLE   GLEN DALE
VELMA WAYNE and ROY BRADLEY
Music by JED WARNER'S
Columbia Recording Orchestra

Theatre handbill.

Larry rushed into the phone booth to warn Moe that their train was about to leave and saw him crumpled over, crying. Since Moe never showed his emotions, Larry cracked to Curly, "Your brother's nuts. He is actually crying." Moe didn't explain the reason for his sudden emotional breakdown until he got aboard the train.

It was when Howard arrived back in Hollywood that he learned the details of Healy's death from a writer friend, Henry Taylor. He told Moe that Ted had been out drinking at the Trocadero night club on Sunset Strip and an argument broke out between him and three college fellows. Ted had called them every vile name in the book and offered to go outside the club to take care of them one at a time. But once outside, Ted didn't have a chance to raise his fists; the

Ted Healy with real life and MGM film girl friend, Bonnie Bonnell.

our homes and envied the fact we were all married and had children. Healy always loved kids and often gave Christmas parties for underpriviledged youngsters and spent hundreds of dollars on toys."

At the time of Ted's death, the Stooges—Moe, Larry and Curly—were at Grand Central Station in New York preparing to leave for a personal appearance in Boston. Before their departure, Moe called Rube Jackter, head of Columbia Pictures' sales department, to confirm their benefit performance at Boston's Children's Hospital. During the conversation, Jackter told Howard that the night editor of *The New York Times* wanted to talk to him.

Moe phoned the *Times*. The editor, without even a greeting, queried curtly, "Is this Moe?" Howard replied, "Yes." Then the editor asked, "Would you like to make a statement on the death of Ted Healy?" Moe was stunned. He dropped the phone. Then, folding his arms over his head, started to sob. Curly and

Curly, Larry and Moe welcome Ted's sister Marcia Healy to the set of *The Sitter-Downers*.

three men jumped him, knocked him to the ground and kicked him in the head, ribs and stomach. Healy's friend, Joe Frisco, came to the scene and picked him up from the sidewalk and took him to his apartment, where Ted died of what medical officials first claimed was a brain concussion.

According to Moe, even in the heyday of his stage career, Ted refused to put any money away and spent every dime of his salary as fast as he received it. Healy was also a heavy drinker, loved the horses and enjoyed hunting and fishing; his favorite reading matter was race track charts.

Moe had often said that Ted's drinking led to outbreaks of violence, such as the night of his tragic, untimely death. When sober, he was the essence of refinement. Ironically, liquor had killed Ted's father and uncle and ruined the life of his sister, Marcia. As a result, Ted made a pledge when he was very young

never to touch liquor, but the strain of show business life got him started and he was never able to stop.

As a salute to Healy and his many contributions to the world of show business as a comedian, Helen Howard, Moe's wife, wrote the following poem to Healy on one of his birthdays:

> The poet, the scholar, the painter
> Each in their own art reign
> But we don't chant much of the actor
> Who has slowly risen to fame.
> Of the man who uses his talent
> To make us laugh as he'll joke
> While deep in his heart there's an aching
> And 'round his neck is a yoke.
> We lounge in our chair at the theatre
> And laugh at his merriment

16

Then when it is o'er we go to our homes
Feeling light-hearted and content.
But when the curtain drops
And we leave the man who clowns
The greasepaint of smiles is rubbed away
And naught is left but the frowns.
So let's drink a toast to a "comedian"
Who has reached the heights to which not
    many soar
Health, happiness and long life, Ted Healy—
Could we wish you anything more?

Healy, married twice, was survived by his widow, the former Betty Hickman, whom he married on May 15, 1936, and a son, John Jacob (who was baptized in St. Augustine's Church, across from MGM, a week after Healy's death).

The legendary success of Ted Healy can best be explained in a remark the comedian made to actor Jimmy Stewart. "Never treat an audience as customers—always treat them as partners."

Newlyweds Ted Healy and his second wife, Betty Hickman, a UCLA alumna, in a May 16, 1936, photo.

Ted Healy with Mabel Todd in his next to last film appearance, *Hollywood Hotel* (1937).

Moe Howard

Moe Howard, the irascible one with the world-famous bangs, was born on June 19, 1897, in Bensonhurst, New York, a small Jewish community on the outskirts of Brooklyn. His real name was Moses Horwitz (only later did he adopt the name Harry), son of real estate entrepreneur Jennie Horwitz and clothing cutter Solomon Horwitz. Moe was the fourth eldest of the five Howard brothers, all but two, Jack and Irving, having entered show business.

Throughout Moe's career, columnists the world over tried to find words to describe his unusual haircut; buster brown, spittoon, Sugar Bowl, Rose Bowl and Beatle were but a few. His hair color changed with the years from black in his youth to reddish-brown (when he dyed it) to silver-white (its final natural color) during the seventies. He had a marvelous mop of hair until the day he died, but during grammar school days it was the bane of his existence. He was constantly taunted by his classmates over his head of shoulder-length curls—which his mother adored, having always wanted a girl. One day, tired of fighting with his school chums, Moe grabbed a pair of shears and hacked off the curls that encircled his freckled face; the resulting hairstyle was a raggedy version of the one that became his trademark.

Moe was an extremely bright child and at a very young age displayed an ability to quickly memorize anything. This ability carried over into later life, making him a quick study during his acting career. Brother Jack reminisced about his youth and his love for books: "I had many Horatio Alger books and it was Moe's greatest pleasure to read them. They started his imaginative mind working and gave him ideas by the dozen. I think they were instrumental in putting thoughts into his head—to become a person of good character and to become successful."

Moe carried his penchant for learning and a love of the theatre right with him to school, acting in a play he dramatized, directed and appeared in, *The Story of Nathan Hale*. He was fascinated with acting and played hookey to catch the shows at the melodrama theatres during the week. As his interest in the theatre grew, Moe's excellent marks in school began to suffer. In spite of his truancy, he graduated from P.S. 163 in Brooklyn, but he attended Erasmus High School for only two months, never completing his high school education. This greatly disturbed his parents, who were not in favor of his show business aspirations and urged him to go into a profession or some kind of trade. Moe tried to please them and did take a class in electric shop at the Baron DeHirsch Trade School in New York. His interest was short-lived, however, and within a few months he gave up all thought of school to pursue the career that was closest to his heart, show business.

Years later, recalling his lost schooldays, Moe said: "I used to stand outside the theatre knowing the truant officer was looking for me. I would stand there 'til someone came along and then ask them to buy my ticket. It was necessary for an adult to accompany a juvenile into the theatre. When I succeeded I'd give him my ten cents—that's all it cost—and I'd go up to the top of the balcony where I'd put my chin on the rail and watch, spellbound, from the first act to the last. I would usually select the actor I liked the most and follow his performance throughout the play."

His love for show business indelibly fixed, Howard embarked on a film career in 1909 at the Vitagraph Studios in Brooklyn, where he earned his entree into filmmaking by running errands, "for no tips," for such performers as Maurice Costello. As a result of his persistence, Moe soon appeared in films with such silent stars as John Bunny, Flora Finch, Earle William, Herbert Rawlinson and Walter Johnson.

In 1909 Moe met Ted Healy for the first time. They became close friends and together in the summer of 1912 joined Annette Kellerman's aquatic act as diving "girls." This job lasted through the summer.

Then in 1913, Moe and Shemp tried their hand at singing, using the family room at Sullivan's Saloon to gain their much-needed experience in front of an audience. The Howards sang along in a quartet with the talented bass singer of that time, Babe Tuttle, and an Irish tenor, Willie O'Connor. Moe sang baritone, while Shemp sang lead. Together, the foursome har-

Moe Howard in the twenties—a real Dapper Dan.

monized such popular old songs as "Dear Old Girl," "Oh, You Beautiful Doll," "By the Light of the Silvery Moon," "Heart of My Heart" and "I've Been Through the Mill, Bill." Moe and Shemp continued to sing every night until nine or ten o'clock, until their father found out what they were doing and soon put a stop to it.

The following year, in 1914, Moe, feeling a bit of Huck Finn in his blood, wangled himself a job with a performing troupe on Capt. Billy Bryant's showboat, *Sunflower*. For two summers Howard acted with the company in the same melodramas he had seen as a kid, performing his favorite roles in *Bertha, the Sewing Machine Girl, St. Elmo* and *Ten Nights in a Barroom*, all at the age of seventeen. Before answering Ted Healy's call in 1922 to become a stooge, Moe worked a blackface act with Shemp, touring the country. Besides stage work, Moe also appeared in 12 two-reel shorts with baseball great Hans Wagner.

Late in 1922, Moe renewed his acquaintance with Ted Healy and together with Shemp formed a partnership that, except for a few short breaks, would last for almost ten years.

On June 7, 1925, Moe married Helen Schonberger, a cousin of the late Harry Houdini. In 1926 Helen urged Moe to leave the stage and Ted Healy in order to spend more time with her, as she was expecting a child. Moe acquiesced and left show business to work in real estate for a year. When that didn't work out he opened a small retail store and attempted to sell distressed merchandise, which turned into an hysteri-

Moe Howard with part-time Stooge, Kenneth Lackey.

Moe Howard lifeguarding in the early twenties, flanked by Helen and her sister Clarice.

cal fiasco. During 1927 Moe worked intermittently at the Jewish Community House in Bensonhurst, producing and directing plays. One of his early efforts, *Stepping Along*, was reviewed by a critic at *The New York Times*, who wrote, "A Musical Dream in Three Episodes was probably as good a description as anything else and it was a dream from which none wanted to awaken."

Sorely missing the old gang and unable to make a living in the workaday world, Moe rejoined Healy a short time later, appearing in a J.J. Shubert production, *A Night in Venice*, in addition to vaudeville engagements and numerous films for MGM. When Healy decided to star in features at Metro and the Stooges left to star in their two-reel comedies at Columbia, Moe became the permanent leader of the group—a leadership that would last through the Stooges' contract with Columbia for 24 consecutive years; the longest single contract ever held by a comedy team.

In many ways Moe's off-screen persona was far removed from the character he played on screen. In the theatre or before the cameras, Moe would open up and let his nervous energies flow, but at home he was a very different man. While Larry was gregarious, Moe was introverted, very serious and very nervous, a man who found it very hard to relax. He also had difficulty expressing his true feelings and emotions and bought gifts for family and friends as a means of expressing his love. Moe felt his inability to demonstrate his emotions stemmed from his family upbring-

Larry Fine's impression of Moe in a pencil sketch.

Moe and his six-month-old daughter Joan.

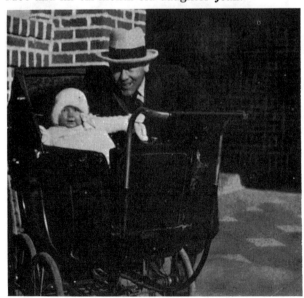

Moe reminds daughter Joan that it's never safe to steal the silverware.

ing. As he once wrote: "I recall that my father rarely kissed my mother and that I rarely kissed them. Expressing our love for one another was difficult."

As his son-in-law Norman Maurer explains it: "If he liked you, he would do anything for you. Like his mother, he worked for charity organizations and loved to watch people's faces when they opened their gifts. On one occasion during the Hanukkah/Christmas season, Moe went grocery shopping for Emil Sitka and his family of seven and delivered the groceries himself. Howard made the gesture without being asked. Sitka, a character actor who had played in many of the Stooges' comedies, was surprised to come home and find the cupboards and refrigerator packed with groceries. Emil expressed his gratitude to the comedian in a letter he wrote: "The oil burns for eight days during Hanukkah—but my torch burns in gratitude for you forever."

Moe's desire to give a helping hand to the needy continued throughout his life—as a member and three-time president of the Spastic Children's Guild, playing Santa Claus·for the Guild's palsied children, rounding up their gifts and committing himself and the other two Stooges to hundreds of benefit performances whenever and wherever he was asked.

Despite his tough demeanor on screen, at home he

Moe and Curly prepare to use Joan to fuel their fire engine.

Moe mugging with his son Paul.

Moe, Curly and an innocent spectator get all wrapped up while hooking a rug.

was quite softhearted. His wife Helen remembers with nostalgia the different ways Moe liked to mark their wedding anniversary each year. As she recalled, "He was a very sentimental man and wrote me hundreds of love poems when we were first married. On our tenth wedding anniversary, the phone rang and a strange voice on the other end asked me if I would take Moe Horwitz for my lawful, wedded husband. The voice then proceeded to perform the entire wedding ceremony with me on one end and Moe, the mystery voice, on the other. He was also a

Helen, eyeing Moe in drag on set of *Self-Made Maids*.

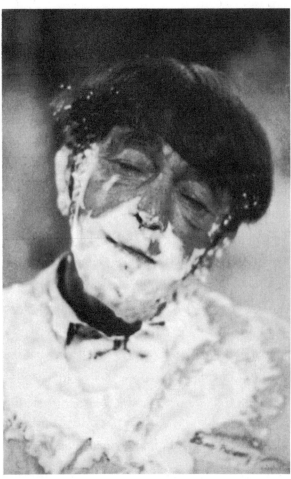

Moe and Helen on their 25th wedding anniversary.

Moe gets it on the set of *The Three Stooges Meet Hercules*.

Director and Moe's son-in-law, Norman Maurer, having a gentlemanly disagreement with the Stooges on the set of *The Outlaws Is Coming!*

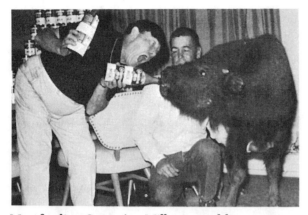

Moe feeding Carnation Milk to a real-live contented "buffalo."

singer and at the end of the ceremony, in a beautiful baritone voice, he sang, 'Oh Promise Me,' the song sung at our wedding."

Moe was also the businessman of the team, ran the group and made most of the team's decisions. Curly and Larry were carefree individuals, never priding themselves on punctuality and with absolutely no regard for money. Moe did the worrying for all of them.

Although Moe was cautious in certain directions about saving money, he would go crazy in other directions. Norman Maurer nicknamed him "Wholesale Charlie," since his fondest pleasure was buying clothes for all the members of his family. He'd buy everything by the dozen (it seemed that all his boyhood friends had wound up in the wholesale garment business). Norman felt that he wasted a good

deal of money on these spending sprees, but Moe got untold enjoyment out of them.

Despite his inability to relax and enjoy life to its fullest like Curly and Larry, Moe's goal in life was to give his family their every wish, and this he did. He and his wife Helen traveled to just about every city in the world, where they were treated like royalty by their fans.

Director Edward Bernds, who knew him for 40 years, felt the businesslike side of Moe certainly helped on the set. "Moe was all business, but he was interested in making the film as good as he could. He didn't take anything away from the director but he did see to it that the boys shaped up. He liked making suggestions and was very creative."

Moe's social life was quite different from Shemp's, as he rarely mingled with a show business crowd.

Moe enjoying another hobby, fishing, with son-in-law, Norman Maurer, and friend, Bud Basolo (1963).

Most of his friends, as strange as it seems, were judges, lawyers and doctors and any people his wife befriended. Although he loved his profession, Moe's first thoughts were for his family and he dreaded the separation caused by hectic shooting schedules and personal appearance tours.

After the loss of his brothers, Curly and Shemp, Moe once remarked that he had mixed feeling about watching his brothers in television reruns of their Stooges comedies. As he said, "How strange it is that people can laugh at comedians who are dead and never give it a second thought. At the same time, it's good to think that Shemp and my kid brother, Curly, are still remembered."

There was more to Moe's life than bopping and slapping his fellow Stooges. He had a wide range of

Moe enjoying one of his favorite hobbies, ceramics.

interests over the years which included travelling, gardening, ceramics and cooking. (He could whip up a mean *cioppino* and a marvelous lasagna—neither of which he ate. He cooked them because his wife loved them.)

In his younger days, he enjoyed going to the fights, football games and midget auto racing and had hobbies that included hooking rugs and stamp and coin collecting. Moe even tried the art of wine making. His daughter Joan, about ten at the time, recalls vaguely what happened: "It seems that my father decided to make wine. Never one for reading directions carefully, he made a radical mistake somewhere down the line. Something to do with not removing the bung from the wine barrel at the right time... or maybe not removing it at all. When the day arrived for my father to taste his wine, he pulled out the bung and all hell broke loose. The entire contents of the barrel—wine, skins and seeds—exploded out like they were shot out of a cannon. The room, which had white walls, was splashed with vivid red, but the strangest sight of all was my father. He was wine red from head to toe and peppered with grape seeds. They were stuck to him everywhere: his ears, his nostrils, his hair. Even the walls of the room were plastered with seeds. My dad was able to take a bath after and clean himself up, but that house must still have telltale signs of what went on that fateful day."

Moe's favorite music was quite diverse. It included anything sung by a barber shop quartet, the music of Andre Segovia, and his favorite song, "How Deep Is the Ocean." His favorite Stooges comedy was *You*

Moe practicing one of his greatest skills on Dick Albain, special effects man, between scenes of *The Three Stooges in Orbit*.

Nazty Spy (1940). For exercise there was golf and a brisk two-mile walk every morning.

Moe had two children: his first, Joan, and eight years later a son, Paul. He was married almost 50 years to his wife, Helen, who died six months after him on October 31, 1975.

When once asked how long the Stooges would remain in show business, Howard replied, "Forever is a long time, but with a little luck, we just might make it."

The last photograph of Larry and Moe taken together in summer of 1974.

Larry Fine

THE TEAM'S MIDDLEMAN, Larry Fine, was born Louis Feinberg on October 5, 1902, in the south side of Philadelphia, Pennsylvania. His father, Joseph Feinberg, and mother, Fanny Lieberman, owned a watch repair and jewelry shop.

Larry was the first of four children; he had two brothers, Morris and a younger brother, Philip, who died prematurely, and a sister, Lyla, who became a school teacher. He wasn't even a year old when his parents and friends started treating him like a celebrity. He stole the show as an entertainer while still in diapers. One time, at just two years of age, his father propped him up on top of a jewelry showcase to show relatives how well he could dance. Larry managed to do a few dance steps before losing his balance and falling backward through the glass top of the display case. Luckily, he emerged unharmed.

Morris Feinberg recalls that Larry had another close call in his youth. "Larry wasn't so fortunate the next time he got into trouble. It happened when Dad was testing metals to see which were gold. He used a powerful acid that when applied to base metals would turn them green or burn a hole in them. Gold, however, was not affected by the acid. One day Dad had removed the stopper from the acid bottle, leaving it uncovered. A thirsty Larry stood unnoticed at his side. As he reached for the bottle of acid to raise it to his mouth and drink, Dad saw him out of the corner of his eye and smacked the bottle from his hand, splashing acid on his left arm and burning it badly."

Larry required immediate medical attention and a skin graft was done on his arm. After the surgery, doctors recommended that he be given violin lessons as a form of therapy. It was believed that the action of drawing the bow over the strings would strengthen his damaged arm muscles. Little did Larry realize that the violin would become an important tool in his career.

In his teens, Larry had aspirations of becoming a comedian—even a star. He enjoyed putting on shows for anyone who would watch him. As a result, he gained valuable experience. Larry's skill as a violinist became so impressive that he was asked to play professionally. At age ten, as a student at Southwalk Grammar School, he soloed at a children's concert at the Roseland Dance Hall in Philadelphia. Backed by Howard Lanin's orchestra, he played "Humoresque" on his violin.

Morris remembers that Larry eventually became a versatile musician. "He was a natural-born performer and could play any instrument he got his hands on—piano, clarinet, saxophone and brass. He even constructed a violin out of a cigar box and a broom handle. He played its single string like a cello, holding it between his knees."

Music now in his blood, Larry played on the bill of local theatre amateur nights, taking top prizes in most of these contests. Which didn't surprise his peers, since he was certainly good at his craft. During this period he interspersed his musical talents with pugilistic skills, earning money as a lightweight boxer, fighting over 40 bouts. By age fifteen, he started singing along with movie slides at Philadelphia theatres—the Keystone, Alhambra, Broadway, Nixon's Grand and the Allegheny—where he received two dollars for each performance. All of this was accomplished while he was still a student at Central High School. In later years, he would go on to develop an act in which he would do a Russian dance while playing the violin.

In 1921, Larry landed a job in Gus Edwards' Newsboy Sextette, playing the violin, dancing and telling jokes in a Jewish dialect. On the bill with him was Mabel Haney, who would later become his wife. Mabel, with her sister, Loretta, joined Larry in an act called "The Haney Sisters and Fine." The trio worked together in vaudeville until 1925, playing the RKO, Orpheum, Keith-Orpheum and Delmar Circuits and the Paramount Theatre in Canada.

It was during a playdate in Chicago, in 1925, at a night club called the Rainbow Gardens, that Larry was first asked to become a stooge. Ted Healy, Moe and Shemp Howard took in Larry's performance one evening, at which time Shemp informed Healy that he planned to leave the act. Moe suggested that perhaps Larry could replace Shemp. Healy liked the

27

idea and at the conclusion of the show the trio went backstage to meet with Fine. Ted made him an offer: $90 a week to become a stooge and an extra $10 a week if he'd throw away his fiddle. The next day,

Mabel and Larry in 1933.

Joan (3rd from left) helps Larry's daughter Phyllis (extreme right) celebrate her birthday.

Larry accepted the offer and this was the beginning of what would eventually be "The Three Stooges"; Shemp would return later, as his stint away from Healy did not pan out.

The trio, Moe, Larry and Shemp, first opened on Broadway in *A Night in Venice* and later appeared in

A theatre manager fills in for Larry Fine during a publicity photo session with Moe and Curly-Joe as a result of Fine's tardiness.

20th Century-Fox's comedy *Soup to Nuts* (1930). The rest of Larry's career would parallel Moe's. When the team left MGM in 1934, the Stooges were comprised of Moe, Larry and Curly. They went on to star in two-reel comedies for Columbia Pictures, where the team remained for 24 years.

Offstage, Larry was a social butterfly. He liked a good time and surrounded himself with friends. Larry and his wife, Mabel, loved having parties and every Christmas threw lavish midnight suppers. Larry was what some friends have called a "yes man," since he was always so agreeable, no matter what the circumstances. As film director Charles Lamont recalled after directing Fine in two Stooges comedies, "Larry was a nut. He was the kind of guy who always said anything. He was a yapper."

Larry's devil-may-care personality carried over to the world of finance. He was a terrible businessman and spent his money as soon as he earned it. He would either gamble it away at the track or at high-stakes gin rummy games. In an interview, Fine even admitted that he often gave money to actors and friends who needed help and never asked to be reimbursed. Joe Besser and director Edward Bernds remember that because of his free spending, Larry was almost forced into bankruptcy when Columbia terminated the Three Stooges comedies in 1958.

Norman Maurer recalls that Larry was surrounded by friends, some of whom were ready and waiting to take his money. "Larry would wait around at the end of a booking during personal appearance tours. Then, the minute Moe would go to the theatre manager to get their money, Larry would take his cut and ten minutes later it was gone. It would be spent on life's luxuries: diamond rings, fur coats and on the horses. Or if one of his friends would say, 'Larry, I've got a deal—this non-sinkable bathing suit...all we need is $15,000'—-Larry was had!"

On another occasion, Larry convinced Moe to finance a fast-food restaurant in Glendale called Mi Patio. Larry's two friends, who conceived the idea, planned to sell Stoogeburgers, which would be served in little plastic baskets with the Stooges' faces printed on the sides. After several months of so-so business the partners skipped town with everything they could get their hands on, including the burgers. As a result, Moe and Larry were left holding the bag.

Because of his prodigal ways and his wife's dislike for housekeeping, Larry and his family lived in hotels—first in the President Hotel in Atlantic City, where his daughter Phyllis was raised, then the Knickerbocker Hotel in Hollywood. Not until the late forties did Larry buy a home—a splendid, old Mediterranean structure in the Los Feliz area of Los Angeles.

Larry's screen personality was as laid back as his real life one, and thus his character was never forced. Prior to the filming of a scene he'd come up with a gag idea that he'd toss at the director; he would always shrug it off when his ideas were ignored. He was said to be a bit of a whiner, sometimes complaining about the smallest things. If he stubbed his toe on a chair during a scene, he'd carry on until the propman cushioned the chair leg with a sponge pad to protect him from injuring the toe again. In the early days,

At Moe's son Paul's wedding: (clockwise) Larry, Mabel, Joe DeRita, Phyllis Lamond (Larry's daughter), Don Lamond (Larry's son-in-law), Jeffrey and Michael Maurer (Moe's grandsons), Claretta White, Sam White (Jules White's brother), Norman Maurer, Joan Howard Maurer, Bill Dyer.

Larry remembers to duck during the "Maharaja" sketch in *The Three Stooges Go Around the World in a Daze.*

Stooges comedies. As he put it: "I think Larry was the best actor of the three. I used to argue with Moe about giving him more lines because Larry was good, but Moe was against it."

Larry had two children, a son, Johnny, who died in a tragic automobile accident on November 17, 1961, at age 24, and a daughter, Phyllis. His wife Mabel died on May 30, 1967, during the Memorial Day weekend while the Stooges were on tour. Larry left the show when he learned of his wife's death and, in true show business tradition, Moe and Curly-Joe carried out the team's three-day engagement.

Fine's favorite hobbies included teaching serious music, preferably jazz, the kind Andre Previn, Percy Faith, Morton Gould and Andre Kostelanetz popularized. His favorite Stooge: Curly. As he once commented, "Personally, I thought Curly was the greatest because he was a natural comedian who had no formal training. Whatever he did he made up on the spur of the moment." Larry's favorite sport was baseball, the Los Angeles Dodgers his favorite team. He also enjoyed going to the boxing matches.

Larry's favorite actors were Spencer Tracy, Clark Gable and Peter Falk, while Milton Berle, Jack Benny and Redd Foxx were his choice for comedians. His favorite Stooges films were *Scrambled Brains* (1951) and *The Three Stooges Meet Hercules* (1962). Runner-up favorites included *You Nazty Spy* (1940) and *I'll Never Heil Again* (1941).

Larry takes it like a man.

Larry would put on an act in public, trying to appear aloof, to make people believe he was a serious intellectual—a complete opposite of his screen persona. But this false front disappeared as he matured.

Fine was also known for his tardiness. He rarely got to the set on time, or to any other engagement. Several times during his career, Moe had to cover for him until he showed up. Tardiness was definitely one of his foibles, which even the cast's call-sheets bear out. In fact, one time while performing in Atlantic City, a newspaper photographer had arranged a photo session with the Stooges in advance of their engagement. When Larry forgot the appointment, Moe had to ask the theatre manager to take his place.

Ed Bernds, who directed Larry in numerous Stooges films, recalls that he wasn't as dedicated to his career as the other Stooges. "He tended to be a bit of a goof-off." Bernds said. "But not a real goldbricker; he just wasn't as dedicated as Moe was."

But Norman Maurer believes that Larry's talent as an actor and comedian were commonly overlooked in

Larry's last public appearance, along with a chimp
friend, at California's Lion Country Safari.

Curly Howard

CURLY HOWARD, the one with the shaven head which Moe referred to as "looking like a dirty tennis ball," was the most popular member of the Three Stooges and the most inventive of the three. His hilarious improvisations and classic catch-phrases of "N'yuk-n'yuk-n'yuk!" and "Wooo-wooo-wooo!" have established him as a great American cult hero.

His real name was Jerome Lester Horwitz, born to Jennie and Solomon Horwitz on October 22, 1903, in Bath Beach, a summer resort in a section of Brooklyn, He was the fifth and youngest of the Horwitz sons and weighed eight and a half pounds at birth. He was delivered by Dr. Duffy, the brother of Moe Howard's six-grade school teacher. Curly-Jerome, to complicate matters, was nicknamed "Babe" by his brother Moe.

Curly was a quiet child and gave his parents very little trouble. Moe and Shemp made up for him in spades. Moe recalls one mischievious incident when Curly was an infant: "We took his brand-new baby carriage, removed the wheels, made a pair of axles from two-by-fours and built our own version of a 'soap box racer.' We put Curly in it and dragged him all over town. It was a lucky thing we didn't kill him. When our parents found out we had the devil to pay."

When Curly was about four, Moe and Shemp started to instill in their brother the idea of becoming a comedian. Quite frequently they would stage small theatre productions in the basement of their friends' homes; the cast would usually consist of Shemp, Moe and Curly. There was a charge of two cents for admission, but the ventures could not have been very lucrative, as the boys had to split the take three ways. It is believed that during these performances Curly got his first taste of comedy.

Moe also recalled that Curly was only a fair student in school. A boyhood friend, Lester Friedman, remembers that he was a fine athelete, making a name for himself on the elementary school basketball team. Although Curly never graduated from school, he kept himself busy doing odd jobs, following Moe and Shemp wherever they went.

As a young man, Curly loved to dance and listen to music, and he became an accomplished ballroom dancer. He would go regularly to the Triangle Ballroom in Brooklyn, where on several occasions he met George Raft, who in the early days of his career was a fine ballroom dancer. Curly also tried his hand at the ukulele, singing along as he strummed. As Moe once said, "He was not a good student but he was in demand socially, what with his beautiful singing voice." Moe continued to influence his kid brother's theatrical education, taking him along with him to vaudeville shows and the melodrama theatres, but Curly's first love was musicals and comedy.

During this period, sometime in his late teens, Curly found another love and married a young girl whose name remains a mystery to this day. His mother, Jennie Horwitz, the matriarch of the family, was against the idea of Curly's marrying at such a young age and, before six months had gone by, had the marriage annulled.

In 1928, Curly landed a job as a comedy musical conductor for the Orville Knapp Band, which, to that date, was his only stage experience. Moe recalls that his brother's performances usually overshadowed those of the band. "He was billed as the guest conductor and would come out and lead the band in a breakaway tuxedo. The sections of the suit would fall away, piece by piece, while he stood there swinging his baton."

Young Curly's interest in show business continued to grow as he watched his brothers, Shemp and Moe, perform as stooges in Ted Healy's act. Joe Besser, who worked with them in *The Passing Show of 1932*, recalls that Curly liked to hang around backstage. "He was there all the time and would get sandwiches for all of us in the show, including Ted Healy and his Stooges. He never participated in any of the routines but liked to watch us perform." During this period Curly remained in the shadow of his brothers, and watched as their careers began to skyrocket them to stardom along with Healy.

It was in 1932, during J.J. Shubert's *Passing Show*, that Healy had an argument with Shubert and walked off the show, taking Larry and Moe along with him. Shemp, disenchanted with Healy's drunken bouts and practical jokes, decided to remain in the Shubert show.

Later that afternoon, Moe suggested to Healy that his kid brother, Babe (Curly), was available and would make an excellent replacement for Shemp, since he was familiar with the act. Ted agreed, asking Curly to join the act, but under the condition that he shave his head. At the time, Curly sported long, wavy brown hair and a moustache. In an interview, Curly recalled the incident: "I had beautiful wavy hair and a waxed moustache. When I went to see Ted Healy about a job as one of the Stooges, he said, 'What can you do?' I said, 'I don't know.' He said, 'I know what you can do. You can shave off your hair to start with.' Then later on I had to shave off my poor moustache. I had to shave it off right down to the skin."

Curly's wacky style of comedy started to emerge, first on stage and then on screen when Healy and his Stooges starred in numerous features and comedy

Curly Howard (top left) at about fifteen, with his school's basketball team. At his feet, friend Lester Friedman.

shorts for MGM. Later, in 1934, Curly played an integral part in the team's rise to fame as the Three Stooges at Columbia Pictures, where he starred as a Stooge in 97 two-reel comedies.

But success virtually destroyed Curly. He started to drink heavily, feeling that his shaven head robbed him

of his sex appeal. Larry Fine once remarked that Curly wore a hat in public to confirm an image of masculinity, since he felt like a little kid with his hair shaved off. Curly was also unable to save a cent. When he received his check he'd rush out to spend it on life's pleasures: wine, women, a new house, an automobile or a new dog—Curly was mad about dogs. Since Curly was certainly no businessman, Moe usually handled all of his affairs, helped him manage his money and even made out his income tax returns.

Curly's homes were San Fernando Valley showplaces and most of them were either purchased from or sold to a select group of Hollywood personalities. One house Curly purchased was on Cahuenga Boulevard and Sarah Street in North Hollywood and was purchased from child star Sabu. Later Curly sold the property to a promising young actress of the forties, Joan Leslie. Curly also bought a lot next door to Moe Howard's palatial home in Toluca Lake, expecting to build on it, but he never did. It was eventually sold to film director Raoul Walsh.

As to Curly's personality, he was basically an introvert, barely speaking on the set between takes, the complete antithesis of his insanely hilarious screen character. Charles Lamont, who directed Curly in two Stooges comedies, related in an interview that "Curly was pretty dull. This may not be a very nice thing to say, but I don't think he had all of his marbles. He was always on Cloud Nine whenever you talked to him."

Clarice Seiden, the sister of Moe Howard's wife, Helen, saw Curly off screen whenever there was a party at his home. She remembers him as being far from "a quiet person." Seiden said: "Although he

Elaine Ackerman (Curly's bride-to-be) shows off her engagement ring to a delighted Curly, Jennie and Solomon Horwitz.

Moe and Curly touring the British Isles (1939).

wasn't on (stage) all the time, I wouldn't call him a quiet person....he was a lot of fun. He was quiet at times but when he had a few drinks—and he drank quite a bit—he was more gregarious."

Curly's niece, Dolly Sallin, agreed with Mrs. Seiden that Curly liked people but shared Lamont's viewpoint that he could be quiet at times. "I can remember his wanting to be with people. He wasn't a recluse and I wouldn't call him dull. He wasn't an intellect nor did he go in for discussions. But when I think of someone as dull, I'd think of them as being under par intelligence-wise, and Curly wasn't that."

Friends remember that Curly refrained from any crazy antics in private life but reserved them for his performances in the comedies. However, when he got together with his brothers, Moe and Shemp, it was a totally different story. As Irma Grenner Leveton, a friend of Moe and Helen Howard, recalls: "Yes, Curly did clown around, but only if Moe, Shemp and Larry were with him. Or if his immediate group of friends or family were there. But the minute there were strangers, he retreated."

But Curly's main weakness was women; to paraphrase an old adage, "Curly couldn't live with women, or live without them." Mrs. Leveton remembers that women were his favorite pastime for a

number of reasons. As she said: "He just liked a good time and that was it. And women...he loved women. I don't have to tell you...not always the nicest women. You know why, because he was so shy. Curly didn't know how to speak to a woman, so he would

Larry, Curly and Moe mugging. Their straight man is brother Jack Howard.

wind up conversing with anyone that approached him."

Dolly Sallin viewed his love for women in a similar manner: "I can remember his wanting to be around people, and that included the current woman in his life. That was the most important thing—if she was good, bad, or whatever. If he decided she was interesting, that was that! As long as there was a woman around the house, he would stay home instead of running around. He seemed restless to me."

Director-producer Norman Maurer first met Curly in 1945 and remembers that he "was a pushover for women. If a pretty girl went up to him and gave him a spiel, Curly would marry her. Then she would take his money and run off. It was the same when a real estate agent would come up and say, 'I have a house for you,' Curly would sell his current home and buy another one. It seemed as though every two weeks he would have a new girl, a new car, a new house and a new dog."

But as much as Curly loved women, they were his downfall. He married three times after his first marriage was annulled. On June 7, 1937, he married Elaine Ackerman. In 1938 Elaine gave birth to Curly's first child, a daughter, Marilyn. Due to the addition to their family, Curly and Elaine moved to a home on the 400 block of Highland Avenue in Hollywood, near where Moe lived at the time. But slowly the marriage began to crumble and Elaine filed suit for divorce on July 11, 1940, after only three years of marriage.

During the next five years, Curly ate, drank and made merry. He gained a tremendous amount of weight and his blood pressure soared. On January 23, 1945, he entered the Cottage Hospital in Santa Barbara where he was diagnosed as having extreme hypertension, a retinal hemorrhage and obesity. He remained at the hospital for tests and treatment and was discharged on February 9, 1945.

Eight months later, while making a personal appearance in New York, Curly met Marion Buxbaum, a petite blonde woman with a ten-year-old son from a previous marriage. Curly instantly fell in love with her and they were married in New York on October 17, 1945. It was felt that Marion used Curly to her advantage. He spent a fortune on her—everything from fur coats to expensive jewelry. Curly even bought her a new home on Ledge Street in Toluca Lake. As Marie Howard, Jack Howard's wife, recalled: "She was just after his money."

It didn't take long for Curly to find out that Marion wasn't for him. After a miserable three months of arguments and accusations, Marion and Curly separated on January 14, 1946, and Curly sued for divorce. The divorce was quite scandalous and notices were carried in all the local papers. Dolly Sallin recalled: "It was horrible. She tried to get everything she could from him and even accused Curly of never bathing, which was totally untrue. Curly was fat but he was always immaculate. That marriage nearly ruined him." Marion was awarded the decree on July 22, 1946, less than nine months after they were married.

Irma Leveton remembers that Moe talked Curly into the marriage with Marion since he, Moe, did not like the kind of wild life his brother was leading. Moe wanted Curly to settle down and take care of his health. As Leveton remarked: "Moe fixed them up— Marion and Curly. He wanted Curly to get married and pushed him into it. He wanted Curly to quit the life he was leading, as he was getting sick. Curly had very high blood pressure and that marriage to Marion

Curly and Moe share a laugh with brother Shemp on the Columbia lot.

Curly, Larry and Moe with the "Mysterious Wrestler."

didn't help. It was very aggravating for Curly and a very unhappy time for all concerned."

With his third marriage a disaster, the question surfaced as to why Curly's marriages had failed? Irma Leveton believed that it was a combination of Curly's immaturity and a succession of mismatched marriages. As she remarked: "He couldn't contribute anything to a marriage. Most likely his wives married

restless. He seemed to need women to soothe his restless quality, not just for sex. I would guess that he was restless and that nothing seemed to help."

It was soon after his separation from Marion that Curly's health started its rapid decline. On May 6 (not May 19), 1946, he suffered a stroke during the filming of his 97th Three Stooges comedy, *Half-Wits' Holiday* (1947). Curly had to leave the team to recuperate from

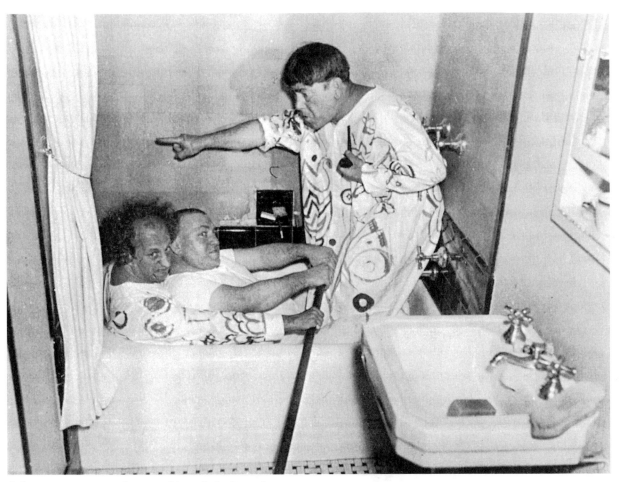

A happy moment at home taking their Saturday night bath.

him because he was a (film) personality. But he had nothing to back it up. There was no substance of any kind. He always seemed to be in a trance ... kinda dopey. Once in awhile he would come out with something very funny. And I can't even imagine him saying, 'I Love you,' to any woman."

But Dolly Sallin brought to light another point of view. She said: "I don't think Curly ever grew up. He couldn't make it in a one-to-one relationship. He was sweet and loving but not really mature. He was very

his illness. His condition began to improve and a year later, still not fully recovered from his stroke, Curly met a thrice-married widow of thirty-two who really seemed to care for him—Valerie Newman, whom he married on July 31, 1947.

Valerie was Curly's fourth wife, a very caring woman who nursed him through those last, awful years. Although his health worsened after the marriage, Valerie gave birth to a daughter, Curly's second child, Janie. As Irma Leveton recalls: "Valerie was the only decent thing that happened to Curly and the only one that really cared about him. I remember she nursed him 24 hours a day."

Finally, in 1949, Curly's health took a severe turn for the worse when he suffered his second in a series of strokes and was rushed to Cedars of Lebanon Hospital in Hollywood. Doctors contemplated doing spinal surgery on him since the stroke had left him partially paralyzed. But the final decision was not to operate.

Curly was confined to a wheelchair and doctors put him on a diet of boiled rice and apples. It was hoped that this would bring down his weight and his high blood pressure. As a result of his illness Curly's weight dropped dramatically. As Norman Maurer recalls: "I'll never forget him at this point in his life. His hand would constantly fall off the arm of the wheelchair, either from weakness or the paralysis, and he couldn't

get it back on without help." When Curly's condition failed to improve, Valerie admitted him into the Motion Picture Country House and Hospital in Woodland Hills on August 29, 1950. He was released after several months of treatment and medical tests on November 15, 1950. Curly would return periodically to the hospital, up until 1952.

Curly returned home confined to his bed, where Valerie nursed him. When his health worsened, in February 1951, she made a request for a male nurse to help her. In that same month, Curly was placed in a nursing home, the Colonial House, located in Los Angeles. In March, he suffered another stroke and Moe had to move him, out, due to the fact that the nursing home did not meet state fire codes.

In April of 1951 Curly was moved to North Hollywood Hospital and Sanitarium. In December, the hospital supervisor advised the family that Curly was

Curly in a world of his own on the Western set of *Phony Express* (1943).

Curly, after his first stroke, at Joan's wedding in 1947.

becoming a problem to the nursing staff due to mental deterioration and that they could no longer care for him. It was suggested that he be placed in a mental hospital, but Moe would not hear of it. On January 7, 1952, Moe was called from the filming of a Stooges comedy, *He Cooked His Goose* (1952), to help move Curly again, this time to the Baldy View Sanitarium in San Gabriel. He died 11 days later on January 18, 1952. He was forty-eight years old.

Curly Howard is gone and one can only wonder what it would have been like if he had lived and worked with the Stooges through the 1960's. Imagine Curly starring in full-length features in color and black-and-white. Stooges cartoons could have been voiced with the original Curly "N'yuk-n'yuking" and "Wooo-woooing." Television audiences could have realized the true genius of Curly Howard on talk and variety shows. When the Stooges' popularity suddenly burgeoned in 1959, Curly could have been around to take the bows with Moe and Larry.

Hopefully, if there is a Stooges' heaven Curly will be there watching, seeing his talent, his art of comedy and his contributions as a Stooge continue to be enjoyed by millions throughout the world.

40

Shemp Howard

SHEMP HOWARD, his hair slicked down over lov-ing-cup ears, became one of the most famous comedy stooges in the history of stage and screen. The third eldest brother of Moe Howard, the team leader, Shemp was born Samuel Horwitz in Brooklyn, New York, on March 17, 1895 (not 1900 as listed in studio biographies).

Moe once recalled how his brother acquired the name Shemp. "Shemp was given the Hebrew name Schmool, after his mother's grandfather. Schmool was Anglicized to Samuel and then shortened to Sam. When his mother, with her broad European accent, would call him, the name 'Sam' came out 'Sams,' and if you weren't listening carefully it could sound like Shemp...which it did! So from the time he was seven that's what his family called him. It was Shemp in school and in the world of the theatre. In later years, no one knew it was anything else."

Shemp was a very mischievious child, and Moe recalled his favorite pastime was stuffing everything from woolen stockings to sweaters down the hallway toilet. "I remember one time when Shemp tore the pages out of our brother Irving's history book and jammed them into the toilet in our home in Ben-sonhurst," Moe chuckled as he recalled, "Because of this he had to run the family gauntlet: a smack from Mother, a belt across the head from Dad, a shove from Irving and a kick in the fanny from me."

When Shemp reached the age of thirteen, he was a completely different person and had outgrown most of his mischief-making. Moe remembers that friends of the family had always predicted that Shemp was going to be an actor or a great comedian. But Shemp thought otherwise and never seriously entertained the idea of entering show business. Moe, on the other hand, worked like a demon at it, planned his future, and eventually made it to the footlights before his brother.

Shemp graduated from P.S. 163 in Brooklyn, the same grammar school his brother Moe attended, and got as far as starting New Utrecht High School. Since he and Moe failed to finish school, their parents, Jennie and Solomon Horwitz, urged them to go to a trade school. Late in 1911, Moe and Shemp enrolled at the Baron DeHirsch Trade School in New York, where Shemp took up plumbing and Moe studied to be an electrician. While Moe learned the definition of an ampere, an ohm and a volt, Shemp learned the basics of threading and cutting pipe. Neither of the boys ever finished these courses but instead put their lessons into practice in a rare act of mischief.

Moe remembers that while learning the tricks of their trade they got the tricks down pat: "Neither Shemp nor I ever finished the course, but we did find a use for lesson #1—"The Push-Button Door Latch." We wired it into our apartment so that by pushing a concealed button we could open the front-door latch when we got home late at night without our parents being the wiser. I'd just reach under the door step, press the button, wait for the click of the latch and open the door from the outside. This worked well until Dad found out. One night we came home very late, and reached for the button, but the button wasn't there. That particular evening Shemp and I had borrowed Jack and Irving's new long-pants suits to go to a party. We came home about three in the morning and there was no way to get in without waking our parents. Then I got the bright idea of going to the back of the house. The bathroom window was open and I climbed through the darkened opening, head down, arms outstretched and probing, right into a half-filled tub that either Irving or Jack had left from that night's bath. I landed face down in the water. I rolled over and sat up laughing hysterically. I had forgotten all about Shemp and letting him in. A moment later he climbed in and found himself in the same boat. There we were when my father entered, the two of us sopping wet with our brothers' good clothes on. Somehow our father's smacks on our wet faces sounded much louder and were more painful than on a dry face."

In recalling his school days, Moe has said that Shemp was not athletically inclined and as a student he was nil. He tried to pay attention in class but seemed unable to concentrate. Jack and Irving tried to help him with his schoolwork, but Shemp was already playing the comedian. He'd laugh everything off with a cute remark, draw funny drawings, or make faces at the other students to make them laugh and get them in trouble along with himself. Shemp craved attention.

Moe also recalled that Shemp was industrious for his age. The two brothers worked together at many different neighborhood jobs. First, they tried the plumbing business, but when Shemp burned his hand on hot solder he quit. The Howards next tried setting up pins in a local bowling alley, then deliver-

Shemp in his teens, on stage with a fellow vaudevillian.

A frame blow-up from a 1930's home movie featuring Shemp with wife, Gertrude, and son, Mort.

ing newspapers for the *Brooklyn Eagle*. This continued until, finally, Shemp realized there was nothing left for them but the theatre.

In the hope of acquiring some stage experience, Shemp agreed to do an act with Moe at dancehalls and theatre amateur nights in the area. Comedy was neither Moe nor Shemp's forte at the time. Moe had been directing his energies toward dramatic theatre while Shemp, except for fooling around at parties, had practically no theatrical experience. The two boys wrote a short skit, rehearsed it and went on stage at an amateur night at the Bath Beach Theatre. Three minutes into their performance, they were thrown bodily out of the theatre. Needless to say, Shemp was terribly discouraged but Moe felt it was a step in the right direction....Shemp had finally performed on a stage.

Charlotte Shurman, an old Bensonhurst friend of the Howards when they were in their twenties, watched many of their performances around the neighborhood. She recalled: "They were just starting out in dancehalls and everyone got a big kick out of them and the shows they put on. Shemp and Moe worked together and I followed them around wherever they went ... because I was so proud. I remember Shemp. He was a riot ... simply a riot. And it came so naturally."

Sometime during the course of World War I, Moe and Shemp formed a blackface vaudeville act which disbanded for a brief period when Shemp was drafted into the army. He was discharged after only a few months (he was discovered to be a bedwetter) and rejoined Moe in vaudeville. In 1917 Shemp and Moe took their comedy act back to the boards and played on both the Loew's and RKO circuits, managing to work for the rival outfits through a ruse: They played a

Shemp proudly displays his first paycheck from Fox Studio in 1930.

blackface routine for RKO and a whiteface one for Loew's. They continued with their stage appearances through 1922. Shemp jokingly recalled the blackest moment of his life as the time he was working blackface in a minstrel show and the manager skipped with the payroll and the cold cream. Despite his show business desires, Shemp once said, "My parents wanted me to grow up to be a gentleman."

Then, one afternoon in 1922, Shemp got his biggest show business break. A former schoolmate and vaudeville comedian, Ted Healy, was playing at the Brooklyn Prospect Theatre and needed a replacement in his current act. He prevailed upon Moe and then Shemp to come up out of the audience and perform in the show. The Howards went on stage with Healy and fractured the audience with an entirely ad-libbed routine.

The act with Healy and his Stooges kept up its frantic pace from that night on. A short-lived problem arose at the beginning of the brothers' careers. Their mother, Jennie Horwitz, was totally against the idea of her sons joining Ted Healy.

Jack Howard remembers what Ted Healy said to persuade her to change her mind. "It seems my

Moe and Shemp in blackface, in stock with Margaret Bryant Players, summer 1919.

mother did not want Shemp or Moe to be actors. She thought it would be much better if they became professionals. Ted Healy came to the house one day to plead with my mother to let Moe and Shemp join the act. He was getting nowhere. Suddenly, Ted said to my mother, 'Jennie, I'll give you $100 for your synagogue building fund if you let the boys come with me.' She thought about the good that the money would do and agreed, reluctantly."

Following his debut as a stooge, Shemp's association with Healy continued to prosper. He was prominently billed in such J.J. Shubert musicals as *A Night*

Shemp in costume from *A Night in Venice*, 1929.

in Spain and *A Night in Venice*. In 1925, Howard married Gertrude "Babe" Frank. She gave birth to a son, Morton, in 1927. (He died on January 13, 1972, of cancer.) In this same year, Larry joined Healy, Moe and Shemp.

Then, in 1930, it was off to Hollywood to co-star in Rube Goldberg's critical sensation *Soup to Nuts*. A short time later Larry, Moe and Shemp left Healy to form an act of their own, "Three Lost Souls." But a year later they returned to Healy to star in *The Passing Show of 1932*, a J.J. Shubert Broadway revue. Healy left the show over a contract dispute, taking Moe and Larry with him. Shemp decided to stay behind.

Leaving the team gave Shemp a chance to use his wide-ranging talents in various film productions, including features and featurettes. He went on to star in countless two-reel comedies for Vitaphone in 1932 and he later played the role of Knobby Walsh in the Joe Palooka series. Shemp's leaving the act also gave his

43

Shemp readies himself to jump over the candlestick in *Fiddler's Three* (1948).

kid brother Curly the opportunity of a lifetime—to become the world's favorite Stooge.

In 1937, Shemp Howard returned to Hollywood, this time to open the "Stage One" nightclub (now Andre's restaurant on Wilshire Boulevard) with actor/partner Wally Vernon. Shortly after the club opened, Shemp signed a contract to do a comedy series at Columbia and later feature film roles at RKO, MGM and Monogram. In the 1940's, he was given numerous roles in such Universal films as *Buck Privates, The Bank Dick* and *Hellzapoppin!* He also worked in films starring Abbott and Costello, W.C. Fields, Broderick Crawford and John Wayne.

When times were good, Shemp and his wife Gertrude's greatest pleasure was entertaining actor friends in the movie community. The Howards' parties at their North Hollywood home included such guests as Morey Amsterdam, Phil Silvers, Harry Silvers, Huntz Hall, Gabe Dell, Martha Raye and Murray Alpert. On rare occasions, brothers Moe and Curly would drop by with their wives, but when things went sour work-wise, some of Shemp's friends were known to abandon ship. Clarice Seiden, Moe Howard's sister-in-law, recalls: "I remember when Shemp's contract was not renewed with Universal, the partygoers that were always at his house disappeared. When his contract was renewed everyone would come back."

Whatever the situation, no matter how unnerving, Shemp was always a warm, caring, understanding man, though a bit of an introvert at times. Once he was at ease with people, Shemp opened up and the jokes and humorous anecdotes poured forth. Dolly

Sallin, daughter of Jack Howard, remembers Shemp as informal and casual. She says, "Shemp was really a quiet, family man who had evening get-togethers where friends would drop in. He was quite devoted to his wife and son. Moe was the one who kept up on world affairs and kept his mind active, while Shemp simply didn't care. He wanted things to be easy and uncomplicated." Friends also reveal that Shemp was not a businessman and spent most of his time sitting at home listening to his favorite radio show or, in his later years, watching television.

Shemp also shared many intimate moments with his son Mort, who was an only child and bore more resemblance to his mother than to Shemp. Irma Leveton, Helen Howard's friend, remembered that Shemp liked to go fishing with Mort. Dolly Sallin added that Shemp and Mort used to produce their own tape-recorded music on a reel-to-reel recorder Shemp owned.

Norman Maurer, who first met Shemp in 1945, remembers the comedian as always being jovial and never without a kind word. Maurer recalls: "Shemp was a delightful man. He was the funniest of the three brothers ... he was a riot. He would just open his mouth and he was funny. He was also the world's greatest environmentalist. He couldn't step on an ant."

Shemp also had his share of phobias that he was never able to outgrow—a fear of heights, a fear of driving or being driven in a car and a fear of water.

Shemp with his wife, Gertrude.

Moe told of the time that Shemp insisted he was getting seasick...just standing on the dock fishing. The Stooges always traveled by train whenever they went across country on personal appearance tours because of Shemp's paranoia; it was impossible to get him on an airplane. Irma Leveton recalled Shemp's fear of dogs, even though he had a dog of his own, a collie named Wags. As Leveton said: "He used to walk down the street with a stick in his hand to protect himself. If a dog ever came near him, he would have fainted. There was no way he would ever hit a dog. He couldn't kill a fly. It's hard to imagine that a man with a face like that—he looked like a killer—was really a gentle man."

Emil Sitka, who worked with Shemp in many comedies, remembers his fear on the set of *Hold That Lion* (1947). "We had a lion in this film who was so sickly he would fall asleep in the middle of a take. When Shemp heard that there was a lion on the set, he was really panicked. I thought he was kidding, but he wasn't. When he finally shot the scene the technicians had to put a glass plate between the lion and Shemp ... he was that scared."

Another anecdote concerning Shemp's phobias occurred during the filming of *Africa Screams*, a 1949 romp featuring Shemp and starring Abbott and Costello. In it was another future Stooge, Joe Besser. Charles Barton directed the epic and remembers that Shemp's fear of heights and water seemed funny to everyone but Shemp:

"I remember when we did *Africa Screams* together, there were some funny scenes between Joe Besser and Shemp Howard where they were sitting on a raft floating down a river and Shemp was beside himself with fear and refused to get on the raft, even though the water wasn't up to his knees. I had to literally carry him onto the raft. When it started moving, he was so afraid of falling off, he kept clutching at Joe Besser's shirt. This brought on a lot of teasing from the cast and crew. After the scene, they left him sitting on

Larry and Moe in one of their last photographs with Shemp.

the raft as a gag. And he kept yelling, 'Will someone get me down from here? How much longer do I have to stay here? I'm getting sea-sick!' Everybody just laughed."

Joe Besser, who replaced Shemp as a third Stooge, was his good personal friend. During production on *Africa Screams*, Besser recalls an incident which illustrated the comedian's inborn fear: "Every night Shemp would wait outside the studio for a cab. One time I stopped to give him a lift. He seemed nervous and didn't want to go with me. Finally, I convinced him to get in the car but he couldn't relax. In desperation, I took his hands and made him hold them as if he was holding an imaginary steering wheel, hoping that would help. He seemed more at ease but when I took off down the street, he started madly turning his hands back and forth as if he were actually driving the car!"

Shemp loved spectator sports, the more aggressive the better. It was probably a form of release for his fear and tension. He also filled his leisure time fishing, attending the fights and listening to Cole Porter's music. Richard Arlen, Andy Devine and Horace MacMahon were his favorite actors, Patsy Kelly his favorite actress and Fred Allen his choice for radio comedian. His favorite Three Stooges comedy was *Fright Night* (1947), his first comedy with the Three Stooges and which, coincidentally, dealt with boxing.

Shemp's mother wished her son to be a gentleman ...and according to everyone who knew him he certainly was a *gentle man*!

The Stooges, Larry, Moe and Shemp, all caring men, entertain some youngsters at a children's hospital.

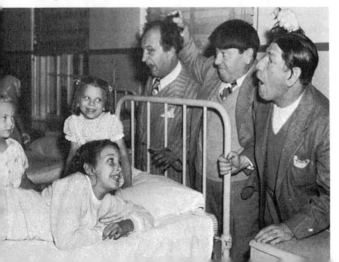

46

Joe Besser

JOE BESSER, who replaced Shemp Howard as the third Stooge in 1956 (not 1955), caught the attention of theatre-goers with his impish grin and child-like demeanor. He was certainly a comedian in his own right.

Joe's stooging began as a youngster growing up in St. Louis, Missouri, where he was born on August 12, 1907, to Fanny and Morris Besser. His parents, orthodox Jews, had moved to the United States from Poland in 1895 where Morris worked as a baker. Joe became the ninth child (two died before his birth) in a family comprised of seven daughters: Rose, Esther, Molly, Lilly, Gertrude, Florence, Henrietta, and an older brother, Manny, who entered show business as a comedian and Jewish dialectician.

Joe became enthralled with magic and show business at an early age and was encouraged by his parents. They might have thought twice about this had they known their son would spend more time watching vaudeville matinees than attending Glascoe Elementary School. Besser once remarked: "I learned more in the theatre than I did in school."

For his age, Joe was a very independent and enterprising young man, working as a Western Union delivery boy, a song-plugger for the Waterson, Berlin and Synder sheet music store and as a distributor of handbills for the Fox Theatre Circuit in St. Louis. By age 13 Joe decided to become a professional magician. His favorite magician was Howard Thurston who appeared in St. Louis annually. Whenever Thurston was in town, Joe eagerly went backstage to ask the world-renowned magician if he could join his act. Each time Thurston replied, "When you get a little bit older, we'll talk about it." Thurston gave Besser the same answer for five years!

Finally, in 1920, the night Thurston's act closed in St. Louis, Joe watched avidly as the stagehands loaded all the scenery and trunks into a nearby freight train. Besser remembers: "I was so anxious to join his act that I stowed away that night on the train with Thurston's act on board, heading for Michigan. The following morning as the train pulled into Detroit, Thurston and his manager found me fast asleep on top of the lion's cage. They wired my folks to tell them where I was and from that day on I was part of the act." On stage, Joe would comically foil Thurston's feats of legerdemain. He would tip-toe in from the audience and reach into Thurston's coat pocket, yanking out trick flowers and other magic-shop props.

In 1923, once Besser discovered that comedy was his forte, he decided to leave Thurston and went on to serve as magician's assistant to Madame Herrman; six months later he became prop assistant to Queenie DeNeenen, a circus tightrope performer. Eventually, Joe teamed with several vaudeville acts, including the popular comedy team Alexandria and Olsen. This was John Olsen, the brother of Chic from the comedy team of Olsen and Johnson.

Joe's career was quickly finding a direction; his current pursuit, in 1928, was that of a solo comedian. While on tour, he was introduced to an Allan K. Foster dancer, Erna Dora Kretschmer (who shortened her name to Erna Kay—then was nicknamed "Ernie"). They courted for four years and were married on November 18, 1932. Ernie served as a choreographer on the 1929 Paramount film *The Coconuts*, featuring the Marx Brothers.

In 1930, Joe toured the Keith Theatre Circuit with a new act containing two hilarious skits, "Wild Cat Duggan" and "Spanish Omelet." Sam Critcherson (known on stage as Dick Dana) signed as Joe's first professional straight man. By 1938, however, Besser broke in a new act with nightclub singer Lee Royce, who sang a baritone rendition of "Ol' Man River." Then, two years later, Besser took Columbia Pictures contractee Jimmy Little on tour as his straight man. These acts weren't billed jointly, but as "Joe Besser with An Added Attraction." Soon Besser became a headliner on the Orpheum, RKO, Paramount and Loew's theatre circuits. He also appeared on the Broadway stage in two J.J. Shubert revues, *The Passing Show of 1932* and *The Greenwich Village Follies*. (In 1946, Besser returned to Broadway in *If the Shoe Fits*, a Cinderella story.)

Joe's portrayal of an exasperated, whining child earned him a spot in Olsen and Johnson's long-running Broadway Show, *Sons of Fun*, and a chance to spring his act on audiences everywhere. In times of mass confusion, his retort was a simple wave of his hand and a sputtering assault of such catchphrases as "Not so fast!" and "You crazy you!" He was occasionally booked to bolster Fatty Arbuckle's personal appearance tours (Arbuckle, before his untimely death, entertained thoughts of starring Besser as his younger brother in a series of comedy shorts), but *Sons of Fun* was the biggest break of his career.

It was Columbia producer Irving Briskin and director Charles Barton who, upon seeing Besser during *Sons of Fun*, urged the studio to sign him. Barton

Joe Besser at age five.

recalls his initial reaction to Besser's antics: "I had never seen anything so wild in my whole life. Irving's and my reactions were 'Get the little guy...get him...' because he was so cute."

Columbia Pictures signed Besser to an exclusive contract and cast him in features and comedy two-reelers. He made his screen debut in a 1938 All-Star Comedy short for Columbia, *Cuckoorancho*. His credits at Columbia include *Hey, Rookie!* (1944) with Ann Miller and Larry Parks, and *Eadie Was a Lady* (1945) and *Talk About a Lady* (1946) with Jinx Falkenburg.

Slowly Besser made his climb to stardom. Soon radio comedians like Jack Benny, Fred Allen, Eddie Cantor and Milton Berle were all clamoring to have him on their shows. Besser made frequent appearances on *The Jack Benny Show, The Fred Allen*

Show, The Eddie Cantor Show, Tonight on Broadway (a summer replacement show in 1946), *The Vaughan Monroe Show* and, from 1945 to 1949, as the delirious character, Mr. Know It All, on *Let Yourself Go*, starring Milton Berle.

Besser's television debut came on Standard Brands' variety series, *Hour Glass*, the first live, hour-long entertainment series of any kind produced for network television. It aired on NBC, May 9, 1946. Besser stole the opening with his hilarious military sketch, "The Rookie."

Television producers of the 1950s then clamored for Besser, casting him on *Hollywood House* with Jim Backus, *The Ken Murray Show, The Private Eyes* (a never-shown pilot which teamed Joe with Sheldon Leonard), *Mr. District Attorney, The Abbott and Costello Show* (as a malevolent brat named "Stinky" in 13 episodes), *The Spike Jones Show*, Alan Young's *Saturday Night Revue, My Favorite Story* (as a Small-town Mayor in "No Tears") and *My Little Margie* ("Vern's Butterflies").

Joe also wowed audiences on such television programs as *The Millionaire* (in "Harvey Blake," the premiere episode, which was directed by Stooge alumnus Edward Bernds), *The Martha Raye Show, The Damon Runyan Theater* ("The Mink Doll"), *I Married Joan, The Jack Benny Show* (a record seven appearances, his most memorable being with Tennessee Ernie Ford), *The Ray Milland Show, Private Secretary, The Dennis O'Keefe Show, December Bride, Willy*, and even *The Gene Autry Show*.

Joe continued making his own comedy shorts for Columbia before joining the Three Stooges in 1956. His series' straight man was Jim Hawthorne, who went on to produce and narrate a series of television blackouts called *Jim Hawthorne's Funnyworld*. Hawthorne has nothing but high praise when speaking of Besser. He credits Joe with helping him develop

Joe is presented with an "Oh you crazy" cake, backstage, during a vaudeville engagement.

Joe with straight man Jimmy Little.

into a comedian: "I believe Joe gave of his talents what others would jealously guard. I felt the relationship was short lived, but a fascinating one for me, with fond memories. I think Joe and I might have developed into a good comedy team which could have replaced the Stooges. The comedies were really fun to make and he was so good in them."

Director Jules White produced and directed most of Besser's solo comedies. He also believed Besser and Hawthorne were a natural combination. "Joe was the little boy with the temper who clenches his fist, threatens, backs away, runs and never really wants to fight you. That was Joe's character," White explained. "This fellow Hawthorne was a good foil for Joe. He was a comic straight man. They were two dummies, each telling the other how dumb they are and neither believing each other. This was a good combination."

Behind the scenes, Joe got along with everybody on the set. Such directors as Jules White and Charles

Barton have said that Besser didn't make demands as to how his character should be played. "Joe was a real gentleman," Jules White said in an interview. "He had good ideas for his character. But if I asked him to do something that wasn't quite right, although he wasn't happy at first, he'd never let me down once we talked things out."

Joe didn't do much socializing after or during working hours. He got strictly down to business when it came to performing. Seldom did Besser take the initiative in starting up new friendships. He just went to the studio, did his job and returned home for the quiet life. Concerning his association with the Stooges, whom he didn't see off screen, Joe has nothing but fond memories. Besser recalls, "Moe and Larry were great. We had a lot of fun and I had no problems with them. I knew them when they were with Ted Healy. So we all went back some years together. After the Healy days, I continued to follow

Joe after leaving the popular comedy team Alexandria and Olsen in 1928.

Joe Besser pictured with his off screen friend, Lou Costello, on the set of *Little Giant* (1946).

Show from 1962 to 1965 as the apartment superintendent, Jillson, in an astronomical 88 episodes.

After Besser's memorable association with the Bishop show ended, he was continually called upon to grace the small screen in cameo roles on: *The Hollywood Palace* (three appearances, twice with Milton Berle), *Batman* ("His Honor the Penguin"), *The Danny Thomas Special* ("It's Greek to Me"), *The Mothers-in-Law* ("How to Manage a Rock Group," "The First Anniversary Is the Hardest" and "Two on the Aisle"), *That's Life* ("Bachelor Days"), *That Girl* ("Eleven Angry Men and That Girl"), *The Don Rickles Show,* and *The Jerry Lewis Show.*

Joe also evoked laughs in *My World and Welcome to It* ("The Night the House Caught Fire"), *The Good*

Joe with his first love, *children*!

their careers. I'm glad I did join the Stooges and I have never regretted it."

Leaving the Stooges in 1958, Besser went on to star in feature films for 20th Century-Fox, in Jerry Lewis comedies, and served up laughs on many more popular 1960s television shows, including: Spike Jones's *Club Oasis, The Kraft Music Hall* (twice with Milton Berle), *The TV Guide Awards Show* with Fred MacMurray and Nanette Fabray, *The Shirley Temple Theatre* (joining comics Carl Ballantine and Jerry Colonna in "Babes in Toyland"), *General Electric Theater* hosted by Ronald Reagan (as Charles Bronson's fight manager in "Memory in White" co-starring Sammy Davis, Jr.) and *The Alvin Show* (as the voice of a Fire-Breathing Dragon).

His popularity, however, soared to new heights when Joe became a regular on the *The Joey Bishop*

The character Joe's voice made famous: Babu, from Hanna-Barbera's *Jeannie*. (© Hanna-Barbera Productions.)

Guys ("Win, Place and Kill" and "No Orchids for the Diner"), *Arnie*, *The Bing Crosby Christmas Special* (of 1970), *The Monk* (a made-for-TV movie), commercials for *Off!* insect repellent and *Scope* mouthwash, and *Love American Style* (four appearances, his funniest being as a Toupee Salesman in "Love and the

Joe with his wife Ernie in 1980.

Lady Barber" (1971), with his customer the late Frank Sutton of *Gomer Pyle* fame).

Joe enjoyed spending his time building toys for neighborhood children and gardening with his wife Ernie. He was also a camera buff. His favorite comedians were Jack Benny and Abbott and Costello, and Ann Miller was his choice for actress. Joe never saw all of his Stooges comedies, but his favorite was *Flying Saucer Daffy* (1958). (His fans prefer *Hoofs and Goofs* (1957) and *A Merry Mix-up* (1957).

On March 1, 1988, Joe Besser's life ended sadly. He was found dead in his North Hollywood home of heart

Joe as he looked offscreen.

failure. Fourteen months later, his wife Ernie succumbed on July 1, 1989, as a result of septic shock, at the Motion Picture and Television Hospital in Woodland Hills. She was 89.

Admittedly, the one element that kept Joe going in later years was the knowing that fans still loved him

"I love working for kids. They are my best fans, my best audience and my best friends," he said. "My biggest thrill is having kids like me. As long as this happens, I've got it made."

Joe DeRita

THE YOUNGEST MEMBER of the Three Stooges, Joseph DeRita—whose real name is Joseph Wardell—was born July 12, 1909, in Philadelphia, Pennsylvania. Of French-Canadian and English ancestry, he is the only one of the Stooges who came from a show business family. His mother, Florenz DeRita, was a dancer and his father, Frank Wardell, was a stage technician.

From age seven, Joe accompanied his parents on tour, going with them from theatre to theatre across the country. He made his stage debut with his sister Phillis at a Topeka, Kansas, Red Cross benefit during World War I. Joe remembers this act: "We did an esthetic dance. I had a wreath around my head and a toga and gave her a rose...that kind of stuff. I was quite small in those days. Of course, they called me Junior.

"We had a small-time act, we never played any major circuits. In those days there were the Western Vaudeville Circuit, the Bert Levy Circuit and the Junior Orpheum Circuit which the smaller acts played."

Then, for seven seasons, Joe played the title role in a stage version of *Peck's Bad Boy* with his mother and father. By age eighteen, with his mother retired and his sister married, Joe decided to do a comedy single in which he sang and danced. As DeRita recalls: "I originally started out as a dancer because my mother was a dancer. Then I went into burlesque in 1921 because vaudeville was just about gone. At least my type of vaudeville was gone. I never worked too risqúe."

Joe continued to play the New Columbia Burlesque Circuit until 1942, after which he went to California to headline in a show at the Music Box Theatre in Hollywood. His notices were so good that MGM signed him to a contract. His actual film debut, however, was in *The Doughgirls* (1944) with Ann Sheridan for Warner Brothers. During this same period of his career he made two other feature films, *The Sailor Takes a Wife* (MGM, 1945) and *People Are Funny* (Paramount, 1946). He performed in shows for the USO and in 1946 starred in a series of two-reel comedies for Columbia; he made four shorts in all.

In speaking of his Columbia shorts, DeRita has said, "My comedy in those scripts was limited to getting hit on the head with something, then going over to my screen wife to say, 'Honey, don't leave me!' For this kind of comedy material you could have gotten a bus boy to do it and it would have been just as funny."

During World War II, Joe started working for the USO and toured the South Pacific with his good friend Randolph Scott as his straight man. He made several tours, going overseas with Bing Crosby to entertain servicemen in England and France, this time with Crosby as his straight man. After returning to the States, Joe played the Hollywood Casino in Los Angeles and made guest appearances on two radio shows with Crosby, *Philco Hall of Fame* and *Cavalcade of America*. He also appeared on radio with Burns and Allen, Andy Russell, Ginny Simms and appeared for 13 weeks on *The Fred Brady Show*, a summer replacement for Bob Burns. Before joining the Stooges in 1958, he had a major role as the hangman in *The Bravados* for 20th Century-Fox, which starred Gregory Peck. DeRita ran the gamut in films, as well as making guest appearances on such television shows as *The Desilu Playhouse, This Is Alice* and *Bachelor Father*.

Up to this point, Joe DeRita's name was far from a household word. It was his 12-year association with the Three Stooges that catapulted him to stardom. As director Norman Maurer explains, "He was the best Curly replacement the Stooges ever had. Joe was great on adlibs. He was like Curly in several respects, with his weight and his ballet-like grace despite his weight. Joe could do a little shuffle—not quite like Curly—but just as graceful, and it was hard to believe a guy that big was doing it."

On the set, however, there were times Curly-Joe had his share of bad days. "Every now and then Joe would become temperamental, but it was a passing

Joe as a dancer at age eight.

Joe, sister Phillis and mother Florenz in the act
"DeRita Sisters and Junior."

Joe, with Moe and Larry backstage following a
1960 Philadelphia nightclub appearance.

Joe with Larry and Moe during a lighter moment on the set of *Have Rocket, Will Travel.*

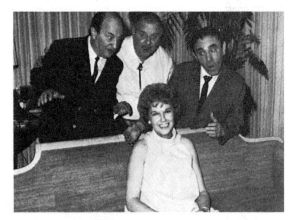

Larry and Moe, with Joe and Jean in Moe's home a few months after their marriage in 1966.

Joe, Larry, Moe and Moose take in the scenery between filming on *Kook's Tour.*

Curly-Joe today.

thing," Maurer recalls. "In most cases, Joe was a good sport and got the job done."

Now retired, Curly-Joe leads a rather quiet life. Even during his years as a Stooge, Joe recalled that he seldom saw Moe and Larry off the set. "We never socialized much, unless it was a film promotion, a premiere or a business meeting. Moe knew judges, doctors, wealthy people—he had his circle of friends. Larry had his friends. And I knew some people out of Hollywood—friends of mine that I'm fond of, and I enjoy their company. But I don't go out of my way to meet people."

Joe resides now in North Hollywood with his wife, Jean Sullivan, whom he married on December 28, 1966. He spends most of his time reading and watching television, but his favorite pastime is listening to classical music. As to Joe's likes and dislikes: He considers Hollywood's three worst actors to be George Raft, Buster Crabbe and Johnny Weismuller. His favorite Stooges film, *The Three Stooges Go Around the World in a Daze* (Columbia, 1963).

Caricature of Ted Healy and His Gang.

1

Historical Overview

For over five decades, fans have been roaring with laughter at the wild, two-fisted, knockabout antics of the Three Stooges. It is their trademark blend of slaps in the face, bops in the head and pokes in the eye that continue to fracture audiences of all ages and all races and creeds throughout the world. Although success was not easily attained, the Stooges, like wine, have improved with age.

The winning formula that catapulted the Stooges into the limelight was first conceived in 1922 when Ted Healy, booked into the Brooklyn Prospect Theatre in New York, ran into trouble with his German acrobatic act. They walked out before their scheduled performance because of an argument with Healy. Now, minus the acrobats, Ted called on two boyhood friends—first Moe and then Shemp Howard—to come up from the audience and join him on stage. The Howards and Healy went on to fracture their audiences with their ad-libbed routines. From theatre circuit to theatre circuit, the crowd's reaction was always the same, instantaneous laughter.

According to an interview with Larry, Healy and his Stooges toured the vaudeville circuits for four years before Shemp decided he wanted to change. He had the opportunity to form a new act with an old friend and vaudeville comedian, Jack Waldron. Shemp broke the news to Healy during a visit to the Rainbow Gardens nightclub, in 1925, when the boys took a break from their scheduled performance to catch a new act on the bill: a song-and-dance team, "Haney Sisters and Fine." Loretta and Mabel Haney sang and danced while Larry Fine played the violin and did a Russian dance to the tune of "My Old Kentucky Home."

During Fine's performance, after Shemp had informed Ted of his decision to leave the act, Moe turned to Healy and suggested that Fine might make a perfect Stooge replacement for Shemp. Ted agreed, and after the show was over, Healy, Moe and Shemp went backstage to visit Larry. Inside Larry's dressing room, Ted made him the offer to become a Stooge.

Even though the Haney act was breaking up, Larry reminisced, "I was hesitant about accepting Healy's offer. I had never done comedy before and was afraid of the outcome." Healy agreed to give Larry some time to think the offer over.

The following evening, Larry returned to the Rainbow Gardens, his mind preoccupied with whether or not to accept Healy's offer. That night, however, Larry's decision on Ted's contract offer was made for him. Since Prohibition was in effect, the serving of alcoholic beverages was against the law, and the nightclub had been shut down because of drinking on the premises. To compound matters, the nightclub manager, Fred Mann, feeling the incident had stained his image, committed suicide. As a result of the club's closure and Mann's death, Larry was released from his nightclub contract.

Immediately, Larry hailed a taxi to take him to the Cohan Theatre where Healy, Moe and Shemp were performing. Backstage, Fine dashed into the wings where he hoped to catch Healy's attention. Larry once recalled in an interview what happened when Ted saw him: "Ted was quick-witted and sharp. The moment he saw me, he signaled to Al Jolson, who was also in the show, to push me out on stage. To my surprise, there we were, ad-libbing the entire scene together. In the excitement I actually didn't know what Healy was saying. He would talk to me out loud and then whisper in my ear what I should answer. I can't remember what happened but the audience was laughing like hell. After the show, Shemp came up to Healy and said, 'You don't need me anymore. You've got a great replacement in Larry.' And that's how I became a Stooge."

(Incidentally, it should be pointed out here that reports that Healy's original Stooges were comprised of Shemp Howard, Lou Warren and Dick Hakins are untrue. However, from 1922 to 1924 another performer, Kenneth Lackey, did on occasion replace Shemp. Lackey finally quit Healy to join Earl Carroll's *Vanities* and several years later returned to his home in Indiana to serve as a district court clerk.)

It took Fine several months to become comfortable with his new role as a Stooge and as a comedian. Soon Healy and his Stooges' raucous style of roughhouse shenanigans caught on and the team played to sell-out crowds in vaudeville theatres across the country.

Of one stage engagement at Loew's Rochester Theatre, a critic enthused: "There's a lot of what might be called 'broad comedy' in Healy's contribution to the new combination screen (movie) and vaudeville. The majority know Healy as a good entertainer and he does not disappoint in his present offering. He is particularly fortunate in having such capable comedy assistants. They keep the fun moving, and while it is moving, the audience gets plenty of entertainment."

Healy's troupe continued to live up to the critic's praise, playing top vaudeville circuits throughout the nation. The team was usually billed as "Ted Healy and His Racketeers" (sometimes "Ted Healy and His Laugh Racketeers"), "Ted Healy and His Three Southern Gentlemen" and "Ted Healy and His Gang." But Healy's ensemble was never called "Ted Healy and the Three Stooges." (Larry Fine erroneously reported in his book, *A Stroke of Luck*, that he, Moe and Shemp were billed in vaudeville as the Three Stooges, which is completely false.)

Postcard promoting *A Night in Venice*.

In 1927, Healy, Shemp and a gang of funsters frolicked on Broadway in J.J. Shubert's musical revue, *A Night in Spain*, Moe left the act to be closer to his family, as his daughter was due to be born that year,

Program from *A Night in Venice*.

while Fine married his former vaudeville partner, Mabel Haney. Healy and Shemp Howard, despite the loss of Moe and Larry, appeared in the Shubert revue, along with Betty Healy, Phil Baker, Sid Silvers and Helen Kane.

Larry and Moe returned to join Healy's act in time for the Broadway revue *A Night in Venice*, which opened at the Shubert Theatre in New York on May 21, 1929. Healy and his Stooges—Moe, Larry and Shemp—had a permanent place on the bill after a successful tryout engagement in New Haven, Atlantic City and Akron. The lavish revue, with 25 dazzling sketches, was directed and choreographed by Busby

film, which had them playing several roles: part-time firemen who aid Healy in crashing a society affair, and soldiers from the Mexican Revolution. Lou Breslow wrote the film's screenplay from Goldberg's original story and Benjamin Stoloff directed. (It is interesting to note that, several years later, Breslow worked with the Stooges at Columbia when he directed the team's second comedy, *Punch Drunks* (1934).)

While the feature was less than sensational, Fox was tremendously impressed with the Stooges and studio executives offered them a seven-year contract to star in features. Up until then, Moe, Larry and Shemp answered to Healy with respect to all contracts, since

New York *Daily News* cartoon from *A Night in Venice*. (Mark Hellinger)

Berkeley. *The New York Times* reported that Healy's hilarious trio were "three of the frowziest numbskulls ever assembled." *A Night in Venice* closed, due to the onset of the Depression, after 175 performances.

Although it lacked longevity, *A Night In Venice* pointed up the Stooges' record-breaking performances, drove their careers to new heights and attracted interest from Hollywood talent scouts, who came *en masse* when Healy and his Stooges were booked at New York's Palace Theatre in 1930. Fox Studios, the forerunner to 20th Century-Fox, was among the film studios represented.

The Fox scout, impressed with the team's performance, immediately signed Healy, Moe, Larry and Shemp to star in Rube Goldberg's comedy, *Soup to Nuts*. Xylophone player Freddie Sanborn, who was also at the Palace Theatre, was billed in the film as one of "Healy's Racketeers" along with Moe, Larry and Shemp. The Stooges' crazy antics were utilized in the

their working agreement with Ted was a verbal pact of faith. This was an unusual set-up, with Healy and not the studio or vaudeville theatre manager paying the Stooges their weekly salaries. Ted's salary to star in *Soup to Nuts* was a third less than his usual vaudeville salary, but was lucrative enough at $1250 per week. Out of this, Healy paid each Stooge $150 per week to star in the Fox film. When Healy learned of the studio's offer of an exclusive contract to the Stooges, he stormed into the office of Fox's studio head, Winnie Sheehan, arguing that the contract was invalid without his approval. In a rage, Ted took the contract from Sheehan's desk and tore it to shreds.

Moe, Larry and Shemp soon caught wind of Healy's latest double-dealing and left the act immediately to form one of their own under the name of Howard, Fine and Howard and billed as the "Three Lost Souls." The trio performed on the West Coast and worked their way back to New York. In 1931, the

59

Jack Walsh, straight man, seen with "Three Lost Souls," Shemp, Moe and Larry.

Stooges hired Jack Walsh as their straight man and together wreaked havoc on the stages of the RKO-Keith Theatre Circuit. On the same bill were such prominent vaudeville performers as Adelaide Hall ("The Crooning Blackbird"), magician Fred Keating and the Hazel Mangean Girls.

The Walsh-Stooges combination was making headlines. Critics reported that Walsh complemented the trio's broad, physical style of comedy to perfection. The Stooges' act with Walsh had many routines from the Healy days but an additional bit of nonsense had them constantly interrupting his singing of "Shine On, Harvest Moon." One theatre critic raved, "Howard, Fine and Howard have one of the most amusing acts in show business. The way they punch each other (apparently) right in the eyes and slap each other around is nobody's business but we should make it ours if we were on the receiving end. They have a straight man, Jack Walsh, whose handsome presence and easy style make a strong contrast."

During this period Ted Healy, wanting to regroup the Stooges, tried to steal first one Stooge and then all three of them back, using a number of underhanded methods. First, he filed a legal suit against the team for promoting themselves in newspaper ads as "Howard, Fine and Howard—Former associates of Ted Healy in *A Night in Venice*." Healy claimed the use of his name, combined with the Stooges' use of his comedy material in their act, was illegal. But a U.S. District Court ruled in favor of the Stooges, claiming that Healy had no rights to the material.

The material that Healy filed suit over was skits taken from portions of the Stooge's performance in *A Night in Venice*. However, Moe Howard, always the team's manager, secured permission from the show's producer, J.J. Shubert, to use certain pieces of material from the show and incorporate it into their act. Healy's Irish temper was slow to cool and in frustration he resorted to threats in a vain attempt to stop the Stooges from continuing their use of any of his material.

Because of Healy's constant threats, Moe, Larry and Shemp became concerned for their own well-being and decided to change some of the material, hoping to pacify Ted. Before one engagement, working at fever pitch, the Stooges in one evening sketched out about a half-dozen new routines. As Larry Fine recalled: "We worked in between the first and second show, and did a complete turnabout. We worked out an old bit where we were musicians and faked a riot, breaking instruments over each others' heads and staging a fight. The audience just loved us, and so did the manager, who booked us for eight more weeks."

Even with their act revamped, Shemp continued to fear Healy and became so concerned over what action the comedian might take next that he stressed his desire to leave the act. Moe, trying to entice Shemp to stay, agreed that he and Larry would raise his salary and pay him more than they were making. According to Moe, Shemp took 36 percent of the team's salary while he and Larry retained 32 percent apiece. The trio then divided, using this new formula, the lucrative salary of $900 a week.

Somehow Shemp must have had a sixth sense about Healy, who, continuing with his threats, warned them to quit using their comedy material or he would actually sabotage one of their engagements with a bomb. Ted was the kind of person who, if he were mad enough, would carry out his threats. But as the comedian's temper began to cool, his threats also waned.

In the meantime, the Stooges continued to fracture audiences, young and old, and critics continued to acclaim the team's growing success as vaudeville

Caricatures of Ted Healy and His Stooges—Shemp, Larry and Moe.

Artist's conception of a scene from *A Night in Venice* (1929).

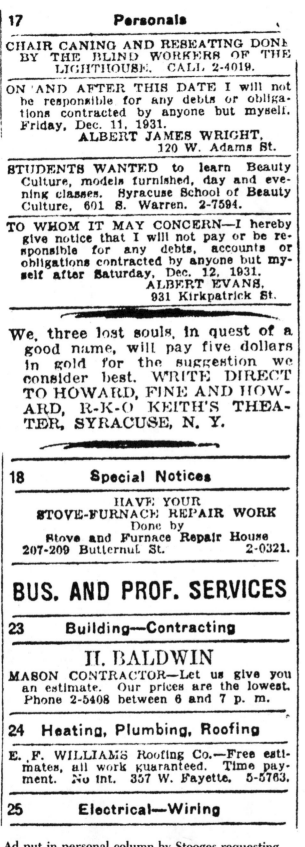

Ad put in personal column by Stooges requesting suggestions for a new name for the team; circa 1931.

comedians. Some critics went so far as to say that Moe, Larry and Shemp "remind us somehow of the Marx Brothers. Their humor is natural and unforced and they have good gags."

Watching Howard, Fine and Howard climb the ladder of success, Healy realized his act wasn't the same without them and kept begging them to come back. But the Stooges refused, since they had grown tired of Healy's shenanigans. In desperation, Ted hired three novice comics as *his* Stooges—Paul "Mousie" Garner, Dick Hakins and Jack Wolf, who with Healy floundered about in Billy Rose's new musical, *Crazy Quilt*. Critics reported that Healy's three new knockabout comics "don't equal the comedian's original Stooges in any professional way." Suddenly, Ted came to the realization that this new act was not working and begged Moe, Larry and Shemp to forgive and forget.

By now, Moe Howard had become the team's manager and the Stooges' driving force. He made the decisions when it came to theatre bookings and the team's salaries, so he also reviewed the matter of Healy's offer. Shemp was reticent but Larry was willing. So Moe gave Ted an ultimatum: If he wanted a deal, with all three of them returning as his Stooges, he had to stop drinking. Ted vowed never to take another drink, and in 1932 the Stooges made the deal official.

When the Stooges, Moe, Larry and Shemp, returned to Healy's act, the comedian let Garner, Wolf and Hakins go. Six years later in 1938, when Moe, Larry and Curly became the famous "Columbia's Three Stooges," Garner, Wolf and Hakins filed a law suit against the trio, claiming that they had stolen the name "Three Stooges" from them and kept them from achieving a like success. However, research and a legal document signed by Moe Howard, Larry Fine and Curly Howard has proven that the name "Three Stooges" was first conceived by the original Stooges, Moe, Larry and Curly. (It should also be noted that Mousie Garner has claimed that Wolf, Hakins and himself starred in Vitaphone comedies as Stooges before the Three Stooges were featured in their own series at Columbia. He has also maintained that he occasionally spelled Shemp Howard as a third Stooge during Shemp's association with Ted Healy, Moe and Larry. Research has found these claims to be untrue.)

When Healy and his original Stooges got together again, J. J. Shubert immediately booked the team into his new Broadway show, *The Passing Show of 1932*. But after four weeks of rehearsal, an argument ensued between Healy and Shubert over a loophole in the comedian's contract. Evidently, Healy's personal manager, Paul Dempsey, noticed that Ted's contract didn't contain a closing date for the show, thus making it void. Healy broke his contract with Shubert to take an offer from the Balaban & Katz Circuit for $6,000 a week (Shubert was only paying him $2800 a week). The Stooges, meanwhile, went back to their original salary of only $100 a week. Shemp did not want any part of Ted's deviousness and refused to leave the Shubert musical. (Also on the Shubert bill with Shemp was another comedian, who later became a Stooge himself, Joe Besser.) Not long after this, Shemp starred in Vitaphone comedies and later established himself in the role of Knobby Walsh in the *Joe Palooka* series.

Moe and Larry went along with Healy to work for Balaban & Katz, and as a temporary replacement for Shemp, Healy hired xylophonist Freddie Sanborn (who had worked with the Stooges before in *Soup to Nuts*) for the team's exclusive six-week engagement. Despite Shemp's departure, Ted and his Stooges drew packed houses every night and continued to leave the audiences in stitches. Once the engagement ended, Sanborn left the group and returned to his xylophone playing.

With Sanborn gone, Moe decided to recruit his brother Jerry, later nicknamed "Curly," to take over the cornerstone of third Stooge. Curly at that time sported long, wavy-brown hair and a waxed moustache. Legend has it that when Jerry joined the team, he shaved off both his hair and moustache, but photographs of the early team show that Curly shaved his head but kept his stubby moustache. He snipped off the moustache when the Stooges and Healy landed their contract to star in films at MGM. With Curly aboard, it should also be pointed out that the team's salary structure changed. Curly received $75 a week while Moe's salary climbed to $140 and Larry took home $125 a week. Curly's theatrical experience was limited to a brief stint as musical conductor for the Orville Knapp Band. Yet, inexperience did not inhibit him from becoming a tremendous asset to the act. In his first stage appearance, Curly's nervousness caused him to speak in a very high-pitched voice. That voice became his trademark as well as his silly grunts and squeals which he used to cover up his inability to remember his lines. Moe recalls that Ted was concerned about Curly's inexperience. "What Curly did for the first three weeks was just run across the stage in a bathing suit, carrying a little pail of water. That's all he did, run back and forth, until we gradually worked him into the act," Howard said.

It was during the team's performance at the New York Cafe, in 1933, that an MGM scout discovered and signed Ted Healy and His Stooges to a studio contract. As explained earlier, Healy signed the contracts for all of them.

Unlike the Stooges' previous journey to Hollywood

Artist's conception of Stooges from MGM film *Plane Nuts* (1933).

Nitrate film clip of a deleted scene from the MGM short *Plane Nuts*.

for the Fox film, this time the team's trip west was for keeps. MGM executives had laid plans to star Healy and His Stooges in musical comedies and features. The madcap trio's first, joint feature appearance was in MGM's *Turn Back the Clock* (1933) with Lee Tracy and Mae Clark. They were next featured in *Meet the Baron* (1933) with Jimmy Durante, ZaSu Pitts and

wood Party (1934), along with Jimmy Durante, Mickey Mouse, Polly Moran and a comedy team in their own right, Laurel and Hardy.

Besides blockbuster feature-length movies, Healy and His Stooges also starred in five musical-comedy shorts which co-starred Ted's real-life girl friend, Bonnie Bonnell. Bonnell had also worked with Healy

Shemp as Knobby Walsh demonstrates a "knockout" punch for Joe Palooka (Robert Norton) and his second (Johnny Berkes).

Edna May Oliver, followed by their roles in *Dancing Lady* (1933) starring Joan Crawford and Clark Gable. Also cast in the picture were Franchot Tone, Nelson Eddy, Robert Benchley and Fred Astaire. Metro next used the Stooges and Healy in *Fugitive Lovers* (1934) and then spotted them in a comedy feature, *Holly-*

and His Stooges on stage during their vaudeville days. Of the team's five comedy two-reelers, two of them were filmed in two-strip experimental color—*Nertsery Rhymes* (1933), their first musical short, and *Hello, Pop!* (1933). Jack Cummings was the series' producer and director. The films were a combination of new comedy sketches starring Healy and the Stooges and stock footage of dance extravaganzas lifted from MGM musicals.

Curly Howard also made a cameo appearance in *Roast Beef and Movies* (1934), another experimental color short. Larry Fine recalls that Metro tried to reproduce the Stooges by pairing Curly with two other comedians, George Givot and Bobby Callahan. This didn't pan out, even though the film was a critical success. Curly also appeared in another MGM comedy, this one with Moe Howard, called *Jailbirds of Paradise*, which was released in color on March 10, 1934.

Just four months prior to the release of *Jailbirds of Paradise*, Universal Pictures' film producer Brian Foy signed Ted Healy, Moe, Larry and Curly to star in four feature-length films commencing with *Myrt and Marge* (1933). Research has found, contrary to previously published reports, that the Stooges do appear in this Universal film, portraying Ted Healy's bumbling stagehands. Al Boasberg, whom the trio worked under at MGM, directed the team in the film. For reasons unknown, however, the Stooges never fulfilled their contractual obligation with Universal by starring in the other three features. (Universal also tried to cast the Stooges in *Gift of Gab* (1934) during the trio's tenure at Columbia, but studio head Harry Cohn nixed the deal. Instead, producer Ryan James sought out three stooges of his own for the roles.)

In addition, the team had agreements to star, jointly or separately, in the following productions: *The Gang's All Here* (a working title for a film based on the

Bonnie Bonnell, Ted Healy and His Stooges in MGM short *The Big Idea* (1934).

Larry, Curly and Moe with Marjorie White on the set of *Woman Haters* (1934), their first Columbia short.

popular Broadway show), a film version of Billy Rose's *Crazy Quilt; Going Hollywood* (1933) with Bing Crosby and Marion Davies; and *Employment Agency for Stooges* (written by Herman Timberg and planned first as a feature, then as a short). According to Hollywood trade paper reports, *Employment Agency* was meant to launch the team's career in features as "filmdom's successors to the Marx Brothers." Unfortunately, for reasons unclear, the Stooges never pursued any of these projects.

During this period of their careers, the Stooges' onscreen shenanigans carried over off-screen. There was just no way these classic film clowns could refrain

65

Moe in a solo film appearance with Leo White in a scene from MGM short *Jail Birds of Paradise* (1934).

from livening up their social affairs. A prime example of their comedic, offstage antics happened when Healy and His Stooges attended the Los Angeles premiere of *Dinner at Eight* (1933), which was being screened at Grauman's Chinese Theatre in September 1933. Limousines arrived carrying filmdom's top celebrities while Healy and his trio could be seen pedaling up to the theatre on a bicycle-built-for-four! Ted sat on the first seat gloriously resplendent in a white top hat with feathers, boots, breeches and bright-colored tails. Taking up the rear were comrades Moe, Larry and Curly, garbed in high hats and immaculate evening clothes. The Stooges were definitely the hit of the evening.

The riotous antics of the team didn't stop here, however. Backstage at Metro, as all was quiet on the set, Moe, Larry and Curly broke new ground with their slapstick-brand of tomfoolery. Wearing ghoulish make-up, the Stooges wandered over to another MGM sound stage and ran smack into Greta Garbo. Witnesses reported that it was hard to tell who was the most nonplussed, Garbo or the Stooges. It is also

An ad from the *Motion Picture Herald* informing exhibitors that *Gents Without Cents* is available for booking.

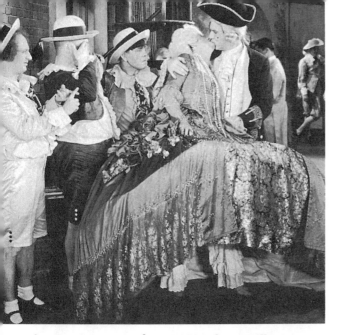

Stooges in a scene from MGM short *Hello Pop* (1933).

Evidently, Moe, Larry and Curly did some soul searching as to their remaining with Healy, but their meager salaries became the deciding factor. As Moe once remarked in an interview: "In the early days, what Ted paid us was laughable. And there were times when Ted didn't get paid, so we didn't get paid. This was later reflected in the period at MGM, where some weeks Ted would give me one hundred, some weeks only fifty dollars. I went along with it since I understood his financial situation was such that he couldn't pay us what he owed us." But as time wore on, and Healy's lapses in payment continued, Moe found it an impossible situation, as did his partners, Larry and Curly. They all wanted out.

believed that the Stooges' monster make-up scared Garbo, who came out with her then-famous line, "I vant to be alone!"

Even Curly got into the act while making a personal appearance in Philadelphia. Ted had just bought a dozen very expensive imported shirts that he was simply mad about. In fact, he loved them so much that he warned the Stooges not to lay a finger on them. One evening, during a performance, Curly grabbed Healy by the shirt and, for a comedic effect, literally tore it off Healy's back. Ted, not realizing until the act was over that he was wearing his favorite shirt, never thought to stop Curly.

Since Metro never really utilized Ted Healy and His Stooges to their full potential, it was not surprising that Hollywood trade papers reported on May 16, 1933, that Healy had signed a deal with Columbia Pictures to star in a series of two-reelers. A *Hollywood Reporter* article revealed that Healy, Moe, Larry and Curly were set to star in a series of Columbia comedies, starting with *We're in the Money.* Ralph Staub was signed to direct this two-reel effort which would have changed the entire story of the Stooges' history at Columbia Pictures if the film had gone into production. But, at the last minute, Metro stepped in and voided the Columbia deal since Healy had not fulfilled his Metro contract. Consequently, the film was never produced.

Although the team continued to ride on a wave of successes at Metro, the Stooges were very unhappy with their position strictly as Healy's comic relief. On March 6, 1934, when Healy's contract was up for renewal, the Stooges decided to break with him.

A scene from *Beer and Pretzels* with Ed Brophy as a theatre manager.

In a meeting with Healy and Paul Dempsey (Healy's agent), Moe induced them to draw up a paper releasing him and the Stooges from working with Ted. Finally free, it was off to find out whether there was a place for the boys in the movie industry. Ted did try, on several occasions, to get the Stooges to come back, but they just weren't interested.

It was with sadness that reporters in the trades noted the Healy/Stooges break-up. As one columnist wrote: "Sad note. Ted Healy and his completely mad Stooges have unfortunately come to the parting of the ways. The Stooges felt they could make more money

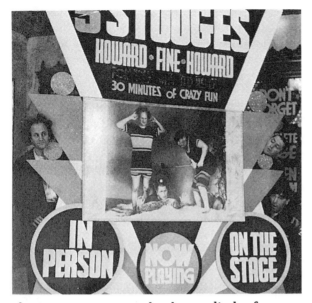

The Stooges peer around a theatre display for one of their stage appearances.

Men in Black, the team's third comedy, was a spoof of the MGM/Clark Gable film, *Men in White*, and the only film for which the Stooges received an Academy Award nomination. Even though the film was worthy of the honor, *La Cucaracha*, an RKO color musical short, won the Oscar.

History has also cited that *Men in Black* was the

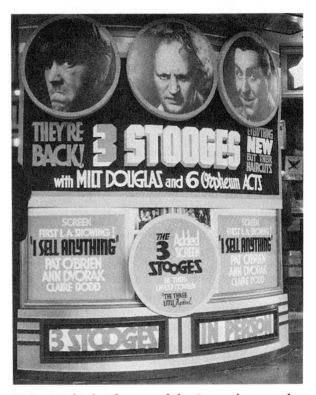

A theatre display for one of the Stooges' personal appearances.

and get along better sans their discoverer. Wezel see."

The Stooges made their historic jump from Metro to Columbia Pictures on March 19, 1934 (not June 1934), when the trio signed a one-picture contract, with additonal comedies to be made if reception was favorable for the first one. Columbia inserted into the team's pact a 60-day waiting period that would be used to decide whether to exercise their option to star the Stooges in additional comedies following release of their first film. The contract also provided that, if Columbia did request further production of Stooge comedies, the team would film eight two-reel comedies in a 40-week period with 12 weeks off (which could be used for any sort of work other than films).

Eight days after studio approval of the team's contract, Columbia cast the Stooges in *Woman Haters* (1934) opposite a rising contract starlet, Marjorie White. In the film, the Stooges were not billed as the Three Stooges, but as Howard, Fine and Howard. The name Three Stooges was not officially conceived until June 1, 1934. Besides being the team's first starring film without Ted Healy, *Woman Haters* was Walter Brennan's first screen role; he played a bit part as a train conductor.

In their next two-reeler and second film in the series, *Punch Drunks*, the trio received story credit and clearly showed promise as film comedians. It also was the first film in which the team was billed on screen as "The Three Stooges." Incidentally, the eight-page treatment the Stooges wrote was entitled *A Symphony of Punches*, an original copy of which still remains.

turning point in the Stooges' film career. Jules White, the film's producer, has stated that the film convinced Columbia to keep the Stooges on, since one of their films was nominated for an Academy Award and proved to the studio the comedians' worth to the industry. The Stooges' salary for starring in *Woman Haters* was a paltry $1,000 split three ways. But as the team's popularity grew, Columbia increased their salary to as much as $7,500 a week for the team, divided equally.

Next, the Stooges starred in a college football comedy, *Three Little Pigskins* (1935), featuring a new contract player, Lucille Ball. Years later, in a *Look* Magazine interview, Ball recounted what it was like working with the Stooges: "The only thing I learned from them was how to duck!"

In their films following *Woman Haters*, the Stooges were able to convey their real, newly found screen personalities. Moe was the bullying, self-appointed leader of the trio. Curly was an enigma, happily lost in his own magical world and frustrated when the harsh, real world intruded. And Larry was the ultimate middleman, existing only to serve his two stronger-willed partners.

Along with character development, Stooges comedies also managed to mirror many social and political themes that are still with us; crises of government, war, unemployment and crime made headlines then as often as they do today. Stories also included the basic line of the Stooges poking fun at the upper classes, during a time when America was experiencing the aftershocks of the Great Depression. Audiences identified with the lower-class Stooges conquering the highest reaches of society, working as plumbers in ritzy mansions, seeking elegant employment and spoofing the United States' military brass in World War II.

Besides timely satirical and social themes, Moe had remarked that it was a combination of slapstick and "the upsetting of dignity" that gave them a basic foundation for their comedy. "We subtly, the three of us, always went into an area of life which we were not

A newspaper ad for one of the Three Stooges' many stage appearances.

The Stooges ham it up during an MGM photo session.

supposed to understand. If we were going to go into society, the picture would open with us as garbage collectors. We would take a man with a high hat, a monocle and spats, and smash him in the nose with a pie, thus bringing him down to our level. I think that we appealed to all age brackets and all class brackets. We did stupid things but they were excusable because we didn't know any better."

In 1939, during a hiatus from their two-reel comedies, which had proven to be immensely popular, the Stooges were signed to tour the British Isles. Their first stop was England, to play a two-week engagement at the London Palladium which was held over. Their tour through the British Isles continued with further stops in Blackpool, Dublin and Glasgow. Then, it was back to the United States to open as

Broadway stars in *The George White Scandals of 1939*, which was tried out in Atlantic City and opened in New York at the Alvin Theatre on August 28, 1939. The production lasted for 120 performances and marked the Stooges' first Broadway show in over seven years. The boys performed for the first time a new sketch called "The Stand-In," a parody of the Hollywood stand-in that included a very messy pie-throwing battle at its finish. The all-star cast that grabbed laughter and applause in this first-rate entertainment also included Willie and Eugene Howard, Ella Logan, Ben Blue and a young dancer by the name of Ann Miller. As critic Robert Coleman of the *New York Daily Mirror* wrote, "...(The Stooges) come through with flying colors and faces dripping with gooseberry pies....They lured laughter from the first nighters like a wringer does water from damp shirts."

In addition to their comedies, the team appeared in many Columbia feature films as comedy relief. Usually, their appearance was a five-to ten-minute cameo in such films as *The Captain Hates the Sea* (1934), *Start Cheering* (1938), *Time Out for Rhythm* (1941), *My Sister Eileen* (1942) and *Rockin' in the Rockies* (1945). The team was also set to appear in two more features, *Chinese Hooey* (1938) with Joe E. Brown, and *Right Guy*, which was re-titled *Good Luck Mr. Yates* (1943). In the Joe E. Brown film, the Stooges were going to perform material written by Moe's wife, Helen Howard, but production was cancelled. In the *Mr. Yates* feature, scenes were filmed on April 16, 1943, on Stage 8, of the Stooges performing "Niagara Falls," with Jules White directing *only* the Stooges' routine; Ray Enright was the feature's over-all director. Footage of the Stooges, however, was cut from the final release print and was shelved until a story could

A lobby card from *Hoi Polloi* (1935).

The Stooges prepare to board a train for a cross-country tour.

be written based around the scenes. Later this entire sequence became the premise for the Stooges comedy, *Gents Without Cents* (1944). The boys also appeared in an independently produced feature for Monogram Pictures called *Swing Parade of 1946*, which featured the team throughout the entire production.

The Stooges continued to enjoy their newly discovered success in movies but found that audiences were divided roughly into two groups: one made up of persons who laughed at them and the other of those who wondered why. There were several reasons why filmgoers liked the Stooges' antics in films. The trio's spontaneous slapstick routines and insane antics were usually improvised, resulting in a balanced blend of ingenuity and creativity. Rival comedy teams, like Abbott and Costello and Laurel and Hardy, stuck mainly to the script. Moe felt that improvising added to the spontaniety in a given scene, unless the Stooges went overboard. But usually that wasn't the case. Larry and Moe were good studies when it came to knowing their lines. Moe, however, was the only one to memorize every player's lines, including his own; he did this for the sake of pacing and timing. Curly was the antithesis, terrible at remembering his lines, and consequently improvising the most. As Moe related in an interview: "If he forgot his lines, it was a temporary thing. I could tell, because his eyes would roll around a little bit and he'd fall to the floor and spin around like a top—or do a backward kick, or go on his back and move like a snake."

71

Curly's reliance on ad-libbing usually accelerated the already frantic pace of the team's comedies and many times was their savior. Tempo was vitally important in these broad, slapstick comedies and brisk pace and split-second timing was crucial—unlike the films starring Laurel and Hardy, who worked at a much slower pace.

Laurel and Hardy, for instance, took several minutes to build up to one laugh-riot moment, while the

The Stooges do a "triple take" when they come face to face with a musclebound menace.

Stooges' wham-bam style elicited ten times the guffaws in a single scene. Moe remarked that the team abided by three rules to keep the tempo moving: "Our three rules for working were watch, listen and plan. We watched the tempo of the act, listened to the other member when one was in the spotlight and planned our routines. There was a lot more to it than just going up and telling funny stories and smacking each other around. We checked the slapstick carefully in order not to overdo it. If comedy goes on too long, the audience begins to think about it. We aimed not to give anyone time to think."

But besides the customary teamwork, as Moe calls it, the Stooges' stock company of players brought many additional memorable scenes to the screen. Hollywood usually recognizes the stars of a long-running series but forgets the incidental players. Moe was one of the film industry's few comedians to give

recognition to the secondary players during interviews, since he realized their presence was of immeasurable value to the team's films.

Columbia's stock company was comprised of veteran character actors from silent films (Keystone and Sennett stars) and the legitimate stage. Bud Jamison and Vernon Dent, who started out in silent comedies, were in many Three Stooges films and made every scene count. Symona Boniface, who launched her career in legitimate theatre, invariably wound up as the perfect dowager and got a pie in the face for her efforts. Christine McIntyre, the fans' favorite heroine and villainess, played in dozens of Three Stooges shorts. In the film *Micro-Phonies* (1945), McIntyre made her singing debut as she belted out the lyrics to the tune "The Voices of Spring," which unfortunately was never produced as a record single. Dorothy Appleby, Kenneth MacDonald, Gene Roth, Phil Van Zandt, Gino Corrado, Fred Kelsey, Dick Curtis, Emil Sitka and Harold Brauer were among the many dramatic-actors-turned-comics in Stooges films. Even people like Lloyd Bridges, Walter Brennan, Lucille Ball and Jock Mahoney used Stooges comedies as stepping stones in their careers.

A competent staff of writers and directors was also behind the success of each Stooges film. Felix Adler, Clyde Bruckman and Elwood Ullman were just three of the team's prominent screenwriters. Del Lord, Preston Black (his real name was Jack White, Jules White's brother) and Ray McCarey were the team's first directors. The Stooges' staff of skilled directors also featured the likes of Charles Lamont and Charley Chase and, later, Edward Bernds and Jules White. Recognition is also due such staffers as propman Ray Hunt, sound effects editor Joe Henrie and script girl Dorothy Cumming.

According to Moe and Larry, the violence quota per film depended on the director making the two-reeler. People like Del Lord and Charley Chase were more interested in slapstick and visual gags than outright violence. Edward Bernds also relied on visual gags but even more on coherent stories. Jules White, who produced many Columbia two-reel comedies, earned the distinction of leaning heavily on unnecessary violence in the films. White enjoyed injecting many grotesque and overly cruel gags into their films, such as using scissors, mallets and saws on areas of the human anatomy that should be given a little respect.

A greater risk of injury befell the Stooges themselves, however, in films that contained a higher measure of violence. According to Moe, the Stooges sustained a variety of bumps and bruises and injuries by the dozens; broken noses, fractured ribs, sprained ankles and cracked teeth.

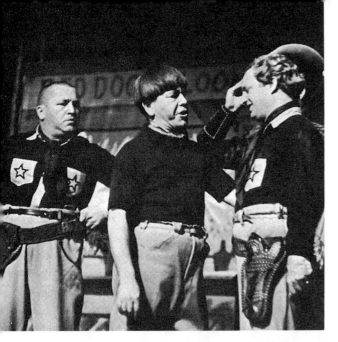

Columbia propman, Stan Dunn, was present several times when the Stooges were injured on the set. The first time, Dunn said, was when Moe broke his nose when he missed his timing going through a revolving door. On another occasion, Curly broke his big toe when he delivered a swift kick at Larry and hit a table leg instead.

(Dunn also recalled a story concerning Larry Fine's periodic hunger pangs. As Dunn remembers: "Fine was always hungry. He spent his money on wine and women, but not on food." Dunn had set aside a dish of dog food for a trained dog who was to appear in a scene with the Stooges. Larry was famished and gobbled the dog food right out of the dish. When Larry found out what he had eaten, he allegedly turned green, then quipped, "That was great! What brand was it?")

Moe reminds Larry that he has just insulted the sovereign state of Texas (clap-clap-clap!).

A publicity still from *The Ghost Talks* (1949).

The Stooges were also concerned over the development of story situations and gags written for them in the scripts. Moe always found it was of paramount importance to hold story conferences with the writer and director. His reason: "All we asked of the writers was a situation. We would look for certain sequences where we could put in some satire and still make it part of the story. It was very important for us to be part of the story and not just be dragged into it. After

when it came to brainstorming new ideas. As director Edward Bernds, who started directing the Stooges in 1945, said: "Moe was good at adding ideas but needed help when it came to constructing a good story line. Larry's suggestions were usually off-target but once in a while he would come up with a gem that would get us started on something. Curly was usually more subdued at these meetings."

Stooges script sessions ran right through pre-pro-

After rejoining the team, Shemp made only one feature film appearance with the Stooges, in *Gold Raiders*, co-starring George O'Brien (1951).

all, we were naturally the best judges of what lines and actions were most appropriate for each of us in any given situation."

When it came to actively providing creative input for these conferences, Moe was the guiding force of the team as far as writing new gags and ideas. He was an inveterate doodler and scribbled many of his ideas down on hotel letterheads, matchbooks and note paper. The least resourceful were Larry and Curly

duction. The Stooges were usually asked to report for a run-through of the script's first draft, then suggestions were made. Edward Bernds, who wrote many Stooges comedies as well as directed them, once explained what transpired at these meetings: "We'd usually have a kind of bull session in which the boys would wander all over the place, ad-libbing routines, reminiscing and I would make notes. I would borrow from old scripts, too, but mostly I listened. I would

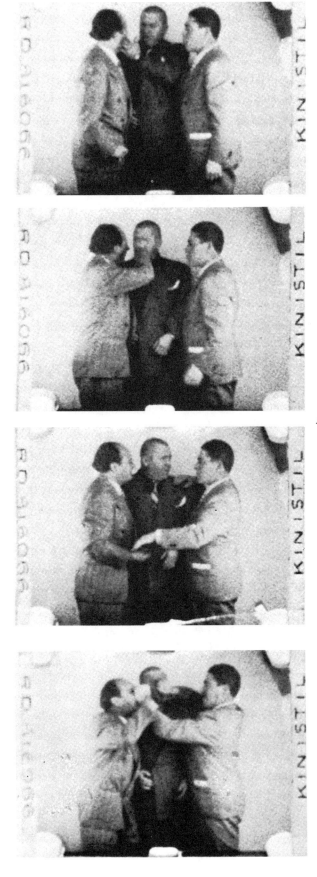

Even during moving day with Curly and his new bride, Elaine, the Stooges can't quit their crazy antics.

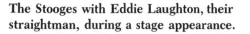
A still photographer captures the Stooges in action.

The Stooges with Eddie Laughton, their straightman, during a stage appearance.

stockpile routines, devise some sort of framework for them to hang on. I would then write a rough draft script and call in the Stooges. They would go through the first draft. It gave them other notions and I would make cuts and additions and somehow hammer out another draft. It was pretty much agreed upon by the time it went into final draft."

Stooges screenwriter Elwood Ullman recalls that ideas for Stooges comedies didn't come easily. "It took me a great deal of time to get used to writing their comedies. I thank Del Lord for providing me with some guidance. But ideas for these scripts weren't easy to conceive. I'd be at my desk perusing *Variety* when the boss, Jules White, might buzz me and say. 'There's an English manor set on Stage Two that's available to us. Take a stroll through the set and see if

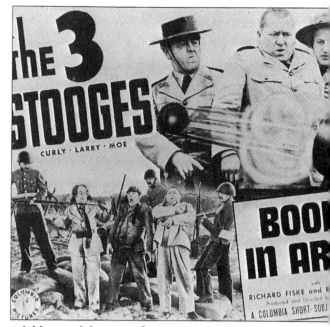

A lobby card from *Boobs in Arms* (1940).

Curly, Larry and Moe during a tense moment on stage.

you can come up with something for the Three Stooges.' There were many nervous times when I would pace all over until I finally struck on an idea."

By the mid-forties, however, the Stooges started facing problems. Curly's physical appearance began showing signs of deterioration in the films. His vitality and mobility had begun to languish. He was unable to do the brilliant physical comedy that had been his forte. No longer could he fall on the floor, and spin like a top. His high-pitched squeal of a voice had become a hoarse croak. He couldn't even muster up enough strength to do his ever-popular "Wooo-wooo-wooo."

The Curly Howard moviegoers saw in 1946 was, as Larry Fine later remarked, "a shell of a man." The critical reason for Curly's sudden decline was a series of minor strokes he had suffered.

Director Edward Bernds joined the ranks of Stooges directors in 1945 and became acutely aware of Curly's worsening physical condition while directing *A Bird in the Head* (1946). As Bernds recalls: "I had seen Curly at his greatest and his work in this film was far from great. The wallpaper scene was agony to direct because of the physical movements required to roll up the wallpaper and to react when it curled up on him. It just didn't work. As a fledgling director, my plans were based on doing everything in one nice neat shot. But when I saw scenes were not playing, I had to improvise and use other angles to make it play. It was the wallpaper scene that we shot first, and during the first two hours of filming, I became aware that we had a problem with Curly."

When Norman Maurer was on leave from the Navy in 1945, he paid a visit to the set of the film *Rhythm and Weep* (1946). Maurer remembers that Curly was having problems even then. "He was having trouble with his coordination. He was supposed to pop pills in his mouth during the scene," Maurer said, "but the scene was switched to Moe putting the pills into Curly's mouth because of Curly's physical problems."

According to doctors' theories, people can suffer a series of minor strokes and not know it. Bernds and Maurer agree that Curly probably suffered many little strokes which would account for his decline, but not one great enough to disable him. The fact that Curly drank heavily could have contributed to this; one of his strokes could have been passed off as a hangover. As Larry Fine once stated, "We think that Curly had many small strokes in 1945, but was afraid to tell us because he was afraid that we would have to break up the act."

In agreement with the doctors' theories about strokes, Bernds has said that Curly's physical problems changed from day to day. In an interview, Bernds recalled the progression of Curly's decline in each of the films in the order in which they were shot. "I don't remember having any great difficulty with him in *Three Troubledoers*. Then in *Micro-Phonies* he was suddenly the old Curly. I can't think of a fault; he was himself again. Then, in *Monkey Businessmen* he was at his worst. Moe coached him the way one would a child, getting him to repeat each line after him. We had to shoot Curly repeating one line at a time. Then,

The boys show off their Motion Picture Exhibitors "Laurel Awards" which they won for many years in a row.

The Stooges reprise their acrobatic act from their days with Ted Healy, during a stage appearance with Curly.

in *Three Little Pirates*, he was terrific. It was the last flash of the old Curly," Bernds said.

Bernds was able to pinpoint these events from his diary, which he kept sporadically during this period of Curly's decline. He remembers the strokes started about January 31, 1945, and continued until Curly had

77

his major stroke. It was Moe who remembered that fateful day; Curly suffered a massive stroke on May 19, 1946, during filming of the Stooge's 97th short, *Half-Wits' Holiday* (1947). But Bernds' diary and the film's shooting schedule prove otherwise. Curly suffered the stroke that impaired his health for the rest of his life on May 6, 1946.

The untimely, tragic loss of Curly's services as a Stooge came at a time when Bernds had just finished writing the team's next comedy, *Pardon My Terror*, the forerunner to Bernds' later Stooges comedy, *Who Done It?* (1949). Because of Curly's sudden illness,

Moe's and Larry's screen wives react in horror to the boys' culinary catastrophe, in *Husbands Beware* (1956), one of the last films to feature *new* footage of Shemp.

Bernds re-wrote the script and cast Columbia's Gus Schilling and Dick Lane as leads in this two-reel film. The premise concerns two detectives hunting for clues to the mysterious death of millionaire Jonas Morton. Filming commenced four days after Curly's stroke and the two-reel comedy was released September 12, 1946.

Character actor Emil Sitka also starred in *Half-Wits' Holiday* as a high society butler in what was ironically his first Stooges comedy and Curly's last. Sitka recalls that word of what happened to Curly was never

A newspaper ad for a Stooges stage appearance with Shemp.

78

The Stooges use the tricks of their trade on director Jules White between takes of *The Ghost Talks* (1949).

One of Moe's favorite give-away photos was a reproduction of an actual handbill used in *Merry Mavericks* (1951).

revealed to the film's supporting cast. "Nobody was informed. Curly was doing a scene, then all of a sudden we were told there was going to be a big pie fight in the end. Moe and Larry—even Jules—never said a thing. We did the whole scene thinking that Curly was coming in later. He never did. If we had been told, we all would have probably been downcast."

The Stooges saluting some "top brass" at an Air Force Base appearance.

Moe and Larry were hoping that Curly would recover and return to the team, but he never regained his old stamina. Moe believed that, even though his brother couldn't return, the Three Stooges had to continue. So he suggested to Columbia's executives that Shemp Howard, his older brother, replace Curly. At first, Columbia was opposed to the idea since Shemp looked too much like Moe. But he was the obvious candidate because he was so well acquainted with the trio's routines. Shemp agreed to join the team, but first Larry wanted it understood that all three of them would take $50 out of each week's salary and send it to Curly. Moe was extremely touched by

79

Larry, who, although he wasn't a brother, acted like one with his generous act.

Shemp had a tough act to follow, since he had the thankless task of replacing the enormously popular Curly. As far as the transition went, Edward Bernds felt that Shemp was a natural for the job. "Shemp was a trouper, a very willing guy. He was always prepared. It was a delight to work with him. Comparing him to Curly is not fair. He could never be Curly, and never tried to be. Basically, he was a very good actor. I don't think Curly could have been anything but Curly of the Three Stooges. The transition, as far as I was concerned, was all for the good. From then on, I approached the Stooges with anticipation and pleasure," Bernds recalled.

Bernds enjoyed letting the cameras roll at the end of Shemp's scenes, since he gave everything he could to his performance. According to Bernds, Shemp

Stooge stand-in Joe Palma fills in for Shemp Howard in one of four comedy remakes. A scene from *Rumpus in a Harem* (1956).

The loss of Shemp forced Moe and Larry to go it alone in four film remakes. A scene from *Hot Stuff* (1956).

didn't know when to quit. He recalls one incident while shooting *Brideless Groom* (1947) that demonstrates Shemp's method: "In the story, Shemp had a few hours in which to get married if he wanted to inherit his uncle's fortune. He called on Christine McIntyre, who mistook him for her cousin and greeted him with hugs and kisses. Then the real cousin phoned and she accused Shemp of kissing her, as it were, under false pretenses. At this point, she

Columbia Pictures announces the signing of comic Joe Besser as the third Stooge.

was supposed to slap Shemp around. Lady that she was, Chris couldn't do it right; she dabbed at him daintily, afraid of hurting him. After a couple of bad takes, Shemp pleaded with her. 'Honey,' he said, 'if you want to do me a favor, cut loose and do it right. A lot of half-hearted slaps hurts more than one good one. Give it to me, Chris, and let's get it over with.' Chris got up her courage and on the next take, let Shemp have it. 'It' wound up as a whole series of

slaps—the timing was beautiful; they rang out like pistol shots. Shemp was knocked into a chair, bounced up, met another ringing slap, fell down again, scrambled up, trying to explain, only to get another stinging slap. Then Chris delivered a haymaker—a right that knocked Shemp through the door. When the take was over, Shemp was groggy, really groggy. Chris put her arms around him and apologized tearfully. 'It's all right, honey,' Shemp said painfully. 'I said you should cut loose and you did. You sure as hell did!'"

Curly came back in 1947 to make a cameo appearance with the Stooges in *Hold That Lion*. It was the only occasion in which all three Howard brothers appeared together in a film. Curly was the train passenger wearing a derby over his face and a clothespin over his nose. The Stooges put Curly in the film to build up his morale, but it didn't help. Curly Howard passed away after suffering a major stroke on January 18, 1952, at the age of forty-eight. He was buried at Home of Peace Memorial Park and Cemetery in Whittier, California.

Despite Curly's tragic death, the quality of the comedies picked up; with Shemp aboard, his seasoned performances were instrumental in keeping production going at a rapid pace. The series, during Shemp's tenure, received the Motion Picture Exhibitors' Laurel Award for the top two-reel moneymakers for the years 1950, 1951, 1953, 1954 and 1955.

The Stooges, as in the early films, continued to poke fun at social and political issues in their comedies with Shemp. Although his style did not resemble Curly's, he was able to interject his own special brand of insanity into a scene: exaggerated mugging, hilarious double-takes and his own high-pitched, frightened cry of "Heeep-heeep-heeep!"

Shemp not only made 77 Stooges shorts, but also a feature film, *Gold Raiders* (1951). This film was reissued overseas as *The Stooges Go West*, and the Stooges never saw a dime for their participation in the picture other than their salaries. Unlike most of their other feature films, where they appeared only for comedy relief, the Stooges displayed their antics throughout this film. A Hollywood trade paper article reported that the Stooges' appearance in *Gold Raiders* was to mark the first of three features planned for them by United Artists. The other two films were *Tuscon Joe* and *Gasoline Alley*, both starring George O'Brien, who was featured in *Gold Raiders* as well. But according to the film's director, Edward Bernds, Hollywood puffery clouded this article and no additional United Artists/Stooges features were scheduled for production.

Even though the popularity of the Stooges' films remained relatively constant, Columbia Pictures

The Stooges rehearse their old vaudeville act in
***Fifi Blows Her Top* (1958).**

started looking for new methods to increase the team's appeal. Consequently, in 1953 producer Jules White decided to produce two 3-D comedies, *Spooks* and *Pardon My Backfire*. Contrary to erroneous reports in other publications, Columbia Pictures did release both films to theatres in 3-D, not just *Spooks*. Columbia even issued to movie theatres exhibitor one-sheets which were displayed during bookings of these films.

Joe Besser ogles Greta Thyssen on the set of the Stooges' last released short, *Sappy Bullfighters* (1959).

But critics were less than enthusiastic about these new Stooges offerings, as was Columbia, and it abandoned the idea of producing additional 3-D shorts.

Suddenly, the Stooges' popularity started to decline, and to make matters worse, a major disruption of the staff took place. Director Edward Bernds, producer Hugh McCollum and screenwriter Elwood Ullman left Columbia to pursue other interests. Ullman and Bernds accepted an offer to write and direct Allied Artists' Bowery Boys features while McCollum went on to produce several Jack Wrather television series. The absence of Bernds and Ullman was strongly felt in Stooges comedies, especially as White took over complete control of Stooges production. As Ullman explained: "I just had to get out of those shorts. No prestige in shorts. I had to get out if I wanted to stay in the business." Bernds' departure stemmed from the fact that there was no love lost between him and White. As a result, White fired Bernds after letting producer Hugh McCollum go on to greener pastures.

As if losing Bernds, Ullman and McCollum were not enough, death again visited the Stooges. During a break in filming at Columbia on November 23, 1955, Shemp went out with friends to his favorite sporting event—boxing at the Hollywood Legion Stadium. Shemp had reason to celebrate, since he had finished filming four out of eight new two-reelers with the Stooges for their newly signed contract. After the fights were over, Shemp hailed a taxi cab to take him to his North Hollywood home with friend Al Winston. Shemp sat back and lit up his cigar. Suddenly he slumped over into Winston's lap, burning Al with the stogie. It was a heart attack, and Shemp was dead at the age of sixty. On November 24, 1955, he was buried at Home of Peace Cemetery in Whittier, the same cemetery where his brother Curly was laid to rest.

Shemp's death was another crushing blow to Moe and Larry—first Curly, now Shemp. Moe admitted that he found it difficult to accept the deaths of his brothers and seriously considered breaking up the act. But this was impossible since the Stooges' Columbia contract called for Moe and Larry to star in the balance of the comedies—with or without Shemp. Larry and Moe honestly considered making the addi-

The Stooges give Birdie (Tony the Wonder Horse) a bath in *Hoofs and Goofs* (1957), Joe Besser's first short with the Stooges.

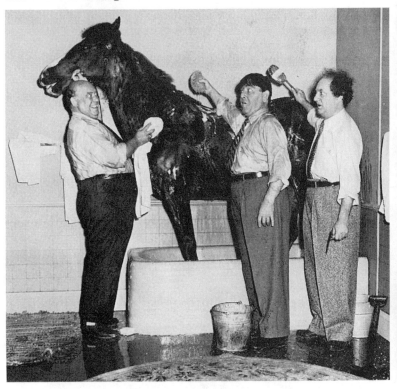

A newspaper ad for Joe Besser's only personal appearance with the Stooges.

tional shorts without a third Stooge. Larry later revealed that there had been some talk of starring Moe and him in comedies as the Two Stooges but that Columbia balked at the idea. Fine asserted afterwards that Columbia was probably right—"Comedy always comes in threes."

Four of Shemp's eight comedies produced for the 1956 season featured him in new footage to be inserted in remakes of old shorts. After Shemp's death, however, four comedies were left and Stooge stand-in Joe Palma was pressed into service made up to look like Shemp for the new footage. Palma had been around the Columbia lot since the mid-thirties. His most notable appearances were in *Three Loan Wolves* (1944), and as Mad Bill Hookup in *Guns A-Poppin'* (1957). Ironically he also appeared in guest shots in several of Shemp Howard's and Joe Besser's films.

Palma was used temporarily as a Stooge so that new footage could be shot to adapt the four films to their new story lines. Palma's face was never seen; his back was always to camera. His four films with the Stooges were *Hot Stuff, Rumpus in the Harem, Scheming*

Moe and Larry say goodby to Joe Besser and director Jules White as they ended their 24-year Columbia Pictures short subject career on December 20, 1957.

Schemers and *Commotion on the Ocean*. The other shorts were remakes with Shemp and were changed from *The Ghost Talks* (1949) to *Creeps* (1956), *Who Done It?* (1949) to *For Crimin' Out Loud* (1956) and *Hocus Pocus* (1949) to *Flagpole Jitters* (1956).

It has long been asserted that Joe Besser quickly stepped in to replace Shemp in 1955, but his old studio contract hadn't run out yet. Moe had drafted a

Columbia Pictures' release of Three Stooges comedies to TV in 1958 proved to be a gigantic moneymaker.

legal agreement with Larry and Curly, then later with Shemp, which gave him the right to select any Stooge replacements. Therefore, any claims to the effect that Columbia's executives or that Jules White picked the Stooge successors are totally erroneous. Columbia's only involvement was to approve Howard's selections and make them official.

Moe chose Besser for the new third Stooge and Besser signed an official contract to that effect on

Joe Besser ends his career as a Stooge on a high-note in *Sappy Bullfighters (1959)*.

Moe, Larry and Joe De Rita—in his only appearance with the Stooges with a full head of hair—in a publicity still promoting a 1958 Pennsylvania nightclub appearance.

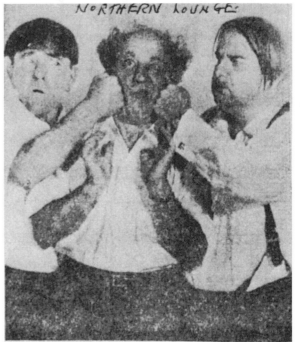

'STOOGES' AT NORTHERN LOUNGE — Famed for their television and movie comedy, the Three Stooges will be starred in the supper club entertainment this week at the Northern Lounge in the Northern Lights Shoppers City. Two shows will be presented each evening, Wednesday through Saturday. Vin Vincent's Orchestra will play for dancing. Featuring knock-about comedy, eccentric haircuts, weird sounds and slapstick, the Three Stooges are popular entertainers from coast to coast.

85

January 1, 1956. However, Besser's contract was signed separately from the Stooges', since he claimed he made more money ($3500 a film) that way, and he inserted a provision that withheld Moe or Larry from "slapping or causing him bodily harm." Besser's reason for this contract stipulation was, "I wasn't used to doing that wild kind of slapstick—and felt rather uncomfortable about it, since I usually played the kind of character who would hit others back." As a result, Jules White had Larry take all the hits and knocks in the head in Besser's place. Larry told Joe, "Don't worry. If you don't want Moe to hit you, I'll take all the belts."

Besser also introduced another dimension to the team. He suggested that Moe and Larry comb their hair back in the comedies in order to make them appear more like gentlemen. Although Jules White approved of the idea, he had to use the new hairstyles sparingly if he wanted to be able to match the old stock footage.

A real innovator, Joe was one of the only Stooge replacements to dare to hit Moe back in the films, not accidentally, but in self-defense. His feisty, little-kid

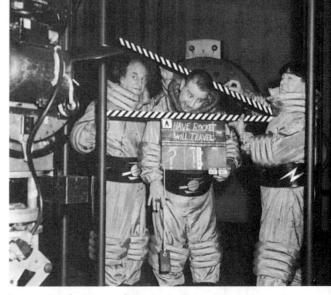

Larry, Curly-Joe and Moe clowning around on the *Have Rocket* set.

character was incorporated into stories that fit his personality. Besser's character was the direct opposite of any previous third Stooge's and presented an interesting contrast when combined with Moe's and Larry's. Joe was perfect as the impish, childlike Stooge because he created the necessary friction between Moe and Larry which was mandatory in making even the weakest films play for laughs.

Columbia Pictures was wise to approve Moe Howard's selection of Besser as Shemp's replacement, for several reasons. The Stooges series had all but run its course and needed a real boost; Besser's vibrant energy onscreen brought that boost. Columbia could ill afford to let Moe pick a lesser-known, less-capable, less-proven comedian than Shemp and Curly. Besser had that track record, as proven by his successful roles in features and his own two-reel series for Columbia.

With Besser aboard, Stooges comedies took the form of television situation comedies. Remakes of the old films were usually shot in one or two days, while others took the maximum three days.

In 1957, Besser made his first and only personal appearance with Moe and Larry at the Paramount Theatre in Los Angeles. A couple of Three Stooges comedies were shown prior to the Stooges' taking the stage to sign autographs and hand out a promotional ballpoint pen that bore the inscription: "Stolen from the Three Stooges, Larry Moe and Joe." It was the only promotional item distributed during Besser's tenure as one of the Stooges.

The Three Stooges finished their last short with Besser and with Columbia on December 20, 1957 (not in January, 1958). The studio had come to a decision that since costs had risen in film production and since there was almost no market for the short subject (Columbia was the last studio to have such a department), the contract's option for the Stooges was not

The Stooges' supper club appearance that was responsible for their comeback.

picked up. The boys' careers had suddenly come to an end. They were at Columbia one day and gone the next—no "Thank yous," no farewell party for their 24 years of dedication and service and the dollars their comedies had reaped for the studio.

Moe Howard recalled that a few weeks after their exit from Columbia, he drove to the studio to say goodbye to several studio executives when he was stopped by a guard at the gate (obviously, not a Stooges fan) and, since he did not have the current year's studio pass, was refused entry. For the moment, it as a crushing blow.

began racking up respectable television ratings during their first months of release, the Stooges' resurgence in popularity did not materialize for almost a year.

In the meantime, Moe and Larry began searching for a new third Stooge to replace Besser. Larry recommended an old vaudeville comedian and erstwhile cronie, Paul "Mousie" Garner. Moe rehearsed with him for three days, later remarking, "He was completely unacceptable." Then, while on vacation in Las Vegas, Larry caught the *Minsky's Follies of 1958* featuring comedian Joe DeRita. Larry informed Moe on his return from Vegas that DeRita might make a

The Stooges broke a 76-year attendance record by appearing before a crowd of 85,000 at the Canadian National Exposition on August 19, 1963.

During the weeks that followed, Moe and Larry discussed their future plans with Besser. They told him they were considering making personal appearances throughout the country; but Joe's wife had suffered a heart attack and he was unwilling to leave her. Besser's decision was difficult but he had to quit the team. (Shortly thereafter, Joe signed a five-year pact with Fox to co-star in a number of feature films. His first was *Say One For Me* with Bing Crosby.)

Moe and Larry then seriously contemplated retirement. Moe had invested his money wisely in real estate and would be able to survive financially. Larry, on the other hand, was on the verge of bankruptcy. In an interview, Larry recalled that Besser's departure left them with very few options. "Moe and I thought of retiring after Columbia let us go. Moe was thinking of quitting show business altogether, since he was pretty well off. I was thinking of managing apartments."

Then, the unexpected happened. In January 1958, Screen Gems released a package of 78 Three Stooges comedies to television. Although the old comedies

good "Curly." Moe then contacted DeRita's agent and set up a meeting.

DeRita recalled in an interview that this meeting was the first time Moe had asked him to join the Stooges. Throughout the years, distorted reports have surfaced that DeRita was asked several times before to become a third Stooge, even following Curly's stroke in 1946. But as DeRita said, "It sounds good. It adds a lot of romance to the story. Around 1958, Moe and Larry wanted to do some personal appearances and they contacted me for the very first time about working with them. We met at an agent's office and I agreed to work with them." Before joining the team, DeRita wore his hair parted down the middle like Shemp. Early publicity photographs show that Joe did not shave his hair off until two months after he joined the Stooges.

Moe tested DeRita's comic expertise in a nightclub engagement. The team's first appearance was at Bakersfield, California, for two weeks starting on October 16, 1958. Moe recalled that the playdate was a disaster and that DeRita wasn't working out. The owner of the club, seeing that the Stooges weren't drawing, tried to suspend their engagement as well as asking them to take a cut in their $2,500 a week salary. Moe was now having second thoughts about the team's future.

Fortunately, the Stooges stuck it out. DeRita continued to rehearse his new role, cut off his hair prior to the trio's next appearance and took on the nickname "Curly-Joe."

The Stooges' next nightclub engagement—the Holiday House in Pittsburgh—was the most successful one of their career and a turning point in their revival. The boys were held over for three weeks and played to capacity crowds.

Suddenly, the Stooges were on the top of the heap with offers pouring in every day for appearances at fairs, shopping centers, even the Shrine Circus—and at ten to 20 times their previous salary. The Stooges' earnings skyrocketed from $2,500 per week in Bakersfield to $25,000 for *one day* to dedicate a new shopping center in Rochester, New York.

Television stations were now reporting high ratings in Three Stooges comedy re-runs in such cities as Philadelphia, 33.3; Nashville, 22.0; Pittsburgh, 25.3;

One-sheet from *Snow White and the Three Stooges* (1961).

A newspaper ad for *The Three Stooges in Orbit* (1962), boasting the trio's hectic, personal appearance schedule.

The Three Stooges discover the camera between filming scenes for *Three Stooges in Orbit* (1962).

The Stooges drown in fan mail as TV-kiddie show host, Paul Shannon, and Curly-Joe look on.

Buffalo, 27.7; and Cleveland, 23.3. It should be pointed out that Popeye cartoons were the number-one children's TV property and that within a period of several months the Stooges knocked Popeye out of the box as king of children's television. Popeye dropped in the ratings to an average television viewing audience percentage of 13.8 in those markets that were playing Stooges comedies.

When Columbia saw that these old films were clicking with new audiences, studio officials strung together several Stooges shorts with Joe Besser and booked them as a feature entitled *Three Stooges Fun-O-Rama* (1959). Then, by popular demand, Columbia's television subsidiary, Screen Gems, released 40 more Stooge comedies to television. Now as many as 156 television stations were running the comedies nationwide. Hollywood trade papers reported that

The Three Stooges at Disneyland.

Columbia made $12 million profit from the first release of Stooges shorts to television.

But despite the astronomical revenue Stooges shorts created for Columbia, Moe and Larry didn't receive a dime in residuals; this because of a Screen Actors' Guild ruling that only post-1960 films broadcast on television would earn residuals for actors.

Even though Stooges films were drawing a large share of TV audiences, parental action groups and other concerned organizations wanted TV stations to pull the Stooges comedies from their daily programming. The National Association for Better Radio and TV found the films "objectionable" and claimed that these comedies "degraded the dignity of man." Moe rebutted these claims in interviews, remarking that Stooge comedies were less violent than Popeye cartoons and old westerns. As he said: "We were not as sadistic as westerns, which to my mind are as violent as gangster movies. Kids don't mind seeing somebody get it over the head as long as they know that that person will get right up." Even Margaret Meade (world-famous anthropologist) agreed with Moe on this point.

Taking it easy between takes, Stooges style.

Columbia Pictures, the same studio that booted the Stooges out a year earlier, offered the team a one-picture deal to star in a feature called *Have Rocket, Will Travel* (1959), which was directed by David Lowell Rich. For their efforts the Stooges received $30,000 and had to split one-half of producer-agent Harry Romm's 50 percent of the net profits derived from the film's distribution. Later when the Stooges and Norman Maurer formed their own production company, Normandy Productions, their salary up front was $50,000 per film and 50 percent of the net profits.

The Three Stooges in Artiscope costume and make-up from *Three Stooges in Orbit* (1962).

Have Rocket, Will Travel opened to mixed reviews but was successful at the box-office and made a profit for Columbia. The film rolled up $127,000 during the first five days of a multiple-theatre engagement in the Los Angeles area. The Stooges feature was double-billed with *The Legend of Tom Dooley*, a low-budget Civil War film. *Rocket* was produced on a $380,000 budget.

Harry Romm, the producer of *Have Rocket, Will Travel*, was also the Stooges' agent and manager for many years. However, during production on the film, a rift between Moe and Romm—over decision making—began to grow and culminated in Moe terminating Harry's services as the team's manager and producer, and naming Norman Maurer as his replacement.

Due to the fact that *Have Rocket* was a money-

Fans await the big moment—the arrival of the Stooges.

On tour for *The Three Stooges Meet Hercules*, the boys raid a refreshment counter in a New York movie theater to peddle "Slow Poke" candy bars.

The Three Stooges were never too busy to find time for their fans.

maker, Columbia decided to make a sequel, and the Stooges, realizing their new-found popularity, asked Romm for $50,000 and 75 percent of his share of the profits. Romm was anxious to make another feature deal but he wanted his usual 50 percent and turned the Stooges down. Instead, Romm went directly to Columbia, piecing together old footage from several Stooges comedies with Curly and bridging them with new scenes of ventriloquist Paul Winchell and his dummies; the film was *Stop! Look! and Laugh!* (1960).

Incensed, the Stooges, with the help of their manager Norman Maurer, took Romm and Columbia to court, protesting the film was illegal since Columbia had no right to cut up old Stooges comedies and re-use them in a new form without the team's permission. The judge agreed and issued an injunction preventing release of the film. Columbia settled out of court, awarding the Stooges a cash settlement and a contract to make a new feature for $50,000 and 50 percent of the profits, with Norman Maurer producing and sharing equally in the profits.

Before starting production on their new Columbia deal, the Stooges made a feature for 20th Century-Fox, *Snow White and the Three Stooges* (1961), which featured 1960 Olympic Skating Champion Carol Heiss as Snow White. Moe often called this film a "Tech-

The Stooges on stage with Joe DeRita.

nicolor mistake." Originally, Frank Tashlin was set to direct the film at a budget of $750,000, but Fox replaced him with Academy-Award-winning director Walter Lang and gave Lang carte blanche. As a result, the budget of *Snow White* skyrocketed to 3.5 million dollars.

At about this time, Joseph E. Levine came out with the blockbuster *Hercules* and was already in production on a sequel. Norman Maurer recalled the success Abbott and Costello had with their series of "meet" films and offered Columbia *The Three Stooges Meet Hercules* (1962) as the team's next feature. Columbia thought it was a sensational concept and Maurer commenced to write the story and produce the film.

The Three Stooges Meet Hercules was completed in 1961 at a budget of under $450,000 and was a blockbuster, outgrossing *Have Rocket, Will Travel*. It also should be noted that the release of *Hercules* followed

Snow White and, theatre by theatre, outgrossed the $3.5 million Fox feature.

With the success of *The Three Stooges Meet Hercules*, Columbia immediately signed Maurer and the Stooges to another feature. This time the Stooges took to warding off Martians Ogg and Zogg in *The Three Stooges in Orbit* (1962). *Orbit* was followed by the team's Jules Verne spoof, *The Three Stooges Go Around the World in a Daze* (1963). The Stooges were then signed for guest appearances in two independent productions, Stanley Kramer's *It's a Mad, Mad, Mad, Mad World* (United Artists, 1963), where they did a short cameo role as firefighters, and *Four for Texas* (Warner Brothers, 1963) starring Dean Martin.

Profits on the Columbia-Three Stooges features started to dip after their successful film *The Three Stooges in Orbit*. Norman Maurer recalled, "The boys' popularity had reached its peak with *Hercules* and *Orbit* and then as production costs took an upswing their popularity took a nose dive. No other studio was making children's films and with increased production costs it was an uphill battle to recoup negative costs from the kids' 25-cent admissions. Accordingly, Columbia wasn't too anxious to produce another Stooges feature." Maurer, however, wrote a new story and convinced Columbia to star the team in one last round-up, *The Outlaws Is Coming!* (1965). Many fans consider *The Three Stooges Meet Hercules*, directed by Edward Bernds, as the Stooges' best feature, while others prefer the two that Maurer directed, *The Three Stooges Go Around the World in a Daze* and *The Outlaws Is Coming!*

In the feature films with Joe DeRita, the Stooges went through a noticeable change in their slapstick routines. Moe made the boys tone down the violence and eliminate some of the slapping and hitting, trying to establish the Stooges as family-oriented comedians. Moe even agreed to discontinue his famous two-finger poke in the eyes, since he felt it set a bad example for the kids. Thus, when the Stooges were making features, there was very little deliberate violence in the context of their routines.

In reviewing the point of view which the Stooges' comedy took, Joe DeRita explained in an interview that he didn't think the Stooges had one. As he recalled, "I don't think the Stooges were funny. I'm not putting you on, I'm telling the truth—they were physical, but they just didn't have any humor about them. Take, for instance, Laurel and Hardy. I can watch their films and I still laugh at them and maybe I've seen them four or five times before. But when I see that pie or seltzer bottle, I know that it's not just lying around for no reason. It's going to be used for something. I was with the Stooges for 12 years and it was a very pleasant association but I just don't think they were funny."

But Larry Fine disagreed. He believed that the mystique of the Stooges' comedy was centered around the question, "What's going to happen next?" Larry remarked in an interview that the Stooges were not method actors but did what came to mind, not what they had been trained to do. He saw the Stooges' comedy as a comedy of anticipation. As Larry stated: "Everyone in the audience anticipates that when you reach that door the tray of dishes you were balancing will topple and crash to the floor. So give the audiences what they expect. The door swings open, the tray tips over and the plates fly in all directions and everyone gets a laugh. That was our comic foundation—we gave people what they expected."

Sandwiched in between the team's released features, the Stooges planned several other productions that never got off the ground. In October 1960, Norman Maurer drafted an 11-page treatment for *The Three Stooges Meet Pinocchio* which was to star Jimmy Durante as Geppetto and continue Maurer's plan for a "Three Stooges Meet..." series. The film never got past the treatment stage, however. Other features Maurer planned were to include *The Three Stooges in King Arthur's Court, The Three Stooges Meet Robin Hood* and *The Three Stooges Meet Captain Bligh*, which MGM stopped because it was producing the remake of *Mutiny on the Bounty* at that time. Maurer also developed a unique starrer for the Stooges called *The Three Stooges Meet the Mobsters* which was to pit Moe, Larry and Curly-Joe against such famous underworld criminals as Al Capone, John Dillinger, Bonnie and Clyde and Baby Face Nelson. Again, no deal could be made since the market for children's films had vanished.

A short time later, Maurer met with Dick Brown, who produced Cambria Studios' *The New Three Stooges* color cartoons. Brown and veteran animator Dick Detiege had written a feature film script for the Stooges entitled *The Flying Hutch* (later retitled *Bush Pilots* and *The Three Stooges Meet the Gang*.) The production was to be filmed in Vancouver, Canada, where Brown owned his own production company.

The Stooges leave in style after visiting the Movieland Wax Museum in Buena Park, California.

Basically, the plot cast the Stooges as laborers working in a Los Angeles junkyard. A telegram informs Curly-Joe that a long-lost uncle in Canada had died, leaving him the sole owner of UCA Airways in Vancouver (Curly-Joe later learns that UCA stands for Uncle Curly's Airways). Naturally, the Stooges believe they'll become tycoons and so burn all their bridges.

A relaxed moment on the set of *Around the World in a Daze*: (clockwise) Larry, Jay Sheffield, Norman Maurer (director), Moe, Curly-Joe and Joan Freeman.

But the airline turns out to be less prestigious than the Stooges first think. A broken-down, single-engine, bush-pilot's flivver turns out to be the sole aircraft of UCA. From here on out, the Stooges turn

the film into a sweeping romp, constantly struggling at odd jobs to make a few bucks and keep their single-engine wreck airborne.

Edward Bernds rewrote the Brown-Detiege script, which consisted mainly of "cartoon-type gags," and Bernds was also set to direct the picture. But production and other problems arose. First, Bernds was never paid the $7,500 Brown had promised to deliver for his services. Brown was unable to obtain sufficient financial backing and the film was scrapped. A year later, Gerald Fine of Gerald Fine Productions offered the Stooges $160,000 to star in four features, or $40,000 per picture. But the offer turned out to be typical Hollywood talk and no deal resulted.

The Stooges made their first film appearance after *The Outlaws Is Coming!* (1965) in a 20-minute United States Treasury Department sales film called *Star Spangled Salesman* (1968). Norman Maurer produced and directed the film. Carl Reiner acted as M.C. and the film featured an all-star cast of such favorites as Carol Burnett, Milton Berle, Howard Morris, John Banner, Werner Klemperer (both of TV's *Hogan's Heroes*), Rafer Johnson, Tim Conway, Harry Morgan and Jack Webb. The services of the producer, director and all the actors were donated free to the government. In this, the team's fourth color film appearance, Howard Morris convinces the Stooges to join the government's payroll savings plan.

After a short hiatus, in September 1969 the Stooges started filming a TV comedy-travelogue called *Kook's Tour*, in color. In the film, Moe suggests they retire and see the rest of the world, since they've been stars for 50 years and have never seen the outside of their dressing rooms.

This film is really what not to do when going camping and fishing—and with the Stooges there are a lot of *what nots*! But during the final days of filming, on January 9, 1970, Larry Fine suffered a stroke which left him paralyzed on the left side of his body. He was admitted to the Motion Picture Country House in Woodland Hills, California, for care and treatment, and the uncompleted *Kook's Tour* was never released to television.

Even though Larry's illness had crippled the team, Moe was not about to abandon the Three Stooges act. In April 1971, Jeff Maurer, Norman's son, completed writing a new Three Stooges feature, *Make Mine Manila*, with the Stooges trapped in a concentration camp even though the war is over (the script was later retitled *Make Love Not War*). Since Larry was incapacitated as a result of the stroke, Moe asked veteran Stooges foil Emil Sitka to join the team as Larry's replacement.

In the meantime, Norman Maurer and Moe held

serious negotiations with producer Alan J. Factor of Bedford Productions and the Philippine government which was going to finance the film. With Sitka signed as a Stooge, Alan Factor set up a meeting at the Friars' Club in Beverly Hills with Moe, Joe and Emil. During the meeting with Factor, Maurer reviewed the plans for production of the film, but remembers that Sitka's actions at the lunch meeting may have contributed to Factor's backing out of the production.

Maurer recalls: "Alan Factor brought in his finance people to join us at lunch. Moe, Joe and I were shocked at the way Emil acted at the meeting. Suddenly, it was star time. While executives announced what days we would be filming in Manila, Emil said, 'Well, I don't know if I'm available,' and 'I'll need a limousine.' Moe and I were slack-jawed.

The *new new* Three Stooges who never saw the light: Curly-Joe, Moe and long-time Stooges foil, Emil Sitka, filling in for Larry.

The Stooges and Howard Morris kidding around during filming of *Star Spangled Salesman* (1968), a color, 20-minute sales film for the U.S. Treasury Department.

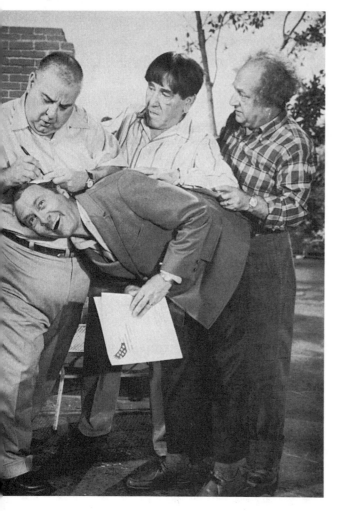

Joe was shocked." Maurer never heard another word on the Philippine film after that meeting.

A short time later, Moe abandoned the idea of continuing as part of a Stooges team and concentrated his energies on pursuing dramatic roles. He made a cameo appearance as a single in the Cinerama science-fiction release, *Doctor Death, Seeker of Souls* (1973). Even though Moe had very little to do in the film, he was excited at the idea of working again. He kept active, playing golf occasionally, taking long walks in the morning and going to a ceramics class twice a week. Then, in between his moments of leisure, Moe would appear on such television programs as *The Mike Douglas Show*, on which he made five appearances, and toured colleges with his own special Three Stooges show. Moe screened several classic Stooges comedies for the audience, then answered their questions afterwards. He played to standing-room-only audiences in colleges everywhere. His last campus appearance was at the University of Buffalo in Buffalo, New York, on September 24, 1974.

Two months later, in November 1974, Columbia Pictures paid tribute to the Stooges by releasing a program to theatres containing unedited Stooges comedies. Called *The Three Stooges Follies*, the program consisted of three of the Stooges' comedies with Curly and several shorts from the 1930s and 1940s.

Larry was the life of the party at the Motion Picture Country House in Woodland Hills where he lived until his death. Of the many social activities the hospital sponsored, Fine's favorite was the annual Wheelchair Parade in which patients decorated their wheelchairs in accordance with that year's theme. In fact, he participated in the event every year and garnered most of the awards.

One year, with Favorite Movie Titles as the theme, 40 patients entered the parade, including Larry. He dressed up as a baby and was supposed to represent the movie title *What Happened to Baby Jane?* Seated in his wheelchair, Fine was decked out in diapers and held an empty whiskey bottle that had the nipple from a baby's bottle on top. Instead of winning the "Most Humorous" category which he did each year, Larry took first place for having the "Most Original" costume.

Larry wasn't surprised that he was often judged the winner. He once said, "Hell, I *can't* lose. All of my friends are judges on the panel. There's Jerry Colonna, Chill Wills, Harry Ackerman and Walter Pidgeon.

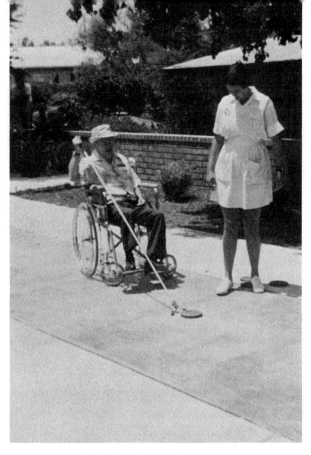

Larry Fine making his final concert appearance at Loara High School on March 2, 1974.

Larry in a shuffleboard match at the Motion Picture Country House and Hospital (July, 1973).

If you ask me, I think it's *fixed*!" But Larry also said that the awards were given to the wrong people and that the decorator of his wheelchair (and his escort for three years), Peg Hart, deserved the awards that he had won. Each year Hart spent over two hours helping Larry with his wheelchair in preparation for the parade.

Besides wheelchair parades, Larry was active in stage productions as one of the *Ding-A-Lings*, a choir composed of patients from the hospital. Twice yearly the choir staged a variety show composed of skits and songs which was held at the Louis B. Mayer Theatre and was open to the public. Famous celebrities were invited to guest star in the shows and participate in skits and songs with the choir.

Every year Larry invited Moe to come and perform a routine with him on stage. One year, Moe couldn't make it, which really put Larry on the spot. He had been accustomed to performing with Moe for over 40 years, and it had been an eternity since he went on stage as a single. But he did, delighting the audience by comically reciting a nursery rhyme: "Mary had a little lamb. It's fleece was black as soot. And every where that lambie went, his sooty foot he put." He was, of course, the hit of the show. As Larry said afterwards, "I was never so scared in all my life. I felt lost without Moe at my side." A year earlier, Moe and Larry had fractured audiences with their version of "Take Me Out to the Ball Game."

Although Larry was able to speak, his voice was thick and his pronunciation was somewhat garbled. Later, Moe admitted that when he went to see Larry,

At his final concert appearance on March 2, 1974, Larry assures his fans he'll walk again by standing for them.

tears would well up in his eyes and it became more and more trying each time, but he went as often as possible. One time, when Moe was over 40 minutes late, Larry quipped, "Who knows where Moe's been? Knowing him, he could get lost in a paper bag!"

Despite his handicap, Larry brought delight to high school and college audiences with his own Three Stooges show. He appeared at several colleges in the San Fernando Valley area and on many occasions took with him actress Babe London, who also resided at the Motion Picture Country House and had co-starred in the Stooges comedy *Scrambled Brains* (1951). Larry assured the fans that he would walk again and during several performances he stood up in his wheelchair for the crowds. As Fine once said, "It only takes five minutes to have a stroke, but it takes five years to recover."

Larry also appeared on several talk shows in the Los Angeles area and wrote a book, *A Stroke of Luck*, which covers his life from childhood to his years as a resident at the Motion Picture Country House. *Stroke of Luck* was published privately by James Carone who helped Larry compile the book. Fine pulled it from distribution when Carone failed to pay him his share of the profits. The book, which was rife with errors, is no longer available.

As Larry approached his seventy-second birthday, his health had improved markedly. But on October 4, 1974, one day before his birthday, Fine suffered another stroke and was rushed to the J-Ward of the hospital, which treats the critically ill. Two weeks later, he was alert and talking again, but his speech was more garbled and slurred than before. Then on the same day that Jack Benny died, Larry suffered a massive stroke which put him into a coma. Two weeks later, Larry suffered no more; he died on January 24, 1975. Funeral services were held at Forest Lawn Memorial Park in Glendale, California.

Moe sobbed when he heard the news of Larry's death, but despite the loss of his former partner, Howard tried to remain active. About a month later, it was announced that Moe, Curly-Joe and Emil Sitka (playing the role of Larry's brother) were set to star in an R-rated comedy, *The Jet Set* (retitled and released as *Blazing Stewardesses*). The Stooges rehearsed their roles and met with the film's producer at the Sheraton-Universal Hotel in Hollywood. Moe was to play a hairdresser, Curly-Joe a masseur and Emil a manicurist. Moe appeared rundown, thin and sickly at the meeting. His voice was barely above a whisper. But despite his failing health, Moe never let on that he was ill. During the meeting, his mind was as sharp as ever, spouting out dozens of gags and routines that the Stooges could perform. The producer was pleased

97

Program cover for Larry's last high school concert appearance to raise funds for the school's stage equipment.

Moe during a 1972 interview.

with the meeting and filming was to begin in Palm Springs a week later.

Although Moe was now seriously ill, he continued to call DeRita and Sitka each week telling them that filming was postponed. Sitka recalls, "The next call I got was from Moe's son. He told me the sad news...that Moe was dead."

Larry waiting to participate in annual Wheelchair Parade at the Motion Picture Country House and Hospital (1973).

On May 4, 1975, at the age of seventy-eight, Moe Howard died of lung cancer. He was buried two days later at Hillside Memorial Park in West Los Angeles.

As Norman Maurer told reporters when interviewed after the comedian's death. "When Moe died, the act died with him."

Despite the loss of Moe Howard and Larry Fine, the memory of the Three Stooges' comedy still lingers on. Their countless films continue to fracture audiences young and old on television stations around the world. In terms of laughs the Stooges remain the kings of comedy. These mechanics of mirth held no secret to success, other than that they were funny and not out to win any popularity contests. Maybe that's why the Stooges are appreciated today more than any other comedy team in history.

Even though the Stooges never won *that* Oscar for their achievements, they have, at least, won the hearts of millions of filmgoers everywhere, and will continue to do so as long as society has that one, basic need...laughter.

An early photograph with Ted Healy backstage during a vaudeville tour.

Theatrical poster promoting the Pillsbury toy
projector.

2

Three Stooges Merchandise

A POTPOURRI of Three Stooges merchandise has been manufactured for over five decades—with many items becoming brisk sellers. Consequently, fans were able to realize another dimension in the team's worldwide appeal through purchase of these many merchandise novelties.

In 1935, the appeal of Three Stooges merchandise first became apparent with the promotion of a cardboard moving picture machine featuring Moe, Larry and Curly. The Pillsbury Company sponsored the construction of this merchandise item and distributed it at movie-theatre matinees across the country. The "picture machine," which was made out of heavy, die-cut cardboard, included a double set of Three Stooges paper movies. The movies were actually frame blow-ups from Stooges comedies printed on squares of cardboard. These frames moved in full action when cranked through the camera-shaped machine. Theatres involved held weekly matinees to provide film-goers with the opportunity to win one of several of these clever gadgets, while consolation prizes were awarded to everyone else in attendance—five-by-seven autographed photographs of the Stooges, signed by Moe, Larry and Curly.

Theatre managers also received as part of the Pillsbury promotion a handsome campaign packet from which to advertise the Three Stooges "picture machine." The kit was composed of a deluxe sound trailer (featuring the Stooges demonstrating the item), a lobby poster, autographed photographs of the Three Stooges for everyone in the audience, follow-up circulars and short film trailers for subsequent matinees. The Pillsbury Company also promoted the Three Stooges tie-in campaign through colorful displays in grocery stores across the country, through its radio program *Today's Children* (which was broadcast daily over thirty-five NBC stations and affiliates) and through newspaper advertising and Sunday comic supplements which reached over ten million homes. Despite the rarity of the Stooges-Pillsbury "picture machine," reports continue to surface periodically

that many of them have been found and sold at collectors' auctions around the nation.

Also, in 1935, the Stooges imparted their comical likenesses to a beautifully crafted set of hand puppets designed by a well-known Italian artist. When the puppets were first made available to stores, Columbia's publicity department took several promotional stills of the Stooges holding their puppet look-a-likes, and additional stills of the studio's feature film stars playing with the Stooges puppets as well. Larry Fine once recalled that the puppets were a losing venture for the toy company, since the cost of this item was outrageously high.

In 1949, the Stooges again broke new ground in the field of merchandise when Jubilee Publications published two issues of a Three Stooges comic book series starring Curly. The series, however, was short-lived.

Although very little merchandise came out on the original film trio, no merchandise at all was manufactured when Shemp replaced Curly in 1946. Columbia received no firm offers from toy and game manufacturers, the one exception being a comic book for the St. John Publishing Company, which was licensed to publish another Three Stooges comic book series in 1953, featuring Shemp.

Though they could not be considered true merchandise, Moe Howard ordered a fancy deck of Three Stooges playing cards through a Chicago firm for himself and the other Stooges. They had the faces of Moe, Larry and Shemp on the backs of each card. Although originally conceived by Moe as a Christmas gift, he mailed many of them to politicians, lawyers and doctors for publicity purposes. The cards are rare since Moe ordered very few sets and they were never distributed to stores.

When Joe Besser replaced Shemp Howard in 1956, Columbia again had no offers from game and novelty manufacturers to produce additional Stooges merchandise. Columbia Pictures, however, in a wise promotional move, did manufacture hundreds of fountain pens that were inscribed with the words: "Stolen

A mob of fans proudly display their Three Stooges Moving Picture Machines and autographed Stooges photos.

A potpourri of Three Stooges merchandise from the 1930's to 1950's.

In 1959 a real treat for moppet members of the Stooges fans was Stooges Beanies.

Very popular collectibles were Three Stooges
bubble gum cards.

Three Stooges finger puppets, manufactured by
Wilkening Manufacturing Company, circa 1959.

Stooges mugging with an innocent fan promoting
the Pillsbury toy projector.

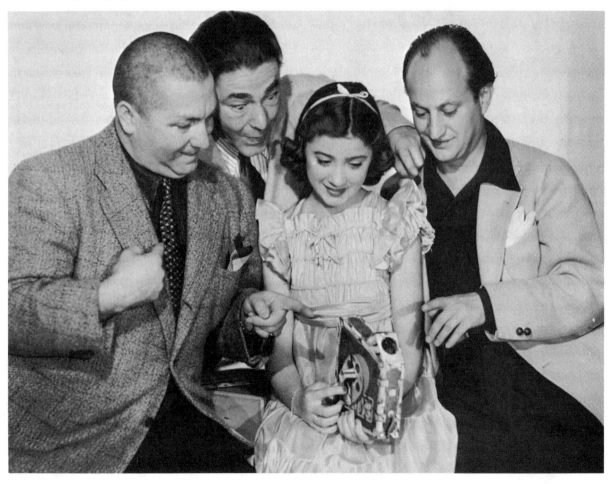

from the Three Stooges, Moe, Larry and Joe." The Stooges handed these out at a personal appearance in Los Angeles, in 1957. Like the playing cards, the pens received no national distribution to gift shops or novelty stores.

In 1958, Three Stooges merchandise exploded onto the scene when Columbia released the Stooges shorts to TV and Joe DeRita, who resembled Curly Howard, joined the team and was nicknamed "Curly-Joe." Because of the trio's sudden rebirth in popularity with children and adults, Norman Maurer Productions licensed Henry Saperstein of Television Personalities, Inc., to merchandise the Three Stooges' names and likenesses. Saperstein's firm did an excellent job and many merchandise deals were made with advances of $1,000 and more plus 5 percent of the gross sales of all items bearing the Stooges' names or likenesses. The year 1959 was a record sales period for Three Stooges merchandise. Under the expert guidance of Saperstein and Norman Maurer, over 36 different toys and games were distributed and sold worldwide.

Norman Maurer recalls that the most popular and most successful merchandise item was Three Stooges Bubble Gum Cards, produced by the Frank H. Fleer Company. Stooges screenwriter, Elwood Ullman, wrote the captions for the gum's full-color trading cards (with stills of Stooges action scenes), which sold in stores for five cents a packet and generated over $20,000 as the Stooges' share.

Another super-successful merchandise item was the first Three Stooges Fan Club, which Norman marketed out of his own home in Los Angeles. Henry Saperstein, who was a genius when it came to making merchandise deals, turned down Maurer's initial proposal for the Stooges Fan Club, since his company had lost money when it marketed their unsuccessful Elvis Presley Fan Club. Confident that the Stooges club would make a profit, Maurer spear-headed the operation on his own and advertised the club on the back cover of Dell's Three Stooges comic books. Fifty cents entitled applicants to an official Three Stooges Fan Club card, an engraved special club certificate, two large photographs of the Stooges, a set of Three Stooges stamps and a personal letter from the team as well.

Maurer recalls that the initial fan reaction was tremendous. Thousands of pieces of mail flooded the Hollywood Post Office. In an interview, Maurer remembered the comical situations these pieces of mail presented:

Three Stooges hand puppets—Larry, Moe and Curly.

"On one occasion the response from an announcement on Sally Starr's TV show in Philadelphia was so great that I almost collapsed from dragging a bag of mail down the post office steps. You can imagine the size and weight of a mailbag with almost $3,000 in assorted coins. Often kids sent in 50 pennies and we had to pay heavy postage-due penalties. Sometimes the kids sewed their coins to cardboard and more often glued them into the envelope."

On another occasion, Maurer also experienced difficulty at a local bank when he asked the head teller to count the coins received from the fan club applications in the bank's automatic coin counter. Evidently fans took extreme care when enclosing the coins with their club applications. They used everything from Scotch tape to Wilhold glue. These sticky substances, were never completely removed from the money and jammed the coin machine. The bank's president was dismayed when he heard the news, called Norman into his office, returned the bag of coins and ordered him never to darken the bank's doors with his definitely filthy lucre.

While Saperstein remained skeptical over the club's chances to turn a profit, Maurer proved his merchandise representative wrong. The Three Stooges Fan Club netted an astronomical $22,000 during the first year of operation and the earnings continued to increase as more fans learned of its existence.

Many other merchandise novelties and games were produced during 1959: Three Stooges Hats (Clinton Toy Co.), Candy Taffy Kisses (Phoenix Candy Co.), Boxed Board Games (Lowell Toy Manufacturing Co.), Three Stooges Magic Coloring Books (Funbuilt Toys, Inc.), Three Stooges Finger Puppets (Wilkening Manufacturing Co.). Other novelties included: Three Stooges Punching Bag Balloons (Van Dam Rubber Co.), Three Stooges Nutty Putty (Nadel and Sons Toy Corp.), Three Stooges Bowling Set and Spinning Top (Empire Plastic Corp.), and Three Stooges Flicker-Action Rings. Additional games and toys distributed that same year were: Three Stooges Jigsaw Puzzle (Colorforms), Three Stooges Silly Riddle Game (Colorforms), Three Stooges Colorforms (Colorforms), Three Stooges Plastic Gum Dispenser (L.H. Becker and Co.), Three Stooges Pin-On Action Pictures (L.H. Becker and Co.), Three Stooges Stuffed Dolls (Juro Novelty Company, Inc.), Three Stooges Coloring Book (Lowe, Inc.), and Three Stooges Inflatable Vinyl Punchos (Hampshire Manufacturing, Inc.).

In 1960 and 1961, a smaller but fun-packed batch of merchandise also spilled into the toy and game marketplace. The items included: Easy Show Projector 8mm Film Strips (Kenner Products, Inc.), Three Stooges Papier Maché Figurines, Three Stooges Ce-ramic Drinking Mugs and Three Stooges Savings Bank (Mahana Importing Co.), Three Stooges Halloween Costumes and Masks (Ben Cooper, Inc.), Three Stooges School Bag and Loose-Leaf Ring Binders (Carry-Case Manufacturing, Co.) and Vinyl Inflatable Toys and Hand Puppets (Ideal Toy Corp.).

Stooges mug with their puppet lookalikes.

In 1962, another unique item was marketed, a Three Stooges TV Viewer and Film Strips (Acme Toy Corp.), followed by another Kenner Products game, the Three Stooges Water Color-Paint Sets, in 1963. In 1964, Whitman Publishing took advantage of the

A sampling of Three Stooges playing cards, circa 1950.

Movie film clips of the Stooges were issued as part of a Three Stooges toy movie viewer.

Newspaper ad of Curly-Joe, Moe and Larry promoting a Three Stooges Colorforms Set.

Three Stooges bubble gum card holder, circa 1959.

Second set of Three Stooges bubble gum cards.

Columbia Pictures home movie division marketed this 3-D version of *Spooks* (1953) retitled *Tails of Horror*.

Original sketch by Norman Maurer for Three Stooges hat, circa 1959.

Stooges' popularity with children and produced a Three Stooges Coloring Book. Whitman also manufactured a fine array of additional Stooges merchandise such as: Three Stooges Punch-Out Book; Three Stooges Cut-Out Book, Three Stooges Stamp Book and Three Stooges Sticker Fun Book. Then, in 1965, the Frank H. Fleer Company produced a second series of Three Stooges Bubble Gum Cards with scenes from Columbia's Pictures' and Normandy Productions' Stooges features on each card. When assembled, the backs of the entire collection of cards made a poster-size, color photograph of the Stooges from the movie *The Outlaws Is Coming!* (1965).

By the late 1960s,. however, the flow of Three Stooges merchandise had diminished. But despite the fact the team's popularity had begun to wane, Columbia Pictures' 8mm Division marketed for home movie use silent, 8mm, abridged versions of Three Stooges comedies with Curly and Shemp. These Stooges films were stocked by discount houses as well as camera stores who carried other Columbia 8mm offerings as well. In 1974, Columbia then expanded the Stooges film series to include unedited 8mm sound versions of Three Stooges comedies featuring Curly and Shemp. These sound films retailed for $39.95, as compared to the original retail price of $12.95 for Columbia's earlier silent formats.

Around 1965, *Snow White and the Three Stooges*, a non-Columbia Stooges feature, appeared on the 8mm home-movie market under the Americom banner.

Comic book ad for the Three Stooges Foto Club.

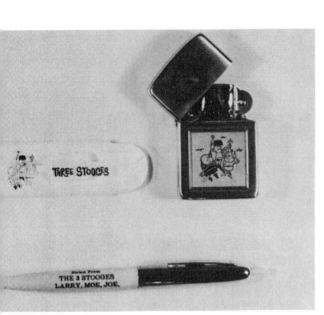

Three rare Stooges collectibles: plastic toothpick and case, cigarette lighter and pen.

The Three Stooges Meet Hercules giveaway photograph.

Carry-Case Manufacturing's version of a Stooges School Bag for child and teenage fans.

Three Stooges punch-out book, complete with cut-out figures of the Stooges.

Three Stooges Fan Club kit, 1959.

Curly-Joe, Moe and Larry mugging with a mock set of Three Stooges balloons, circa 1959.

Three Stooges rings.

Columbia Pictures and Norman Maurer Productions licensed Three Stooges statues.

Columbia Pictures' popular line of Three Stooges video cassettes featuring comedies with Curly.

What do you think I am, a pair of pants?

I told you to turn off the fan!

A group of Three Stooges photographs offered as merchandise by Columbia Pictures.

I could have sworn I just shaved him yesterday.

Sample strip of the Fleer edition of Three Stooges bubble gum cards.

Curly-Joe, Moe and Larry caught up in a jungle of Three Stooges merchandise that flooded the marketplace in 1959.

Americom were producers of films with record soundtracks and obtained permission from 20th Century-Fox, who produced *Snow White*, to release a ten-minute version of the Stooges feature in color and black-and-white. The abridged black-and-white versions sold for $9.95 while the ones in color were $15.95. The films were accompanied by a record soundtrack that could be played along with the film to provide the movie's dialogue and music track in sync with the picture. In 1973, however, Americom went bankrupt and the company's entire library of films was liquidated.

Unlike the late 1960s, the 1970s and 1980s were more promising for Three Stooges-related merchandise. In 1977, General Foods offered, gratis, six different posters of the Stooges in boxes of Post Sugar Crisps. One year later, Norman Maurer Productions and Hanna-Barbera Productions licensed the use of Maurer's animated TV cartoon characters, *The Three Robonic Stooges*, to be published in a Robonic Stooges and Skatebirds Coloring Book. Then, in 1980,

The comical antics of the Stooges reprised in T-shirts.

Columbia Pictures released a collection of video tapes, containing full-length features, cartoons and comedies, all on video cassette tapes. Among the impressive list of Columbia favorites were three volumes of Three Stooges comedies on tape for $59.95.

By 1981, Three Stooges Merchandise entered a new phase of production under the direction of Columbia Pictures' Merchandising Department. In January 1981, Norman Maurer Productions, which retains all rights to the Three Stooges' names and likenesses, signed an exclusive five-year merchandising contract with Columbia Pictures, entitling the New York-based company to merchandise Three Stooges products.

Glenn Dyckoff, Columbia's Merchandising Director, has reported that over 5,000 wholesalers, nation-

The Three Stooges Photo Printing Set.

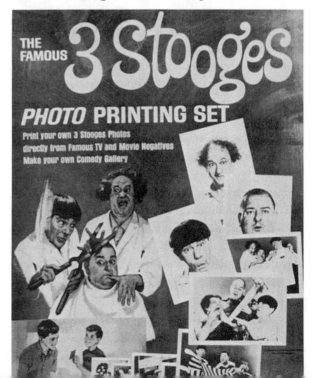

Two examples of Three Stooges super-8 sound home movies marketed by Columbia Pictures' 8mm division.

Gold Raiders, the Stooges' only feature with Shemp, saw additional distribution in a super-8 home movie version, released in England. This item is a rare collector's find.

A set of official Three Stooges 3-D stickers, 1981.

wide and abroad, sell Three Stooges merchandise. Several products, Dyckoff says, were introduced during Columbia's first trial-run year as Stooges merchandise representatives. Items included; Three Stooges Statues (Moe, Larry and Curly, each 37 inches high), Three Stooges Stick-Ons, a Three Stooges wrist watch (which tells time backwards), Three Stooges Posters and Three Stooges Greeting Cards. Columbia Pictures and Norman Maurer Productions also licensed the first Official Three Stooges Fan Club for the purpose of offering new Three Stooges merchandise to fans, as well as providing information about the Stooges through a bi-monthly journal.

In light of the team's impressive marketing history and their constant commercial appeal as attested to by toy and game manufacturers, it would appear that the Three Stooges' niche in the field of merchandising is safe and secure for some time to come.

Flier promoting Niles Films' licensed 8 mm version of *Kook's Tour*, the Stooges' last film.

A young Norman Maurer putting the finishing touches on a Three Stooges comic book panel.

3

Comic Book Stooges

GENERATIONS OF COMIC BOOK BUFFS like to remember the time they purchased their first comic book. But how many comic enthusiasts of old recall a series made in 1949, featuring the Three Stooges?

The idea of using the Stooges in comic books was spawned in May of 1947. Norman Maurer, who later managed the Three Stooges and wrote, produced and directed their feature-length films, was at that time a well-established comic book illustrator, working on *Daredevil* comics, *Boy Comics*, et al. His boyhood pal, Joe Kubert, had a deal with Archer St. John, owner of Jubilee Publications, to produce and edit a number of comics. Joe called Norman and asked him to be a partner and suggested they use the Stooges as one of the comic book series.

Norman started negotiations with the Stooges for licensing the rights to publish Three Stooges comics featuring Larry, Moe and Curly. It should be pointed out that even though Curly left the team in 1946, Columbia continued to distribute the shorts in which he appeared.

On May 28, 1947, the Stooges granted permission for a Three Stooges comic book and Moe, Larry and Curly entered into an agreement with Norman Maurer and Jubilee Publications entitling Maurer and the Stooges to 5 percent of the net profits from the comic book sales.

Maurer wrote, illustrated and edited the Stooges comics. The stories were adapted from actual Three Stooges comedies and utilized the same titles as the Stooges shorts.

The premiere issue of the Three Stooges comic book series was published in February, 1949. Each story held the readers' interest and definitely captured the trio's madcap humor. For a mere ten cents, comic enthusiasts got two Three Stooges stories and a special adventure featuring detective Mark Montage in *The Eyes of Kali*, illustrated by Joe Kubert.

Uncivil Warriors, the first of two story adaptations in issue number one, is a re-working of the 1935 Stooges film of the same title. In this version, however, the boys are three nutty Union spies—

Lieutenant Al Mond, Captain Ches Nutt and Major Phil Bert—assigned to infiltrate General Cornligger's headquarters at a Confederate Army Camp and liberate Operator 13 (who turns out to be a luscious blonde named Miss Draindrop Ansby). Curly's initial reaction to Ansby's shapely figure is—what else?— "Wooo-wooo-wooo!"

When Confederate informants learn that the Stooges are Union spies, a message is delivered to headquarters to notify General Cornligger (played by Bud Jamison in the film version). Curly takes the top-secret message from the messenger and starts reading it to himself. He instantly realizes that their cover has been blown and tries hiding the confidential note from General Cornligger despite constant demands for him to surrender it. In order to appease the general, Curly follows orders and starts to read the message over a burning candle, turning it to ashes.

Through some clever maneuvering, the Stooges free Miss Draindrop Ansby and dash off, with the Confederates in pursuit. They comically shake off their pursuers by hiding inside a hollow tree trunk. They're sure they'll be safe when the Union starts its attack. Instantly, rebel soldiers dash to the hollow log and pull it away, revealing that it was used to camouflage a huge cannon. Kabloom! They blast our heroes back to the friendly confines of Union headquarters.

The second adaptation, *Hoi Polloi*, also sticks relatively close to the story line of its film predecessor. The boys are garbage collectors, who dump rubbish on two upper-class citizens, Professor Duzz and Professor Kool (Rich and Nichols in the two-reeler).

Professor Kool wagers $10,000 with Professor Duzz that he can turn persons of the lowest strata into social lions. Duzz believes Kool is talking about the impossible. He really is when he chooses the Three Stooges as guinea pigs for his experiment!

The Stooges are given a series of lessons in order to transform them into gentlemen. Miss Fox Trotter teaches them how to dance, with disastrous results. During the lesson a fly crawls down her back, making her wriggle uncontrollably with the Stooges comically imitating every step.

Further lessons are provided in reading, eating and walking. Finally, after days of tutoring, Professor Kool, confident of success, unleashes the Stooges on a swank, high-society party. Slapstick bedlam reigns and a pie melee breaks out with the trio caught in the middle as usual. Duzz not only wins his bet with Kool, but gets something he wasn't expecting—a pie in the face.

The second Three Stooges edition, published in May 1949, has as many laughs as the first issue, if not more. Unlike the first book, the Stooges headline only one story, *Three Missing Links*, which is also the last film adaptation in the series. This issue also

Moe Howard with Norman Maurer and Maurer's brother, Leonard, co-creator of the 3-D comic book process.

contains another cliffhanger featuring detective Mark Montage.

Three Missing Links resembles the film version more than the previous adaptations. Every facet of the strip is identical, except for names of the characters and studio. The boys work as janitors for Carnation Pictures (for contented actors) in Hollywood and aspire to become actors. Marlena Marlena, the studio's famed leading lady, is being cast opposite a gorilla in a new epic, *The Gorilla Girl*. But studio president, B.O. Botsfiddle, finds himself in a pickle over who to cast as the male lead.

The Stooges, meanwhile, have trouble impressing Botsfiddle, who fires them for not drying off a hall floor he slipped on. As the Stooges plead for a second chance, Botsfiddle notices that Curly has all the right physical features necessary to play the gorilla and signs him to a contract. Moe and Larry are rehired as Curly's co-stars.

Everything set, they head for Africa and begin filming. Before production gets under way, the Stooges visit a cannibal medicine man who casts hungry eyes on Curly (and envisions him on a platter surrounded by garnishes). Moe swiftly changes the subject and inquires about the medicine man's ancient pottery. The cannibal informs him that their contents vary: poison in one and love candy in another. Curly, who must feed his constant craving for food, pilfers some candy before leaving the witch doctor's straw hut.

The crew is about to start shooting when the zipper on Curly's gorilla suit gets stuck. Meanwhile, as Curly struggles with the zipper, Kongo, a *real* gorilla ambles onto the set and starts to play Curly's big scene: Moe and Larry think the real gorilla is Curly. When Curly comes on the set dressed as a gorilla he tries making friends with Kongo, feeding him love candy. Instantly, the candy's potent formula overpowers Kongo, who falls in love with Curly and starts chasing him through the wilds of Africa. Moe and Larry have to rescue him, and after a series of comical scenes the Stooges ward off Kongo's affection and win out in the end.

Although both issues achieved a reasonable success, publication was suspended when Jubilee cut back on its schedule of publications. Later, in 1953, Archer St. John changed the company name from Jubilee to St. John Publishing Company and hired Joe and Norman to do a new series of comics, and Norman was back to the drawing board for a new crack at Three Stooges comic books.

Despite the long gap between issues, fans were not disappointed in these new Stooges comics. In September 1953, comics were still a dime and readers were treated to three hilarious yarns featuring the three makers of fun.

There was also a greater number of comedy routines in these issues which featured Shemp. Although Norman had seen many Three Stooges comedies, it took working with their characters to fully grasp a complete feeling for the team's unique personalities and humor. Thus, over a period of time, Maurer developed many fresh and clever ideas—unseen in the Stooges films—and incorporated popular Stooges sketches as well.

In addition, the Shemp comics were far superior in terms of design and story. Colors were rich and bright and the artwork was lavishly detailed. Stories were

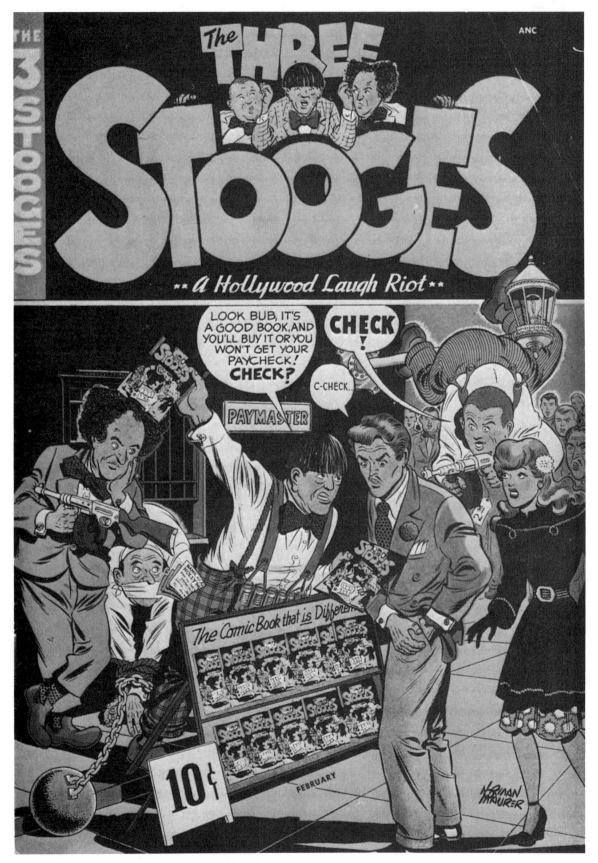

Cover for the first Three Stooges comic book.

A sampling of the Stooges' humor in comic strip form.

especially creative and had intelligent and carefully orchestrated gags. The previous Curly comics relied more on coherent stories and less on gags. The new series also featured a perfect foil for Moe, Larry and Shemp, one Benedict Bogus, a shiftless con-man constantly out to swindle the Stooges.

Furthermore, the first Shemp comic book has a more personal touch than preceding issues. In the inside flap, Norman and Joe introduced themselves to readers in cartoon form, inviting fans to send in suggestions on how to improve their work. The front cover had a nervous cartoonist (obviously Norman) fidgeting with his pen as the Stooges complain that they're not ordinary morons and, therefore, they shouldn't be drawn as ordinary morons.

The first strip, *Bogus Takes a Beating*, casts our trio as proprietors of the *Flop 'n' Sop Cafe*. Inside, the cafe is deserted save for the Three Stooges dressed in soiled waiter's uniforms. Thoroughly depressed, they stand behind a counter laden with huge stacks of unpaid bills for food and supplies.

Suddenly, the boys are startled by an outside sound. They turn to see a crowd of well-dressed businessmen hastily heading toward the front door. Elated they shout, "Customers! Roll out the businessmen's lunch!" Moe remarks that he knew all the time that if they stuck it out, they'd make a success of the business.

As the door swings open, an angry mob of creditors pour in, making violent threats, demanding that their bills be paid immediately. Outside, Benedict Bogus peers in through the cafe window. He reasons that if these stupid characters could operate a cafe with all these richly dressed customers, it surely has to be a gold mine. Thus, he approaches the Stooges and swaps them a bogus deed to the National Firecracker Factory (a recently abandoned property) for ownership of the cafe.

Moe, Larry and Shemp then turn in their dirty chef's linens and run down to view their new property. Meanwhile, word breaks out that two crooks—Trigger Mortise (also a character used years later in *The Outlaws Is Coming!* a 1965 Stooges feature) and Stiletto—have pulled a million-dollar gold heist and are using the fireworks company as a hide-out to grind the stolen gold bricks into gold dust and stuff it into firecrackers. The Stooges, of all people, walk right into trouble and believe the criminals' alibi that they are making fireworks with shiny explosive powder.

Later, while Shemp is snooping around, a bag of gold powder falls on his head, knocking him unconscious. Moe revives him, but the glowing powder refuses to come out of Shemp's hair, which is now golden-blond.

Suspicious, the Stooges mail a gold filled firecracker to Police Lieutenant Holmes of the 14th Precinct. Obviously, the Stooges have done business with him before! Holmes receives the package and discovers a firecracker that busts wide open, exposing a mound of gold powder. The lab checks the powder and discovers it is from the heist, leading Holmes to crack the gigantic gold caper. The Stooges get a $50,000 reward for their efforts and Bogus ends up with all the bill collectors he thought were customers.

This issue of fun-for-all ingredients concludes with two additional Stooges episodes. *Big Brush Off* has them as house painters who mix up a street address and ruin a millionaire's mansion with paint remover. And in *Bell Bent for Treasure*, a $1,000 reward is offered to anyone capable of recovering the Lost Bell of Adonomo. The Stooges accidentally find the bell, win the money and help a financially crippled widow send her son to a hospital for a leg operation. Sub-plot was adapted from the Stooges comedy, *Cash and Carry* (1937).

Issues number two and three were even more illustrious, since they employed a new three-dimensional process for comics.

3-D films were a huge success and comics were the next logical art form in which to experiment. Norman, Joe Kubert and Maurer's brother Leonard were directly responsible for developing the method for producing 3-D comics, a revolutionary process that opened new avenues for comic books.

3-D Illustereo, as it was called, operated under the same principle as 3-D film. In films, Polaroid glasses enabled two images to be superimposed as one. In this case, however, red and green glasses were substituted for Polaroid to create the full three-dimensional effect.

In the midst of refining their new concept, Maurer, Kubert and Maurer developed a makeshift pair of glasses in order to test their new process. The glasses were constructed out of cardboard with red and green cellophane for lenses. Norman remembers what it took for them to find the cellophane. "We had worked all night and I'll never forget how we waited on the street for the Woolworth's store in mid-town Manhattan to open because we figured we could get red and green cellophane from lollipop wrappers. We bought two packages and made a funny pair of glasses which, believe ir or not, worked perfectly."

From there Norman and Joe rushed over to show the 3-D concept to Archer St. John, who was pessimistic about the idea since he believed it was impossible. Confident, Joe and Norman handed him the 3-D sketches and makeshift glasses. Maurer recalls that St. John leaned back in his chair for more light with

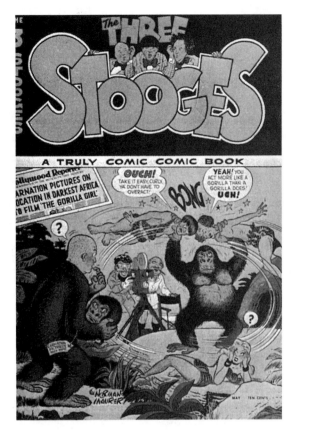

Cover for the second Three Stooges comic book with Curly.   Series of comic strip panels showing the comic book remake of a Stooges comedy.

Cover for first Stooges comic with Shemp.

Inside flap showing cartoonist Norman Maurer and Joe Kubert in cartoon form.

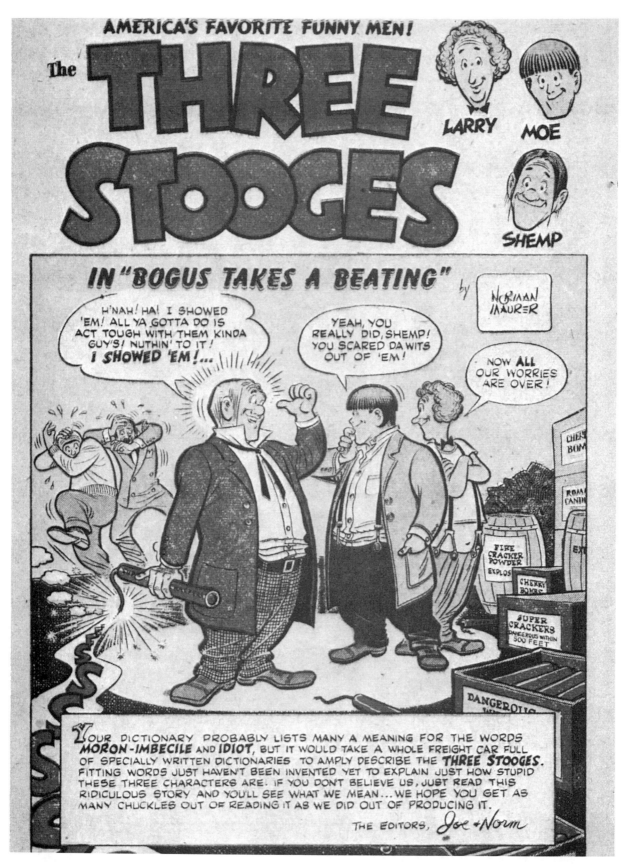

The Stooges took on a new character featured in the Shemp comics, Bogus Benedict, in *Bogus Takes a Beating*.

Panel from the first Stooges comic with Shemp.

Second Stooges comic book issue with Shemp.

which to view the art and almost fell out of the window when he saw the drawings which literally popped out from the paper.

Keenly aware of its potential, St. John bought the idea and first used the process in a 1953 *Mighty Mouse* comic book, produced and drawn by Norman and Joe. It was the Mighty Mouse book which sold millions at 25 cents a copy that inspired Maurer and Kubert to follow suit with the Three Stooges. Around this time, Joe and Norman increased production on the number of comics they produced and created for St. John. They had four series being drawn at once: *The Three Stooges, Meet Miss Pepper, Whack* and *Tor: 1 Million B.C.*

Due to increased production costs, Stooges comics were trimmed down to 32 pages from their original 64. Maurer estimates that each book took as long as one month to produce. Production stages included writing the story, doing the artwork and lettering and coloring the silverprints. Each series was bi-monthly.

As successful as 3-D Comics and films were, Joe and Norman begged St. John not to overproduce, since they felt it was just a fad that would soon fizzle out. Archer St. John disagreed. He saw 3-D as a huge money making device that would last for years. Profits were so tremendous on Mighty Mouse and the

Stooges (actual figures do not exist) that St. John wanted to put out 35 additional books in 3-D. He believed if he flooded the market it would generate millions for his company and for him personally.

To maintain his increased production schedule, St. John expanded his New York offices on 220 West 42nd Street from one to two floors and rented hotel rooms for additional working space. Maurer recalls how St. John's super expansion turned into an unforgettable fiasco. "Joe and I warned him this was a temporary fad. He wouldn't listen. He put 50 girls to work inking and painting artwork. He dumped in every penny he had and borrowed to put a mess of 3-D books out. The demand stopped and he was stuck with the books and lost a fortune which eventually caused him to go bankrupt."

In the interim, between the 3-D fiasco and the demise of St. John Publishing Company, four more (non-3-D) issues of Three Stooges Comics hit the newsstands.

Following the two 3-D issues, a fourth regular Three Stooges comic book was published in March 1954, and evoked the same zaniness that permeated the other editions. The Stooges brought their romps

The Stooges mistake an atom bomb for a carburetor in *Up 'n' Atom*.

125

Third Stooges comic book edition with Shemp.

126

Shemp turns bullfighter in *Alotta the Bull*.

The third Stooges comic book with Shemp featured a new addition, *The Adventures of Li'l Stooge*, a character designed after Moe Howard.

up to date in two new capers while Norman created another new feature, *The New Adventures of Li'l Stooge*. The lead character was a prankish, small-fry version of Moe, written by Michael Brand.

Up 'n' Atom opens this edition with Benedict Bogus conning the Stooges into overpaying for a broken-down jalopy which he claims is a super race car. The Stooges drive off to compete in the big race in Reno, Nevada, and get stranded in the middle of a desert sandstorm. In looking for a gas station, Shemp discovers a sign which reads: "Atom Bomb Testing

Consequently, when Moe turns the starter key, a terrifying ear-shattering atomic blast bursts from the car's exhaust pipe. The smoke clears to reveal the car and the Stooges charred black as they zoom over the horizon at incredible speed with a mushroom cloud spewing from their tailpipe. (Years later, Norman used this original gag of mixing up an atom bomb for a carburetor in the feature film *The Three Stooges in Orbit*, for which he wrote the story and which he produced for Columbia.)

Later, the Stooges enter the big race in Reno. Their

Fourth Stooges comic book with Shemp.

Cover for fifth Stooges comic book with Shemp.

Grounds No Admittance Beyond This Point!" Squinting through the sand, Shemp shouts back that there is a town called "No Admittance" just beyond this point. The boys drive on and their car conks out right next to a miniaturized atom bomb that is about to be detonated in a test.

In a frenzy of slapstick action, Shemp removes a mountain of assorted parts from the engine. They are strewn all over the desert sand. In putting everything back together, Shemp mistakes the miniaturized atom bomb, which is shaped like a carburetor, for the real one and attaches it to the car's engine. Meanwhile, the real carburetor lies harmless and unnoticed on the sand.

souped-up, atomic hot rod overpowers all competition to set a new racetrack record and they win hands down. A team of foreign spies learn that the new mini-bomb is in their car and are ordered to steal it from the Stooges. They succeed when Moe sells them their car for ten times what they paid for it. When the spies bring the bomb to their leader, he is furious since it looks like a harmless carburetor. He becomes so livid that he throws the bomb to the floor. The end result is an explosion unmatched since Hiroshima!

In the second feature, *Medical Mayhem*, the boys are psychiatrists out to cure Benedict Bogus of a rare disease: klepto-swindliac-skeetzo-frinnic. This is a disease which only habitual swindlers and shoplifters

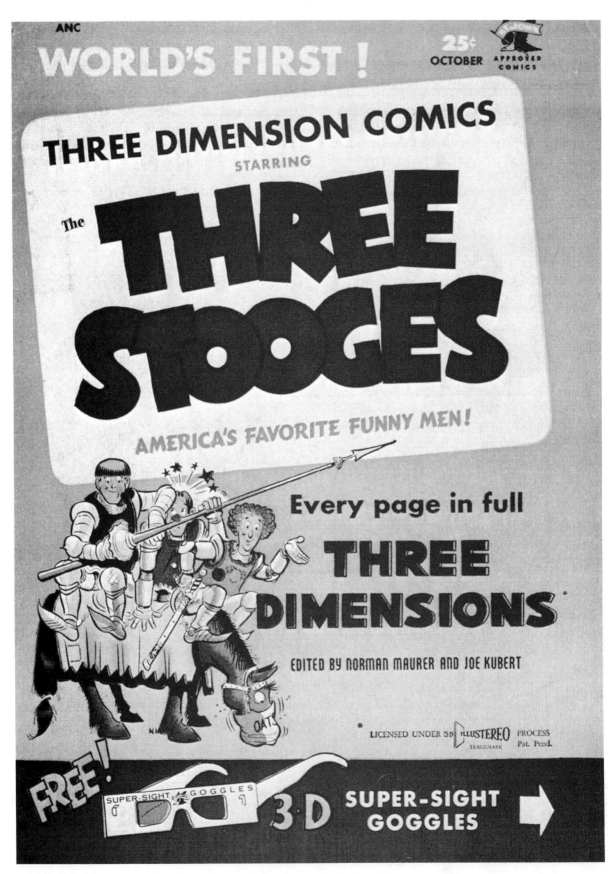

Cover for first 3-D Stooges comic book.

Cover for second 3-D Stooges comic.

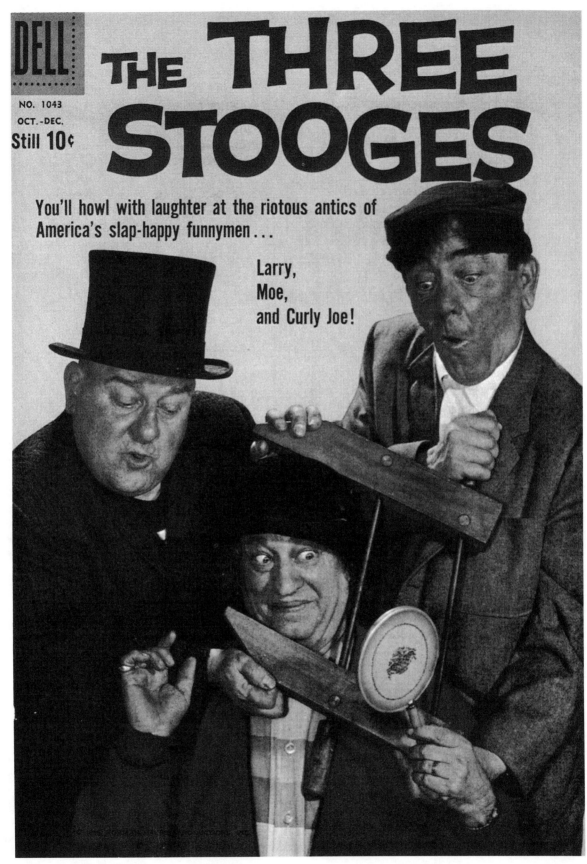

Cover for first Dell Three Stooges comic.

Dell cartoonists introduced the Stooges to readers with a page featuring the trio in cartoon form.

Panel from the first Stooges comic with Curly-Joe.

Back page advertisement on first Dell Stooges comic promoting the team's film, *Have Rocket, Will Travel*, and the first Three Stooges Fan Club.

like Bogus can contract. Moe, Larry and Shemp put Bogus through a series of tests and operations that are totally successful. Bogus is born anew and super honest. No temptation seems to crack him. But Bogus always loses in the end. At the windup of this episode, he gets arrested at the scene of a bank robbery following his attempt to return a $100 bill the crooks accidentally dropped.

Another solid comic book was the June 1954 issue, in which the Stooges continue to thwart Bogus. In *Alotta the Bull*, our trio lose their jobs at the S.O. Seedy Florists, when Shemp ruins $3,000 worth of orchids by eating garlic and breathing on them. A process server chases the Stooges who think he's from their boss and is going to sue them for damages. In a panic, they head for Benedict Bogus's place for help. For a price, Bogus provides them with his usual bogus passports and plane tickets to Mexico.

The Stooges' wild attempts to elude the process server fail as he chases them all the way to Mexico City where Moe, Larry and Shemp duck through a wooden door. They slam it behind them and bolt it from the inside. Instead of winding up safely away from the process server, they panic as they realize

Moe, Curly-Joe, and Larry mugging over a sandwich on another Dell comic.

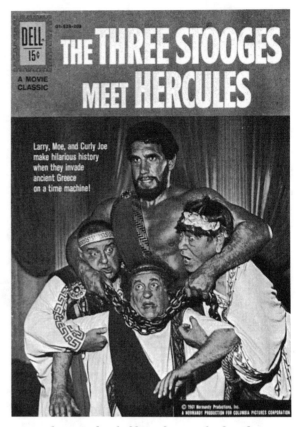

A special comic book film edition of *The Three Stooges Meet Hercules.*

they're inside the unsafe confines of a bull ring with a snorting bull thundering toward them.

Moe and Larry scram as the bull approaches with a full head of steam. Nibbling on his garlic, Shemp stands his ground, smiles and remarks, "Imagine, being scared of a little black cow!" Just as the bull is about to slam into him it sniffs his powerful garlic breath, snorts, grimaces, coughs, squints, vibrates, screeches to a stop with a gasp and keels over. The audience cheers wildly and "El Shempador" becomes an instant hero. Within weeks, El Shempador becomes the most famous matador in all Mexico. Pablo Diablo, the jealous, former world-famous bull-fighter, grows suspicious and discovers Shemp's garlic secret and sets out to find a bull immune to the smell of garlic. He discovers Alotta the Bull and pits her against Shemp. Back in America, before the big fight with Alotta, Bogus learns of Shemp's huge success and income and decides to become Shemp's manager. He hops the first plane to Mexico and convinces Shemp's agent to sell him a half-interest in El Shempador. It costs Bogus $5,000, but, to his mind, a mere pittance considering the profits he'll make. His plans to cash in, however, turn sour in the fight between Alotta and

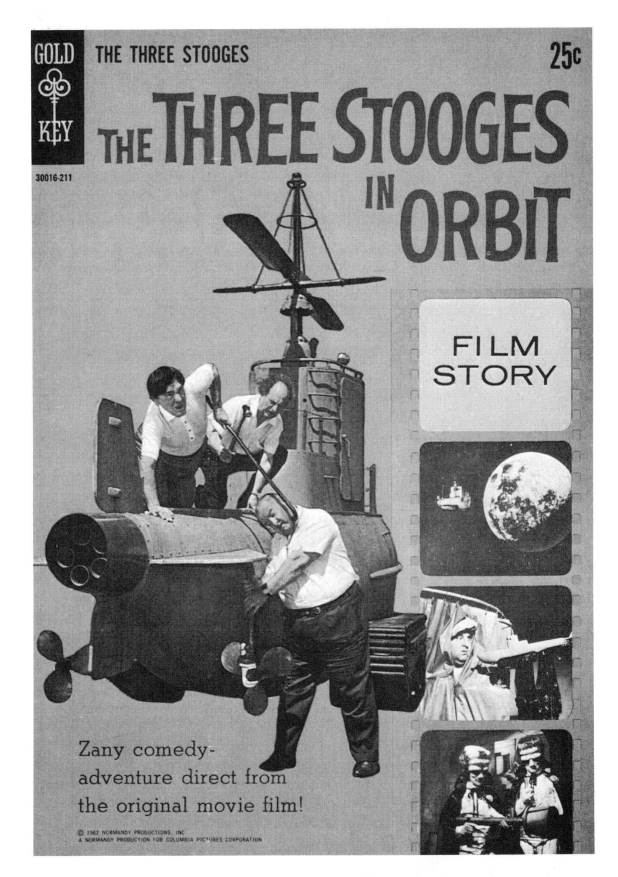

Stooges wreaking havoc on the cover of a *Three Stooges in Orbit* comic.

Zogg suddenly puts the machine into a steep climb, causing Joe to lose his balance and jam his head into the mouth of the cannon.

With Larry working to free Joe, Moe stops Ogg from using the cannon by pouring a bag of water down the periscope into his face.

A last desperate tug pulls Joe's head out of the cannon's mouth. "Quick," yells Moe. "They're getting ready to shoot this thing again. Help me turn it." The three boys use their combined strength to swivel the deadly weapon upwards, away from the city.

The film/comic book of *The Three Stooges in Orbit* actually featured panels of frames from the film telling the story.

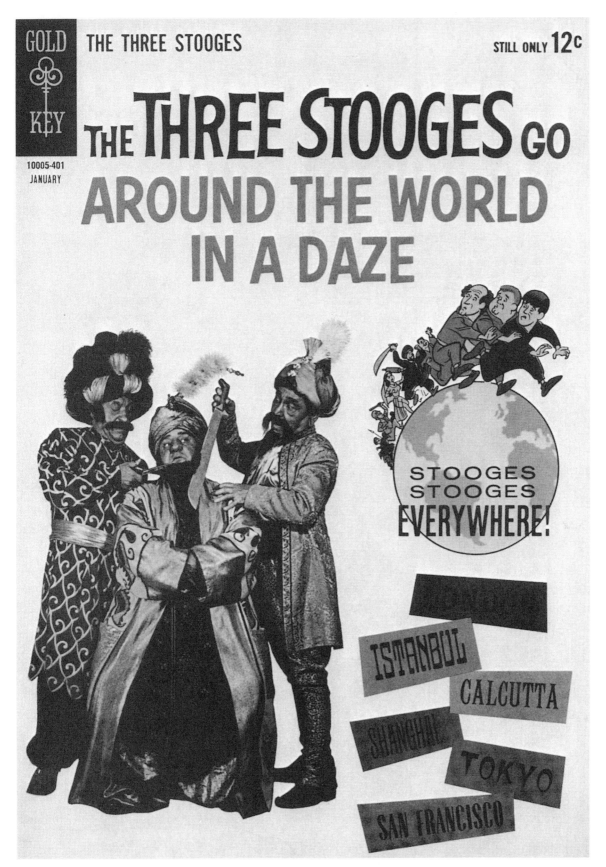

Comic book cover for *The Three Stooges Go Around the World in a Daze.*

Gold key comic book on the Stooges' last released film, *The Outlaws Is Coming!*

Shemp as Alotta, immune to Shemp's garlic breath, plasters him all over the ring.

With disappointed fans chasing after them, the Stooges and Bogus are fortunate to get out of Mexico alive. With our heroes back home, the process server (who isn't a process server at all) finally catches up with them and informs them that their ex-boss wants to give them a $500 bonus. It appears the smell of Shemp's garlic only temporarily affected the orchids. Afterwards, it made them grow five times their normal size!

Another hilarious yarn, $99^{44}/_{100}\%$ *Puritan*, transports Bogus and the Stooges back to London during the year 1681. This is the first of a new series exploiting Bogus in flashbacks to various times in history. The idea is reminiscent of James Thurber's popular story *The Secret Life of Walter Mitty*, because of Bogus's daydreamer sequences. In this adventure, however, Bogus sees himself as a real estate tycoon, pioneering the New World and buying an island—Manhattan—from the Indians.

The Stooges, leading jewelry merchants in the New World, team up with Bogus for an expedition to buy an island on the West Coast. Moe also operates *Moe*hawk Real Estate ("If you Got Beads, We Got Deeds"). In the process of guiding Bogus to his dream island, they accidentally stumble into Indian territory and break up an important crap game. The Indian Chief becomes upset and orders the foursome burned at the stake.

They will be spared, however, if they will marry three old squaws and the chief's 16-year-old daughter. The Stooges convince Bogus that marriage is better than death. Thus, a parade of women emerge from a tepee to meet their future husbands. Moe, Larry and Shemp whistle deliriously and gawk lasciviously as their brides turn out to be curvacious brunettes. Bogus gasps in horror as he gets stuck with the Chief's rotund, plain-Jane daughter who has all the markings of a rump roast. When marriage looks like much less of a bargain, Bogus and the Stooges are tied to stakes and flames lick at their feet. Shemp pours gunpowder into the flames and, stakes and all, they blast away like four antique rockets. In the wind-up, Bogus buys his island, which turns out to be Alcatraz and the prison is built right around him.

If myths and traditions don't make good stories, age-old problems of ghosts and goblins and of wealth and matrimony do. In issue number six, published August 1954, the Stooges poked fun at both. *Fluke Spook* has Moe, Larry and Shemp helping Bogus run a Kentucky plantation that was willed to him. There they meet some frightening characters who are out to steal the deed. And in *Bogus Takes a Bride*, Benedict joins the Matri-Moe Lonely Hearts Club, hoping to snatch a wealthy bride. He finds one all right, a stuffy old dowager who's as broke as Bogus.

This edition also features the first of a special new satirical series that would continue in future issues. Norman and Joe began spoofing time-honored comic strips and films. Their first attempt was *Bringing Up Mama*, satirizing George McManus' *Bringing Up Father*. Norman even credits himself as George McMaurer.

The final Stooges strip in this issue was a mini-version of the 1934 film, *Punch Drunks*, containing some minor alterations. Shemp enters the world of boxing and draws his power in the ring from hearing a popular ballad named "Dixieland" (in the original film it was "Pop Goes the Weasel"). Another change from the original has a jukebox in place of Larry's broken violin as the means by which they play the fight-inspiring song. The jukebox fails and Shemp loses the fight, while in the Columbia two-reeler, Curly wins.

The seventh issue was published in October 1954 and brought the second series of Three Stooges comics to an abrupt close, despite plans for an eighth issue. Issue number seven dealt out some wild stuff with the Stooges as *Nautical Nitwits* vacationing on a gambling ship, *S.S. Betchalife*. The boys go from rags to riches, of course, while Bogus gets a no-way ticket to the poor farm. Their penchant for messing up situations continued as publisher's assistants in *The Memoirs of Benedict Bogus*. The final story was a tantalizing special feature titled *The Crisco Kid*, which spoofed the Cisco Kid movies.

St. John's entire line of comics died on the vine, so to speak, with the death of owner and publisher Archer St. John. A short time later, Maurer left the comic book field to pursue a career in motion pictures. Kubert, his long-time partner, continued to illustrate comic books and several years later started an art school in New Jersey.

Comic book buffs were not treated to another Three Stooges series until 1959. As part of a full-scale merchandising plan and because of the team's enormous popularity, Western Publishing was granted a licensing agreement by Norman Maurer Productions to publish a quarterly series of Stooges Comics. These books were published by Western but distributed by Dell Publishing, which had the ability to get comic books onto the newsstand and into the markets. Once the series proved itself, Western went bi-monthly with their Three Stooges comics. The issues revolved around new adventures with Moe, Larry and Curly-Joe, and the first issue was published in October-November 1959.

Twelve cents won comic enthusiasts two freshly

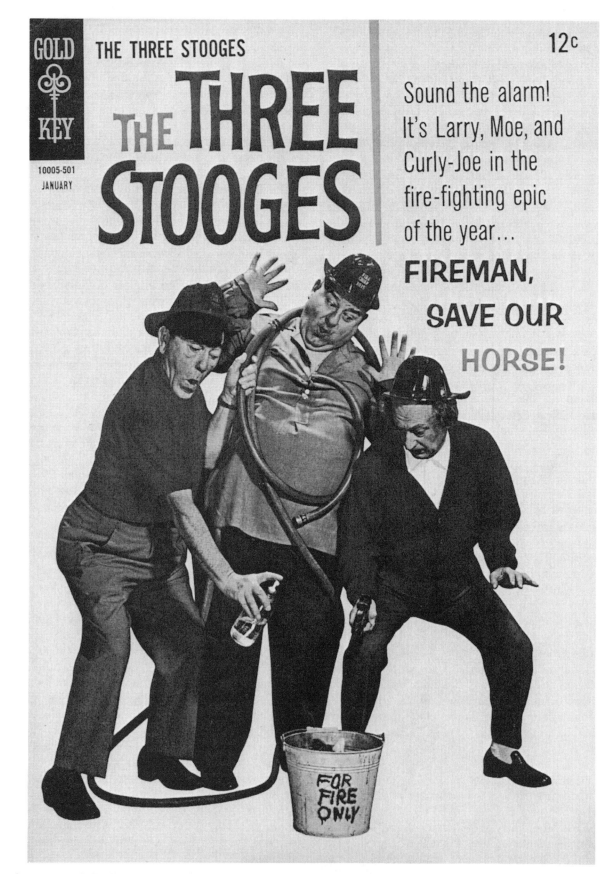

The Stooges help fuel a fire on the cover of a Gold Key comic book.

Norman Maurer introduced The Little Stooges in a series of Gold Key comics. Cover for first edition.

The Little Stooges in a remake of a Shemp comic book story, *The Bull-Dozers*.

written stories with the boys in each issue. Another alternating installment was *Professor Putter* and *The Little Monsters*. Fan questions were answered as well by the team in a bi-monthly column labeled *Dear Stooges*, and the boys offered safety tips in another special feature.

These editions were quite inferior to the St. John series in many ways. Perhaps their best asset was the full-color photographs of the Stooges on the cover of every issue. Some fans consider the covers priceless, more so than the strips inside. Stories were nonsensical and contained much play upon words in its dialogue. Customary slapstick, quite prevelent in the St. John books, wasn't as apparent in an effort to tone down the Stooges' violence and appease parents.

Western employed their own artists and writers to do the strips and it definitely showed! Unfortunately, character drawings of the Stooges were inconsistent, ranging from fair to mediocre. Curly-Joe was as appealing as the Pillsbury Doughboy. Moe, actually, came the closest to looking like himself, while Larry appeared as though he had gone through a character change—his frizzy hair was less rumpled and his nose lost its prominence.

Had Maurer been supervising the series, artists would have done a much more credible job. The Western/Dell books just didn't have the same charisma as the earlier St. John editions. Stories were short on gags and the few that were included were abysmal.

Western continued to publish the Three Stooges series, producing ten issues plus a special comic album. In 1962 Western decided to distribute their own books and used the name *Gold Key* as their logo. Western/Gold Key went on to publish 45 issues over a period of 13 consecutive years.

In addition to regular comic books, Western published adaptations of such Three Stooges feature films as *The Three Stooges Meet Hercules, The Three Stooges in Orbit, The Three Stooges Go Around the World in a Daze* and *The Outlaws Is Coming!* The comic adaptation of *Three Stooges in Orbit* was an unusual oddity since it incorporated actual frame blow-ups from the film to tell the story. Western/Gold Key also published another Three Stooges series called *March of Comics*, which was originally published by K.K. Publications as half-sized comics handed out at shoe stores. Nine *March of Comics* issues were distributed by Western/Gold Key.

Copies of the special movie editions have become collectors' items and sell for as much as $7.50 in mint condition. By contrast, St. John editions with Curly go for $75, while 3-D Stooge editions range from $35 to $45. Western published from 450,000 to 700,000 books per issue. Stooge comics ranked second to Walt Disney comics in circulation, printing almost one million copies every month.

When Western dropped the Stooges comics in 1972, Norman Maurer proposed a new series starring the Little Stooges and the first edition was published under the Gold Key logo in September, 1972. In many respects, *The Little Stooges* was more entertaining than the Three Stooges series (for Western), mainly because Maurer was once again writing the stories and doing the artwork. The stories were fresh and clever. Even Norman's son, Jeff Maurer, wrote several of the stories. Norman began each story with the young Stooges—under the watchful eye of their fathers—picking up where the elder Stooges left off. Their sons prove to be just as clumsy footed and just as nit-witted. The characters' problems dealt with adolescent trials and tribulations: How to survive while growing up during the teen years. In order to satisfy the ardent Stooges fan's appetite for traditional slapstick gags, a bit more slapping and hitting prevailed where necessary. In *Prisoner in a Candy Factory* (Little Stooges, #4) all six Stooges gather to celebrate Curly-Joe Jr.'s birthday at a swank restaurant and the stage is set for the kind of slaphappy Stooges antics fans remember.

Some of the stories featured in the Little Stooges series were adaptations of the best titles from the earlier series featuring Shemp. Re-used were such favorites as *99⁴⁴/₁₀₀% Puritan, Alotta the Bull* (changed to *The Bull-Dozers*) and *The Fluke Spook.* As for character design, teen-age Moe, Larry and Curly-Joe had a charming, hip look about them. Their attire was a reflection of the early 1970s: mod hairstyles, beads and freaky clothes. Trouble ensued wherever they went, but they usually emerged from their misfortune victorious.

Introduced in issue number one was Moose, the Little Stooges canine retriever. Moose was actually Maurer's own Labrador retriever and made his screen debut in the Stooges' final film, *Kook's Tour* (1970). Maurer revived another stock character, his personal favorite, Benedict Bogus, in the form of his son, Benedict Jr. Young Bogus was just as devilish, in fact more scheming than Benedict Sr. In the traditional fashion of his father, Bogus Jr. was unsuccessful in conning the Little Stooges and always got it in the end. The young Stooges also featured girl friends; Moon, a typical girl next-door; Pixie, the richest girl in town; and Lovey, a cute, chubby gal who shares Curly's weakness for chocolate sodas.

But despite the success of the Little Stooges series, it had a formidable obstacle in the changing economy. Comic book companies were treading on bad times

Norman Maurer's caricature drawings of the entire cast from the Gold Key Little Stooges comic book series.

BENEDICT BOGUS

CHEATER'S DIGEST

THE FAMOUS FATHERS

BENEDICT BOGUS, JR.

LITTLE LARRY

GES

A young trio of Stooges go ape in another Gold Key comic.

Sample of a special hand-sized series of comics published on the Stooges.

and sales throughout the industry were down. Their struggle to survive was mirrored in comic book prices: an inflationary twenty cents! And that was for just one story per issue!

Despite economically troubled times, *The Little Stooges* did well enough to warrant seven issues, equaling the output of issues from the St. John series. The last edition was published in March 1974, thus ending the Stooges' 14-year association with Western Publishing, which is quite a successful run for a comic book series.

But the Three Stooges' history as comic strip characters may not be over. As this book goes to press,

Norman Maurer is preparing a new newspaper comic strip called *Larry, Moe and Curly*, by the Three Maurers. The Three Maurers are none other than Norman, who is doing the artwork, and sons Jeffrey and Michael, who are writing the gags.

With a good possibility of another Three Stooges success in the publishing field, we come to the realization that the team has been tops in whatever field of endeavor it has been associated with. As the years have passed, this success has not diminished but has multiplied, and without a doubt has catapulted these three crazy comics into the world of legend.

Curly-Joe, Moe and Larry singing "Heart of My Heart" during their famous operation sketch on *The Ed Sullivan Show.*

CHAPTER

4

The Three Stooges on Television

IT WAS THE GROWING POPULARITY of television, in 1946, which helped give longevity to some comedians' careers and cut short others. The Three Stooges came to television with a special purpose—they wanted to explore another horizon in the realm of comedy.

The Stooges—Moe, Larry and Shemp—first appeared before the tube-watching public on Milton Berle's *Texaco Star Theater*. The show was broadcast over NBC on October 19, 1948. Neither a kinescope of the show nor a script are available for review, so, unfortunately, the material used on their television debut will remain an unknown quantity. However, according to Larry Fine, the show was well received and fans wanted to see more of their antics on the small screen.

Larry once remarked that television's lack of rehearsal time hampered the Stooges' style. In a 1950 radio interview, Fine explained the team's feelings about television. "It's new—hard to get used to—but we like it. The difficulty is, it doesn't give us time to prepare our act and to put on the kind of show we're used to doing and that people expect from us. I imagine TV would be pretty tough to do every week."

Although vaudeville had fallen out of public favor in the early 1940s, television seemed to have revived it for a time as it became the stage for a pastiche of popular vaudeville and burlesque routines. A mighty legion of comedians, including the Stooges, were responsible for the revival of many of these tried-and-true vignettes. The trio came to television with routines that had been lifted from their films and vaudeville. Hardly ever was fresh material written for them, at least during the primitive stages of this new entertainment medium.

The Stooges' first use of new material was a television pilot they starred in, filmed on October 12, 1949, and titled *The Three Stooges*. Moe, Larry and Shemp applied their skills hoping to land a weekly television series. The pilot was shot at ABC and was produced by Phil Berle, Milton Berle's brother. Henry Taylor was hired to scipt it and George McCahan took the helm as director.

The story revolved around the Stooges and their inability to hold a job (a similar device was later employed in a weekly TV series featuring Abbott and Costello). Emil Sitka and Symona Boniface were hired in supporting roles as a high society couple and Joseph Kearns (Mr. Wilson from the *Dennis the Menace Show*) performed a memorable cameo as a pressure-cooker salesman from Punxatawney, Pennsylvania.

In the show's opening, the announcer speaks in a high bubbling pitch as he introduces the Stooges individually. Interspersed with the announcer's remarks, we hear the boys introducing themselves to the audience. The announcer continues to gush: "Yes, ladies and gentlemen, it's the Three Stooges! For mirth and madness—"

The camera cuts to Moe grinning as he intones, "I'm Moe!" The announcer then interjects, "Simple and screwy!" Turning to the camera, Shemp announces, "I'm Shemp!" The announcer continues, "Looney and lunatic!" Up pops the last Stooge, "I'm Larry!" This acts as a cue for the notes of the show's theme song, "Crazy People," to ascend while the camera pulls back to a three-shot of the Stooges in painters' overalls. The announcer continues his spiel: "Yes, the Three Stooges are versatile gentlemen! When it comes to any kind of business, they're as spry as monkeys. Let us look at their spry monkey-business now."

The boys turn up in the show as painters and wallpaper hangers. Mr. Pennyfeather (Emil Sitka) prevails on the boys to re-decorate his opulent mansion. A typical gag results after Pennyfeather makes his entrance into the Stooges' office and asks, "Pardon me, gentlemen. Are you painters and paperhangers?" Larry begins to talk in circles, "Are we painters and paperhangers?" Then Moe chimes in, "Are we painters and paperhangers?" A puzzled Shemp queries, "Are we?" Moe stamps on his foot, causing Shemp to smack the top of a desk with his hand, sweeping off a bottle of ink onto Pennyfeather's three-piece suit. Livid, Pennyfeather eyes his soiled clothing, then glares at Shemp. Moe, apologetic, tries wiping off the ink stains, but, instead, spreads them all over the suit's expensive-looking jacket. Larry, trying to help out, runs over and picks up a gallon-can of ink remover and pours out the entire contents onto Pennyfeather's suit. The potent liquid removes more than ink, as it burns away portions of the jacket as well.

Pennyfeather's temper rises as he takes out his vengeance on Shemp, pouncing on him. His assault is stopped in its tracks as Moe steps in to reprise one of his favorite routines, "Insulting the State of Texas." Strutting up to Pennyfeather, Moe spouts, "Just a minute! Do you realize that you have just struck one of the toughest men from the state of—"(all three clap their hands) "—Texas! Go ahead, tell him, Tex!" Shemp sidles over to Pennyfeather and manages to

squeal, "Yeah, I'm" ... Pennyfeather hauls off and wallops him again. Moe steps back in front of Pennyfeather in the same fashion as before, "Sir, you have again sullied the fair name of the great, sovereign state of—" (the usual four claps) "—Texas!" Motioning to Shemp, Moe says, "Order him off the premises!" The boys proceed to throw Pennyfeather out of the door, paint remover can and all.

The phone rings and it's Mrs. Pennyfeather, calling the Stooges to come over to paint her house. The boys agree to go, not realizing they just brutalized her husband. Enthused over the chance to prove their worth as interior decorators, Larry dashes to the three-drawer file cabinet to find their book of color samples.

Moe spots Larry struggling to open the middle

The Three Stooges appear with Eddie Cantor and Pat Dennie on his TV show *Eddie Cantor Comedy Theatre*. It was Shemp's last TV appearance with the team.

Larry making capital of his appearance on *The Ed Wynn Show*, 1950. Shemp and Moe look on.

drawer of the file cabinet. Infuriated, Larry bangs the top drawer with his fists which sends the bottom drawer flying out, cracking him on the shins. While Larry hops about in pain, Moe takes over remarking, "How did you ever get so stupid?" Larry snaps back, "I gotta charge account—what's your excuse?" Shoving Larry aside, Moe shouts, "Remind me to lower your salary and raise your forehead. Out of the way!"

Of course, Moe quickly proves he's as brainless as the rest of the Stooges. He tugs fruitlessly at the middle drawer—it won't budge. Furious, he kicks the bottom drawer closed. Whap! The top one flies out smashing him in the face.

And now it's Shemp's turn. "Step aside, boys. Let an intelligent man show you how." Moe is angry now and shouts, "Intelligent? What makes you so smart?" Shemp remarks, "I graduated from college—Swedish Massage College." Moe queries, "Then why didn't you go into the business?" Shemp chuckles stupidly, "I couldn't find any Swedes to massage!"

Following a series of comedy miscues, Shemp gets the file drawer open and mistakes a folder plainly marked *Culinary Art Book* for the book of wallpaper and color samples. He drags it along as the Stooges go to Pennyfeather's house. Mrs. P. knows she's in big trouble when Shemp, reading from his cook book, suggests tomato red as the color for the living room.

Aside from the customary slapstick tomfoolery, Moe, Shemp and Larry recreate another famous routine from the Stooges' 1938 comedy, *Tassels in the Air*. The boys are asked to refinish an expensive antique table, but instead ruin it.

The show's ending comes as no surprise when Mr. Pennyfeather finally returns to find the Stooges destroying his house. Reminiscent of their films on high society, Pennyfeather gets back at them for creating their mess by dumping paint over their heads and physically assaulting them.

This scene segues to the weary trio leaving their office; they are in a sorry state. Moe has a bandage on his head, Larry has his arm in a sling and Shemp is walking with a crutch and has band-aids on his face. Suddenly, we are interrupted by the announcer, who says, "And so ends the episode in which our Three Stooges tried their luck as interior decorators but met with misfortune. However, will they be cowards and never try it again? Are they spineless jeffyfish? Quitters?" The boys quickly turn to camera and snap back an answer: "Ya betcha life we are!"

Although their performances were adequate, a good deal of the Stooges' antics were missing. The direction was extremely poor and the film lacked the spontaneity of their shorts. In addition, the writers crammed too many routines into one show, which actually bogged it down.

The pilot, which took one day to film, was never aired. B.B. Kahane, Columbia Pictures' Vice-President of Business Affairs, stopped the show from being broadcast. Kahane warned the Stooges that a contract stipulation restricted them from performing in a TV series that might compete with their two-reel comedies. Columbia further threatened to cancel the boys' contract and take them to court if they tried to sell the series. To avert a legal hassle, the pilot was shelved and the project abandoned.

Although the Stooges were contractually forbidden

The Stooges reprising the "Stand-In" sketch on *The Steve Allen Show*.

from doing a TV series, personal appearances were permitted and they appeared in a guest shot on *The Ed Wynn Show*, sponsored by Camel cigarettes and telecast on CBS on March 11, 1950. Wynn's program was the first live Los Angeles-based variety show. In this particular show, the Stooges played CBS executives (Moe as Mr. *C*, Larry as Mr. *B* and Shemp as Mr. *S*). They order Wynn to overhaul his entire program, from its comedy material to its studio sets. The show was telecast "live" and the boys were a tremendous hit with the studio audience.

In the show's opening scene, Moe introduces Larry to Wynn, informing him that Larry is vice-president in charge of network soap operas. Larry proves it by blowing a stream of bubbles from his mouth. Later on in the show, the Stooges mess up a dramatic sketch and Wynn attempts to rid himself of the trio by positioning them below sandbags, hanging high overhead, determined to clobber them. Helen Forrest, a popular singer of the day, guest-starred along with William Frawley.

Following the Wynn show, the Stooges were invited to appear April 29, 1950, on NBC's *Damon Runyon Memorial Fund* telethon to benefit the American Cancer Society. The show was hosted by Milton Berle. Afterward, Berle asked them to appear again on *The Texaco Star Theater*, airing May 2, 1950. The

Berle series was broadcast on NBC every Tuesday from 8 to 9 p.m. Sharing the spotlight with the trio were the Lee Sheldon Dancers, Victoria Troupe, Rose Marie, Robert Alda, Sid Stone and Morton Downey (who earlier took the Stooges on an extended nationwide tour).

In the better part of one hour, the Stooges employ many of their tried-and-true routines. In the middle of their opening sketch, Shemp interrupts Berle,

The Stooges, mugging broadly, displaying their oversized scrapbook from *Three Stooges Scrapbook*.

Moe and Curly-Joe capturing the butler, disguised as a haunted-house monster, from *Three Stooges Scrapbook*.

advising him that they are running out of time. Here, Shemp cleverly slips in a comedy bit the Stooges had been using since their days with Ted Healy, "Telling Time." Berle notices that Shemp is wearing three watches on his wrist and asks him why he's wearing them. Shemp explains, "Oh, I use those to tell time. Ya see, this one is 20 minutes slow—and this one is ten minutes fast—and this one is stopped at two o'clock." Alarmed, Berle inquires, "Then...how do you tell the time?" Shemp says, smirking, "Well, I subtract the ten on this watch from the 20 on this watch, then I add them all together and divide by two..." Berle interrupts, "Oh yeah! Well then, what time is it?" Shemp yanks out a fourth watch from his coat pocket, checks the time and retorts, "Eight-twenty!" After finishing the bit, Moe, Larry and Shemp convince Berle to let them sing "Sawanee River."

A couple of acts later, they return in a Foreign Legion sketch which features Robert Alda as their commanding officer. Only Moe and Shemp have lines of dialogue, while Larry remains mute. Alda gets into the act by asking Shemp, "Have you been in the

A slapstick publicity still of the Stooges from their popular operation sketch.

Foreign Legion before Pearl Harbor?" Shemp cracks, "I've been in the Foreign Legion before Pearl White!" (a famous actress from the early days of film). Shemp snickers at his own remark as Moe shouts, "Put out your hand!" He smacks Shemp's hand which swings around and clobbers Shemp's skull.

Berle was so pleased with the trio that he called them back for a third guest shot on October 10, 1950. The guest stars included Bert Gordon, the Weavers, Alice Pearce, Yogi Berra, Evelyn Knight, Sid Stone,

Walter Winchell and George Price. Moe, Larry and Shemp performed another stock routine on the show. They used their famous "Maharaja" sketch for the first time on television. While Curly was superb as the near-sighted Maharaja in *Three Little Pirates* (1946), Shemp's performance was just as convincing, and the time-tested Maharaja sketch had the audience howling.

Again, the Stooges hit pay dirt in this riotous moment of lunacy. Shemp, as the Maharaja, enters

155

wearing an Indian turban, a garish Indian costume and glasses with thick, beveled lenses that give him the appearnce of a startled owl. As you would lead a blindman, Moe guides the Maha out onto the stage. Shemp comically bumps into tables and chairs during his absurd entrance. Shemp finally stops, his back to the audience, and bows as Moe spins him around to face the throng, pushing him into a chair. Then Moe inquires, "Like to talk to people?" Shemp chuckles, mutters, "Razbanyas yatee benee-futch ah skidoo kiddo." In the midst of Moe's questions, Shemp gets up from his seat and begins to wander. Moe orders him to sit down. Shemp reacts to his command, searches aimlessly for the chair, sits, misses the seat and falls flat on his duff.

Moe keeps the act moving as he continues his spiel to the audience, "The Rajah never on any occasion uses any helper, assistant or confederate but for this particular group of tricks, he'd like to have a young..." Before Moe finishes Larry dashes up on stage from the audience shouting, "Here I am!" Berle enters the scene as Larry asks, "What does the Maharaja do?" "Yeah, what does he do?" shouts Berle. "We shall see!" Moe chimes in.

Seating himself next to Shemp, Moe shouts, "Ma-ha!" Shemp looks dazedly in several directions, finally spots Moe and stammers, "Ah-ha!" Moe answers with his patented doubletalk, "Razbanyas yata benee futch ah timiney heronha dot pickle-head askee taskee wateecha fertziek you goddit?" (Translation: Moe wants to know what trick Shemp will perform.) Shemp replies, "Nyothing!" Flabbergasted, Moe remarks, "Nyothing??" Moe regains his composure, grabs Larry by the hair and shouts that the Maharaja is an expert sharpshooter and for his first trick will shoot a raisin from the top of this gentleman's head. Given his trusty rifle, half-blind Shemp points it directly at the audience, who scream in panic. Moe twirls him around, helps him aim toward Larry. Kablam! He impresses all, shooting the raisin cleanly off Larry's head.

Larry's cowardice and the Maharaja's blindness are put to the test again in a wild, knife-throwing demonstration. Shemp blindly throws knives which miss the target completely and send Larry into a trembling panic. Finally, Moe shouts to the audience, "The Rajah says the next blade will come within one-eighth of an inch of the victim's brain." The victim, being Larry, quips, "What brain?" Berle, squeamish, runs off stage to escape from the firing line. Shemp then throws his last knife which sails off stage in Berle's direction. A beat and Berle emerges screaming with the trick knife piercing his head.

Berle was a long-time admirer of the Three Stooges

Moe, Curly-Joe and Larry try amusing an eccentric professor (Emil Sitka) in a scene from *Three Stooges Scrapbook.*

Curly-Joe, Moe and Larry stranded as sailors in a scene from *Three Stooges Scrapbook.*

Hollywood Reporter ad saluting the cast and of *Three Stooges Scrapbook.*

TV'S NEWEST BLUE-CHIP OFFERING

THREE STOOGES SCRAPBOOK

PAR VALUE - LOW COST PER THOUSAND

This Certifies that _____ PLEASE PRINT _____ IS THE
OWNER OF RECORD OF A QUARTER-CENTURY OF PROVEN COMEDY SUCCESS.
ALL SHARES NOW SPECIALLY ISSUED FOR THE TELEVISION FAMILY AUDIENCE.
JAM-PACKED WITH LAUGHS, SPILLS, ROLLICKING CARTOONS AND FUN-FILLED MAYHEM.

25 YEARS OF CONTINUOUS DIVIDENDS - NOW PAYABLE WEEKLY DURING 1960 1961

IN COLOR! CARTOONS, TOO!

SEE OUR BROKER — **MERRILL, PIERCE, WILLIAM, MORRIS & AGENCY**

THE SLAP-HAPPY TEAM

SIDNEY MILLER CRAZY DIRECTOR

NORMAN MAURER TIRED, WORE OUT PRODUCER

ELLWOOD ULLMAN CRAZY WRITER
PAUL DUNLAP MAD MUSIC COMPOSER

TV SPOTS MADE THE CRAZY CARTOON

SINCERE THANKS **NORMAN MAURER PRODUCTIONS, INC.**

157

An animated version of the Stooges in a cartoon scene from *Three Stooges Scrapbook*.

and their comedy. His rapid-fire delivery was akin to Ted Healy's and Bud Abbott's. Larry recalled that "Berle was kind of like Healy. He was fast with the jokes and would slap us around. We got into all kinds of messes, of course. And Milton liked having us on the show."

Television producers often used the Stooges as comic relief in musical-variety shows, such as *The Texaco Star Theater*. Ted Collins, Kate Smith's personal agent, signed the trio for NBC's *The Kate Smith Hour*. The team appeared twice on the program, first on October 13, 1950, and then on May 18, 1951. Smith's series was a live weekly variety show which featured Broadway and Hollywood stars in musical numbers and comedy sketches, and the Stooges fit quite well into her format.

Following their success on the Kate Smith show, the boys appeared on NBC's *The Colgate Comedy Hour*. They made their debut on Sunday, December 16, 1951, at the El Capitan Theatre in Hollywood. Other performers who headlined the series at one time or another were such top-name comedians as Abbott and Costello, Fred Allen, Martin and Lewis and Ed Wynn. Carmen Miranda, Alan Young (who played Wilbur Post on *Mister Ed*) and Roy Rogers were hired to guest on the program featuring the Stooges. Kingman Moore directed and Jack Paar hosted.

Moe appearing on a Mexican TV show version of *What's My Line?*

In many respects, the Stooges surpassed their previous television performances, since most of their material for the Colgate show was new. Their first sketch had Larry cast as the manager of Fay's Department Store. As he prepares for a big Christmas Sale, we see a crush of customers outside, anxiously waiting to get into the store. Larry forces his way through the mob, unlocks the doors and is trampled on by a stampede of patrons trying to get in. (Jerry Lewis later reworked this same gag in *Who's Minding the Store?*)

The camera cuts to Larry, flattened on the ground. Moe, a floorwalker, shouts, "Five minutes after nine and he's sleeping already. Come on, Sleeping Beauty, get up!" Moe grabs a handful of Larry's hair and pulls him to his feet. Then, pointing to a table full of miscellaneous goods, shouts, "Here's a bunch of junk we haven't been able to sell all year. *You* are going to sell it!" Larry whimpers, "But where are we going to find someone *stupid* enough to buy this stuff?"

On cue, Shemp (a customer) enters, garbed in an ill-fitting suit and sporting thick-lensed eye glasses. Moe and Larry believe they've found the perfect sucker to take their useless junk. But Shemp isn't interested. All he wants is a full refund on the faulty fountain pen he bought. Inspecting the pen carefully, Moe asks, "What seems to be wrong with the article?" As Shemp pulls open the fill-lever and says, "When I do this..." Zap! Moe gets a faceful of ink. Shemp continues, "...it squirts all over." Moe responds angrily, wiping the ink off his face, burning. "So it does," He belts Shemp with his inky hand.

Moe and Larry refuse to refund Shemp in cash and instead offer their worn-out merchandise in exchange. Shemp remains adamant; he wants a cash "refund." On the word "refund," Moe's violent temper is ignited and he punches Shemp around uncontrollably, trying to change his mind. Shemp won't concede—he wants his money back. In the same vein as "Niagara Falls," another reaction-on-word sketch, Moe reacts violently each time he hears the word "refund." He wallops Shemp so hard that he is nearly out on his feet. As he staggers around comically, about to fall, Moe catches him, holds him upright and in the process feels for Shemp's wallet. He yanks it out and removes a sheaf of bills, moves them close to his ear and riffles them. Moe counts out 98 dollars and pockets it as payment in full for the worthless sale items. Moe and Larry then stuff the junk merchandise and the dazed Shemp into a crate. The the camera zooms in on the words "Do Not Open Until Christmas!"

In their second sketch, Roy Rogers introduces the Stooges as renowned chefs and explains that they are preparing delicacies for a lavish party. Typical bits of

Curly-Joe, Moe and Larry, along with bandleader Skitch Henderson, reprising the "Maharaja" routine on *The Ed Sullivan Show*.

business include: Shemp stuffing a turkey by throwing in eggs and oysters—shells and all—and canned items still in the can. Meanwhile, Larry cleans lettuce in dirty dish water and hangs the leaves to dry on a clothes line. To make things worse, all three accidentally spike the punch with tabasco sauce. Of course, their cooking erupts into an outrageously wild melee which not even the show's announcer can bring under control.

As a result of their successes on *Texaco Star Theater* and *Colgate Comedy Hour*, the Stooges' services were in constant demand. One of their finest achievements was their work on *The Frank Sinatra Show*, a one-hour weekly series for CBS, broadcast January 1, 1952. The series was telecast live from Hollywood and

159

featured celebrated guest stars and plenty of singing by Ol' Blue Eyes. Such noted luminaries as Louis Armstrong, CBS president William Paley, George DeWitt and Yvonne DeCarlo were cast opposite the Stooges.

Larry, Moe and Shemp appear as servants at Sinatra's New Year's Eve party. The Stooges brighten up the sketch in their patented, slapstick manner, messing up the simple task of taking coats from partygoers. They toss the guest's clothing about with Shemp finally flinging everything out the window. Sinatra keeps the show moving at a fast clip, hosting and singing songs to the delight of the audience.

Coming off the Sinatra show, the Stooges received

The Stooges sing along with Mary Costa, Don Ameche, Johnny Mathis, (?), and Frances Langford on her 1960 TV special.

Moe and Curly-Joe failing to repress Larry's torrent of tears in a scene from *The Frances Langford Show*.

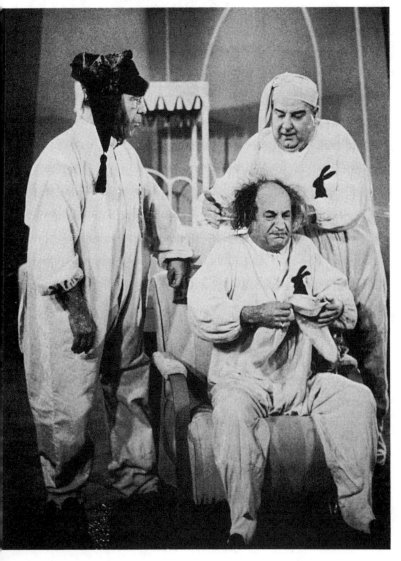

an offer to star in a weekly series of their own. Two friends of Shemp's—Al Winston and Edwin Gale—conceived *We Wuz There* (with the alternate title *Where Were You*), a spoof of the title of Walter Cronkite's famous CBS series, *You Are There*! The main setting was to be a schoolroom with the Stooges as students recounting historical events to their teacher. In the midst of the Stooges' story-telling the show would flashback to the actual event with the Stooges in the lead roles. The series never materialized and one wonders if their previous warning from Columbia had something to do with it.

The Stooges' next TV appearance was on April 29, 1955, as guests on *The Eddie Cantor Comedy Theater* in an episode titled, "What Do You Want in a Show?" (Cantor frequently admitted that he was a Stooges fan and was delighted at the opportunity to finally work with them.) At first glance, the story takes off like the old Mickey Rooney-Judy Garland MGM musicals, where Rooney dreams up all kinds of grandiose, moneymaking ideas with Garland. Cantor employs similar tactics, coming up with the idea of producing a stage revue to save his theatre from bankruptcy. The Stooges star as crooks, Butch, Lefty and Spike, in a production titled "A Night at the U.S. Mint." The show within a show is a financial triumph and lifts Cantor's theatre out of debt.

This was the Stooges' last TV appearance with Shemp, who died of a heart attack seven months later.

Following Shemp's death, Joe Besser was asked on January 1, 1956 to join the team and take over the role of third Stooge. Besser came close to making a new series of television shows with the Stooges when Moe seriously considered abandoning their two-reel deal with Columbia to do a weekly television comedy-news program. On August 14, 1957, *Daily Variety* reported that Moe Howard took this proposal to Columbia Pictures' executives and met with instant rejection, since the shorts were still turning over profits for Columbia. (Moe was slightly ahead of his time: The nightly news programs were spoofed over 20 years later with the creation of TV's *Saturday Night Live*.)

In January 1959, a year after Joe DeRita's replacement of Joe Besser, the Stooges experienced a sudden resurgence in popularity and television producers vied for their services. Norman Maurer also tried to take advantage of the skyrocketing rise in the team's popularity. He took to the networks the idea of using his 1954 animation process, *Artiscope*, for an animated series starring the Stooges.

Maurer's initial creation of this new and revolutionary method was first financed by Moe and subsequently by the Wall Street firm of Mabon and Company. Artiscope was a revolutionary automated animation system that filmed "live" actors and utilized an optical-chemical process to transform each frame of the film into line drawings that looked like they were hand drawn. The result was a high-fidelity animated cartoon, literally drawn by machine, with no artists needed except for minor touch up.

In 1958 Maurer formed a production company called Illustrated Films, Inc., with Moe as vice-president. Plans were made to star the Stooges in a weekly TV series which would utilize the team live and also in Artiscope cartoons.

The series, titled *Stooge Time*, had a unique format, with each show opening with a snappy Three Stooges theme song over titles that were a combination of cartoon and live Stooges. This was to segue into a seven-minute Stooges live-action, slapstick-comedy film, followed by a 30-second routine of them squirting each other with seltzer bottles. The bottles' spray would magically transform them into Artiscope animated characters to introduce "Cartoon Time," and the first seven-minute Stooges cartoon.

Two cartoons were to be included in each half-hour show, along with a healthy amount of new live footage of the Stooges. Twenty-six half-hours, containing a combination of 78 live and animated films, were proposed. Norman planned to have Edward Bernds direct the live segments, and Academy-Award-winning cartoon director Friz Freleng supervise the Artiscope cartoons. Moe Howard and Felix Adler were set as story writers, with Maurer producing. Unfortunately, Norman's original concept didn't sell to television. Network executives refused to believe that the revolutionary Artiscope process could actually produce thousands of drawings without artists.

Incidentally, at the time Norman first devised his Artiscope concept, in 1954, he filmed a test reel

The Stooges as cockamamie ballet dancers, with a hysterical Mary Costa on *The Frances Langford Show*.

starring Moe Howard and Don Lamond titled *Captain Lafitte*. The test was photographed in Moe's garage with Moe and Don clashing swords as two swashbucklering pirates. Lamond, of course, later narrated and appeared in the team's feature films in the 1960s.

Although Norman's pioneering, live-cartoon show didn't sell, other television producers deemed the Stooges sure-fire entertainment for their own series. Comedian Steve Allen was one of them. The trio made three highly publicized guest shots on *The Steve Allan Show*, originating from New York and broadcast over NBC. On January 11, 1959, the trio performed a hysterical "Hospital Operation" skit which was later reprised on *The Ed Sullivan Show*.

After the Steve Allen show, Moe, Larry and Curly-Joe appeared on the television panel quiz show *Masquerade Party*, hosted by Bert Parks. Internationally known celebrities were disguised in elaborate costumes and contestants were asked to identify them. The Stooges dressed as the Gabors—Jolie, Eva and Zsa Zsa—and fooled the experienced panelists, Faye Emerson, Sam Levenson, Audrey Meadows and Lee Bowman. The show was broadcast on CBS, January 15, 1959.

Following this quiz show, the Stooges began rehearsals on their second Steve Allen appearance, which aired on February 22, 1959. Moe's wife Helen accompanied the team and recalled how Moe came down with pneumonia hours before he was to appear on the show. "Moe had rehearsed all day for the Allen show and returned to the hotel to go to bed. There he was with no voice and a high fever and dictating the entire 'Stand-In' routine to a script girl. I remember his adding that hysterical bit where they attach candles to each side of the camera and every time the director shouted, 'Cut!' Moe would shout. 'Save the lights!' And the crew would rush in to blow out the candles. Moe's voice cracked and squeaked throughout the show. And those who loved him—and there were untold numbers—suffered with him."

The Stooges first performed the "Stand-In" sketch during the Broadway stage run of the *George White Scandals of 1939*, featuring a young newcomer, dancer Ann Miller. Matty Brooks and Eddie Davis, who occasionally supplied material for the Stooges, wrote the original sketch.

In "Stand-In" Moe plays the director of a feature movie, Larry is the film's star and Curly-Joe is Larry's stand-in. Each time Larry is about to get involved in a wild action scene, Moe yells, "Cut!" Curly-Joe then takes Larry's place and gets clobbered. Similar slapstick action continues as Curly-Joe takes the brunt of everything from saloon fights to pies in the face and spotless Larry gets all the credit for the terrific scenes. Curly-Joe burns.

In the finish, Larry is to be buried alive in a big box by the villains. Just as he is about to be shoved inside the box, Moe yells, "Cut!" Curly-Joe is shoved inside and the box is nailed shut. At this moment a lunch whistle blows and Moe calls out, "Okay! Lunch, everybody!" As the crew leaves, one of them points to the box and asks, "How about the stand-in?" Moe snaps his fingers, "Holy smoke, I almost forgot about him!" He runs up to the box, raps on it a couple of times and shouts, "Hey! Take an hour for lunch!"

Moe's spirits and health improved after the success of the Allen show, and an offer to reappear prompted him to dictate material for the trio's third Allen show appearance, which aired April 5, 1959. To the delight of millions, Moe, Larry and Curly-Joe reprised their world-famous "Maharaja" sketch.

Suddenly, one of the hottest television acts, the Stooges became the topic of conversation in all circles of show business, including the prestigious Academy Awards show of 1959. It was during the conclusion of the show that the Master of Ceremonies, Jerry Lewis, quipped, "Now nobody leave yet! The management told me that they're going to show a Three Stooges comedy for the losers!"

By 1960, sponsors clamored for the team to endorse their products. The trio's first TV commercial was for Hot Shot Insecticide, a product of the Amsco Chemical Company. This was quickly followed by a fondly remembered commercial for Chunky Chocolates.

But the commercial that rises above them all was for Simoniz Car Wax. This 60-second spot contained some bright moments. It opens with the Stooges as scientists experimenting in a research laboratory. Moe is mixing chemicals while Larry announces that he and Curly-Joe have developed a new product to wax cars. "We've found a way to combine Simoniz Car Wax with Simoniz Car Cleaner," says Larry, beaming with pride. "And just what is that, nitwit?" says Grumpy Moe. "Come here and we'll show you," Curly-Joe remarks as he and Larry drag Moe to an automobile, squirt liquid from a can onto the hood, watch as it powders, then wipe it off. "And look at that shine!" Joe enthuses, "We'll be millionaires!"

"But what will we call it?" Curly-Joe asks wisely. Larry, thinking he has a clever name for the product, queries, "How about Instant Simoniz?" Moe, scowling, cracks, "You idiots, there's already Instant Simoniz!" In a close up he whips out a can of the company's product. Disappointed, Larry retorts, "Boy, they think of everything!" Moe concludes, "Simoniz always thinks of everything." On his words the commercial freeze frames on the product.

The Stooges were paid $8500 for this commercial which aired nationally on March 15, 1960. It was this

The Stooges appear fascinated by a childhood poster-size photograph of Doris Day on *The Frances Langford Show*.

brief segment which caught the attention of film-maker Frank Tashlin who was writing and directing *The Frances Langford Show* for *Sunday Showcase* on NBC. *Showcase* featured different forms of entertainment weekly, including variety, drama and comedy formats. Langford was teamed with Don Ameche, her former co-star in radio's *The Bickersons*. This program, which was telecast on May 1, 1960, saluted the mothers of famous motion picture personalities. The Stooges added their special style of slapstick in several segments. The show's theme concerns Langford's troupe of stars making a trip to Hollywood to stage an honorary show for the "Hollywood Motion Picture

The Stooges prepare to demonstrate a can of Instant Simoniz in a TV commercial for the company.

Curly-Joe, Larry and Moe mugging with Mary Costa in a publicity still for *The Frances Langford Show*.

Mothers." A sentimental sequence features the Stooges preparing for bed while Larry is crying pitifully, emitting a cascade of tears as he recounts how they never had a mother. Curly-Joe tries to comfort him with words of encouragement, but fails. Then Moe steps in and places a handkerchief over Larry's eyes to contain the torrent of tears. But the hanky does little to alleviate the situation as the tears literally explode out of Larry's ears. Curly-Joe tries covering Larry's ears with his hands, trying to stop the flow as another leak breaks out from the top of his

head. Joe cracks, "Hey, Moe, maybe we can charge admission and call him Old Faithful!"

In another segment, Mary Costa comes on and sings her rendition of the Dave Rose recording "Holiday for Strings." During the last eight bars of the tune, the Stooges break up this serious melody by prancing on stage in their cockamamie version of ballet costumes. They not only break up the song's dramatic tempo but Costa and the audience as well. Charles Wick, who also produced *Snow White and the Three Stooges*, produced this hour special and a promotional soundtrack album which featured such top stars as Bob Cummings, Johnny Mathis and Hermione Gingold.

The Stooges' popularity was growing so rapidly that the William Morris Agency urged the Stooges to produce a pilot for a weekly half-hour color television series. Norman Maurer and the Stooges pooled their resources and their own company, Normandy Productions, started work on the 39 shows that would combine live segments with animated cartoons about the Stooges' involvement in important events in our nation's history. TV Spots, Inc.—makers of *Crusader Rabbit* cartoons—agreed to animate 78 five-minute cartoons. Two animated segments were planned for each episode; one with the Stooges and a slippery con-man, Benedict Bogus, who was previously a steady character in the Three Stooges comic books, and the second starring the Li'l Stooges and Muff, an ensemble of juvenile Stooges and their kooky dog.

Trade paper reports indicated that the show's volume of violence and deliberate head banging was to be reduced to a minimum. In an interview, Moe echoed these same sentiments. "In the live portions of these films, we will cut out the deliberate physical horseplay and substitute unintentional violence—if you have to call it violence. In other words, I won't purposely clunk Larry or Curly-Joe, but if I'm carrying a ladder, let's say, and I make a quick turn, it could accidentally clip Curly on the bean. The deliberate stuff will only be seen in the cartoon segments. That will make everybody happy." Moe obviously meant his closing remark for network censors and parental action groups, who often criticized the boys' films as "too violent."

In accordance with network censorship codes of the day, cartoons were allowed greater freedom when it came to violent slapstick humor. Cartoon producers

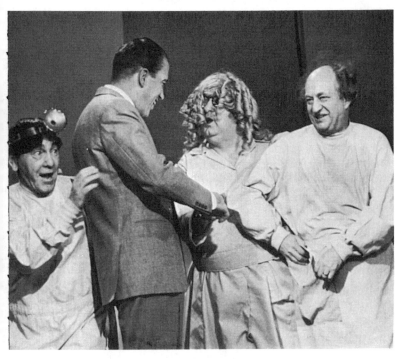

The Stooges with Ed Sullivan, following their successful operation sketch.

and animators were able to get away with intentional violence—a la the *Roadrunner* cartoons—while live performers were condemned for the same actions. The idea of casting the Stooges in a format combining live wraparounds and cartoons alleviated two problems: the trio would be able to star in parent-approved weekly situations, yet exhibit their two-fisted humor in cartoons.

The formula for *Three Stooges Scrapbook*, as the show was to be called, seemed to have all the earmarks of being a winner. Yet television sponsors interested in the series were unable to acquire the proper time slots from networks to broadcast the show. Three times *Scrapbook* was sold, but all three

times, the only available time slot was after 10 p.m. A late night slot was unacceptable to the sponsors, since the Stooges' audience was composed mainly of children. Subsequently, the sponsors withdrew their bids and a short time later *Scrapbook* was shelved permanently.

Surely television viewers and Stooge fans alike missed out on what might have been a hit series. *Three Stooges Scrapbook* was a combination of many elements that made it shine as a top-flight production; it's one dull spot—the cartoon. The pilot, financed by Normandy Productions, was the first time the Stooges appeared on film in color since *Nertsery Rhymes* in 1933. The live action sequences generated their share of laughs as the Stooges take up residence in an old haunted mansion. Then, animated Stooges emerge in a cartoon about Christopher Columbus' discovery that the world is round. But a surprise addition was the title song, *I Wanna Be a Stooge*, written by Academy Award winner George Duning with Stanley Styne.

As the opening credits roll a symphony of *sproinging* springs and hollow clunks could be heard over the following lyrics:

> Larry, Moe, Curly-Joe
> they're the funniest guys we know.
> Golly Gee, that's for me,
> I wanna be a Stooge.

The Stooges seem unfazed by Martha Raye's meeting a gorilla on NBC's *Danny Thomas Special*.

A pie-besmirched Danny Thomas tries restoring order during the Stooges' appearance on his NBC Variety Special.

Well, you can be, like those three
if you don't use common sense.
Yes indeed, all you need
is a high intelligence.

Yes, sir-ree, they're the three
musketeers of comedy
They have fun,
we have fun,
I wanna be a Stooge.

Following this hilarious animated title, the camera fades in on "Hollywood, glamour capital of the world, where Valentino and Pickford wrote the first pages of movie history. But changing times have resulted in the formation of a new medium—television. And bringing their brand of humor to it...The Three Stooges."

The pilot, titled "Home Cooking," opens with the boys rehearsing for their weekly television show, and is actually the same twenty minutes of footage reprinted in black and white and used in the 1962 feature *The Three Stooges in Orbit*. Inside their apartment, with no cooking allowed on the premises, Curly-Joe is preparing lunch while the other two Stooges go over their lines for their weekly TV series.

Despite their attempts to disguise the smell of their cooking, the landlady, Mrs. McGinnis (Marjorie Eaton), manages to sniff them out and evicts them. The story is the same as *In Orbit*, with the boys finding residence at Creepy Manor in Lompoc, California. Here, Professor Doyle (Emil Sitka; Danforth in *In Orbit*) has devised a new-fangled, multi-purpose war machine—a combination tank-helicopter-submarine which Norman Maurer designed and for

which he drew the actual blueprints that appeared in the scene. A monster with a lobster-like claw haunts the mansion in an attempt to steal the plans. Naturally, after several wild, spooky sequences, the Stooges foil his efforts and expose him. You guessed it; he's the butler!

Finally, after escaping from Creepy Manor, the Stooges make it to the studio for their TV show and relate their experiences to their viewers. Then they

Moe, along with Larry and Curly-Joe, surveys the premises in a live-action scene from their TV cartoon series.

proceed to pull out an oversized scrapbook, turning to a page containing one of their favorite stories, recalling the time they set sail with Columbus in 1492. This segues to a live introduction with the boys dressed as sailors where they argue over whether the world is round or flat. Curly-Joe adds further confusion to the scene by clutching a square desk globe.

Suddenly, an animated parrot named "Feathers" flies into the scene to dispel this flat versus round theory. He lands on Joe's shoulder and whispers in his ear. The parrot informs them that Columbus needs

A scene of the animated Stooges from one of their Cambria-produced color cartoons.

tribe in his quest to learn the world's real shape. The Stooges, however, abandon all hope of immortalizing themselves as ship's mates and dive overboard. They take to swimming across the high seas bound for safer waters. But to their surprise their watery journey comes to an abrupt halt as the ocean suddenly drops off vertically, proving that the world is square after all.

Once the cartoon fades out, the live Stooges reappear and Moe and Larry express their disbelief at the idea of anyone believing the world is square. "You mean it ain't?" Curly-Joe remarks innocently. Moe yanks a round globe from behind his back and smashes it over Curly-Joe's head. The globe now looks like a crumpled paper bag. They stare at it in disbelief. It's not round or square!

The end credits roll and the march song returns once again, only this time with slightly different lyrics:

> Larry, Moe, Curly-Joe
> they're the funniest guys we know
> Golly, gee, that's for me,
> I wanna be a Stooge.
>
> Larry clowns, Moe he frowns,
> Joe makes all those crazy sounds,
> What a scream,
> What a team,
> I wanna be a Stooge.

three sailors to help him on a historic expedition, and that Mr. C. promises to pay them union scale and a thousand Blue Chip stamps to make the journey. Or, in the words of the Godfather, Columbus makes the Stooges an offer they can't refuse.

In an episode titled *The Spain Mutiny*, the trio sets sail—in cartoon form—to prove that the world is round. As Moe stated earlier, the cartoons would have a good deal of violence throughout—and he was right. Some examples of it include Moe taking the ship's anchor and using it to clobber Larry. In another violent scene, Moe grabs Larry and Joe off the ground, crushing their heads together.

The cartoon's production values were poor and the animation was flat and grotesque. The Stooges' facial expressions were distorted beyond recognition, with the only recognizable feature being their trademark haircuts.

The Stooges must have realized their cartoon debut was a bust. In one scene, Moe becomes tired of the sailor's life and remarks, "Wait a minute! You guys havin' fun?" Larry chimes in. "No, I'm not havin' fun!" Joe quips. "This isn't fun!" Neither would the cartoon have been fun for viewers, since the movement of the Stooges as animated characters is rickety and the end result seems lifeless. It is bottom-of-the-barrel animation which makes the Stooges' Cambria-produced cartoon series of 1965 look like an award-winner.

As the episode winds down, "Feathers" takes over the expedition and gains support of a local Indian

Although the pilot never sold, the Stooges were always in constant demand. Still to come was "a really big shew!"—the first of three appearances on *The Ed Sullivan Show*, broadcast over CBS, May 14, 1961. Due to their heightened popularity, the Stooges received $8500 and three air fares for their guest appearance, which was good money for its day.

Sullivan made a classic goof when he introduced the Stooges as the Three Ritz Brothers, but later added, "who look more like the Three Stooges to me." The boys didn't disappoint anyone in their debut, including Sullivan. He certainly had no problems remembering their name after the show.

In answer to many requests, the Stooges reprised the highly renowned "Stand-In" sketch—which they had previously performed on Steve Allen's TV show—working to gales of audience laughter. In the wake of this newest triumph, George White filed a law suit against the Stooges, claiming he owned all rights to the "Stand-In" sketch. Rather than enter into a lengthy, drawn-out court battle, White agreed to settle out of court for a marginal fee. Undaunted by the preceding legal action, the Stooges took their treasure chest of comedy material over to NBC. There they were signed for a July 27, 1961, guest appearance on the celebrity interview show *Here's Hollywood*, co-hosted by Dean Miller and JoAnn Jordan. Two additional appearances followed on talk and participant format shows, such as *Play Your Hunch* hosted by Merv Griffin and *The Tonight Show* hosted by Jimmy Dean, which aired on January 24, and July 10, 1962, respectively. The "Stand-In" sketch was later used in a CBS film compilation from the Sullivan shows titled *Ed Sullivan's 15th Anniversary Special*, which was broadcast February 10, 1963.

It wasn't long after this that the Stooges made their second appearance on *The Ed Sullivan Show*, performing the "Hospital Operation" sketch. The program was telecast, June 23, 1963. This scenario lampoons the finest in TV medical shows—*Ben Casey, The Nurses* and *Dr. Kildaire*—with Moe as Dr. Ben Crazy and Curly-Joe disguised as his near-sighted nurse. Larry is hastily brought in to fulfill Moe's request for a patient. Larry, as he's prepped for surgery, asks for the day's special. Curly-Joe holds up a menu which reads: "Liver 75¢. With onions $1.00." Larry wants a bargain and "takes the works." Curly-Joe shoves him down and starts applying the anesthesia. He begins with ether, which doesn't work, followed by a mallet to Larry's head which does. The operation proceeds smoothly until the actual removal of Larry's heart. At this point, Moe shoves his hands under the sheet and comes out with a rubber heart which he holds up as the other two Stooges join him in a chorus of "Heart of My Heart."

A commercial, and Moe returns to the business at hand. He continues with the operation until he's suddenly interrupted by a patient who asks him, "Are you Ben Crazy?" Moe replies, "Why, yes, I am!" The

A hilarious scene of the Stooges as artists in a scene from their color cartoon series.

Moe and Larry's advanced ages started to show during filming of *The New Three Stooges* color cartoon series.

The Stooges introducing their next cartoon during a scene from their TV cartoon series.

Curly-Joe, Larry and Moe playing around with an innocent beachgoer during filming of their TV cartoon show.

Larry, Curly-Joe and Moe on ABC's *The Joey Bishop Show*.

Director Ed Bernds (foreground) and, right of light reflector, Norman Maurer and Dick Brown (wearing cap), watch the Stooges rehearse for their cartoon show.

patient grumbles, "You were to operate on me two hours ago!" Fuming, Moe shouts to Larry, "You imposter, what are you doing here?" Larry protests, "I don't know from nothing—I came to deliver a telegram." The scene fades out as chaos prevails inside the operating room.

The Stooges' fourth appearance on the Sullivan show was on October 6, 1963. They took this opportunity to do the "Niagara Falls" sketch, the search by a man for his estranged wife. With this appearance, their salary climbed to $10,000 for a single television guest shot. The boys graced the Sullivan stage one last time on May 9, 1965.

Despite their advanced ages, Moe, Larry and Curly-Joe performed admirably, still comedians of the highest caliber. People have always maintained that watching the trio is like watching an animated cartoon. Thus it came as no surprise when Normandy Productions agreed to work in association with Heritage Productions and Cambria Studios on 156 five-and-a-half-minute color cartoons called *The New Three Stooges*. Cambria president, Dick Brown, spearheaded the project and completed all the necessary arrangements to animate the films. Budget was set at $1.5 million and the Stooges and Norman Maurer received $163,000 in advance of their efforts.

Forty, live-action wraparounds, some of which were filmed at the Balboa Bay Club in Balboa, California, contained many of the Stooges' traditional routines. These segments were used to open and close each cartoon. The Stooges began filming on July 13, 1965, averaging four live shows per day and completed filming 40 segments in six and a half weeks, an incredible job.

The pilot cartoon, *Little Old Bombmaker*, was a free-lance animation job and was originally titled *The First World War*. When the series sold, Cambria took over the animation and the style changed radically. The pilot's style of animation was much like Jay Ward's *Rocky and Bullwinkle*, in that it was more comically exaggerated.

Curly-Joe DeRita remarked that the 40 live-action segments presented some problems. "There were 156 cartoons and we made only 40 live-action segments. So after they ran the whole 40, they'd just start over by using these same introductions on *new* cartoons. This turned out to be misleading because the viewers would say, 'Oh, I've seen this one before,' and they'd turn off the television. They didn't know it was a new cartoon."

With the Stooges in these live segments were a small group of character actors. Emil Sitka played a variety of roles in most of the live sequences. Norman Maurer's son Jeff, and Dick Brown's wife, Peggy (famous for her role as Charles Ruggles' TV daughter), and children—Cary, Tina and Eileen—also appeared in various episodes.

Norman Maurer was executive producer of the live-action segments and Edward Bernds directed them; he also wrote many of the stories. Animator Dick Detiege, from Warner Brothers, served as animation director, while Lee Orgel secured distribution of the cartoons to over 45 television stations. The films were syndicated nationally by Heritage Productions in October 1965. In accordance with their contract, Cambria's distributor was supposed to forward quarterly statements to the Stooges reporting the series' profits. Norman Maurer recalls receiving only one or two statements over a period of five years. Consequently, the series became grounds for a law suit filed by the Stooges—which they lost. It was a bad break for the Stooges, as the presiding judge knew absolutely nothing about the film business and ruled in favor of Cambria's distributor.

Losing the initial court battle, the Stooges appealed to a higher court in 1975 and won. Despite this belated victory, nothing changed with regard to the distributor's failure to provide statements.

About a month after the cartoons premiered on television stations throughout the country, Danny Thomas invited the Stooges to appear on his NBC special *What Makes People Laugh?* This hour program, which aired on November 8, 1965, showcased the Stooges rather prominently. As a critic for *Daily Variety* wrote: "The Stooges do what comes naturally and this only compounds the insanities." The insanities arise in the form of three sketches. The first one finds the trio attempting to perform Shakespeare, but getting derailed because of interruptions from passersby. Then the Stooges wander out into the audience and attempt to drive three members of the audience from their seats, resorting to pie throwing as a means of persuasion. In the last sketch Moe, Larry and Curly-Joe meet their match in Martha Raye. The all-star line-up of guests included the Spike Jones' Band (formed by Spike Jones, Jr., 16-year-old son of the band leader), Tim Conway and Bill Cosby. Critics lauded the special as "wild and orgiastic" and delightfully entertaining.

At the end of the sixties, the Stooges' popularity began to fade and fewer offers crossed the desks of

The Stooges demonstrate the art of pie making on *The Joey Bishop Show*.

their agent, William Morris, and their producer-manager, Norman Maurer. Maurer has said that the decline in popularity was due to several factors: their vast army of young fans had grown up...rising production costs had rendered children's films economically impossible...and the Stooges were getting on in years. Many producers, when hearing they were available, envisioned them as old men, no longer capable of performing their wild, slapstick antics.

During these slow periods, Moe kept Norman busy contacting producers on whose programs the Stooges wanted to appear. Sometimes the trio would spot a particular show and remark, "Hey, why don't we get on that show!" Moe would then call Norman, who would pursue these different avenues. The Stooges were strongly considered for such hit programs as *Hollywood Palace*, Rowan and Martin's *Laugh-In*, *The Red Skelton Show* and *The Dean Martin Show*, but nothing ever materialized. Maurer also spoke with Columbia Pictures about producing a 90-minute TV special with film clips and interviews called *They Stooged to Conquer*, but this project never materialized either.

Since the Stooges weren't receiving many new offers, Norman tried creating two series himself for the team. He first approached Metromedia Corporation's Los Angeles station KTTV with two unique game show formats, *Obstacle Course* and *The Three Stooges' Junior Olympics*. The idea was to produce these shows in Hollywood and syndicate them through Metromedia's syndication division.

Obstacle Course was the first proposal and had contestants battling their way through a life-sized gameboard of oddly constructed obstacles. Three young contestants would be chosen from the audience and brought up on stage. Their object was to pass through the hazardous maze to the finish line in order to win top prizes. Obstacles were to include a rickety bridge over a shallow tank of muddy water, an automatic pie-throwing machine and a tightrope over a vat of gooey strawberry jam. The Stooges would act as hosts and accompany the contestants on their way down the zig-zag path to victory or defeat.

Junior Olympics was just as wild and inventive and was created fresh on the heels of the country's full-scale physical fitness craze. The Stooges would introduce young contestants from all over the country who would participate in various sporting events. Each week would be like a World Series of Junior Athletic competition. The half-hour shows would include elimination tournaments in such sporting events as bowling and "soap box" derbies. Comedy would result from the Stooges showing off their brand of sports expertise before each segment.

172

The Three Stooges wreak havoc testing out a new line of work clothes in a Dickies Slacks TV commercial

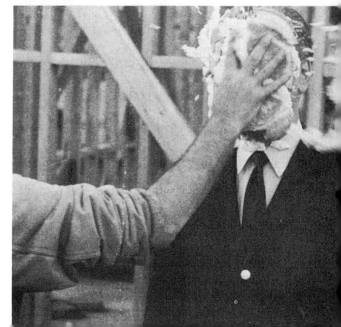

A pilot segment would feature the Stooges giving instructions in bowling. The trio would come out in ill-fitting jerseys, throw their balls down the lane where they would suddenly richochet off the pins and begin racing back towards the Stooges. The boys would turn to run for their lives but the balls would connect and bowl them over. This hilarious sequence would seque into a bowling tournament featuring young bowlers from all over the United States who would compete for the special jackpot of prizes.

Unfortunately, Metromedia didn't see the full market potential for these concepts and turned them down. Both would have been fantastic vehicles for the Stooges, but, unfortunately, it wasn't to be.

Television roles were few and far between for the Stooges until they were signed for a guest shot on ABC's *Off to See the Wizard*. This weekly series was a collection of films geared to children. The trio appeared as "Three Men in a Tub" in an episode titled *Who's Afraid of Mother Goose?* ABC broadcast the show on October 13, 1967. It also starred Maureen O'Hara as Mother Goose, Dick Shawn as Old King Cole and Nancy Sinatra and Frankie Avalon as Jack and Jill.

The Stooges were paid $10,000 for two network runs but their names were pulled from newspaper and television advertisements. ABC made no mention of the team in *TV Guide* listings and half-page announcements. The Stooges were, needless to say, furious over the situation. This was just another example of television executives treating the Stooges as a classless act of has-beens and bowing to the PTA and other pressure groups.

About this time, Continental Baking Company, one of the largest manufacturers of bread products, was planning an extensive campaign to launch a new product called Astro Snacks. Their advertising firm of Ketchum, MacLeod and Grove signed the Stooges for a 60-second commercial. Agency vice-president, Charles W. Llewellyn recalls that the Stooges performed in a stage show in Washington, D.C., to kick off the commercial's campaign for the snack item. The admission was several proof-of-purchase wrappers from the Astro Snacks. Contracts indicate that the commercial was made and telecast on April 1, 1967, and that the Stooges received only $3,000 for their performance.

The television commercial that Stooges fans remember most was for Metropolitan Life Insurance. Larry Fine once recalled that the commercial was filmed in San Francisco and was shot entirely in long shots. Entitled "The Door," it has the Stooges promoting the insurance company's Security Family Plan. What is remembered goes down as classic comedy at

its zenith. A narrator gives his spiel, "...be protected from fire, flood and other calamities and....." The narrator is suddenly cut off as the Stooges enter on cue, driving a beat-up, loaded-down truck and demonstrate just what kind of calamities the narrator is talking about.

Moe pulls up before a house and the Stooges begin unloading axes and mallets. The boys then charge up to the house with tools at the ready and start smashing open the front door. A beat, and the door falls to pieces, followed by the entire house which comes crashing to the ground like a house of cards. This scene-destroying episode prompts the narrator in his spiel on protection from disasters to conclude with "...even the Three Stooges."

Comedian Joey Bishop soon learned how this destructive trio wreaked havoc wherever they went. He invited the Stooges on several of his ABC variety-talk shows, *The Joey Bishop Show*, and each time was assaulted by the Stooges. The most memorable show features the Stooges reprising their "Hospital Operation" sketch under the name of "Hectic Medic." Later they illustrate the art of pie making. The pies find other uses than dessert, of course. Bishop is clobbered when a large-scale pie battle breaks out on stage with pie crust and gooey meringue splattering him and everything in sight. The stage became a mish-mash of meringue and took hours to clean up.

The team's last television appearance was in the form of another commercial, this time for Williamson-Dickie Manufacturers. It was broadcast, March 31, 1969. The Stooges demonstrate the durability of Dickie work clothes and the good sportsmanship of announcer Russel Arms. During this 60-second production, the Stooges get buried in a shower of bricks, swim in wet cement and otherwise demolish one another. "But don't worry," Arms says, stepping into the scene of destruction, "They're wearing Dickie work clothes."

Arms then describes the features which enable Dickies to snap back after rough treatment and shows the Stooges in their tailored, soil-free Dickies. "If Dickies can make the Three Stooges look good, imagine how great you'll look," Arms concludes. The Stooges then show a token of their appreciation, smacking Arms in the face with a pie.

The commercial was filmed in Los Angeles by Elektra Films, and initially aired on ABC's *Wide World of Sports*.

The Stooges next started production on a comedy-travel series for television, produced by Normandy Productions, called *Kook's Tour* (1970). The basic formula was for the Stooges to travel across the United States and later Europe, Japan and Australia. Plans for

Larry watches out for Moose while fishing in a scene from the TV pilot, *Kook's Tour*.

the series were first announced in 1968, with 39 half-hour shows to be filmed. After several changes in the format, producer-director Norman Maurer and the team finally started production on the TV pilot in 1969.

"The boys didn't want to travel outside the country at this point in their lives," recalled Maurer in an interview. "They were older now than when we first planned the series; they wanted to stay close to home." The Stooges also rejected the notion of slapping each other around, because of their advanced ages (Moe was 71 and Larry 67). For this reason the film is not as zany as their old, classic comedies.

Instead, the team created a more relaxed atmosphere in *Kook's Tour* by portraying themselves as retired Stooges, with Moe and Larry wearing their hair out of character.

In September of 1969, the Stooges and the Normandy film unit traveled to Idaho and Wyoming and commenced production on their independently financed pilot. According to Joe DeRita, the Stooges and Maurer pooled their resources and financed the pilot. Scenes were filmed amidst the majestic splendor of the lakes of Idaho and Wyoming. Once location shooting was completed, the cast and crew returned to Los Angeles with three-fourths of the film finished. Maurer planned on lensing close-ups on several integral segments in the Angeles National Forest and at Lake Piru.

On the night of January 9, 1970, in the midst of filming these vital close-ups, Larry Fine suffered a paralyzing stroke which affected the left side of his body and confined him to a wheelchair. Later, he was able to walk with the aid of a cane, but paralysis remained. Obviously, with vital sequences unfinished, all plans for a weekly half-hour television series were cancelled.

"They hoped I would get well enough so they could complete the film by shooting scenes with me from the waist up," Larry once said.

In the tradition of "the show must go on," producer Norman Maurer screened every salvageable inch of film and then edited it together into a one-hour show. He was able to stretch the film's length to 60 minutes by adding extra footage of Idaho's scenic beauty. Maurer hoped that at the one-hour length the comedy-travelogue might be marketable as a TV special.

In 1973, Samuel Gelfman, President of the Cartrivision Corporation, a video tape company, acquired the rights to market a video cassette version of *Kook's Tour*. For a short period of time the cassette was distributed by the Sears-Robuck stores. In 1975, the film went into a minor form of distribution. Niles Film Products, a home movie distributor, signed an agreement with Normandy Productions to market *Kook's Tour* in Super-8 color and sound for a price tag of about $200. But in 1981, Niles went bankrupt. Currently, Maurer is considering plans to edit the film down to its original half-hour format and syndicate it through independent TV stations.

Even though the Three Stooges were no longer working together as a team, in 1973, Moe Howard and Larry Fine started to appear separately in personal appearances and television talk shows. Moe's television performances stand out the clearest, however. He made frequent appearances on the *Mike Douglas Show*, re-creating such fondly remembered routines as "The Maharaja" and "Niagara Falls." His agility was remarkable for his age and his reactions were incredible. Moe definitely knew the old routines inside and out and could have done all three Stooges parts if he wanted (in college appearances he did just that). Douglas said it was a pleasure to work with Moe and he appreciated the fact that Howard bought his own material. Moe participated in the Douglas show sketches with renewed energy and enthusiasm, perhaps because he dreaded retirement and felt he would like to embark on a career as a single.

Moe's first guest shot on the Douglas Show was in July 1973, with Ted Knight and Soupy Sales rounding out the cast. During the show, Moe instructs Douglas and the audience in the technique of pie-throwing. A pie fight ensues when Soupy Sales demands one of the creamy desserts. As a result, Moe blasts the entire cast with pies.

But fans consider Moe's third appearance on the program his most notable. During an interview with Douglas, Moe talks about his charming wife, Helen.

Douglas then urges Howard to introduce her to the audience. Moe willingly steps down from the stage to get Helen, his wife of 50 years. When he reaches her, Helen smashes a pie right into his face!

Helen once recalled that when the show's producer asked her to do the scene, she conceded after some hesitation. "In all our years together, I had never done anything physical to hurt Moe. I was afraid I'd cut him with the pie tin so I put my hand between the tin and the pie and threw chunks of pie in his face," she said.

Douglas was amazed at Howard's ability to undertake such vigorous routines as "Niagara Falls" despite his age. The popular talk show host admired Moe's seasoned professionalism, saying, "My recollection of Moe Howard, from the times he appeared on our show, was that you were immediately aware that he was a man totally dedicated to his profession. He was wonderful!...possessing a great sense of comedic timing and an inspiration to many young performers."

At the same time, Larry appeared on quite a

The Stooges try their hand at camping in *Kook's Tour*.

175

A series of still photographs illustrating a deleted pie-fight scene from the never-released *Kook's Tour* (1970), in which the Stooges comically celebrate Moe's birthday.

176

Moe Howard during the final days of his life in an NBC *Nightly News* interview.

Larry in a Los Angeles TV appearance with Tom Snyder of KNBC's *Sunday Show.*

number of television talk shows in the Los Angeles area. One of them was hosted by KNBC news anchorman Tom Snyder. It was a local, magazine interview program called *Sunday*. On March 4, 1973, Snyder's crew went out to the Motion Picture Country House in Woodland Hills and interviewed resident celebrities, including Larry Fine. Larry discussed his love for painting, showing Snyder his finished works—one of them a pencil sketch of Peter Falk—and mentioned his will to live. Snyder introduced the comedian with a clip from *Men in Black* (1934).

Fine next appeared in an episode of PBS station KCET's *City Watchers*, which highlighted the Motion Picture Country House and the various celebrities who were residents. Sandy Hill, who later found fame on ABC's *Midmorning America*, interviewed Larry when she hosted a program for CBS affiliate KNXT called *Follow-Up*, in what was the comedian's last TV appearance, on November 17, 1974.

Moe Howard's final television appearance came after his death on the *NBC Nightly News*, April 23, 1976. Reporter Jack Perkins taped an interview with Howard several weeks before his death in May, 1975; the interview was a discussion of the team's sudden resurgence in popularity. Perkins also interviewed Joe Besser during this ten-minute report which showcased the talent of young fans who impersonated Curly and the other Stooges.

Even though fans saw the Stooges finish their television careers as separate entities, the Three Stooges, as a team, have never left television; over 400 of their films are being rerun on television stations around the world. Their 190 two-reel comedies continue to play in major television markets while the team's 156 color cartoons and countless features continue to receive broadcast time. Even Norman Maurer's cartoon version of the Stooges for CBS, *The Three Robonic Stooges*, has attracted a large number of viewers and has helped prove the team's worth as one of television's most enduring commodities. To quote Mike Douglas, "It was great that the Three Stooges left their legacy of these wonderful films so that future generations will be able to enjoy their zany antics and learn to love them as we did."

**The Stooges recording songs for their Golden
Records album.**

5

The Three Stooges on Record

THE THREE STOOGES continued to grow as superstars in television and movies—and soon climbed the charts as recording artists.

In 1959, when the Stooges' popularity was rising ever higher, record industry executives awoke to the fact that the Stooges were one of TV's hottest children's commodities, equalling and often rating higher than *Captain Kangaroo, Popeye* and *Yogi Bear*. And so the trio's long but rocky recording career was launched.

While rival record companies kept negotiating with the Stooges, Columbia Pictures' record division beat everybody out with a 45 rpm single of the title song from the team's first *starring* feature, *Have Rocket, Will Travel* (Colpix, CP 120, 1959). This ditty revolves around the Stooges entering the race for outer space. The record, which was originally called *Race for the Moon*, as was the feature, has good tonal quality but, though it glorifies the trio as singers, it didn't make the Top 40. It sold exceptionally well, however, and encouraged other record companies to take a closer look at the boys' vocal talents.

Following the Columbia recording, Golden Records was next to cash in on the Stooges' popularity with distribution of three singles and an album. Golden specialized in children's songs and had a gallery of juvenile favorites already available, such as *Ruff n' Reddy* (Hanna-Barbera cartoon stars), the *Lone Ranger, Smokey the Bear, Captain Kangaroo* and, most popular of all, *Santa Claus*. Since crowds of small fry comprised most of the Stooges' audience, the team was just right for Golden Records and its company of juvenile superstars.

The Stooges' deal with Golden became official in 1959 with the release of *The Three Stooges—Madcap Musical Nonsense at Your House* (GLP 43), a $2.98, 12-inch album containing a dozen songs, complete with a color photograph of the Stooges as band members on the cover. It was an instant hit with children. The "Music Wreckers" supplied the tender musical accompaniment and were also featured on subsequent 45s and 78s. Madcap lyrics were written by producers Bill Buchanan and Dick Cella, who did

a commendable job of adapting children's songs to the team's two-fisted humor.

The album consists of a rich selection of parodies and satirical humor that would appeal to new audiences today. Side One leads off with "We're Coming to Your House" with Moe, Larry and Curly-Joe constantly referring to their small-fry followers and adult listeners as "nice people." This was obviously a vain attempt to clean up their poor image with some adults who were upset over the television rebroadcasts of their violent two-reel comedies.

Lyrics are catchy and clever in the album's title song when all three sing: "We're coming to your house/to have a good time. To bring you some laughter, and happiness, too." Then, Larry ruins the tempo, demonstrating his ability to count ("three/four/five/six/seven"), resulting in some wild knocks on the head by Moe. Another hilarious moment follows after they harmonize: "Though Mommy won't like us/and neither will Dad./We're coming to your house." Troublemaker-Larry interjects in a gruff gangster voice, ". . .to break up the joint!"

This segues to the second cut, "The Concert." Here, the Stooges flex their muscles not on each other but on musical instruments. Of course, the instruments serve as a perfect foundation for a series of comedy vignettes. One in particular, has Moe mastering the banjo, prompting him to ask if he's playing the banjo correctly. Larry surprises Moe with, "You're playing a trombone, not a banjo." A querulous Moe says, "You mean, I know how to play a trombone, too?" The record is full of hokey gags and even contains a few moments of audience participation where the boys invite listeners to pick up their own instruments and join in.

More fun ensues with "At a Baseball Game," timed to the tune of "Skip to My Lou." The Stooges have tickets to a cross-town ballgame which they attend, despite Curly-Joe's remarks that he doesn't like the sport. Joe voices his displeasure while inside the ball park, and Moe tells him to pipe down or he'll quell him with a baseball bat on the head. Insulted, Joe goes away to get some popcorn and doesn't return for hours. When he does, he comes back as a popcorn vendor and tries to sell some to Moe and Larry. It appears to Moe that Curly-Joe has been taking in more food than profits. So Moe shuts Curly up and prevails on him to sit down and enjoy the game. Tired of Moe's demands, Joe races onto the field, kicks out the umpire (voiced by Moe) and smacks a home run to win the game.

Next on the trio's hit parade is "Click Dart's Bandstand," a spoof of Dick Clark's *American Bandstand.* The Stooges receive an invitation to perform on Dart's program. Bearing in mind that Dick Clark was considered TV's "youngster on the block," the Stooges poke fun at this notion in their meeting with Dart by telling him to, "Take a walk, sonny boy!" Finally, convinced he is the *real* Dart, the boys take over the program and belt out their own songs!

Side One's fifth selection is "The Three Chipped Munks," a parody of David Seville's popular children's

stars, Alvin and the Chipmunks. Out for a walk, the Stooges notice that a new theatre program has come to town, *White Snow and the Seven Dwarfs,* featuring a personal stage appearance of the Three Chipped Munks. Mistaken for the singing chipmunks, Moe, Larry, and Curly-Joe serenade the audience with "A-Tisket, A-Tasket" and "Ten Little Indians." Punctuating the satire, the trio finish with their impersonations of the Chipmunks.

An age-old folk song, "Go Tell Aunt Rhody," which has been retitled "Go Tell Aunt Mary," rounds off Side One. The song takes place at a recording studio, where Moe, Larry and Curly-Joe want to learn how a record is produced. Curiosity overcomes Curly-Joe, so much so that he gets caught in a record stamping machine and gets stuck in the disc's actual playing grooves. Helplessly trapped, he screams, "Boys and girls, maybe if you turn the record over you can get me out!" Suddenly, as if his prayers were answered,

Golden Records' 45 rpm release (1959).

THE STORY OF THE MAGIC LAMP

180

the music stops. Then, addressing the listeners who are turning the record over, Larry adds, "Careful! That's it! Don't hurt him with the needle!"

The Stooges' comedy exploits pick up speed on Side Two with, "At the Circus," in which they win jobs as circus clowns. Curly-Joe becomes less interested in clowning and more enthused about climbing a rope ladder. He does, and while in the process, a tiger breaks loose from its cage and rampages through the audience.

Joe loses his balance on the wire, falls, knocks the tiger unconscious and becomes the hero of the day.

The previous cut blends nicely with a similar childhood tale, "At the Toy Store." Here, Curly-Joe clashes with a polite toy store manager. Moe apologizes for his fat partner who seems to be in another one of his sarcastic moods (a trait of DeRita's that permeates most cuts on the album). Salvation is near, however, as the Stooges prevent a spineless criminal

from robbing the store's cash register. A grateful store manager rewards the trio, telling them to take all the toys they want. Since they have a large following of fans, the Stooges back up a truck and haul away the store's entire inventory.

The Stooges first album ends on a sad note with them singing their own rendition of "Auld Lang Syne." Perhaps, they were tugging on the heartstrings of millions of fans, hoping they would want more. But, actually, a more appropriate finish might have been something a little more upbeat. Fans were not accustomed to these zany comedians turning thespians and would have preferred a more comedic ending. However, despite this flaw, the record stands up as top-notch entertainment and showcases the trio's full range of talents.

In Christmas 1959, Golden released three perfect stocking stuffers starring the Stooges: two 45s (one special extra-long playing edition) and the team's first

Golden Records' 45 rpm release, *6 Yuletide Songs* (1959).

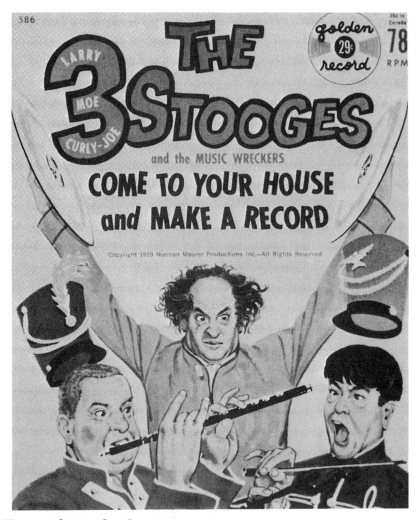

Golden Records' 78 rpm release, *The Three Stooges Come to Your House and Make a Record* (1959).

78 rpm novelty. *The Three Stooges Sing Six Happy Yuletide Songs* (EP 561) was the first release of the three, and was part of Golden Records' EP (Extra-Long Playing) series. The Christmas single begins on a glorious note with "All I Want for Christmas Is My Two Front Teeth," followed by an hilarious novelty, "I want a Hippopotamus for Christmas," and concluding with "I Gotta Cold for Christmas."

Decorating a tree turns into havoc on Side Two, with "Wreck the Halls of Bough and Holly." More comedy results in "Jingle Bells Drag," wherein the Stooges attempt to ride an old-fashioned, ancient sleigh, complete with an old, broken-down horse who, Moe quips, "is older than the sleigh!" In "Down Through the Housetop!" they explore another yuletide tale of how Santa Claus comes down the chimney.

Themes in subsequent records were as topical and appealed to people of all ages. Two yuletide songs,

"All I Want for Christmas Is My Two Front Teeth" and "I Gotta Cold for Christmas" are featured in the team's 45 release, *The Three Stooges Sing* (Golden Records, 559). As in previous recordings, the Music Wreckers add their special style of music to these arrangements. Later, two selections from *The Three Stooges—Madcap Musical Nonsense at Your House* were transformed into a 29-cent, 78 rpm issue of "We're Coming to Your House" and "We're Cutting a Record" (Golden Records, 586).

All four Golden Records—the album and singles—combined to bring the Stooges royalties of over $15,000. The advance on these records was $5,000 and the income was derived from gross sales of all four releases. During that same year, 1959, the team's total earnings reached an all time high: a remarkable $750,000 split three ways, according to a *Hollywood Reporter* article. Their previous income high was reached during their last ten years at Columbia. Moe reported that the trio were each making $70,000 a year, including salaries and personal appearances.

Perhaps their records did so well because of the rare and unusual content and the fact they were sung by the comedians themselves. Who would have ever dreamed of the Stooges heralding themselves as Santa Clauses, or as recording artists, for that matter.

Like all recording stars, the Stooges were bound to have their share of hits and misses and hoped that sooner or later their luck would change. With their next release, a soundtrack of the feature film *Snow White and the Three Stooges* (Columbia Records, 1650), their luck didn't get much better. Incidentally, although the film was released through 20th Century-Fox, the soundtrack was distributed on the Columbia Records label. Twentieth Century-Fox lost its shirt on the film, which was budgeted at over $3 million and the studio had no way of recovering their costs

because the comedy-fantasy was tailored strictly for children who paid only 50 cents admission. This time the Stooges took their manager's advice and came out ahead by opting for $75,000 up front instead of $50,000 and a percentage of the film's profit. It would have taken an audience of over 15 million kids (at 50 cents admission) for the film just to break even. Another problem that led to the film's boxoffice failure was that many adults, believing the film was a perfect baby sitter, dropped their kids off at the theatres and left them there all day; thus, theatres were often filled to capacity but there was no turnover.

The 1960 Columbia Records' soundtrack of *Snow White and the Three Stooges* leaves a much more favorable impression than the feature and actually makes the picture sound like a winner. Copies of this disc are rare, and usually sell for as much as $20. The album is ideal for collectors interested in having a

The Stooges' fourth 45 rpm release for Golden Records (1959).

**The Stooges' Peter Pan 78 rpm release, *The
Princess and the Pea.***

well-produced audio version of the film, sparing them
the tedium of seeing it. The Stooges can be heard in
several dialogue scenes from the film and in a happy-
go-lucky song, "Looking for People, Looking for Fun."

Originally, this happy-go-lucky melody was
planned for a film sequence involving the Stooges as
medicine-show peddlers. However, at the last minute, Fox cut the scene, perhaps, hoping to cut down
the film's length. As a result, they may have trimmed
out the best sequence featuring the Stooges. On the
Snow White album, musical instruments embellish
the lickety-split timing of the Stooges singing the
upbeat lyrics. Dialogue scenes command a good deal
of Side One, which serves as a great reference for
buffs wanting scene dialogue but is less impressive for
musical enthusiasts wanting a collection of songs.

Unknown to record dealers and collectors, Columbia Records was considering the release of "Looking

for People, Looking for Fun" as a 45 rpm single.
Research has found that Columbia Records made a
special recording of the song on a 12-inch acetate disc,
which only took up seven inches of space on the
record (the normal size for a 45 and 78). However, no
single was ever produced and the song's only distribution was within the album's soundtrack. For reasons
unknown, what could have been another historical
Stooge novelty became a shelved artifact.

In 1960 the Stooges then recorded another single
release by Epic Records containing two cuts, "Sinking
of the Robert E. Lee" and "You Are My Girl."
Incidentally, this same single was re-issued some
years later under the Spinit label. The Stooges began
their 1961 record season with another oddity, *The
Three Stooges' Happy Birthday Record* (RCA Records
X4LM-8766). This seven-inch vinyl disc was recorded
in November, pressed for Ardee Records and distrib-

184

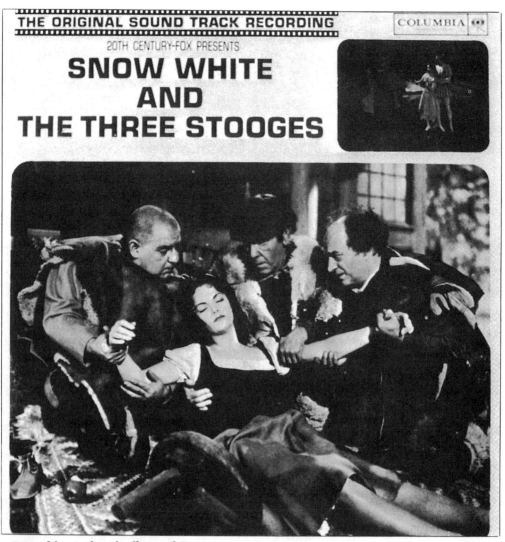

THE ORIGINAL SOUND TRACK RECORDING

COLUMBIA

20TH CENTURY-FOX PRESENTS

**SNOW WHITE
AND
THE THREE STOOGES**

**Columbia Records' soundtrack album of *Snow
White and the Three Stooges*.**

uted through RCA Victor Records. The story focuses around the Stooges performing "Old MacDonald Had a Farm" and "Goldilocks and the Three Bears" at a birthday party, whereupon they sing "Happy birthday" to a lucky youngster. Some old gags (written by Elwood Ullman) surface when the Stooges want to hail a taxi to get to the party. "Call me a taxi!" Moe shouts to Larry and Joe. "You're a taxi!" Larry and Joe shout back. Kids probably got a kick out of these vintage wheezes, while most adults probably held their noses.

Twelve minutes of non-stop song and jokes sold for $1 in department stores and $1.25 through a special mail order firm named Hargo Company. Each record was personalized with a different child's name. In fact, 238 individual children could have happy birthday sung to them by the Three Stooges. Their manager, Norman Maurer, advised them against the idea since

dealers could not stock all 238 names and thus sales could be poor. Despite this advice, the Stooges went ahead with the deal because of their friendship with Harry Harris, the record's producer. Upon its initial release, RCA Records reported the disc was selling poorly just as Maurer had anticipated. Larry stated some years back, "They just didn't go. We didn't make a dime off them. It would have worked if they hadn't personalized each one and had produced just a general, happy birthday record." Incidentally, Harry Harris contracted the Stooges to record another comedy single, featuring "The Milk" and "Hot Dog" sketches (the latter written by Elwood Ullman) but due to the *Birthday* disc's lethargic sales, the team nixed the agreement.

Although their record career had its low period with these two back-to-back flops, the Stooges made up for it beautifully in an album that is still popular

185

with most fans today, *The Three Stooges Nonsense Song Book* (Coral Records, 57289). Of all their recordings, this album has the best orchestration and song selections, Lew Douglas backs the Stooges with his fine orchestra, and the boys display a variety of material, some dating back to the 1900s.

Though some believe Coral spared no expense in making the record or in acquiring the Stooges, reports show that it was just the opposite. The Stooges were paid a smaller advance than they had received from Golden Records, a paltry $1,000, and never received one penny after the album's release. It was the first and last record deal made by their former agent and manager, Harry Romm. William Morris became their agents and Norman Maurer took over as their personal manager and worked out the deal with Golden.

The Coral album was sure-fire entertainment from the first groove to the last, beginning with a revival of

Curly-Joe, Larry and Moe show their displeasure after recording a number for *The Three Stooges Madcap Musical Nonsense*.

The Stooges' first record release, a soundtrack for
Have Rocket, Will Travel.

"Swinging the Alphabet," which was first popularized in the 1938 Stooge comedy *Violent Is the Word for Curly*. Retitled "The Alphabet Song," it has as much flair as the original. In a flashback of sing-song melodies, Moe leads his partners in a sequence of consonants against the vowels, like so: 'B-A Bay/B-E, Bee/ B-I, Bickey, Bi/ B-O, Bo/ Bickey, Bi, Bo, Bee-U-Boo/Bickey, Bi, Bo, Boo" The song becomes progressively sillier as the Stooges swing through the alphabet.

An ancient lyric from the Big Band Era surfaces in

"Three Little Fishies," written by a member of Hal Kemp's Orchestra, Saxie Dowell. With their next entry, "The Aba Daba Honeymoon," a 1914 hit by Arthur Fields and Walter Donovan, it becomes apparent that the Stooges are spending fewer moments on slapstick and more on singing. This welcome change doesn't hurt their performance, or the album. In fact, it proves that their comedy was equally effective minus the roughhouse.

The next theme, "The Merry-Go-Round Broke Down," was first introduced in the 1930s. A speeded-

187

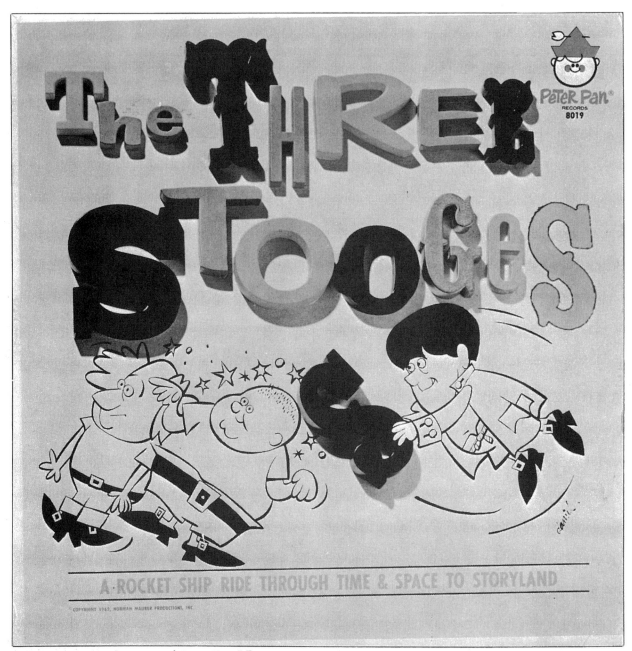

**Album cover for the Stooges' Peter Pan LP
released in 1963.**

up version was used as the opening music for Warner Brothers cartoons. Big Band sounds returned with "Two Little Birdies," a popular tune composed by Dolly Dawn and her Dawn Patrol. The Stooges wind down Side One with "The Children's Marching Song (Nick Nack Paddy Whack)."

Side Two becomes even more of a nostalgic throwback in time, as the Stooges revive sounds from the early 1900s, starting with a novelty song, comprised of a multi-word "patter chorus," called "Peggy O'Neil." Their nonsensical fun reaches its zenith in "Chickery Chick," and they revive Irving Berlin's 1915 classic "Play a Simple Melody." Then it's back to a popular children's song with "Old MacDonald Had a Farm," followed by a silly rendition of "Mairzy Doats."

The human-side of the Stooges surfaces in "Give Thanks." For a brief moment, we envision three slapstick heroes without make-up, impressing listeners with a side of their personalities never seen before. Their fragility and humbleness shines through as they sing:

Give thanks for the wonderful sunshine/

that helps you smile when you're blue
Give thanks for the birds in the springtime/
singing a song to cheer you along
The raindrops bring happy hours/
God's teardrops bless the flowers
Give thanks everyday when you kneel and pray/
and give thanks for your blessings each day.

The Stooges' appeal spread beyond the children's market with this album, due perhaps to the number of old songs it contained, songs that only adults could remember and appreciate. Also, the album's price of $4.98 was steep for that era and more affordable to adults than children. Although not financially successful, the album undoubtedly is their best. We witness not just the Three Stooges as comedians but as true recording artists with an extraordinary range.

In 1967, Vocalion Records re-issued this album as *The Three Stooges Sing for Kids* (Vocalion, 73823), containing ten cuts instead of twelve. The two deleted

The Stooges display their singing prowess on Coral Records' album cover for *The Three Stooges Nonsense Songbook*.

selections were "Two Little Birdies" and "Peggy O'Neil." Customers found the disc mainly on budget-racks or in discount department stores where it did striking business.

Next to 1959, the year 1963 was the Stooges' most productive season for spinning out records. Their talents were put to good use with a new children's release, *The Three Stooges in Storyland* (Peter Pan, 8019B). In 1973, Peter Pan retitled the album, *The Three Stooges and Six Funny Bone Stories*, using a

different illustration of the team on the album cover.

Here, by means of a typically zany rocket ship journey through time and space, the Stooges encounter a host of storybook characters and situations. Stories were written by Ronald Singer, who provides a minimum of humor and a maximum of serious drama in his segments. The story line opens with the trio launching themselves back into history in "The Three Stooges and the Time Rocket." We discover where their space expedition takes them in "The Crash,"

Golden Records' popular LP, *The Three Stooges Madcap Musical Nonsense* (1959).

GLP 43   HIGH FIDELITY   Golden Record   LONG PLAYING TREASURY

THE **3** STOOGES

MADCAP MUSICAL NONSENSE AT YOUR HOUSE

STARRING **LARRY, MOE** and **CURLY**

FEATURING THE MUSIC WRECKERS

WE'RE COMING TO YOUR HOUSE
(ON TOP OF OLD SMOKEY)

AT THE CIRCUS
(JOHN PHILLIP SOUSA MARCH)

AT A BASEBALL GAME
(SKIP TO MY LOU)

THE CLICK DART BANDSTAND SHOW
(MARY HAD A LITTLE LAMB)

THE THREE CHIPPED MUNKS
(10 LITTLE INDIANS)
(A TISKET, A TASKET)

TOY STORE
(A HUNTING WE WILL GO)

HOW NOT TO LEAD A BAND
(THE FARMER IN THE DELL)

THE STOOGES CUT UP A RECORD
(GO TELL AUNT RHODY)

GO TELL AUNT MARY
(GO TELL AUNT RHODY)

WRITTEN and PRODUCED by BUCHANAN and CELLA   © 1959 – NORMAN MAURER PRODUCTIONS, INC. – ALL RIGHTS RESERVED

190

where they wind up in Storyland and match wits with Cinderella. On Side Two, additional storybook characters appear in "The Three Stooges Meet the Ugly Duckling," "The Three Stooges Meet the Princess and the Pea" and "The Three Stooges and the Magic Lamp" (the last two selections were issued in 78 and 45 rpm versions).

The Stooges' swan song (their final LP) was *Yogi Bear and the Three Stooges Meet Dr. No-No* (Hanna-Barbera Records, 1966, 2050). The stock background music from the Hanna-Barbera library, so common in hundreds of Hanna-Barbera shows, is here, as well as some good comedy spoofing James Bond's *Dr. No*.

A caucus of forest rangers is held at Jellystone National Park. President Lyndon Johnson has ordered them to protect Yogi Bear, since he is important to Jellystone's tourism. The rangers vote to use the services of the Three Stooges, who are appointed Yogi's round-the-clock guardians. Nothing must happen to him, or the boys will be sawing trees in

The Stooges' final LP release, *Yogi Bear and the Three Stooges Meet the Mad, Mad, Mad, Dr. No-No* (1966).

191

Alcatraz rather than caring for them in the confines of Jellystone.

"Don't worry, we'll keep seven eyes on him." Curly-Joe reassures his fellow ranger. "How do you get seven," Moe demands. "Everybody knows that two times three equals seven!" Joe proclaims, inducing a

dressed like a sweet, innocent old lady. Noticing he's missing, the boys, on Moe's orders, scour the grounds for footprints, which provokes Curly-Joe to quip, "Yogi doesn't wear any shoes, he goes *bear* footed!"

During their comical search to find Yogi, a storm breaks out and complicates their hunt.

Curly-Joe, Moe and Larry trying out as a new rock group.

slap-in-the-face from Moe, who screams in dead seriousness, "Don't you know two times three equals *eight!*"

Though the story is rather conventional, the Stooges' humor is first-rate. Yogi doesn't stay under the Stooges' careful watch for long. He escapes,

Meanwhile, Yogi finds his way to a mysterious old mansion, high on top of a hill, where Dr. No-No and his not-so-bright assistant, Fang, have been experimenting with a kooky, new invention, the gizmo; a Molecule Mixing Machine which has the ability to re-arrange the molecules of a human body into that of an

192

animal. Dr. No-No has already successfully experimented with animals, but yearns for a human guinea pig. Instead, he must settle for Yogi, who Fang invites in from the cold. The evil No-No prepares to turn him into a chicken as Fang squeals, "I hope it works. We haven't had eggs in days!" No-No succeeds and the Stooges arrive to discover that Yogi has been transformed into a candidate for Colonel Sanders' Kentucky Fryers.

Dr. No-No is elated at the sight of the Stooges, realizing that he finally has three humans for his next experiment. He asks for volunteers. Larry and Curly-Joe instantly suggest Moe, who volunteers because he doesn't believe the crazy machine works. No-No asks them for suggestions as to what he should turn Moe into. Larry cracks, "Turn him into a monkey!"

Larry's suggestion becomes hard fact as Moe emerges from the machine as a full-sized gorilla. Taking advantage of Moe's new physique and Herculean strength, Larry and Curly-Joe come up with a brilliant scheme to save Yogi. They lure Dr. No-No right into the clutches of Gorilla/Moe, who threatens to clobber him if he doesn't return Yogi and himself back to normal (which is quite a challenge if you consider neither of them are). Dr. No-No, panicked, surrenders to Moe's demand but becomes a victim of his own invention when the Stooges turn him into a duck. Back at Jellystone Park, the park ranger inquires as to who was involved in Yogi's disappearance. The Stooges remark, "Why Doctor No-No." In disbelief, the Ranger says, "Well, okay, let's see this Dr. No-No." As they drag in Dr. No-No Duck, Curly-Joe quips, "Whatta ya know—a quacked doctor!"

This record has all the sure-fire material that became Hanna-Barbera's trademark, like the corny but funny ending, typical in all their cartoon shows. As a result, the Stooges are funnier—since they thrive on old puns and jokes—and come across more visual than in any other recording. Their stock-in-trade material lent itself to a visual presentation that didn't need graphics to explain the story. It is too bad, however, that the producers didn't consider making this into an hour Yogi Bear television special. No doubt, combining Yogi and the Three Stooges, probably would have drawn high ratings in prime time; especially because of the James Bond satire.

Charles Show wrote and directed the LP, with Dan Finnerty doing a competent job of editing. Richard Olsen and Bill Getty combined their expertise as recording engineers. And H.C. Pennington offered his sharp art direction.

The Stooges' recording careers ended with the Yogi Bear album and they had come full circle by returning to the comedy, slapstick material they used so successfully in their early records. Their initial albums wisely used standard, comedy Stooges routines. Later, they experimented with a variety of formats and selections both comedic and dramatic. Their most successful were the Golden releases which had more time devoted to singing. The Yogi LP was a departure from both and wins on its own merit as a cartoon story with plenty of action and situations that complemented the Stooges' patented brand of humor and allowed them to wind up their recording careers with a well-deserved success.

In retrospect, Larry, Moe and Curly-Joe were impressive as slapstick-comedians-turned-recording-artists. Despite the army of critics who felt their brand of wild comedy wasn't adaptable to record albums, the Stooges were not fazed by the challenge and proved that their totally visual, insane comedy style could be successfully tranformed into aural form.

**Shemp Howard, Billy Gilbert and Maxie
Rosenbloom** mugging as stooges in Monogram's
Crazy Knights.

6

Three Stooges Impersonators

WHOEVER COINED THE PHRASE knew what he was talking about when he said, "Imitation is the sincerest form of flattery." It certainly applies to the Three Stooges, who have been flattered enormously throughout their monumental career by a parade of imitators.

The Stooges have been "cloned" in a variety of forms, including animated cartoons, newspaper comic strips and television shows, and have even influenced other comedians to imitate their look and style. Some impersonators have done this *not* to cash in on but clearly to salute the Stooges as the unsung heroes of the comedy world. Several comedians have even attempted to establish themselves as members of the Three Stooges team. Specifically, comedians Paul "Mousie" Garner and Sammy Wolfe have linked their past performances with Ted Healy, suggesting that they were part of the original Three Stooges. Their claims are more fiction than fact and nothing could be further from the truth, as the name "Three Stooges" was never used until Larry, Moe and Curly made films for Columbia after they left Ted Healy.

Before elaborating further, it should be noted that the word "stooge" has been a part of the theatre vernacular for over 50 years and has held a specific connotation. Ken Murray had his stooges, meaning actors, who would run up and down theatre aisles, or act as hecklers in box seats. Phil Baker used to bill himself as "King of the Stooges" with Sid Silvers as his stooge.

But Ted Healy's original stooges were altogether different. They were undoubtedly stooges of the highest order, originals who created their special "stooge concept" in vaudeville. They weren't just assistants or actors, but comedians as well, who took some pretty rough punishment for their comic mistakes. Despite other acts that followed, Healy has the distinction of being the first to incorporate stooges in the physical manner as we know them. Included in that legendary *first* were Shemp and Moe Howard, two of the original Stooges. Subsequent stooges were comic cast-offs that copied the broad, physical slapstick inherent in Healy's act.

The earliest and first impersonators came in 1930, when Moe, Larry and Shemp left Ted Healy to form their act "Three Lost Souls." Healy quickly assembled a motley trio as replacements—Paul "Mousie" Garner, Dick Hakins and Jack Wolf. Their comedy was a copy of the original Stooges, in that Healy cracked them over the head and utilized his stock, broad, physical comedy in the act. Their humor had earmarks of Moe, Larry and Shemp, but with some significant differences. Garner explains: "What they did with the smacking, the poking in the eyes, we did with instruments, breaking fiddles across heads, squirting seltzer bottles." Little did Garner and his stooges realize, however, that their association as replacements would be short-lived, since Moe, Larry and Shemp—the original Stooges—would return and rejoin Ted Healy in 1932.

Garner remembers how his team joined Healy. "Jack Wolf, Dick Hakins and I found out that Healy had to replace the Stooges. We went down to the Imperial Theatre where he was holding auditions. There must have been a hundred guys there. What do you think my audition was? Healy smacked me in the head and I jumped on him and bit his ear and grabbed his nose. He said, 'You're great. Get in the corner, you're hired.'"

Hakins, Wolf and Garner went on to star in several Broadway shows with Healy, *The Gang's All Here* and *Crazy Quilt*. Years later, Garner continued to entertain theatregoers with partners Wolf and Hakins as *The Gentle Maniacs*.

The next trio of Three Stooges imitators included none other than—Curly Howard. While making films at Metro, he was cast opposite two comedians—George Givot and Bobby Callahan—in a Technicolor short, *Roast Beef and Movies* (1934). The film was a blatant attempt on the part of Metro to spawn another team of Stooges. It contains a melange of bizarre routines and equally strange dialogue, written by Richy Craig, Jr., a former vaudeville comedian who was considered the Bob Hope of his day.

In the film *Roast Beef and Movies*, Givot and his two comic contemporaries invade the Masterpiece

Film Corporation in the hope of breaking into film-making. Listening at an open transom, they hear someone say that he will pay $100,000 for a good, quality film production. They immediately rush out to produce four films (within the film)—two segments with the Albertina Rusch Dancers. These are screened for the potenial buyers. Some pretty inane sequences result with Givot narrating the films; one contains a Mae West look-alike making love to a house detective in "Prepare to Die." Givot's thick European

Warner Brothers cartoon version of the Stooges, from *Porky's Hero Agency* (1937). (© Warner Bros.)

accent makes some important dialogue inaudible but he is able to deliver the necessary comic punch.

Extremely fascinated by Givot's films, the studio producer acclaims them—fittingly we might add—as "masterpieces" and offers $100,000 for distribution rights. First, however he must consult with the studio's board of directors to approve the pending deal. But the board turns out to be escapees from a local mental institution. Punctuating this funny scene is a shot of the board members making deranged faces and playing with children's toys. Later, a sanitarium attendant orders the supposed studio executives back into the wagon with the rest of the patients, dragging along the producer, Givot, Curly Howard and Callahan. The comedy, interspersed with Busby Berkeley-type musical numbers to bring it to length, loses no spontaneity despite the interruptions.

It is interesting seeing a young Curly Howard in an experimental Technicolor short, sans his usual Stooges ensemble. He and Callahan prove to be an awkward pair as the latter tries to upstage Curly. Basically Curly's involvement is limited to harrassing Callahan and introducing another one of Givot's films. Scattered throughout are some bright moments with Givot, who shows promise as a film comedian. (Incidentally, his previous film experience included appearances in Vitaphone comedies. Callahan went on to make his living in such films as *Men in Black* (1934) with the Three Stooges, and Laurel and Hardy's *Helpmates* (1932). Moe Howard once recalled, after viewing *Men in Black*, that "Callahan made a career out of playing Western Union delivery boys in our pictures and others.") This awkward, new trio offered no great threat to the real Stooges ensemble. MGM gave up any attempt to re-group them.

In March 1934, after the Three Stooges signed with Columbia Pictures, Ted Healy yearned once more for another group of stooges to menace. A short time later, he took a new trio of comedians under his wing—Jimmy Brewster, Sammy Wolfe (whose real name was Sammy Glasser) and Rhett Pearson—and toured the nightclub circuit. Many critics contended that Healy's new act offered nothing original and that they seemed out of place. In 1936, they returned to Hollywood for a bit part with Healy in MGM's *San Francisco*. They appeared in the film as bartenders in a big stage revue.

Even Shemp Howard got into the act, putting his best stooging forward. In 1934, RKO Radio Pictures

The Stooges as a three-headed monster in a scene from *Porky in Wackyland*. (© Warner Bros.)

196

starred him in *A Knife of the Party* and billed him as Shemp Howard and His Stooges. In this musical-comedy revue, Jack Good and Lillian Miles star as singers attempting to pull a hotel out of debt. A critic for *Motion Picture Herald* called the film "fair," but thought "a good portion of the comedy" was provided by Shemp Howard and His Stooges. Howard's rough-house humor reminded audiences of the Three Stooges but it lacked the spontaneity of the original Stooges comedies.

That same year, there was another incident where imposters were used when the producing studio was unable to hire the original Three Stooges. *Gift of Gab* (Universal, 1934) was a musical-comedy feature originally planned with the trio in cameo roles. Lew Breslow, who directed the Stooges in *Punch Drunks* (1934), wrote the film's original screenplay. Producer Ryan James' efforts to secure the Stooges met with misfortune, however, when Harry Cohn of Columbia nixed the deal. Instead, James threw together three comedians named Sid Walker, Skins Miller and Jack Harling and billed them as the Three Stooges.

Animation cartoon producers also decided to jump on the Three Stooges bandwagon, creating caricatures of Larry, Moe and Curly to be used in many animated cartoons. Warner Brothers' cartoon division was no exception. Director Friz Freleng, an avid fan of the Stooges, became the first cartoon director to animate the trio. His *The Miller's Daughter*, a 1934 Merrie Melodies, becomes a bright, gay adventure with the Stooges appearing as statues in a gallery of figurines that come to life.

Curly, Larry and Moe, resplendent in tuxedoes, from Tex Avery's *Hollywood Steps Out*. (© Warner Bros.)

The following year, animators Ben Harrison and Frank Moser inserted the trio in a Color Rhapsody cartoon, released through Columbia Pictures, called *The Bon-Bon Parade* (1935). Naturally, working in close quarters with the Stooges, Harrison and Moser became inspired by the team's antics and cast them as "cupids." The Stooges later appeared in the following Color Rhapsodies as well: *Hollywood Panic* (1937), *Poor Little Butterfly* (1939), *A Hollywood Detour* (1942) and *Cinderella Goes to a Party* (1942).

Producer Walter Lantz's own version of the Stooges—three chimpanzees, Meany, Miny and Moe. (© Walter Lantz Productions.)

Bob Clampett was another Warner Brothers director who loved entertaining audiences with a sprinkling of animated radio and film personalities in his cartoons. In *Porky's Hero Agency* (1937), the Stooges become one of many victims affected by the evil magic of Gorgon. The sorcerer turns the boys into the Wise Monkeys of Japan, or, in other words, hear-no-evil, speak-no-evil and see-no-evil.

Wholly Smoke (1938) was another Warners cartoon featuring Porky and the Stooges, directed by Frank Tashlin. The story concerns Porky's many sleepless nights; among his dreams are hallucinations of the Stooges as cigars who poke him in the eyes.

A year earlier, Walter Lantz produced a new cartoon series, *Meany, Miny and Moe*, consisting of a trio of circus monkeys. Lantz has admitted that the Three Stooges influenced him in his conception. In an

MGM's new version of the Stooges—George Givot,
Curly Howard and Bobby Callahan, from *Roast
Beef and Movies* (1934).

interview, he recalled, "They were more like the
Three Stooges, where their actions were very physical
and broad. They didn't have to speak, because they
were doing the kind of pantomime that Charlie
Chaplin and Harry Langdon did."

Lantz produced thirteen *Meany, Miny and Moe*
cartoons between 1936 and 1937 and released them
through United Artists. Their stories struck a familiar
chord, reminiscent of the world-renowned Stooges
comedies with Curly. In *The Golfers* (1936), the three
make a go of playing golf, with disastrous results.
They not only have a rough time on the green, but
wreck the golf cart, the golf clubs and the golf course.
Only the golf balls come out of this nightmare un-
scathed. In many respects, this cartoon resembles an
earlier Stooges comedy, *Three Little Beers* (1935), in
which the boys tear up a municipal golf course—
sandtrap and all. Lantz also attempted to animate the
Stooges prior to this series in a Cartune Classic,
Candy Land (1935).

Back at Warners, Bob Clampett returned with our
three heroes in *Porky in Wackyland* (1938). The
Stooges were naturals for Bob's crazy anything-for-a-
laugh style of humor. This time around, Porky visits
Wackyland where all creatures are...well, wacky! He
even meets a three-headed monster whose heads
argue among themselves and slap each other violently. It's the Stooges, of course.

Lavish Hollywood parties and film premieres were
even greater backdrops for the Stooges' antics. In Tex
Avery's *Hollywood Steps Out* (Warner Brothers, 1941),
a number of stars make their way to a big Hollywood
bash. Seen in cartoon form for the very first time are
Bing Crosby, Cary Grant, Peter Lorre, James Cagney,
Mickey Rooney and Joan Crawford. But what would a
party be like without the Stooges banging, socking
and crushing each other to conga rhythm. This scene
was used again in a 1975 documentary feature,
Brother Can You Spare a Dime? and a compilation
entitled, *Bugs Bunny, Superstar*.

Ted Healy and his new Stooges in publicity still from MGM's *San Francisco* (1936).

I finished playing the Palladium," Besser recalls, "they came up to me and said, 'Do you mind if we do you?' What could I say. I figured even if I said, 'No,' they'd probably do *me* anyway."

Around this same time, in October, 1938, Mousie Garner, Dick Hakins and Sammy Wolfe began booking themselves at vaudeville theaters as *Ted Healy's Original Stooges.* This alarmed Moe, Larry and Curly so much so that they filed a legal action to stop the new act from using the word "original" in the billing. The dispute was settled out of court, with the American Guild of Variety Artists (AGVA) ruling in favor of the Three Stooges. Joe Smith (of Smith 'n' Dale fame) was a member of AGVA's board of arbitration. Years later, he recalled in a letter to Moe Howard how everyone on the board knew they were Ted Healy's original stooges and that the trio had the unanimous support of the Guild's board.

Then, Shemp Howard started to reestablish himself in Stoogedom in several film productions of his own. As a Monogram contract player, he was starred in three features opposite Billy Gilbert and Maxie Rosenbloom. The first, *Three of a Kind* (1944), utilized these veteran comedians in Stooges-like roles. Their first film mustered up some pretty good box-office and was reissued through Astor Pictures as *Cooking Up Trouble.* They followed their previous triumph with *Crazy Knights* (retitled for television as

Comedians Sam Wolfe, Paul "Mousie" Garner and Dick Hakins as the "Gentle Maniacs" made a career out of impersonating the Stooges.

The Stooges' last Warner Brothers cartoon emergence was in *Dough for Do-Do* (1949), directed by Friz Freleng. A remake of *Porky in Wackyland,* Freleng uses the same footage of the trio as a three-headed monster. This time the cartoon is in Technicolor and Moe's hair has been painted white!

Live performers continued to imitate the Stooges. In England, a trio of comedians gained permission from Moe Howard to bill themselves as the Three Stooges and re-enact the same kind of violent slapstick. This British ensemble played at the Trocadero Theatre in England for six days, beginning July 4, 1938, opposite Archie McKay (who was their straight man). Their use of the Three Stooges name was restricted to boundaries inside the United Kingdom, since billing of another Three Stooges team in America would have been illegal.

Joe Besser recalls that this British trio never impersonated the same act twice. Whoever caught their fancy would become their next impersonation. "After

Shemp's) were in the form of Moe-Howard-type slaps and pokes (without Moe's flair). In one series entry, *Tough as They Come* (1942), member Gabriel Dell actually calls Hall "lame-brain"! Shemp Howard worked with the gang in three films and Hall later cited him as having a tremendous influence on his comedic style. Several of Hall's "Bowery Boys" comedies (with Leo Gorcey) were directed and written by Stooges/Columbia alumni Edward Bernds and Elwood Ullman.

Universal Pictures, in their musical/whodunit *Murder in the Blue Room* (1944), decided to cross the Three Stooges and the Andrew Sisters to create "The Three Jazzybelles," a female vaudeville team who find themselves in an old mansion that houses a mysterious room. Grace MacDonald is the leader, with Betty Kean in what might be termed the Curly-role and June Preisser rounding out the threesome. They

Three innocent fan impersonators at a 1950's masquerade party.

The Stooges as a three-headed monster revisited in a *Beany and Cecil* cartoon, *The Capture of the Dreaded, Three-Headed Threep*. (© Bob Clampett Productions.)

Ghost Crazy) in 1944 and *Trouble Chasers* in 1945. Critics for the *Motion Picture Herald* gave all three of these films a "fair" rating. The trio did not bill themselves under character names but rather as themselves. Because of Shemp's vast background as a former Stooge, his impersonations of the Stooges were more acceptable than those of other imitators.

Film historian Brent Walker has cited several other films that utilized some form of Stooges material. A trace of Stooges influence can be detected in the films of Universal's "Little Tough Guys," a spinoff of the "Dead End Kids" made in the early forties, which are substantially less entertaining than the pictures made by the Warner Brothers and Monogram groups. This conglomeration was led by Billy Halop, whose communications with buddy Huntz Hall (a close friend of

eventually spend the night in the eerie Blue Room and have to share a king-size bed. Naturally, a hand reaches through a hole in the wall and slaps them each on the head, causing them to blame each other for the deed in typical Stooges fashion.

The 1940s were naturally good times for imitating the Stooges. They had reached their first peak and weren't tapering off. But by the 1950s "Stooges imposters" started to slacken. Not until the Stooges' TV resurgence in the 1960s did impersonators resurface.

Bob Clampett got everything rolling again with *The Beany and Cecil Show*. This color, animated series, which was first broadcast in 1961, featured the Stooges as a three-headed monster, called the "Threep," in an episode titled "The Capture of the Dreaded Three-Headed Threep."

The Stooges are drawn in a manner similar to Clampett's original Threep monster in *Porky in Wackyland*. In this episode, however, Capt. Huffenpuff, Beany and Cecil set sail to bring back the Threep Monster to star in its own weekly television series. Clampett does a good job of building suspense as to what his Threep/Stooges look like. Beany blows his beany top when Cecil get three coconuts stuck on his head. The coconuts then cast a gigantic shadow of the Three Stooges' heads on the ground. Finally, Beany ventures into an out of the way cavern where the Threep/Stooges invites Cecil and him for dinner.

Afterwards, it agrees to return with them and do the television series.

Television cartoon producers William Hanna and Joseph Barbera came close to matching the Stooges' violent humor with an award-winning series of *Tom and Jerry* cartoons for MGM. While producing TV's *The Flintstones*, starring Fred, Barney, Wilma and Betty in prehistoric situations, they decided that the Stooges' ancient style of humor would enhance their series. So Joe and Bill decided to include the Stooges in "The Most Beautiful Baby in Bedrock," broadcast April 17, 1964. In this episode, Fred and Barney are appealing for votes from the local citizenry for a Most-Beautiful-Baby Contest; their children, Pebbles and Bamm-Bamm, are entered. It is during their tour from neighborhood to neighborhood that they meet three familiar characters, the Three Stooges, going under the names of Manny, Moe and Jack. Fred and

Moe Howard, Larry Fine and Joe Besser with six stooge impersonators on the set of *Merry Mix-Up* (1957).

The presidential team of the people—stooges Richard (Larry) Nixon, John (Moe) Kennedy and Lyndon (Curly) Johnson.

Barney show the trio photographs of their children and ask them which one is the most beautiful. Unable to agree, the trio begin thwacking and bopping each other around while Fred and Barney make a quick exit.

In 1965, Edward Bernds and Elwood Ullman were contracted to script *Tickle Me*, a vehicle for Elvis Presley, and they wound up utilizing many gags they had used in their Stooge days. The finale takes place

Three Stooges doubles standing off stage in a scene from *Three Stooges Scrapbook* (1960).

in a "haunted house" (Ullman's favorite comedy setting) and features closeted spooks, doors that open to bottomless depths and lots of hallway chases. At one point, a villain throws a knife at Elvis. The King ducks, then reaches back for the handle and makes threats with it, not realizing the blade is still stuck in the wall, which is an old Stooges gag. Elvis continued his Stooges associations with *Spinout* (1966), in which his lead guitarist and bass player are named Larry and Curly. Does this, by chance, make Elvis Moe?

Greater noise and media hoopla was made over the Beatles—Paul McCartney, Ringo Starr, George Harrison and John Lennon—sporting, as some writers called it, "Moe haircuts." Full-page accounts were published in newspapers and magazines on this Liverpool group copying Howard's world-famous, sugarbowl haircut. *Mad* Magazine got into the act as well, running a letter from Moe Howard addressed to the Beatles. This bizarre publicity did the Stooges no harm; it served to add to their recognition.

The 1960s were far from inactive in terms of contributions from Stooges impersonators. A hit rock 'n' roll group and television series, *The Monkees* (1966), characterized some of the same wild situations the Stooges first made famous during the 1930s and 1940s. Storylines were unrealistic and nonsensical, without the knockabout slapstick, but utilized fast motion photography to embellish their comic romps. This fabulous quartet was a cross-between the Stooges and the Beatles. Their zaniness carried slapstick to the absurd.

Japanese Stooges impersonators from *The Three Stooges Go Around the World in a Daze* (1963).

Moe meets his Japanese counterpart impersonator in *The Outlaws Is Coming!* (1965).

Michael Nesmith, Davey Jones, Mickey Dolenz and Peter Tork comprised the Monkees popular foursome. Ironically, these color, half-hour shows were filmed on the Columbia Pictures' back lot, where many Three Stooges comedies were produced.

But being impersonated has had its share of drawbacks, too. For instance, a puzzling but hilarious identity crisis has existed for years regarding the Stooges, ever since a national chain of automobile supply stores, *The Pep Boys*, sprang up. Emblazoned on the stores' facades are three, toothy, grinning auto mechanics, posed like the Three Stooges with their names in bold letters underneath, "Manny, Moe and Jack." Customers—not true fans—invariably point at these ugly dudes and shout, "There's the Three Stooges!"

A humorous incident recently happened to us that points up the Pep Boys-Three Stooges identity crisis.

Larry, Moe and Curly-Joe mugging with a set of Japanese Stooges impersonators. A publicity still for *The Three Stooges Go Around the World in a Daze* (1963).

While we were Xeroxing some photographs at a local copy center, a clerk noticed the pictures and wanted to demonstrate her incredible knowledge of the Stooges. She poked her head around the corner of the machine and blurted out, "Boys, those guys were funny. Good ole' Manny, Moe and Jack."

Hanna-Barbera produced another high-rated cartoon series in 1972 called *The New Scooby Doo*

If you've been watching the covers of Movie Magazines on the newsstands lately, you're probably aware that they all look something like this...

When you get right down to it, all Movie Magazine covers are composed of two basic ingredients: (1) Wild and sensational story-titles, most of which are misleading and/or phony; and (2) Come-on articles and photos dealing with—of all people—JACKIE KENNEDY! Apparently, in the eyes of Movie Magazine editors, Jackie hasn't suffered enough in her life time. Now she is forced to undergo the indignity of seeing photos and idiotically-contrived stories about her in every Film Fan Publication in the country. Which got us to thinking: Since Movie Mags have found the magic success formula, isn't it a matter of time before all the other magazines latch on to the same formula? Here, then, is what we can expect ...

IF OTHER PUBLICATIONS USED THOSE SENSATIONAL MOVIE MAG COVER GIMMICKS
(INCLUDING THE SHAMELESS EXPLOITATION OF JACKIE KENNEDY)

Cartoon satire of the Stooges from an edition of *Mad* magazine.

Movies, featuring the Stooges in two of its episodes, both written by Norman Maurer. Moe, Larry and Curly-Joe were paid $2,000 apiece for the use of their names and likenesses in the shows but didn't provide the voices for their characters. Larry's speech was partially impaired, as a result of a stroke in 1970. After watching these shows, Fine remarked sadly, "I wish they had let us do the voices for the shows. If I was given the lines ahead of time, I could have rehearsed them and sounded pretty much like my old self." The first cartoon had them as proprietors of a run-down amusement park in "Ghastly Ghost Town," followed by "Ghost of the Red Baron," with the Stooges as crop dusters teamed with Scooby and Company to capture the Red Baron.

The 1970s inspired a whole era of hope for Stooges fans. The team's rise in fame and popularity kept increasing—thanks to an incredible nostalgia craze that was sweeping the country. Revival theaters held a series of Three Stooges Festivals, while television stations scheduled Stooges marathons. A Boston television station ran three-hours of non-stop Stooges comedies every day for a solid month! Even comedians Carol Burnett and Rich Little took note and impersonated the team on their weekly television shows.

Four Moe haircut impersonators, who strangely enough made it big as the Beatles. (Courtesy Mike Lefebvre/Pepperland.)

Three doubles wearing Stooges masks take to the ice in *Snow White and the Three Stooges*.

Carol Burnett reprised their antics over CBS in an episode of the 1973 season, co-starring Harvey Korman and Ken Berry. In the sketch, Burnett and her comic associates are founders of *The Three Stooges National Bank*, and can't decide who'll take over ownership. The usual slapstick abounds, with Korman impressive as Moe, Burnett convincing as Larry (frizzy-haired wig and all), but Berry's Curly is not up to par. They re-enact some traditional routines; Korman poking Burnett who raises her hand in front of her nose to stop the attacking fingers. In another good bit of business, Korman orders Berry to put his left fist out; Korman smacks it up driving it into Berry's own forehead. The antics were typical of many scenes from the Stooges' two-reel comedies, including the sound effects. In the final scene, an executive walks in and remarks to the Stooges, "Sorry gentlemen, you're fired. We've hired someone more sophisticated to run the bank." Out of nowhere strut three Marx Brothers look-alikes.

Carol Burnett, Harvey Korman and Ken Berry imitating the Stooges on CBS' *The Carol Burnett Show*.

In August 1973, Norman Maurer held serious negotiations with 20th Century Fox on a series starring the sons of the Three Stooges, tentatively titled *The Three Stooges, Jr.* or *The Little Stooges*. Producer Alan J. Factor and Maurer were set to produce a weekly series through Fox's television division. First and foremost was the task of casting the three lead roles. Maurer set up an office at Fox to hold auditions. Press releases were issued and local radio stations announced that three young actors were needed to play the Three Stooges in a new television series.

What seemed like an easy job wasn't. The producers couldn't find a teen-ager to play Curly; he was supposed to have been the easiest to cast. "What was even worse were the young adults we had coming in to play Moe and Larry," Maurer said. Consequently, Maurer and Factor disbanded the project.

The largest single producer of Saturday morning cartoons, Hanna-Barbera Productions, was next in line, reviewing the possibilities of an animated series on the Little Stooges but no sale resulted. The closest Maurer came to producing the idea was in a series of comic books for Gold Key Comics published in 1972. (Incidentally, Maurer revised this concept from an earlier version, also with three juvenile Stooges, titled *The Li'l Stooges*, with their mischievious companion, Muff the dog. But, unfortunately, as winsome as the first premise was, it was never produced.)

Even high schools and colleges, as well as grade schools, were filled with Three Stooges impersonators. Moe Howard once recalled three students at Loara High School in Anaheim, California, doing their impersonation of "Niagara Falls" in a variety show production. One student went so far as to cut his hair like Moe's while another tousled his curls like Larry. Understandably, the third student refused to shave his head; he wore a bald head-piece to make him look like Curly.

Norman Maurer's proposed idea for a *Little
Stooges* TV cartoon series.

**The Little Stooges and Muff spoof King Arthur's
Court in *The Time Trespassers*.**

Students became so enthralled with their screen idols that some staged pie fights at noontime rallies and re-enacted such favorite Stooge routines as "The Maharaja." Moe enjoyed saving newspaper clippings, sent to him by fans, depicting student activities and fan impersonators.

Perhaps, the least known trio of Three Stooges impersonators was a nightclub act formed by Curly-Joe DeRita in 1974. Moe Howard, who was retired, gave Joe permission to use the Three Stooges name and DeRita called the ensemble *The New Three Stooges*. Hired to complete the trio were Mousie

Rich "Moe" Little, yuks it up in a scene with Stooge partners R.G. "Larry" Brown, Joe "Curly" Baker and their victim Michael Landon, in a sketch from *The Rich Little Show*. (Courtesy NBC.)

Garner and Frank Mitchell. DeRita adapted the act, using a combination of music and comedy with Garner doing his shtick behind the piano. The new threesome opened in Boston and played in several Eastern cities. According to Curly-Joe, the team would have made better seltzer water because it fizzled just as fast.

In the meantime, Rich Little—the man of a thousand impressions—paid tribute to the team in a 1975 episode of NBC's *The Rich Little Show*. Guests Joe Baker and R.G. Brown essayed the roles of Curly and Larry, while Little did Moe in "The Three Stooges Stop Smoking Clinic," and a courtroom sketch featuring Michael Landon.

Little's effort to duplicate the Stooges was met with a strong complaint from the attorneys for Norman Maurer Productions for using the Three Stooges' names and likenesses without permission. An out-of-court settlement was subsequently reached with NBC where they agreed to cease using scenes with the Three Stooges and all previously produced segments were struck from syndicated prints of the Rich Little Show.

Of all the impersonations on record, perhaps the greatest and clearest was in Mel Brooks' *Silent Movie* (20th Century-Fox, 1976). Brooks, Marty Feldman and Dom DeLuise were more sophisticated in their Stooge impressions. Mel was apparently the overbearing boss of the trio. Feldman, replete with bulging eyes and a wild head of hair was a carbon copy of Larry. And DeLuise didn't have a moment in the film where he was without a sandwich to eat—obviously portraying Curly.

Critics had high acclaim for the film, and wrote that Brooks was bringing the Three Stooges act "up-to-date". Mel got away with his brash, nonsensical humor throughout the film, adapting it to the characters. A particularly funny segment occurred when Brooks and his two comrades crash a convalescent home. Following a bizarre mishap, a chase scene results with the boys racing through the grounds in electric wheelchairs (an updated version of a similar scene in the 1937 Stooges comedy, *Dizzy Doctors*).

Norman Maurer's TV cartoon conception of the Little Stooges as a teenage rock band.

208

In light of the other blatant character rip-offs, Brooks did a commendable job in making his tribute to the Stooges honorable and memorable. Film historians have since called it his best film.

Another performer sought to make his particular niche in Three Stooges history as a Curly Howard impersonator. His name is Frank Welker. Welker has joined the ranks of such prominent cartoon voice artists as Mel Blanc and Daws Butler. In 1977, he was asked to voice a lovable, but stupid, white shark in a *Jaws*-inspired Hanna-Barbera (ABC) cartoon series, *Jabberjaw*. Norman Maurer Productions gave ABC permission to duplicate Curly as the Shark. This sharp-tooth mammal, who has the brain of a sardine and the courage of a guppy, served as mascot for four teenagers and their rock group, living in an underwater civilization. Welker shaped his character around Curly Howard, recreating the comedian's unusual mannerisms and falsetto voice in shark form. Bizarre would best describe the sight of an obnoxious shark belting out "wooo-wooos" and "n'yuk-n'yuk-n'yuks."

At this time, Norman Maurer was writing scripts for several Hanna-Barbera shows, most notably *Dynomutt, Dog Wonder*. He then created a new cartoon series format to star the Three Stooges, titled *The Three Robonic Stooges* and featuring the misadventures of a bionic Moe, Larry and Curly. The boys found themselves playing bionic, secret-agent super-

heroes in the typical—and not so typical—Stooges jams to the dismay of their boss, Agent 000. Unlike the old trio, however, these new models were capable of telescoping their limbs, heads and torsos into goofy positions when on assignment. Supplying the voices for the Stooges were Paul Winchell as Moe, Joe Baker

John Candy as Curly, Joe Flaherty as Larry, Eugene Levy as Moe, appearing as Three Stooges impersonators on an episode of NBC's SCTV.

A scene from the Hanna-Barbera, Norman Maurer Productions' cartoon series *The Three Robonic Stooges*.

Dom DeLuise, Marty Feldman, and Mel Brooks
portrayed modern-day Stooges in Brooks' film
Silent Movie (1976).

A Helene Curtis Magazine ad—impersonating the
Stooges.

as Larry and Frank Welker as Curly. Their boss,
Agent 000, was expertly characterized by the late
Ross Martin of *Wild, Wild West* television fame.

At first, Hanna-Barbera produced these five-minute cartoons as part of their live-action series, *The
Skatebirds*. The series debuted on CBS, September
10, 1977. Two *Robonic Stooges* cartoons were shown
every week, along with the *Skatebirds*, *Wonder-
wheels*, *Woofer and Wimper, Dog Detectives* and a
live adventure, *Mystery Island*. The Skatebirds—
Scooter the Penguin, Satchel the Pelican, Knock-
Knock the Woodpecker and Scat Cat—were nothing
more than weak imitations of the studio's former live
foursome, *The Banana Splits*.

The Neilsen ratings indicated that the Stooges
segments received more viewers than any other segment in the show. As a result, the *Skatebirds* show
was cancelled and CBS installed the trio in a half-hour

time slot on their own as *The Three Robonic Stooges* with Woofer and Wimper. The series aired from January 28, 1978, to December 30, 1979. In many parts of the world, stations continued to broadcast these wacky, animated romps, consisting of a total of 32 five-minute Robonic Stooges cartoons with stories ranging from traditional myths to conventional situations.

Previously, another cartoon series was proposed to Norman Maurer Productions using the Stooges. Fine Arts Productions submitted the concept titled *Super Stooges*, which was ultimately turned down.

Impersonations have also appeared in the form of editorial and comic strip art. Periodically, newspaper cartoonists utilize the Stooges' likenesses for topping off specific gags, or as featured performers. They have been satirized in such strips as *Momma*, the *Wizard of Id* and *B.C.* (in the latter the Stooges were used for

to the list was *Chevy Chase's National Humor Test*, a one-hour NBC special which aired May 10, 1979. Chase was one of several young comedians influenced by the masters of comedy—including the Three Stooges. He brought back the Buster Keaton form of pratfalls—notably through his mocking of the former President Gerald Ford—and other trademark shtick from the 1930s and 1940s.

Chase's writers developed the kind of sketch where viewers would least expect the Stooges. He lampoons the trials and tribulations of banking in The First National Funny Bank. Chase narrates the scene, explaining to viewers that perhaps the least humorous times of our lives are spent in an ordinary bank. But one particular branch wants to alleviate this humdrum atmosphere, since it can't compete with the giants in the industry who are offering the same old, serious style of banking.

An unproduced cartoon satire, *Superstooges*.

two weeks straight following Larry Fine's death in 1975). Political satirists have also called on the trio for use in one-column editorial cartoons.

The Stooges impersonators continued to surface in newspapers and in many top television shows. Added

In an attempt to rectify the situation, bank president H.R. "Cuddles" McBride, dreams up the idea of mixing "funny with money." Among the bank's many services are its personal checks. McBride takes great pride in being the only bank to have checks featuring

211

a wide assortment of comedians—everybody from Jack Benny to Pinky Lee to the Three Stooges. Naturally, mentioning the Stooges' names creates the need for an impersonation.

Chase and McBride listen in as a teller (Debbie Harmon) watches her customer (Robert Morris) leaf through samples of the different checks the bank has to offer. When she comes to the Stooges she says, "Then we have the Three Stooges—Moe, Larry and Shemp." (While pointing at the photographs, she confuses Moe for Shemp, and vice versa.) Morris appears totally confused. He says, "Where's Curly?" The teller explains, "I think he came later, it was Shemp first!" Morris, attempting to imitate Shemp, remarks, "Curly was the one who went yeng-yeng-yeng!" The teller corrects him, "No, that was Shemp." She proceeds to reprise Curly's famous catch phrase, followed by the familiar wave of the hand. "Curly was wooo-wooo-wooo!" The best part of this sketch was, naturally, this surprise inclusion of the Stooges, who have been neglected so often whenever a salute to comedians comes up.

Probably the one series of impersonations that ranks in the "poor taste" column appeared on ABC's *Fridays* program. Three comedians—Bruce Mahler (Moe), Larry David (Larry) and John Roarke (Curly)—brought a new dimension to the team as drug-culture comedians. They managed to include the customary slapstick but interwove it around sick, drug-oriented jokes.

In one particular episode, all sorts of incidents occur, opening with the Stooges in bed asleep and snoring (a traditional opening in several Stooges comedies). They awaken and perform what they believe are constructive duties around the house. Curly begins cleaning out a drug instrument of some kind which accidentally squirts ink in Moe's face. This was one of the least offensive gags that appeared in the show. A more typical one was Curly smoking marijuana for the first time, getting high and spinning on the floor like a top. In another scene a pusher tries selling the Stooges some drugs with the boys resisting momentarily, followed by a remark from Curly, "I'll do it when I'm ready?" The pusher whips out a switchblade knife and cracks, "Are you ready?" A frightened Curly gasps, "Yeah, I'm ready!"

Slightly amusing was another episode with George Hamilton in the Ted Healy role. He is at a reunion with his three, long-lost brothers (the Stooges) who

return to visit and leave Hamilton's mansion in a shambles. George vents his anger in the end, performing Moe's triple-slap on the Stooges. Actually, these impersonations could have stood up as timeless masterpieces without the constant drug references. Instead, they were distasteful tributes to three come-

"A glass of fine chablis, a marvelous cheddar, and a Three Stooges festival. Cheers!"

(REPRINTED FROM THE SATURDAY EVENING PO

EVERYONE IN THE WORLD KNOWS **LARRY, MOE AND CURLY!** WE'VE EVEN BEEN IMMORTALIZED IN MAGAZINE AND NEWSPAPER CARTOONS!

A hodge-podge of newspaper comic strips featuring the Stooges. Far left is Norman Maurer's interpretation of the Stooges from his strip, *Larry, Moe and Curly*.

dians who always had good, clean fun and never used foul language in their films. As in the Rich Little stooge impersonations, Norman Maurer Productions' attorneys made a strong protest to ABC for this unlicensed use of the Stooges' name and likenesses and an out-of-court settlement was obtained.

Following *Fridays* string of sketches was another late-night comedy show adding some laughs with a surprise impersonation of Curly Howard in one segment. *Second City Television Network 90* came up with a hilarious satirical sketch entitled "Melvin and Howard." The premise depicted the odd relationship

Even though they don't look like them, Bill, Mark, and Brett—better known as the Hudson Brothers—also impersonated the Stooges on their ill-remembered TV series, *The Hudson Brothers Comedy Hour.*

between gas station attendant, Melvin Dumar (Rick Moranis), and millionaire, Howard Hughes (Joe Flaherty). NBC broadcast the show on May 29, 1981.

This sketch was touted as a Movie-of-the-Week promo, divided into three segments. In each sequence, Dumar and Howard are seen driving on a cross-country trip through the Arizona desert. At each turn, they pick up a passenger with the first or last name of Howard—first, Howard Cosell (Eugene Levy), followed by Senator Howard Baker (Dave Thomas). By now, television viewers realize that another person named Howard will be picked up. The question is, "Who?" The final segment puts to rest all questions, and surprises everyone as Hughes takes over the cross-country driving chores. In the midst of trying to keep his eyes from closing, a hand comes in under them, wriggles back and forth and thrusts downward, smacking Hughes in the face. The camera cuts to our new passenger, Curly Howard (John Candy), looking on innocently as Hughes barks, "Who the hell are you?" Candy replies, "Curly...Curly Howard, N'yuk, n'yuk!" Hughes quickly retorts, "Well, start singing, pea-brain!" Curly first refuses, but Hughes changes his mind with a whack in the mouth. Curly then cries, "Oh, Elaine, won't you come out tonight...at least until the morning's bright. Oh, Cedric's here, your darling Cedric's here..." At this point, Dumar raises his hand to lead

the group as they finish this happy-go-lucky tune together and the sketch as well.

Candy's performance as Curly was not only well-rehearsed but the best on record. He had every mannerism and nuance down to perfection, even Curly's famous "n'yuk-n'yuk" catch phrase.

A final form of impersonations include subtle, throwaway scenes in television shows and motion pictures. Apparently, television and film writers who are Stooges buffs are in agreement. Those writing behind the scenes of TV's *Nurse*, starring Michael Learned, took a line of dialogue straight from *Men in Black* (1934). The routine involved the hospital loudspeaker over which Curly, Larry and Moe would be paged as "Dr. Howard, Dr. Fine, Dr. Howard!". Well, the same exact words graced hospital loudspeakers in one episode as—we hear—"Dr. Howard, Dr. Fine, Dr. Howard."

More apparent was a scene from a low-budget, comedy feature, *Gas* (1981), released to theatres for one week. Featured in this piecemeal cheapie was Steve Furst who made his film debut in such comedies as *Animal House* and *Meatballs*. He stole scenes as a gas station attendant in this movie, notably one in which he eyed the attractive figure of a buxom, female customer. He deliriously reacted by flapping his hand up and down on top of his head and shouting, "Wooo-wooo-wooo-wooo!"

Three Stooges lookalikes promoting a Michigan State lottery.

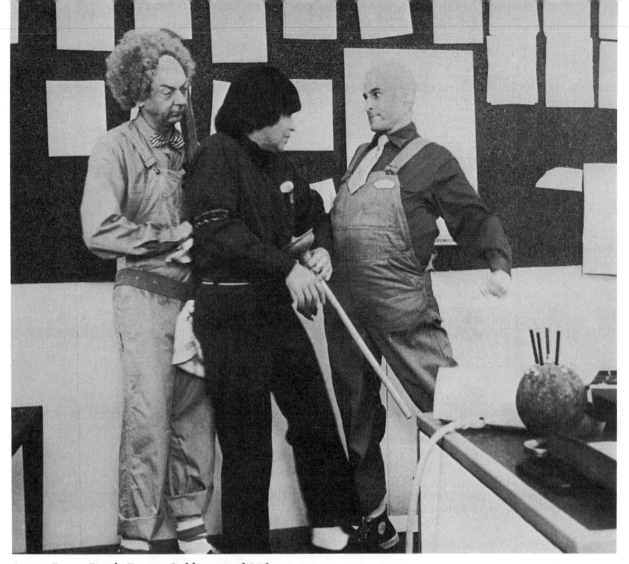

Actors Barry Pearl, Danny Goldman and Mike Tucci impersonating the Stooges in an episode of CBS' *Jessica Novak.*

The most recent impersonation of the Stooges team was broadcast in an episode of CBS' *Jessica Novak* on November 26, 1981. In this segment, written by Ira Behr, a young Stooges fan named Moe Tannenbaum solicits over two thousand signatures, including those of Merv Griffin, Danny Thomas, Joey Bishop and Steve Allen, for a petition to secure the Three Stooges their star in the Hollywood Walk of Fame. Inpersonator/Moe meets up with TV news reporter Jessica Novak in the lobby of a local movie theatre and appeals to her for support, to help inform TV viewers through her broadcast that the Stooges do not have a star in the Walk of Fame. When Novak is unable to help, Moe corners Jessica's cameraman and his assistant and convinces them to let him and his two Stooges-imposters into the newsroom.

In another scene, Moe and his two friends, Ricky and Bonelli, who play Larry and Curly, descend upon the newsroom to reenact some traditional Stooges antics. And at the same time, they convince the producer of the show to give them air time in order to promote their cause. But even their comic antics, though hilarious and well-timed, fail to impress the producer. Resigned, the mock Stooges exit scene with imposter/Curly "wooo-wooing" as the scene fades out. Curly, Larry and Moe were expertly played by Barry Pearl, Danny Goldman and Mike Tucci, respectively.

Surely, the Stooges have been imitated in just about every form known to man. It truly baffles the mind after realizing that the Stooges, perhaps, have been impersonated more than any comedy team Hollywood has known. Despite fan allegations that the team has been constantly neglected, this chapter has shown, without a shadow of a doubt, that the Three Stooges have been fully appreciated for what they are—the grand masters of comedy.

Three Stooges Deli

PO-BOYS DONUTS
GAS GROCERIES

Call-In... Carry-Out

Phone Orders
345-4322
or
345-4528

Po-Boys Sandwiches

Choice of White, Wheat, Rye, Bun

	Po-Boy	Sandwich
BOLOGNA	$1.75	$1.15
SALAMI	$1.90	$1.25
HAM	$1.90	$1.25
LUNCH LOAF	$1.90	$1.25
ROAST BEEF	$2.25	$1.45
TURKEY	$2.00	$1.30
PASTRAMI	$2.35	$1.50
CORNED BEEF	$2.35	$1.50
MEATBALL	$1.60	$1.15
SMOKED SAUSAGE	$1.90	$1.25

(Hot Mild or Italian)

ANY CHEESE ADDED 20¢ EXTRA

Stooges Specials

Choice of White, Wheat, Rye, Bun

	Po-Boy	Sandwich
LARRY'S LOG	$2.25	$1.50
Ham, Salami, Provolone Cheese		
CURLEY'S COMBO	$2.25	$1.50
Ham, Turkey, Swiss Cheese		
DELI DELITE	$2.50	$1.60
Ham, Turkey, R.B., Swiss Cheese		
HAMBURGER	$1.75	$ .75
STOOGES' BBQ	$1.75	$1.00
TUNA FISH	$1.50	$ .90
RUEBEN	$2.60	$1.75
MOE'S MUFFALOTTA	$5.75	$3.00
Ham, Salami, R.B., Provolone Cheese		
STOOGES SUB	$2.25	$1.50
Lunch Mt. Salami, Bologna, Am. & Swiss		

Deli Dinner Specials

Dinners
SERVED WITH BREAD
POTATO SALAD & COLE SLAW

RIB DINNER	$2.75
SMOKED SAUSAGE DIN.	$2.25

A' La Carte

RIBS	LB.	$2.99
SMOKED SAUSAGE	LB.	$2.99

Ask Any Stooge **Assorted Meats & Cheeses Cut to Order** Ask Any Stooge

OPEN 7 DAYS A WEEK — 6:00 A.M. to 12:00 Midnight

Located Across From Hammond Square Mall

I'VE BEEN TO THE THREE STOOGES DELI
GAS, POBOYS, GROCERIES, DONUTS

Menu and bumper sticker for the Three Stooges
Deli.

216

CHAPTER

7

A Growing Cult

IT CAN SAFELY BE SAID that a show business performer cannot achieve prominence without the support of his fans—this certainly is true regarding the Three Stooges. Their legion of fans has been responsible for many record-setting events in the team's history. Their enormous television popularity has been one of them. In spite of the fact the Stooges' films have been televised for almost a quarter of a century, their popularity among viewers has never paled.

Columbia Pictures' merchandising director, Glenn Dyckoff, reports that nearly ninety domestic television markets carry the Screen Gems' syndicated package of 190 Three Stooges comedies. The group's antics are broadcast Monday through Friday in many major cities, including New York, Chicago, San Francisco, San Diego, Philadelphia, Atlanta, Portland, Minneapolis, St. Louis and Dallas.

Various television stations in such prime areas as Chicago (WFLD-Channel 12) and New York (WPIX-Channel 11) air the Stooge comedies during adult viewing hours (as early as 10 p.m. and as late as midnight in half-hour and hour time slots). In the past, station program-directors shied away from scheduling these films in nighttime slots, since they were primarily thought to be for the children's market. Today, however, station managers are discovering that the avid Stooges fans of the 50's and 60's, who are now adults, want to re-experience the team's antics today. A station manager for KVZK-TV in Pago Pago took a survey of programming and found that the Three Stooges ranked number one against such competition as *The Wonderful World of Disney, Hawaii Five-O* and first-run network movies. Besides domestic runs, Stooges comedies are available dubbed in Japanese, Spanish, Portuguese and Italian. (The year 1981 marked the first time that Three Stooges films were seen over Italian airwaves.)

The incredible phenomenon of the Stooges' resurgence encompasses more than scheduled broadcasts of their two-reelers. Additional efforts of significance have been made to pay tribute to the Stooges. On January 25, 1981, KTLA-Channel 5 in Los Angeles broadcast two Three Stooges features, back to back—*The Three Stooges in Orbit* and *The Three Stooges Go Around the World in a Daze*—in a four-hour time slot opposite the Super Bowl game. Norman Maurer appeared on the program and recalled many intimate stories about the team. The next day, program host Tom Hatten advised Maurer that the Stooges features screened were the highest-rated Los Angeles program next to the Super Bowl, beating out all other competition. The films were part of the station's *Family Film Festival*, a program which, according to Hatten, draws primarily adult viewers and movie buffs.

In addition to normal commercial markets, the team's shorts are being played on numerous cable and pay-TV outlets nationwide. Since February 1979, Los-Angeles-based SelecTV, one of the largest subscription television services in the country, has been showing Stooges films ten times monthly after 8:30 p.m. According to Bill Mechanic, program director for SelecTV, the trio's two-reel comedies have a loyal, adult following, continue to outdraw many top feature-film entries and have about a 12 percent viewership rating (which is higher than any other non-feature selection broadcast on the station).

Realizing the potential adult Stooges market, SelecTV double-billed *Miss Sadie Thompson* (1953), starring Rita Hayworth, with *Spooks*, a 1953 3-D short featuring the Three Stooges. Mechanic maintains that *Spooks* drew 30.6 percent of SelecTV's 75,000 subscribers and was the first 3-D film ever telecast. Subscribers wanting to view the film were sent 3-D glasses with their monthly film guide.

Ted Turner's Superstation WTBS, based in Atlanta, Georgia, and broadcasting 24 hours a day, rates the Stooges comedies as the station's number one nostalgic installment which attracts nearly 60 percent of the audience. And speaking of hits, Petry Television, Inc., a firm representing a number of leading independent stations, came up with some interesting data. In a television survey, they list the following

Fan letter sent to Columbia Pictures in 1936—
complete with cut-outs of the Stooges.

titles as the most-watched black-and-white programs: *I Love Lucy, You Bet Your Life* (with Groucho Marx), *Leave it to Beaver* and *The Three Stooges*.

Stoogemania seems to triumph wherever and whenever Stooges related functions prevail, whether on television or in movie theatres. Theatre owners are catching on to the fever that is widespread and are booking Stooges film programs. Mann and United Artist theatre chains started things off by booking the 1974 film *The Three Stooges Follies*, which packed them in at every show.

Noting this remarkable find, revival theatres became keenly aware of the team's commercial value and began scheduling Three Stooges festivals. And fans were willing to shell out the $3 to $5 admission price, despite the fact that many stations broadcast these same films free. The idea of viewing them complete and uncut, in a large theatre atmosphere, piqued the interest of many fans. Even born-again Stooges fans saw these festivals as alternative events to which they could take their girlfriends or go with their boyfriends. Moreover, the greatest advantage was the clarity of the 35mm prints as opposed to scratched, edited TV prints.

Syndicated cartoon spoofing the ABC Monday Night Football commentators Don Meredith, Howard Cosell and Frank Gifford.

Samples of fan's adulation through letters to the Stooges.

One of the most memorable festivals was held on January 26, 1981, at the Tiffany Theatre on Hollywood's Sunset Strip, which featured a one night, four-hour program of Stooges shorts with Curly. Twelve shorts were shown in a program entitled *The Best of the Three Stooges* and both shows were sellouts. Lines started stretching around the block several hours before the first show. At an admission price of $3.50,

Characteristic of the Stooges cult following was Columbia's 1974 film release, *The Three Stooges Follies*.

the 300-seat theatre was filled to capacity—not with children, but with adults. The Tiffany's ticket seller estimated that more than 150 potential customers were turned away and others were undoubtedly scared away by the sight of a line three blocks long.

Because of the festival's success, the Tiffany management wound up extending the engagement of *The Best of the Three Stooges*, which was unheard of even with such classic films as *Dr. Zhivago* and *Singing in the Rain*.

The Tiffany's Three Stooges Festival realized such tremendous boxoffice that additional ones were arranged, including one comprised of comedies with Ted Healy and his Stooges. MGM hadn't issued these musical comedies to theatres since their original dates of release in 1933 and 1934. As it turned out, MGM would have been wiser to have kept them under lock and key, since fans reacted violently to them. A chorus of boos erupted at one showing as a result of too much Healy and not enough Stooges in the films. Understandably, a sizeable part of the audience went home disgruntled, commenting, "I wanted to see more of Curly!" It appears that Curly has joined the ranks of superstar-comedians in an age when superstar-comedians are scarce.

The Stooges newly found popularity was observed at another 1981 festival which took place over the July Fourth weekend. The Balboa Theatre, located in Balboa, California, sponsored a Three Stooges festival similar to the first one held at the Tiffany Theatre. This show was also a sell-out.

In the tradition of previous festivals, fans couldn't wait for the program to start and went berserk when it did. Cheers went up as each film appeared on the screen and the audience turned extremely boisterous—jeering, hollering, screaming with laughter and seeming to go totally bonkers. When a coming-attractions trailer interrupted the program at midpoint, chants echoed throughout the theatre: "We want the Stooges!" and "Stooges! Stooges! Stooges!" The shouting became so alarming that the screening of the trailer was quickly aborted.

But bedlam was reigning in revival theatres all over the country. Dan Weiss, manager of Take One Cinema in Coral Gables, Florida, can attest to this. In 1980, a local radio station, Love 94 FM, sponsored a Three Stooges Festival in his theatre. Weiss's bill was usually comprised of MGM musicals, not comedies. The result of this sudden change in programming...not one empty seat!

The Three Stooges renaissance has also overwhelmed theatre owners in Pittsburgh, New Jersey, Philadelphia, Indiana, Boston, Illinois and New York. Crowds were just as phenomenal, selling out at every program. A chain of several dozen theatres in New York followed the same successful combination of Three Stooges and Little Rascal comedies. The turnout was so tremendous that theatres held the program over for two weeks.

Revival theatres weren't the only ones keen on booking Stooges Festivals. Universities and colleges continue to program similar festivals, securing the films through local rental houses. The University of Michigan, for example, has made it a tradition, since 1966, to schedule an annual Three Stooges Festival.

The parade of Stooges enthusiasts has also invaded church groups. One in West Chester, Pennsylvania, strung together Three Stooges comedies with an organized sporting event entitled *The Three Stooges Olympics*. Soccer with an oversized ball, a well-organized game called "Bedlam" and something known as "Flamingo Football," were all part of this original event. Youths ranging from grades nine through 12 participated.

As a salute to Curly and his appetite for sandwiches, the town of Hammond, Louisiana, sports *The Three Stooges Deli*, serving sandwiches named after the Stooges. A fantastic array of Three Stooges photographs adorns the walls behind the sales counter and at times the owner has glossy reproductions for sale. T-shirts, baseball caps and drink holders are also for sale with the Deli's insignia printed on each. In addition to these novelties, customer-giveaways include Deli-menus, bumper stickers, and for a few cents, Three-Stooges-Deli matches. Some of the Deli's more notable dishes include: Larry's Log, Moe's Muffalotto, Stooges BBQ, Curly's Combo and the Stooges Sub.

These food items could be said to serve a basic need, as does The Three Stooges Fan Club, Inc., formerly operated by Morris Feinberg (Larry Fine's

The Three Stooges Deli, located in Hammond, Louisiana.

brother). The club, now headed by Gary Lassin, was originally established by Ralph Schiller in 1972 because of the increasing demand for information about the team (club address: 701 Collins Ave., Lansdale, PA 19446).

Feinberg was Schiller's successor as president of the club, which was headquartered in his town of Philadelphia until his death in 1985. The club keeps fans abreast of the latest in Three Stooges happenings through a quarterly journal, featuring articles on the team and special reports by correspondents from around the globe.

Another Stooges fan club, The Official Three Stooges Fan Club, was licensed by Columbia Pictures and Norman Maurer Productions in October 1981 and was an instant success. Ira Friedman, who formed the Official Star Wars Club, organized this second Stooges society. The club was set up primarily to promote Three Stooges posters and novelties and to inform and entertain fans through a monthly newsletter with articles written by co-workers and friends of the Stooges. The club has since discontinued its operation.

Although the Three Stooges received world-wide public acclaim and years of uninterrupted success, the Hollywood Chamber of Commerce long ignored recognizing them with a star on its Walk of Fame. The Walk, which consists of bronze stars embedded in the sidewalks of Hollywood Boulevard, are each enscribed and dedicated to a radio, television, recording or motion picture personality.

Matchbook for the Three Stooges Deli.

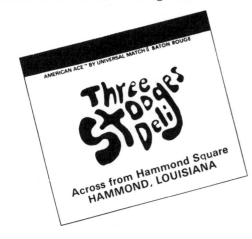

221

**Membership application for the Official Three
Stooges Fan Club, founded in 1981.**

The omission of the Stooges brought about cries
of discrimination throughout the years. The Stooges

**Fans lining up early for another standing-room-
only Three Stooges festival at the Balboa Theatre,
Balboa, California.**

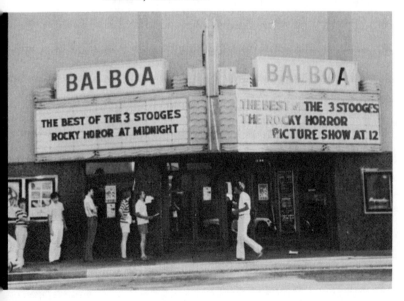

themselves once tried to rectify the situation with
their usual zaniness. In 1964, Moe, Larry and Curly-
Joe came up with the clever idea of painting a huge
gold star, at midnight, in the center of the intersection
of Hollywood and Vine. The boys planned to dress up
in painter's overalls, block off the street and paint
their names inside a gigantic, mock-up of the star.
Moe abandoned the midnight escapade at the last
minute, evidently fearing the police might arrest
them.

Following a six-month letter writing campaign
drive headed by radio/TV personality Gary Owens
and Jeff and Greg Lenburg, founders of "A Star for
The Three Stooges Committee," on August 20, 1983,
the Stooges finally received a star.

Joe Besser, representing the trio, joined Joan
Maurer and Phyllis Fine Lamond in carrying out the
honors of unveiling the star. Hordes of media turned
out to cover the event—newspapers, magazines and
television news crews—plus nearly 3,000 fans, then
considered the largest turnout for a Hollywood Walk
of Fame event. (The star, the 1,767th handed out by
the Walk of Fame, is near the famous corner of
Hollywood and Vine.)

Milton Berle, who worked with Moe, Larry and

Shemp on his 1950s television series, summed up the ceremony best, when the said: "What these men gave to the world is timeless. These great gentlemen, who brought laughter to millions and millions of people, will never be forgotten."

****

The phrase "from the ridiculous to the sublime" fits quite well here. The Stooges have literally run the gamut—from Healy's slap-happy, ridiculous Stooges to playing a sublime part in connection with one of the country's creative geniuses.

Jack Kerouac, considered a unique voice in American literature, wrote a book in 1952 called *Visions of Cody*. And it's amazing to find that Kerouac, in trying to understand America and in looking at it with

Joe Besser leads the cheers as the Stooges finally get a star on the Hollywood Walk of Fame.

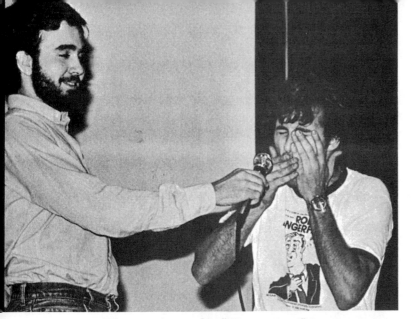

Fan covering up his "Woo-woo-woo" impersonation as a contestant in a Stooge Lookalike Festival. (Courtesy *Surburban Trib.*)

The Stooges are the official mascot of the Indiana University School of Dentistry, as shown in this reproduction of the school's T-shirt emblem. (Courtesy, Lee Prusinski.)

compassion for bygone days, had chosen to write about the Three Stooges.

In one of the passages in his book Kerouac tells his story through the person of one of his characters, Jack Duluoz, whose idol is a character named Cody. Duluoz discusses how he and Cody began talking about the Three Stooges and goes on to describe Moe.

"Moe the leader, mopish, mowbry, mope-mouthed, mealy, mad, hanking, making othersquake; whacking Curly on the iron pate, backhanding Larry (who wonders); picking up a sledgehammer, honk and ramming it down nozzle first on the flatpan of Curly's skull, boing."

Then he goes on to describe Curly and Larry. "All

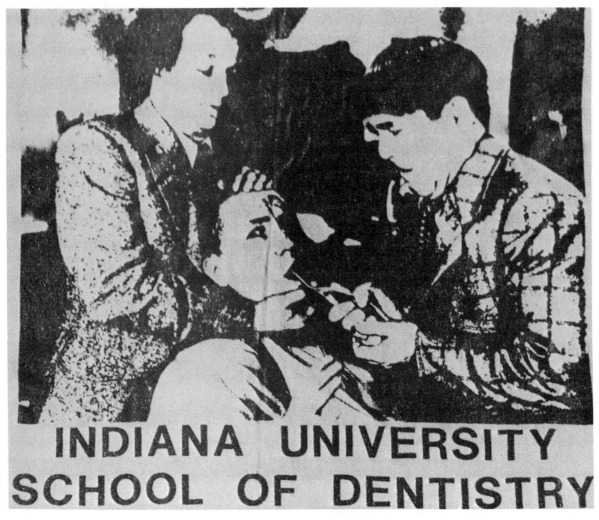

INDIANA UNIVERSITY SCHOOL OF DENTISTRY

A wrought iron weathervane, designed by Helen Howard for their Valley home's bath house as a surprise for Moe. It now rests on the cupola of Joan Maurer's garage.

Tiffany Theatre Stooges festivals.

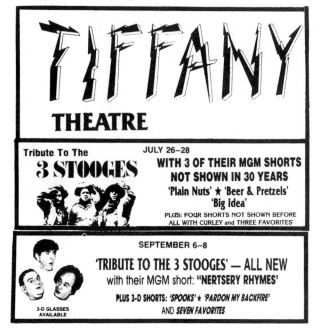

big dumb convict Curly does is muckle and yukkle and squeal, pressing his lips, shaking his old butt like jelly knotting his jello fists, eyeing Moe, who looks back and at him with that lowered and surly, "Well what are you gonna do about it." Under the thunderstorm eyebrows like the eyebrows of Beethoven completely ironbound in surls, Larry in his angelic or rather he really looks like he conned the other two to let him join the group, so they had to pay him all these years a regular share of the salary to them who work so hard with the props."

After this...how can anyone say the Stooges are "second rate"? They've withstood the test of time handsomely. As *Chicago Sun-Times* critic, Gary Deeb writes, "It looks more like Curly Howard, Larry Fine and Moe Howard may have been the cleverest practitioners of farce comedy ever to ply their trade in this country."

It's no wonder...the Three Stooges were really funny.

225

Opening title from Stooges films with Curly.

226

Filmography

The following is a complete listing of films of the Stooges with Ted Healy and the Columbia Three Stooges. Cast listings and roles were determined after exhausting still/script collections, after reviewing available cast call sheets, and after personal viewings of the films. Working titles, shooting days, production footnotes, gag sources and production sidelights are noted where available. Films are rated * to ****.

Abbreviations used throughout the filmography and television listings are defined as follows:

Key to filmography					
a	=	Art Director	m	=	Minutes or Music
ad	=	Assistant Director	md	=	Musical Director
aka	=	Also known as	p	=	Producer
ap	=	Associate Producer	ph	=	Director of Photography
Br	=	Broadcast date	Prod. No.	=	Production Number
C	=	Cast	PS	=	Prod. Sidelight(s)
CNA	=	Cast not available	RI	=	Release date
d	=	Director	RNA	=	Role not available
ds	=	Dance Sequences	scr	=	Screenplay
e	=	Film Editor	SD	=	Shooting Days
eps	=	Episode title(s)	sd	=	Set Decorator
exp	=	Executive Producer	st	=	Story
FN	=	Production Footnotes(s)	synd	=	Syndication date
l	=	Lyrics	SYN	=	Synopsis
			WT	=	Working title(s)

TED HEALY AND HIS STOOGES (Larry, Moe and Shemp)
(Fox Feature, 1930)

1. SOUP TO NUTS ** / Rl. Sept. 28 / Prod. No. 33 / 71m / *ap* A.L. Rockett / *d* Benjamin Stoloff / *st* Rube Goldberg / *scr* Rube Goldberg and Howard J. Green / *ph* Joseph Valentine / *e* Clyde Carruth / *s* Al Bruzler / C: Frances McCoy (Queenie), Stanley Smith (Carlsor), Lucile Browne (Louise), Charles Winninger (Schmidt), Hallam Cooley (Throckmorton), George Bickel (Klein) and Wm. H. Tooker (Ferguson) / SYN: In this smorgasbord of comedy, the Stooges (and Freddie Sanborn) are part-time firemen who break up a swank party, and later appear as members of an army of Mexican revolutionists.

TED HEALY AND HIS STOOGES (Larry, Moe and Curly)
MGM Shorts
1933

1. NERTSERY RHYMES *** / Rl. July 6 / Technicolor / Prod. No. 685 / 20m / *d* Jack Cummings / C: Bonnie Bonnell (Fairy Princess) / SYN: As children, the Stooges are unable to sleep in their oversized crib and ask their father, Ted Healy, to tell them a bedtime story. In order to appease them, Healy croons a comedic rendition of "The Midnight Ride of Paul Revere." When his comical tale fails to put them into slumber, Healy produces a Fairy Princess out of the boys' bedroom closet to put them to sleep with her own fairytale. Her storytelling is a success, and Ted and the Fairy Princess try tiptoeing out of the trio's room to have a night on the town. Curly wakes up, however, spots the couple together and wakes up Moe and Larry, screaming at Ted to tell them another bedtime story. Enraged, Ted brandishes a mallet and wallops his Stooges unconscious as the film fades out. / WT: *Nursery Rhymes.* / FN: *Nertsery Rhymes* was the team's first musical-comedy revue (billed as Colortone Musical Revues) and the first of two experimental two-strip Technicolor shorts for Metro. Ted Healy, Moe Howard, and Matty Brooks collaborated on the original eight-page script, as well as on scripts in the entire series.

2. BEER AND PRETZELS ** / Rl. Aug. 26 / Prod. No. 690 / 20m / *d* Jack Cummings / *m* Al Goodhart / *l* Gus Kahn / C: Bonnie Bonnell (Nightclub Singer) and Ed Brophy (Happy Hour Theatre Manager) / SYN: This brassy comedy is based on Ted Healy's controversial offstage life. Healy and his Stooges are thrown off the bill at the Happy Hour Theatre, since Ted is more interested in women then he is in performing. He promises to give up women but soon spots a statuesque blonde (Bonnie Bonnell) bending over to pick up a handkerchief. Bonnie brushes off Ted, and the Stooges insist that they better find jobs if they are going to eat. When they win jobs as head waiter and three assistants at a local nightclub, Bonnie turns up again as the nightclub's singer and belts out a medley of songs, while Moe, Larry, and Curly wreak havoc in the swank restaurant. With the club left like a battlefield, our story comes full circle when the manager fires Ted and his Stooges for demolishing the restaurant. This time Ted swears off women for good. But his promise is short-lived, as he eyes a beauteous woman leaning over and turning up her stockings. When Healy puts on the charm, however, the lady turns out to be an undercover policemen. / WT: *Beer Gardens.*

3. HELLO POP! *** / Rl. Sept. 16 / Technicolor / Prod. No. 696 / 17m / *d* Jack Cummings / *Song:* "I'm Sailing on a Sunbeam" by Irving Berlin / C: Henry Armetta, Bonnie Bonnell and the Albertina Rusch Girls (Themselves) / SYN: (Since MGM no longer has prints available of this film, the rating and following synopsis was derived from Hollywood trade paper reviews.) While putting on a costume show, Ted is beset by producer problems and aggravated by the undependability of his "pals," the Stooges. The climax comes when the Stooges slip onto the stage underneath the enormous hoopskirt of the featured vocalist, ruining the scene and the show. / WT: *Back Stage, New Musical Short by Suber,* and *Ted Healy Short.*

4. PLANE NUTS **½ / Rl. Oct. 14 / Prod. No. 680 / 20m / *d* Jack Cummings / C: Bonnie Bonnell (Herself) / SYN: In their fourth musical-comedy revue and third in black-and-white, Ted Healy and his Stooges

A newspaper ad for *Meet the Baron* (1933).

rehash their old vaudeville act intact; the film also features several other acts as well. Three-fourths of the production, however, is strewn with musical numbers taken from MGM musicals, or of Ted Healy singing his favorite love song, "The Dance Until the Dawn." The comedy usually hits a feverish pitch when the Stooges interrupt Healy during his singing segments. One sketch that appears in the film of Healy taking a

mental test was later incorporated in several of the Stooges' Columbia comedies. The film dissolves to several army musical numbers near the film's closing. The last dance number features the Albertina Rusch Girls dressed in the form of fighter airplanes! / *WT*: *Aviation Short* and *Around the World Backwards*. / *FN*: Deleted is a segment in which Ted and the Stooges board a plane and embark on a trip around the world—

only backwards. It is believed that the film was originally planned as a three-reel short or a theatrical feature. Photos of this missing sequence may be found on pages 57 and 58 of *Moe Howard & the 3 Stooges*.

1934

5. THE BIG IDEA * / Rl. May 12 / Prod. No. 628 / 20m / *d* Wm. Crowley / *ds* Sammy Lee / *C*: Bonnie Bonnell (Rubbish Girl), Muriel Evans (Becky, Healy's Wife), the Three Radio Rogues (Themselves) and the MGM Dancing Girls (Themselves) / *SYN*: Ted Healy is a frustrated script writer in search of that "big idea." He is working late in the office to finish and deliver one of his new screenplays when a building matron breaks into his office, spilling garbage on the floor and combining it with the rubbish found in Healy's office. Her constant interruptions ruin Ted's intense concentration, but the main series of noisy interruptions occurs when the Stooges enter Healy's office sounding trumpets, then squirting water in Ted's face. This turns into a running gag throughout the film, with the Stooges returning each time with a different instrument, only to douse Healy with water again and again. / *FN*: When *The Big Idea* was later re-issued, new title cards were inserted in the existing preprint material in order for Metro to cash-in on the Stooges' new-found popularity at Columbia, minus Ted Healy. Hence, the billing was changed from "Ted Healy, with Howard, Fine and Howard" to "Ted Healy and His Three Stooges." Gee, those studio people were sure clever. Film clip used in *Hollywood: The Gift of Laughter* (ABC-TV, 5/16/82).

Ted Healy and His Stooges also appeared in the following film shorts:

1933

1. HOLLYWOOD ON PARADE / Rl. by Paramount / 11m / *p* Louis Lewyn / *C*: All-Star / *SYN*: Ted Healy and his Stooges supply the laughs.

2. SCREEN SNAPSHOTS / Rl. Sept. by Columbia / 8m / *p* Harriet Parsons / *d w ph* Ralph Staub / *C*: Jack Holt, Anita Page, Una Merkel, Chico Marx and many more / *SYN*: Screen personalities are seen off the set at a Hollywood nightclub, with Ted, Moe, Larry and Curly performing some slapstick bits.

Feature Films
All were released by MGM unless otherwise noted.
1933
1. TURN BACK THE CLOCK **½ / Rl. Aug. 25 / Prod. No. 689 / 80m / *ap* Harry Rapf / *d* Edgar Selwyn / *st scr* Edgar Selwyn and Ben Hecht / *ph* Harold Rosson / *e* Frank Sullivan / *C*: Lee Tracy (Joe), Mae Clarke (Mary), Otto Kruger (Ted), Geo. Barbier (Evans), Peggy Shannon (Elvins), C. Henry Gordon (Mr. Holmes) and Clara Blandick (Joe's Mother) / *SYN*: Ted Healy and His Stooges make a brief appearance in this film, the story of a retail store owner and his

228

trials and tribulations after marrying his childhood sweetheart.

2. MEET THE BARON **½ / Rl. Oct. 20 / Prod. No. 710 / 68m / d Walter Lang / st Herman Mankiewicz and Norman Krasna / scr Allen Rivkin and P.J. Wolfson / ph Al Siegler / e James E. Newcom / C: Jack Pearl (Baron), Jimmy Durante (Joe McGoo), Zasu Pitts (Zasu), Edna May Oliver (Dean Primrose), Ben Bard (Sharlie), Henry Kolker (Real Baron), and Wm. B. Davidson (Radio Man) / SYN: In this film, Jack Pearl is a pants presser who assumes the identity of Baron Munchausen. Ted Healy is the campus janitor of Cuddles College, and calls on the Stooges, who are plumbers, to mend a leak. "Ted Healy and His Stooges nearly steal the picture" (Times-Mirror).

3. DANCING LADY **½ / Rl. Nov. 24 / Prod. No. 694 / 94m / exp David O. Selznick / ap John W. Considine / d Robert Z. Leonard / scr Allen Rivkin and P.J. Wolfson, from the novel by James W. Bellah / ph Oliver T. Marsh / ds Sammy Lee and Eddie Prinz / Songs Burton Lane and Harold Adamson, Richard Rodgers and Lorenz Hart, and Jimmy McHugh, Dorothy Fields, and Arthur Freed / e Margaret Booth / C: Joan Crawford (Janie Barlow), Clark Gable (Patch Gallagher), Franchot Tone (Tod Newton), May Robson (Mrs. Newton), Winnie Lightner (Rosette La Rue), Fred Astaire (Himself), Robert Benchley (Ward King), Ted Healy (Steve), Gloria Foy (Vivian Warner), Art Jarrett (Art), Grant Mitchell (Bradley, Sr.), Maynard Holmes (Bradley Jr.), Sterling Holloway (Author) and the Stooges (Stage Hands) / SYN: A musical-comedy extravaganza centering on the romance of singer-dancer Janie Barlow with Patch Gallagher and playboy Tod Newton. In several sequences, Healy and His Stooges, as stage manager and stage assistants, are seen with Joan Crawford.

4. MYRT AND MARGE ** / Rl. Dec. 4 by Universal / Prod. No. F8 / 65m / d Al Boasberg / st Beatrice Banyard / scr Al Boasberg / ph J.A. Valentine / Songs: M.K. Jerome / ds Jack Haskell / C: Myrtle Vail (Myrt Minter), Donna Damerel (Marge Spear), Ted Healy (Mullins), Eddie Foy, Jr. (Eddie Hanley), Grace Hayes (Grace), Trixie Friganza (Mrs. Minter), Thomas Jackson (Jackson), Ray Hedges (Clarence), Howard, Fine and Howard (Mullins' Helpers), J. Farrell MacDonald (Grady) and Bonnie Bonnell (Bonnie) / SYN: A meagerly bankrolled musical-comedy troupe is en route to New York where Myrt hopes to discover a savior in the form of a rich financial backer. "Ted Healy and his Stooges, by sticking to their own vaudeville technique, and probably undirected except for Healy, come through with a minimum of stilted moments" (Variety). FN: Reports that Healy, Howard, Fine and Howard did not appear in Myrt and Marge are erroneous. (See Moe Howard & the 3 Stooges, p. 58. Bottom photo is from Myrt and Marge, not Dancing Lady.)

1934

5. FUGITIVE LOVERS **½ / Rl. Jan. 5 / Prod. No. 716 / 84m / ap Lucien Hubbard / d Richard Boleslavsky / st Ferdinand Reyher and Frank Read scr Albert Hackett, Frances Goodrich, and Geo. B. Seitz / a Arnold Gillespie / ph Ted Tetzlaff / e Wm. S. Gray / C: Robert Montgomery (Porter), Madge Evans (Letty), Ted Healy (Withington), Nat Pendleton (Legs), C. Henry Gordon (Daly), Ruth Selwyn (Babe), Larry Fine, Moe and Jerry Howard (Three Julians) / SYN: A chorus girl (Madge Evans) takes a bus trip west in hope of becoming a star. Her unwelcome suitor (Nat Pendleton) keeps following her from bus station to bus station, determined to win her love. A comic drunk (Ted Healy) and three assistant drunks (the Stooges) are also passengers. / WT: Overland Bus and Transcontinental Bus.

6. HOLLYWOOD PARTY **½ / Rl. June 1 / Prod. No. 695 / 70m / d Edmund Goulding, Russel Mach, Richard Boleslavsky (musical sequences), George Stevens (comedy sequences), Sam Wood (one skit), Allan Dwan (added scenes), Charles Reisner (remaining scenes)/ scr Howard Dietz and Arthur Kober / m Richard Rodgers and Lorenz Hart, Walter Donaldson and Gus Kahn, Nacio Herb Brown and Arthur Freed / ds Seymour Felix, Geo. Hale, and David Gould / Animated cartoon sequences courtesy of Walt Disney Productions / Color sequence photographed by Technicolor / ph James Wong Howe / e Geo. Boemler / C: Laurel and Hardy (Themselves), Jimmy Durante (Jimmy), Charles Butterworth (Harvey Clemp), Polly Moran (Henrietta), Lupe Velez (Lupe), Frances Williams (Herself), Jack Pearl (Baron Munchausen), Eddie

In a deleted scene, Billy Wolfstone, "Little Curly," asks his screen father "Big Curly," to explain the climax of the story in *Three Little Pigskins* (1934).

Quillan (Bob), June Clyde (Linda), Geo. Givot (Duke), Richard Carle (Knapp), Ben Bard (Charley), Tom Kennedy (Beavers), Mickey Mouse (Himself) and Ted Healy and His Stooges / SYN: Jimmy Durante throws an elegant Hollywood party, inviting affluent people of all-professional nature. At the same time, however, Durante tries increasing his collection of animal artifacts by influencing Baron Munchausen (Jack Pearl) to sell him his menagerie. Outside Durante's party, Ted Healy and His Stooges, posing as reporter and photographers, try to crash this swank affair. A group of professors mistake the Stooges for prime examples of Cro-Magnon Man! / WT: Broadway to Hollywood. / FN: None of the above mentioned directors received screen credit. Their names were expertly compiled by author Randy Skretvedt. The exact same footage of the Stooges was reused in Robert Youngson's 1964 film compilation, MGM's Big Parade of Comedy.

THE THREE STOOGES (Moe, Larry and Curly)
Columbia Shorts
1934

1. WOMAN HATERS **½ / A Musical Novelty / Rl. May 5 / 21m / Prod. No. 112 / d Archie Gottler / st Jerome S. Gottler / ph Joseph August / e James Sweeney / s Edward Bernds / C: Marjorie White (Mary, Larry's Wife), Monty Collins (Mr. Zero, member), Bud Jamison (Club Chairman), Snowflake (Baggage Man), Jack Norton (Wedding Member), Tiny Sandford (Cop), Geo. Gray (Man on Crutches), Walter Brennan (Train Conductor), A.R. Haysel, Don Roberts, Les Goodwin, Charles Richman and Gilbert C. Emery (Bit Men) / SYN: Larry reneges on the Woman Haters Club's oath when he secretly marries a girl named Mary. Moe and Curly learn of the marriage during Mary and Larry's honeymoon train trip west. While inside Moe and Curly's train berth, Mary informs them that Larry is her husband and that their earlier no-women agreement is no longer binding. To prove her point, she pushes them out the train's window. / SD: 4 (T 3/27 to F 3/30/34) / FN: When the film was originally released, Marjorie White received top-billing over the Three Stooges, who were credited as "Jerry Howard, Larry Fine, and Moe Howard." White was killed in an automobile accident shortly after the production. (See Moe Howard & the 3 Stooges, p. 78.)

2. PUNCH DRUNKS *** / Rl. July 13 / Prod. No. 116 / 17m / d Lou Breslow / scr Jack Cluett / st Jerry Howard, Larry Fine, and Moe Howard / ph Henry Freulich / e Robert Carlisle / C: Dorothy Granger (Girl), Arthur Houseman (Fight Timekeeper), William Irving (Second Plug Ugly), Jack "Tiny" Lipson (First Plug Ugly), Billy Bletcher (Fight Announcer), Al Hill (Killer Kilduff, the Champ), Chuck Callahan (Restaurant Mgr.) and Larry McCrath (Referee) / SYN: Moe, a boxing manager, and Larry, a violinist, discover that when Larry plays

"Pop Goes the Weasel," Curly explodes and starts punching any available target. Consequently, Moe offers to manage Curly as the ring's newest boxing sensation and hires Larry to play "Weasel" at ringside, enabling Curly to win each fight. During the championship bout, Larry's violin gets broken and he returns with a campaign bandwagon, blaring the "Weasel" song, which revives Curly who wins the fight. / WT: Symphony of Punches and A Symphony of Punches. / SD: 4 (W 5/2 to SA 4/5/34) / FN: Punch Drunks is the only Stooges film to credit the Stooges as writers. In the original treatment, Curly turns boxer and wins every fight when Fuzzy (Larry) plays "Stars and Stripes Forever." According to director Lou Breslow, the song was changed from "Stars and Stripes" to "Weasel" because the latter was public domain and "the only song that was half-funny." Curly becoming fighting mad upon hearing "Weasel" was redone in The Three Stooges Go Around the World in a Daze (1963). Remade as A Hit With a Miss (12/13/45) with Shemp Howard. (See Moe Howard & the 3 Stooges, pp. 74-5, 78.)

3. MEN IN BLACK ***½ / Rl. Sept. 28 / Prod. No. 152 / 19m / Stooges No. 1 / d Raymond McCarey / st scr Felix Adler / ph Benjamin Kline / e James Sweeney / C: Dell Henderson (Dr. Graves), Jeanie Roberts (Hiccupping Nurse), Ruth Hiatt (Whispering Nurse), Billy Gilbert (D. T. Patient), Little Billy (Himself), Bud Jamison (Doctor), Hank Mann (Laborer), Bobby Callahan (Messenger), Phyllis Crane (Anna Conda), Arthur West, Joe Mills (Bit Men), Irene Coleman, Carmen Andre, Helen Splane, Kay Hughes, Eve Reynolds, Eve Kimberly, Lucile Watson, Billie Stockton, Betty Andre (Bit Nurses), Arthur Rankin, Neal Burns, Joe Fine, Charles Dorety (Attendants) and Charles King (Anesthesiologist) / SYN: At the Los Arms Hospital, three brainless interns—Doctors Howard, Fine and Howard—promise Dr. Graves, the hospital superintendent, that they will devote the rest of their lives to the glorious cause of "duty and humanity." The first official Three Stooges comedy. Nominated for an Academy Award. / SD: 4 (W 8/29 to SA 9/1/34) / FN: On August 8, 1934, Columbia moved its comedy department from Gower Street to the California Studio on Beechwood Drive. In Men in Black, the Stooges ad-libbed the bizarre medical terminology for their surgical instruments, and several scenes were also cut from Felix Adler's script, including an alternate ending in which the Stooges meet Nell, "their" girl. She turns out to be siamese triplets!

4. THREE LITTLE PIGSKINS *** / Rl. Dec. 8 / Prod. No. 156 / 20m / d Raymond McCarey / st scr Felix Adler and Griffin Jay / ph Henry Freulich / e James Sweeney / C: Lucille Ball (Daisy Simms), Gertie Green (Lulu Banks), Phyllis Crane (Molly Gray), Walter Long (Joe Stacks), Joseph Young (Pete, Joe's Henchman), Wm. Irving (Photographer), Joe Levine (Little Larry), Alex

Hirschfield (Little Moe), Billy Wolfstone (Little Curly), Bobby Burns (Street Man), Jimmie Phillips, Johnny Kascier, Milton Douglas, Harry Bowen, and Lynton Brent (Bit Men) / SYN: Larry, Moe, and Curly are mistaken for the Three Horsemen, Boulder Dam University's top football players. Joe Stacks, a two-bit gangster, wagers his money on these exciting athletes to win the big football matchup of the week. But he soon learns that the boys' knowledge of football is very limited when the Stooges lose the game. Upset over this defeat, Stacks empties his gun into the derrieres of the fleeing Stooges. Loyola University's football team appears in the game-action scenes photographed at Gilmore Stadium in Los Angeles. / SD: 4 (TH 10/25 to F 10/26, and M 10/29 to T 10/30/34) FN: On many occasions, Moe Howard reported that Three Little Pigskins ends with the Stooges relating the climax of the story to their three children. According to an earlier draft script, the scene was planned as an "alternate ending." Stills reprinted in Moe Howard & the 3 Stooges, pp. 6, 7, 68, suggest that the segment was indeed filmed, but evidently, the ending was cut from the final release print. / PS: Larry Fine once recalled that numerous injuries were sustained during production of the film. Curly broke his leg after riding down the dumbwaiter, and Larry lost a tooth when Joseph Young, actor Robert Young's brother, socked him in the jaw. (See Moe Howard & the 3 Stooges, pp. 79 and 81.)

1935

5. HORSES' COLLARS *** / Rl. Jan 10 / Prod. No. 159 / 17m / d Clyde Bruckman / st scr Felix Adler / ph John Boyle / e James Sweeney / C: Dorothy Kent (Nell), Fred Kohler (Double Deal Decker), Leo Willis (Lobo), Fred Kelsey (Detective Hyden Zeke), Allyn Drake (Dance Hall Girl), Slim Whittaker (Cowboy), Nelson McDowell (Bartender), Milton Douglas (Waiter), Johnny Kascier (Moe's Double), Bert Young (Curly's Double), Ed Brandenberg (Larry's Double), Bobby Callahan (Bit Drunk), June Gittleson, Alice Dahl and Nancy Caswell (Bit Girls) / SYN: Double Deal Decker has just robbed poor, sweet Nell of her deed to the ranch, and she hires detective Hyden Zeke to send her three of his best men. Who else comes to her but the Three Stooges. The boys find Decker at a local saloon and here it is disclosed that Curly goes bonkers every time he sees a mouse. When the Stooges attempt to regain the deed, Curly becomes delirious upon spotting a squiggly mouse and clobbers the villains before Moe and Larry can calm him down. / SD: 4 (F 11/23 to SA 11/24, and M 11/26 to T 11/27/34) / FN: Painted-on eyelids gag was later re-enacted in Slaphappy Sleuths (11/9/50).

6. RESTLESS KNIGHTS ***½ / Rl. Feb. 20 / Prod. No. 160 / 16½m / d Charles Lamont / st scr Felix Adler / ph Benjamin Kline / e Wm. A. Lyon / C: Geneva Mitchell (Queen), Walter Brennan (Father), Geo.

Baxter (Count Boris), Chris Franke (Announcer), James Howard (Wrestler), Bud O'Neill (Wrestler), Stanley Blystone (Captain of the Guard), Ernie Young (Henchman), Billy Francy (Attendant), Jack Duffy (Bit Guard), Lynton Brent, Bob Burns, Wm. Irving, Joe Perry, Al Thompson, Bert Young, Dutch Hendrian (Bit Men), Marie Wells, Eadie Adams, Corinne Williams, Dorothy King and Patty Price (Bit Women) /

clubs by mistake. / *SD*: 4 (W 12/19 to SA 12/22/34) *PS*: Charles Lamont, who started directing in 1918 and later piloted many Abbott and Costello features, had his own technique for handling the Stooges: "I made them follow the script. If there was anything I didn't like, I'd cut it out. I was never a great admirer of ad-libs."

7. POP GOES THE EASEL *** / Rl March

into Kraft's College of Arts, ruining the studio with a clay-throwing free-for-all./ *FN*: Moe's daughter, Joan, and Larry's daughter, Phyllis, appear together in the hopscotch sequence. It was the only time the two girls appeared with their fathers in a Stooges comedy.

8. UNCIVIL WARRIORS ***½ / Rl. April 26 / Prod. No. 165 / 20m / *d* Del Lord / *st scr*

Lobby card from *Pop Goes the Easel* (1935).

SYN: The Stooges are appointed the Queen's royal bodyguards but wind up before a firing squad when she is kidnapped. Their deaths, however, are avoided when the soldiers are distracted by a pretty girl undressing near her window. The Stooges quickly escape, as the guards enjoy their peep show, and track down the Queen, who is tied up in a wine cellar not far from her captors. Curly leads the kidnappers, one by one, past Moe and Larry, who clobber them unconscious with their clubs. While all of this continues, the Queen breaks loose of her bonds and strides past Moe and Larry, getting smashed on the head with their

29 / Prod. No. 163 / 20m / *d* Del Lord / *st scr* Felix Adler / *e* James Sweeney / *ph* Henry Freulich / *C*: Bobby Burns (Prof. Fuller), Jack Duffy (Bearded Man), Elinor Vandivere (Dignified Woman), Phyllis Fine, Joan Howard (Girls Playing Hopscotch), Phyllis Crane (Model in Tights) and Wm. Irving (Man Curly Asks for Meal) / *SYN*: Jobless, the Stooges decide that the only way to find employment is to create work. So they grab three brooms in front of a nearby novelty store and begin cleaning up the sidewalks. The store's owner, however, views this act of kindness as an act of robbery and screams for the police, who chase the Stooges right

Felix Adler / *ph* John Stumar / *e* Charles Hochberg / *C*: Ted Lorch (Colonel Filbert), Lew Davis (Bit Orderly), Marvin Loback (Bit Colonel), Billy Engle (Bit Captain), Ford West (Lt. Colonel), Si Jenks (Major), Bud Jamison (General Butts), Phyllis Crane (Judith), Celeste Edwards (Clementine), Lou Archer (Goofy Soldier), James C. Morton (Northern General), Charles Dorety, Heinie Conklin, Jack Kenny (Bit Soldiers), Hubert Diltz, Charles Cross, Geo. Gray, Jack Rand, Harry Keaton (Bit Soldiers) and Wes Warner (Stuntman) / *SYN*: During the Civil War, a Northern General summons three undercover agents, Operators 12

231

(Larry), 14 (Moe) and 15 (Curly), to pose as Southern officers, Lieutenant Duck, Capt. Dodge, and Major Hyde. Their mission is to recover enemy secrets from Colonel Butts's mansion. Later that evening, as part of their plan, the Stooges socialize with the Colonel's daughter, Judith, and Curly offers to help frost a layer cake. He pays more attention to Judith, however, and accidentally frosts a quilted potholder, resulting in an attack of coughing feathers after everyone has eaten the cake. Later, to avoid discovery, Larry and Curly leave the room at separate moments to return disguised as Moe's father and mother. Mr. and Mrs. Dodge. Their masquerade is successful until they are asked the whereabouts of the Dodge's baby. Curly's delirious reaction prompts Moe to dash outside and steal any baby that resembles the real one. Moe finds one alright, only it turns out to be black. / *SD*: 4 (W 3/13 to F 3/15, and M 3/18/35). / *FN*: Initially, the characters of Duck, Dodge, and Hyde were supposed to be called Greps, Burp, and Belch. The "Coughing Up Feathers" gag was redone in *Three Hams on Rye* (9/7/50). "Charlie, the Guy with the Goofy Limp" bit was revived in *From Nurse to Worse* (8/23/40) and *Hold That Lion* (7/17/47).

9. PARDON MY SCOTCH *** / Rl. Aug 1 / Prod. No. 168 / 19m / *d* Del Lord / *st scr* Andrew Bennison / *ph* George Meehan / *e* James Sweeney / *C*: Nat Carr (Mr. Martin), James C. Morton (J.T. Walton), Billy Gilbert (Signor Louis Balero Cantino), Grace Goodall (Mrs. Walton), Barlowe Borland (Bit Scotchman), Scotty Dunsmuir (Bit Scotchman), Gladys Gale (Mrs. Martin), Wilson Benge (1st Butler), Alec Craig (Bit Bagpiper), Al Thompson (Jones), Johnny Kascier (Moe's Double), Symona Boniface, Pauline High (Bit Party Guests), Billy Bletcher, Bill Irving (Bit Men), Ettore Compana (Bit Singer), Nena Compana (Bit Piano Player) and Geo. Gray (Bit Customer) / *SYN*: The Stooges are hired as handymen at Jones's Drugstore to wait on their boss's customers during his short absence. Martin, a local bootlegger, enters the store and asks the trio for a pick-me-up. The boys rush to the pharmacy department and mix every conceivable liquid into an old boot, which Martin guzzles down later. Impressed with the brew, Martin offers the Stooges a chance to make thousands of dollars. All they have to do is masquerade as the McSnort Brothers, three Scottish distillers, and crash a party at J.T. Walton's house to sell their "Breath of Heather" to his distinguished guests. At the party, Martin suggests that the Stooges haul in a keg of their homemade Scotch for everyone to taste. All is well until the trio has trouble driving a spigot into the huge barrel. Impatient, Moe raises his mallet and smacks the cask a tremendous blow, causing the keg to explode into a fountain of foam, dousing the party guests. / *SD*: 4 (TH 4/11 to SA 4/13 and M 4/15/35) / *FN*: The "Point to Your Right" routine was later used in *Four for Texas*. Mixing of liquids in a worn-out boot can also be seen in *Out West*

(4/24/47), *All Gummed Up* (12/18/47), *Bubble Trouble* (10/8/53), and *Pals and Gals* (6/3/54). Likewise, the segment involving flipping grapes into an opera singer's mouth appears (changed to cherries) in *Micro-Phonies* (11/15/45). "Roll on the Fork" gag was lifted from Chaplin's *The Gold Rush* (1925).

10. HOI POLLOI **** / Rl. Aug. 29 / Prod. No. 207 / 19m / *d* Del Lord / *st scr* Felix Adler / *ph* Benjamin Kline / *e* John Rawlins *C*: Harry Holmes (Prof. Rich), Robert Graves (Prof. Nichols), Bud Jamison (Butler), Grace Goodall (Mrs. Rich), Betty McMahon (Nichols' Daughter), Phyllis Crane (Nichols' Daughter), Geneva Mitchell (Dance Instructor), Kathryn Kitty McHugh (Duchess, Curly's Dance Partner), James C. Morton, Wm. Irving, Arthur Rankin, Robert McKenzie, Celeste Edwards, Harriett DeBussman, Mary Dees, Blanche Payson, Geo. B. French, Gail Arnold, Don Roberts and Billy Mann (Party Guests) / *SYN*: In a cafe, two educators are seen discussing what factors influence the de-

Lobby card from *Three Little Beers* (1935).

velopment of human personality. Professor Rich believes "Environment is the keynote to social distinction," while Professor Nichols argues that "Heredity is the backbone of all social life." Nichols then wagers ten thousand dollars that he can produce—through exposure to the proper environment—a regular "social lion" from the lowest strata of life. He picks three rubbish workers, the Stooges, for his experiment. Following months of tutoring, Nichols unleashes the boys at a swank party, but the Stooges' old habits resurface and become contagious with the party-goers, causing a full-scale war. Having had enough of such vulgar behavior, the Stooges exit Professor

Nichols' mansion in tuxedos and top hats. / *SD*: 4 (TH 5/2 to SA 5/4, and M 5/6/35) / *FN*: Remade as *Half-Wits' Holiday* (1/9/47) and *Pies and Guys* (6/12/58). Stock footage used in *In the Sweet Pie and Pie* (10/16/41). Spring on the trousers gag also seen in *Asleep at the Switch* (1923) with Ben Turpin, in the Stooges' *An Ache in Every Stake* (8/22/41) and in *Have Rocket Will Travel* (1959).

11. THREE LITTLE BEERS ***½ / Rl. Nov. 28 / Prod. No. 210 / 17m / *p* Jules White / *d* Del Lord / *st scr* Clyde Bruckman / *ph* Benjamin Kline / *e* Wm. Lyon / *C*: Bud Jamison (A. Panther), Nanette Crawford, Eve Reynolds (Girls on the Golf Course), Frank Terry (Golfer), Harry Semels (Gardener), Jack "Tiny" Lipson (Foreman), Eddie Laughton (Desk Relief Clerk), Geo. Gray (Caddy) and Stanley Blystone (Cement Layer) / *SYN*: The Panther Brewery Co. is sponsoring a big golf tournament and three of its employees, the Stooges, enter the competition even though they have never played the game before! The golf course, however, never looks the same after the Stooges are through practicing. Curly's ball gets stuck in a tree and he chops down the tree in order to retrieve the ball. Larry, meanwhile, gets distracted by a small root sticking out of the ground, and starts tugging on it. He keeps yanking on the root until, finally, the course looks like a disjointed jigsaw puzzle. It comes as no surprise that the Stooges are chased off the golf course. / *SD*: 4 (W 10/9 to SA 10/12/35) / *FN*: The "Press, Press, Pull" gag later appeared in *Even As I.O.U.* (9/28/42). Beer trucks and rolling barrels also can be seen in *What No Beer* (1933) with Buster Keaton.

232

12. ANTS IN THE PANTRY *** / Rl. Feb. 6 / Prod. No. 218 / 17½m / *ap* Jules White / *d* Preston Black / *st scr* Al Giebler / *ph* Benjamin Kline / *e* Wm. Lyon / *C:* Clara Kimball Young (Mrs. Burlap), Harrison Greene (Herman Mouser), Bud Jamison (Prof. Repulso), Isabelle LaMal (Clara), Vesey O'Davoren (Gawkins, the Butler), Douglas Gerrard (Lord Stoke Pogis), Anne O'Neal (Matron), James C. Morton, Arthur Rowlands, Bert Young, Lou Davis, Ron Wilson, Bobby Burns, Lynton Brent, Arthur Thalasso (Bit Men), Phyllis Crane (Debutante), Al Thompson (Dignified Man), Helen Martinez (Maid), Charles Dorety (Bit Man), Hilda Title (Stenographer), Elaine Waters, Althea Henley, Idalyn Dupre, Stella LeSaint, Flo Promise and Gay Waters (Bit Women) / *SYN:* The Stooges are pest exterminators for the Lightning Pest Control company and their boss, Herman Mouser, orders them to start stirring up some business if they plan on keeping their jobs. The Stooges select a swank mansion as their first target in which to drum up some new business. As part of their plan, the trio bugs the house—literally—with ants, mice, and termites and rush in to ward off the pests when the owner, Mrs. Burlap, screams for help. But, as expected, the Stooges are no help at all. Later, however, Moe, Larry and Curly make up for their blunders when they enter Burlap's fox hunt. Curly, suffering from a terrible head cold, temporarily becomes the hero when his sinuses clear upon smelling what he thinks is a fox, but is actually a skunk! / *WT: Pardon My Ants* / *SD:* 4 (W 12/11 to SA 12/14/35) / *FN:* Partially remade as *The Pest Man Wins* (12/6/51). (See *Moe Howard & the 3 Stooges*, p. 81.)

13. MOVIE MANIACS *** / Rl. Feb. 20 / Prod. No. 213 / 18m / *p* Jules White / *d* Del Lord / *st scr* Felix Adler / *ph* Benjamin Kline / *e* Wm Lyon / *C:* Bud Jamison (Fuller Rath),   Lois Lindsey (Sound Stage Girl), Althea Henley (Sound Stage Girl), Kenneth Harlan (Leading Man), Mildred Harris (Leading Lady), Harry Semels (Dir. Cecil Z. Sweinhardt), Antrim Short (Cameraman), Jack Kenney, Charles Dorety, Elaine Waters (Studio Employees), Bert Young (Asst. Cameraman), Hilda Title (Script Girl) and Eddie Laughton (Grip) / *SYN:* With aspirations of becoming movie stars, the Stooges sneak into the Carnation Pictures Studio and; mistaken for the new management team from the East, gain complete control of the lot from the general manager, Fuller Rath. Showing off their new authority, the Stooges invade a movie sound stage and force director Cecil Z. Sweinhardt and his cast to quit. Moe becomes the new director and Curly and Larry fill in as Carnation's romantic screen couple. When Rath learns that the Stooges are imposters, however, he chases them off the set with the help of two studio guards, right into the lion's den. After a narrow escape, Moe, Larry and Curly race out the studio in a limousine, with the lion inside, for parts unknown. / *WT: G-A-G*

Lobby card from *Ants in the Pantry* (1936).

Men. / *SD:* 4 (F 10/25 to SA 10/26, and M 10/28 to T 10/29/35) / *FN:* Deleted is an alternate film ending—the Stooges accidentally burn down the studio.

14. HALF-SHOT SHOOTERS *** / Rl. April 30 / Prod. No. 225 / 19m / *ap* Jules White / *d* Preston Black / *st scr* Clyde Bruckman / *ph* Benjamin Kline / *e* Charles Hochberg / *C:* Stanley Blystone (Sgt. MacGillicuddy), Vernon Dent (Restaurant Man, Dent), Harry Semels (Capt. Burke) and Johnny Kascier (Soldier) / *SYN:* With World War I over, Sergeant MacGillicuddy wakes the Stooges and beats them up for sleeping through the entire war; they receive medals of valor for their wounds. Years later and unemployed, the Stooges accidentally sign up again with the Army and meet up with their old comrade, Sergeant MacGillicuddy, who's assigned to their regiment. The Stooges' first duty is to retrieve ammunition for target practice. During their absence, however, target practice is postponed because Admiral Hawkins' flagship is late in arriving. Unaware of the news, the Stooges fire the cannon and blow up the Admiral's flagship./*SD:* 4 (W 3/18 to SA 3/21/36). / *FN:* The Hague, Holland's film censorship board, blocked both *Half-Shot Shooters* and *Hoi Polloi* from being shown in that country.

15. DISORDER IN THE COURT **½ / Rl. May 30 / Prod. No. 217 / 16½m / *ap* Jules White / *d* Preston Black / *st scr* Felix Adler / *ph* Benjamin Kline / *e* Wm. Lyon / *C:* Susan Karaan (Gail Tempest), Dan Brady (Juror), Tiny Jones (Juror), Bill O'Brien (Juror), Bud Jamison (Defense Attorney), Harry Semels (District Attorney), Edward LeSaint (Judge), Hank Bell (Clerk), James C. Morton (Bailiff), Nick Baskovitch, Arthur Thalasso and Ed Mull (Men in Hallway)

SYN: Kirk Robbin is found dead at the Black Bottom Cafe, with club dancer Gail Tempest found standing over his body holding a gun. Did she kill him? To find the answer, Larry, Moe and Curly are called to appear as star witnesses in the murder trial. Throughout their testimony, a trained parrot and witness keeps repeating, "Find the letter." The Stooges break the case wide open when they recover the letter, which is attached to the parrot's claw and proves the dancer's innocence. / *WT: Disorder in the Courtroom* / *SD:* 4 (W 4/1 to F 4/3, and M 4/6/36) / *FN:* When Moe demonstrates on Curly how Buck Wing shoved Kirk Robbin's skull into a letter press, a rubber head was used to give the effect of Curly's noggin being twisted out of shape. Curly's courtroom testimony is borrowed from *Sidewalks of New York* (1931) with Buster Keaton, directed by Jules White and Zion Myers.

16. A PAIN IN THE PULLMAN **½ / Rl. June 27 / Prod. No. 223 / 18m / *ap* Jules White / *d st scr* Preston Black / *ph* Benjamin Kline / *e* Wm. Lyon / *C:* Bud Jamison (Johnson), James C. Morton (Paul ˙Pain), Eddie Laughton (Train Conductor), Loretta Andrews, Ethelreda Leopold, Gale Arnold (Show Girls), Ray Turner (Porter), Mary Lou Dix (Karen), Hilda Title (Show Girl), Joe the Monkey, Phyllis Crane (Girl Curly Kisses), Eddie Laughton (Train Conductor) and Bobby Burns (Man in Berth) / *SYN:* The Stooges are an unemployed vaudeville act living at Mrs. Hammond Eggerley's boarding house, and later fill in for the Eggnog Brothers in a big musical revue, *The Panics of 1936*. Behind in their rent, Moe, Larry and Curly, with their pet monkey, Joe, sneak out of the boarding house and rush to catch a train containing the rest of the show's cast, including Paul Pain, the leading man

(he wears a toupee). On board Joe and the Stooges prove to be nothing but a *pain* for Pain! Joe complicates matters when he wreaks havoc with the sleeping passengers by pulling the emergency cord to stop the train. / *SD*: 4 (W 4/29 to F 5/1, and M 5/4/36) / *FN*: A remake of *Show Business* (8/20/32) with Thelma Todd and Zasu Pitts, directed by Jules White. Ending was reused in *A-Ducking They Did Go* (4/7/39). (See *Moe Howard & the 3 Stooges*, pp. 81-2.)

17. FALSE ALARMS **½ / Rl. Aug. 16 / Prod. No. 224 / 18m / *ap* Jules White / *d* Del Lord / *st scr* John Grey / *ph* Benjamin Kline / *e* Charles Hochberg / *C*: Stanley Blystone (Capt.), June Gittelson, (Minnie) and Johnny Grey (First Fireman) / *SYN*: Larry, Moe, and Curly are inept firemen, taking showers when the fire alarm sounds, almost losing their jobs as a result. Despite this near-catastrophe, Curly is invited to a party by his girl friend, where two other girls insist that Curly call Moe and Larry to join them. Rather than telephone them, Curly steps outside and triggers the city's fire alarm system, which rings not only at the Stooges' firehouse but at every other station in the county. Moe and Larry make it to the girls house by borrowing the chief's brand new automobile, arriving minutes before the other fire departments respond to the alarm. Disaster strikes, however, when the Stooges and the girls take a pleasure jaunt in the chief's car, totalling it in an accident. / *SD*: 4 (T 5/19 to F 5/22/36).

18. WHOOPS I'M AN INDIAN *** / Rl. Sept. 11 / Prod. No. 226 / 17m / *ap* Jules White / *d* Del Lord / *st* Searle Kramer and Herman Boxer / *scr* Clyde Bruckman / *ph* Benjamin Kline / *e* Charles Hochberg / *C*: Bud Jamison (Pierre), Elaine Waters and Beatrice Blynn (Girls) / *SYN*: In Lobo City, bunco men Moe, Larry and Curly escape a "hanging jury" following some sleight-of-hand tricks during a poker game between them and French-Canadian trooper, Pierre. Back at his cabin, Pierre learns that his wife has left him for Chief Moulting Eagle, an Indian Chief, and vows to kill all Indians. Sometime later at another saloon, Pierre again meets up with the Stooges, only this time they are garbed as Indians. Although he hasn't forgotten his pledge, Pierre soon weakens at the sight of Curly dressed like an Indian squaw and marries him (her). When Pierre realizes Curly is an imposter, however, a chase evolves with the Stooges taking refuge in the city's jail. / *WT: Frontier Daze.* / *SD*: 4 (W 6/3 to SA 6/6/36).

19. SLIPPERY SILKS **½ / Rl. Dec. 27 / Prod. No. 221 / 17½m / *ap* Jules White / *d* Preston Black / *st scr* Ewart Adamson / *ph* Benjamin Kline / *e* Wm. Lyon / *C*: Vernon Dent (Mr. Morgan, Cabinet Owner), Robert Williams (Boss Romani), Symona Boniface (Lady Customer), Elaine Waters, Beatrice Blynn, Martha Tibbetts, Beatrice Curtis (Fashion Show Women), Mary Lou Dix, Gale Arnold, Loretta Andrews (Fashion Show Models), Gertrude Messenger and Hilda Title (Models' Assistants) / *SYN*: Carpenters Larry, Moe and Curly find working in an antique shop difficult, as they break a valuable Ming vase belonging to Mr. Morgan, the irate owner. Later, they inherit

Lobby card from *Grips, Grunts and Groans* (1937).

their uncle's ultra-smart Fifth Avenue Dress Salon and stage their first fashion show, during which they meet up again with the angry vase owner, causing a massive cream-puff melee. / *SD*: 4 (W 6/10 to F 6/12, and M 6/15/36). (See *Moe Howard & the 3 Stooges*, pp. 88 and 95.)

1937

20. GRIPS, GRUNTS, AND GROANS * / Rl. Jan. 15 / Prod. No. 259 / 19m / *ap* Jules White / *d* Preston Black / *st* Searle Kramer and Herman Boxer / *scr* Clyde Bruckman / *ph* Benjamin Kline / *e* Charles Nelson / *C*: Harrison Greene (Ivan Bustoff), Casey Columbo (Tony, the Fight Promoter), Herb Stagman (Pinkie, Sparring Partner), Chuck Callahan (Waiter), Blackie Whiteford (Mugg), Elaine Waters (Perfume Girl), Cy Schindell (Ironhead), Tony Chavez, Budd Fine, Sam Lufkin, Bill Irving and Harry Wilson (Bit Men) / *SYN*: Moe, Larry and Curly win jobs at the Hangover Athletic Club as trainers and sparring partner, respectively, to the World Champion Wrestler, Ivan Bustoff. The night before the big match, Bustoff gets drunk and Curly has a bout with a woman's bottle of *Wild Hyacinth* (a perfume which drives him wild). Before Bustoff's championship bout, Moe learns that Tony, the fight promoter, has wagered a huge bankroll on Bustoff to win. But when Curly and Larry accidentally drop dumbbells on Bustoff's head, the champ is unable to answer the bell and Moe makes Curly take his place, disguised as Bustoff. During the match, however, Curly does miserably until Moe grabs a lady spectator's bottle of *Wild Hyacinth*. The scent of the perfume not only enables Curly to win the fight but to knock out everyone else in sight! / *SD*: 4 (M 11/2 to T 11/5/36).

21. DIZZY DOCTORS * / Rl. March 19 / Prod. No. 263 / 17½m / *ap* Jules White / *d* Del Lord / *scr* Al Ray / *st* Charles Melson / *ph* Benjamin Kline / *e* Charles Nelson / *C*: June Gittelson (Curly's Wife), Eva Murray (Larry's Wife), Ione Leslie (Moe's Wife), Vernon Dent (Dr. Harry Arms), Louise Carver (Lady by Car), Ella McKenzie (Nurse), Bud Jamison (Cop), Cy Schindell (Attendant), Wilfred Lucas, Eric Bunn, Frank Mills, Harley Wood, James C. Morton, A.R. Haysel (Bit Men) and Betty MacMahon (Bit Girl) / *SYN*: With their wives upset at them for not working, the Stooges land jobs with the Brighto Medicinal Company selling Dr. Brighto's *Brighto*, a cure-all medicine which the boys use for *every other* conceivable household task. *Brighto* is the miracle medicine that removes the finish clean off automobiles and burns through the shoulder of a policeman's uniform, as the Stooges find out. Naturally, sales pick up when the Stooges realize that *Brighto* is actually a medicine. They invade the Los Arms Hospital and peddle the stuff to everyone, including Dr. Harry Arms (who lost his hair buying a bottle from the Stooges earlier). He chases them out of the hospital and back home with their wives, where they belong. / *SD*: 4 (W 12/9 to SA 12/12/36).

22. THREE DUMB CLUCKS * / Rl. April 17 / Prod. No. 266 / 17m / *ap* Jules White / *d* Del Lord / *st scr* Clyde Bruckman / *ph* Andre Barlatier / *e* Charles Nelson / *C*: Lynton Brent (Butch), Frank Austin (Guard), Lucille Lund (Daisy) and Eddie Laughton (Chopper) / *SYN*: The Stooges break out of jail to prevent their Pa from marrying a curvaceous blonde named Daisy, who's linked with two gangsters, Butch and Chopper, who plan to kill Pa and collect his money. Curly, who resembles his father (he plays dual roles), doubles for Pa at the wedding in Daisy's penthouse. Complications arise, however, when the *real* Pa arrives during the wedding. As a result, the two crooks chase the Stooges up a flagpole, break the pole and watch the trio fall two stories below on top of Pa, who just happens to be in front of the hotel. / *SD*: 4 (M 2/1 to TH 2/4/37) / *FN*: Remade, with some stock footage, as *Up in Daisy's Penthouse* (2/5/53). Hat routine was also in *Steamboat Bill, Jr.* (1928) with Buster Keaton. On the last day of shooting, Curly fell down an elevator shaft and suffered a severe head wound. (See *Moe Howard & the 3 Stooges*, p. 101.)

**23. BACK TO THE WOODS **½ / Rl. May 14 / Prod. No. 268 / 19½m / *ap* Jules White / *d* Preston Black / *st* Searle Kramer / *scr* Andrew Bennison / *ph* George Meehan / *e* Charles Nelson / *C*: Bud Jamison (Prosecutor), Vernon Dent (Governor), Theodore Lorch (Chief Rain in the Puss) and Bert Young (Indian) / *SYN*: Merry Old England, about 1630. Larry, Moe and Curly are accused of battling with His Majesty's Guard and are sentenced to defend the Plymouth Colonists from the Indians. Here, they meet three lovely ladies: Faith, Hope and Charity. While protecting their fellow man, Larry is captured by savages, prompting a rescue from Moe and Curly. Making their escape, the Stooges hop into a canoe and, with one paddle stroke, cross the lake / *SD*: 4 (W 3/3 to SA 3/6/37) / *FN*: Ending is stock footage from *Whoops, I'm an Indian* (9/11/36).

**24. GOOFS AND SADDLES ***½ / Rl. July 2 / Prod. No. 274 / 17m / *ap* Jules White / *d* Del Lord / *st scr* Felix Adler / *ph* Benjamin Kline / *e* Charles Nelson / *C*: Ted Lorch (Gen. Muster), Hank Mann (Lem), Stanley Blystone (Longhorn Pete), Sam Lufkin (Colonel), Hank Bell (Character), Ethan Laidlaw, George Gray and Joe Palma (Bit Men) / *SYN*: With cattle rustlers becoming a scourge, General Muster sends for his three best undercover agents to wipe these varmints out: Wild Bill Hiccup (Moe), Buffalo Billious (Curly), and Just-Plain Bill (Larry). Their target: Longhorn Pete, the leading cattle thief in the country. Disguised as gamblers, the trio play a wild (and dishonest) game of poker with Longhorn Pete, who eventually sees through their cheating ways and threatens to kill them. The Stooges make their exit in a covered wagon (Rattlesnake Joe's Medicine Show), with Pete and his gang in hot pursuit. Upon

arriving at an abandoned cabin, Curly accidentally dumps a box of bullets into a meat grinder, creating a terrific machine gun that blasts the outlaws, causing them to surrender. / *SD*: 4 (W 4/14 to F 4/16, and M 4/19/37) / *FN*: Footage was reused in *Pals and Gals* (6/3/54—covered wagon escape and ending) and *Stop! Look! and Laugh!* (7/60). Exchanging cards under the table is also seen in *Out West* (4/24/47) and *Pals and Gals* (6/3/54). "Homing pigeon to Headquarters" gag was milked in *The Private Eyes* (1981) with Don Knotts and Tim Conway.

**25. CASH AND CARRY ** / Rl. Sept 3 / Prod. No. 400 / 20m / *ap* Jules White / *d* Del Lord / *st* Clyde Bruckman / *scr* Clyde Bruckman and Elwood Ullman / *ph* Lucien Ballard / *e* Charles Nelson / *C*: Sonny Bupp (Jimmy, the Crippled Boy), Al Richardson (Pres. Roosevelt), Harlene Wood (Boy's Sister) and Lester Dorr (Bit Man) / *SYN*: The Stooges discover that their city dump shack has been taken over by Jimmy, a crippled boy, and his sister. Jimmy needs a leg operation, which costs $500, but doesn't have the money. The Stooges take the boy's lifesavings of $62 and try opening a bank account, thinking it would grow to $500 because of interest. Two con men overhear the Stooges and swindle them out of Jimmy's money by selling them a map to Captain Kidd's buried treasure, located in an old mansion. The Stooges dynamite their way into the building, which turns out to be the United States Sub-Treasury. The Stooges are pardoned after explaining their innocence before President Roosevelt, and arrangements are made for Jimmy's leg operation. / *WT*: *Golddigging in the Treasury*. / *SD*: 4 (W 5/5/ to SA 5/8/37) / *FN*: Remade as *A Miner Affair* (11/1/45) and *Two April Fools* (6/17/54), both with Andy Clyde.

**26. PLAYING THE PONIES * / Rl. Oct. 15 / Prod. No. 401 / 17m / *ap* Jules White / *d* Charles Lamont / *st* Will Harr and Irving Frisch / *scr* Al Giebler, Elwood Ullman, and Charley Melson / *ph* Allen G. Siegler / *e* Charles Hochberg / *C*: William Irving (Higgins), Jack "Tiny" Lipson (Customer) and Billy Bletcher (Announcer) / *SYN*: Flounder Inn restaurant owners, Moe, Larry and Curly, swap the ownership of their restaurant with two city slickers, Higgins and Parker, for the con men's alleged prize horse, Thunderbolt. The Stooges soon learn, however, that the thoroughbred is nothing more than a broken-down, half-starved filly. Curly saves the deal when he accidentally feeds Thunderbolt chili pepperinos (thinking they're peanuts), causing the horse to race around the track at blazing speed. With this sure-fire ingredient, the Stooges enter Thunderbolt in the Benson County Fair Five-Thousand-Dollar Sweepstakes race. Jockey Larry energizes Thunderbolt with a handful of peppers, while Moe and Larry aid the cause, racing in front of the horse with a bucket of water, thus powering her to victory. Afterward, the Stooges wine and dine in their new mansion. / SD: (W 5/12 to F 5/14, and M 5/17/37) / FN: Gag of chasing a dog past a customer ordering franks and beans later used in *Malice in the Palace* (9/1/49) and *Rumpus in a Harem* (6/21/56).

27. THE SITTER-DOWNERS *** / Rl.
Nov. 26 / Prod. No. 402 / 17m / *ap* Jules White / *d* Del Lord / *st scr* Ewart Adamson / *ph* George Meehan / *e* Charles Nelson / *C*: Marcia Healy (Dorabell), Betty Mack (Florabell), June Gittelson (Corabell), James C. Morton (Mr. Bell), Robert McKenzie (Sheriff), Jack Long (Justice of the Peace) and Bert Young (Truck Driver) / *SYN*: Mr. Bell refuses to allow the Stooges to marry his daughters, Dorabell, Florabell and Corabell, causing the boys to stage a sitdown strike. Their strike gains national exposure and fame for the trio, including several complimentary gifts, the best being a house on a lot. As a result of their new fame, Mr. Bell gives his blessing and the Stooges take their brides to their new home, which turns out to be a pre-fabricated house they have to assemble. When the boys refuse to build the house, the wives stage their own sitdown strike, "No House, No Honeymoon!" Eventually the Stooges weaken, construct the house, which crashes to the ground when Corabell carelessly removes one wooden post. / *SD*: 4 (F 5/28, M 5/31 to W 6/2/37) / *FN*: Premise was reworked from Buster Keaton's *One Week* (1920). Clyde Bruckman also utilized this same idea in *Honeymoon House*, the 48th TV episode of *The Abbott and Costello Show* (1953-4). This film also features Ted Healy's sister, Marcia Healy, as Dorabell.

1938
28. TERMITES OF 1938 *** / Rl. Jan. 7 /
Prod. No. 416 / 16½m / *ap* Charley Chase and Hugh McCollum / *d* Del Lord / *st scr* Elwood Ullman / *ph* Andre Barlatier / *e* Arthur Seid / *C*: Dorothy Granger (Mrs. Sturgeon), Bud Jamison (Lord Wafflebottom) and Bess Flowers (Mrs. Muriel Van Twitchett) / *SYN*: Mrs. Van Twitchett is in an unenviable predicament. She's throwing a party for some society matron friends and has no escorts. So Van Twitchett misdials the telephone number for *Acme Escorts*, winding up with the *Acme Exterminators*, also known as Moe, Larry and Curly. The Stooges are more than happy to help and end up dining with some most distinguished people, teaching them an entirely different set of table manners, which the guests soon imitate. Later, the Stooges stage a musical act for the guests and then get to work on exterminating the house. *SD*: 4 (T 10/19 to F 10/23/37). / *FN*: Remade as *Society Mugs* (9/19/46) with Shemp Howard and Tom Kennedy. Gag of playing musical instruments with the aid of a record player was reworked by Abbott and Costello as the famous *All right!* sketch.

29. WEE WEE MONSIEUR **½ / Rl. Feb.
18 / Prod. No. 404 / 17m / *ap* Jules White / *d* Del Lord / *st scr* Searle Kramer / *ph* Andre Barlatier / *e* Charles Nelson / *C*: Bud Jamison (Lieutenant), Vernon Dent (Chieftain), John Lester Johnson (Eunuch) and Harry Semels (Landlord) / *SYN*: Opening title: "Paris. Somewhere in France." The landlord, Mr. Gigi, is tired of harboring three bogus artists, Moe, Larry and Curly, who owe him many months back rent. When Gigi threatens to kill the boys, our trio escapes and seeks financial aid from the American Consul but sign up in the Foreign Legion by mistake. Moe, Larry and Curly are than stationed in Tsimmis, where their commanding officer, General Gorgonzola, is captured by the Chieftain's men. The Stooges, however, rescue the General disguised as Santa Clauses. / *WT*: *The Foreign Legioneers* and *We We Monsieur* / *SD*: 4 (F 11/12, M 11/15 to W 11/17/37) / *FN*: Stock footage and new scenes of the Stooges as Santas were used in *Malice in the Palace* (9/1/49) and in its remake, *Rumpus in a Harem* (6/21/56), using some footage from *Wee Wee Monsieur* (2/18/38).

30. TASSELS IN THE AIR ***½ / Rl. Apr. 1
/ Prod. No. 420 / 18m / *ap* Charley Chase and Hugh McCollum / *d* Charley Chase / *st scr* Al Giebler and Elwood Ullman / *ph* Allen G. Siegler / *e* Arthur Seid / *C*: Bess Flowers (Maggie Smirch), Vernon Dent (Building Superintendent), Bud Jamison (Thaddeus Smirch) and Vic Travers (Elevator Man) / *SYN*: When janitors Moe, Larry and Curly paint occupation stencils on the wrong office doors. Mrs. Smirch accidentally mistakes Moe for Omay, the famous interior decorator. The real Omay also works in the same office building, but the stencil on his door reads "Maintenance Room." The sight of Mrs. Smirch's tassels makes Curly react violently, but Moe calms him down, taking a paint brush to his chin. In the meantime, the Stooges agree to redecorate her house during Mrs. Smirch's bridge game, and ruin her antique table and everything else in the house. Later, when the real Omay drops in, Mrs. Smirch kicks the trio out, since, as Moe says, "Our genuis isn't appreciated." / *FN*: A partial reworking of *Luncheon at Twelve* (1933) with Charley Chase. The gag of painting a cuckoo clock and revarnishing an antique table was later used in *A Snitch in Time* (12/7/50).

31. FLAT FOOT STOOGES **½ / Rl. May
13 (also given as Nov. 25 and Dec. 5) / Prod. No. 439 / 15½m / *ap* Charley Chase and Hugh McCollum / *st scr d* Charley Chase / *ph* Lucien Ballard / *e* Arthur Seid *C*: Chester Conklin (Fire Chief Kelly), Dick Curtis (Fred Reardon, Salesman) and Lola Jensen (Cricket Kelley, Chief's Daughter) / *SYN*: A salesman, Fred Reardon, unsuccessfully tries to sell Fire Chief Kelly of the Midland Fire Department on buying new motordriven fire engines, replacing the station's old, inefficient horse-drawn ones. In an attempt to punish Kelly's stubborness, Reardon sneaks into the department's garage and plants a keg of TNT in the stack of an old fire engine. When the chief's daughter, Crickett, tries stopping Reardon, both parties struggle, knocking each other out. Meanwhile, an innocent duck starts consuming the trail of spilled gun powder, later laying an explosive egg that sets the firehouse on fire. When the fire alarm sounds, Chief Kelly and the Stooges dash off for another location, not realizing that their own firehouse is ablaze. Fortunately, the Stooges notice that their station is burning down and arrive in time to douse the fire, saving Reardon and Crickett from any harm. / *SD*: 4 (M 10/25 to TH 10/28/37).

32. HEALTHY, WEALTHY, AND DUMB
*** / Rl. May 20 / Prod. No. 422 / 16m / *ap* Jules White / *d* Del Lord / *st scr* Searle Kramer / *ph* Allen G. Siegler / *e* Charles Nelson / *C*: Lucille Lund (Daisy), Jean Carmen (Marge), Erlene Heath (Lil), James C. Morton (Hotel Mgr.), Bud Jamison (House Detective) and Bobby Burns (Waiter) / *SYN*: Curly wins a $50,000 radio jackpot, and the Stooges celebrate lavishly, renting an elegant suite at the Hotel Costa Plente (and it does). In a matter of hours, three luscious golddiggers try spooning off the boys' earnings. Then, after the hotel manager delivers the Stooges their whopping bill, Curly receives a telegram informing him that, after tax deductions, only $4.85 remains out of his winnings! /*WT*: *Cuckoo Over Contests*. *FN*: Remade as *A Missed Fortune* (1/3/52).

33. VIOLENT IS THE WORD FOR
CURLY ***½ / RI. July 2 / Prod. No. 423 18m / *ap* Charley Chase and Hugh McCollum / *d* Charley Chase / *st scr* Al Giebler and Elwood Ullman / *e* Arthur Seid / *C*: Gladys Gale (The Dean), Marjorie Dean (Young Girl), Bud Jamison (Butler), Eddie Fetherstone, John T. Murray and Pat Gleason (Professors) / *SYN*: Gas station attendants, Moe, Larry and Curly, blow up an automobile carrying three foreign professors, whom the Stooges replace as guest instructors at Mildew's Girl College. In class, the Stooges teach the girls how to sing "Swinging the Alphabet," and instruct them on the finer points of playing football. But since the college hasn't got an athletic budget, the trio borrow a basketball (loaded with the three professors' nitroglycerin). / *SD*: 4 (M 3/14 to 3/17/38).

34. THREE MISSING LINKS *** / Rl. July
29 (also given as Sept 2) / Prod. No. 426 / 18m / *ap* Jules White / *d* Jules White / *st scr* Searle Kramer / *ph* Henry Freulich / *e* Charles Nelson / *C*: Monty Collins (Director Herbert Herringbone), Jane Hamilton (Mirabel Mirabel), James C. Morton (B.O. Botswaddle) and Naba (Dr. Ba Loni Sulami) / *SYN*: Studio president B.O. Botswaddle is conferring with film director Herbert Herringbone over his trouble in locating a leading man to portray a gorilla, opposite Mirabel Mirabel, in *Darkest Africa*. Who could they find to essay the missing link? Following their meeting, Botswaddle and Herringbone stumble across three studio janitors (the Stooges) rehearsing Shakespeare in the broom closet. Herringbone

236

looks no farther, hiring Curly as the lead gorilla and Moe and Larry as his assistants. The following day, the entire cast and crew shift production to Africa, where the Stooges meet Dr. Ba Loni Sulami, a witch doctor, who sells "Love Candy" (which produces instant passion when consumed). Curly is sold on this taffy-like substance, buying some for his leading lady, Mirabel. While filming a scene, however, Curly (in an Ape costume), has a face-to-face confrontation with a *real* female gorilla. She chases Curly through the jungle and back to the witch doctor's hut. Curly offers the gorilla Love Candy, but the animal doesn't accept his peace offering. Curly then swallows the potent stuff himself and, like a shot from Cupid's bow, springs after his new sweetheart, the gorilla / *SD*: 4 (TH 4/7 to F 4/8, M 4/11 and T 4/12/38).

35. MUTTS TO YOU *** / Rl. Oct. 14 / Prod. No. 427 / 18m / *ap* Charley Chase and Hugh McCollum / *st scr* Al Giebler and Elwood Ullman / *ph* Allen G. Siegler / *e* Arthur Seid / *C*: Bess Flowers (Mrs. Manning), Lane Chandler (Doug Manning), Vernon Dent (Mr. Stutz, the Landlord) and Bud Jamison (Mr. O'Halloran, an Irish Cop) / *SYN*: The Stooges, after a blistering day's work, find an infant left by its mother on the doorstep of their K-9 Laundry store. Thinking the child is abandoned, the Stooges decide to take the baby home. When the newspapers carry screaming banner headlines that the baby was kidnapped, the trio panic. In an attempt to return the tot unobserved, Moe and Larry disguise Curly as the infant's Irish mother. Curly's costume, however, doesn't fool an Irish cop on the beat, Officer O'Halloran, who chases them directly into a nearby Chinese laundry where, minutes later, the baby is reunited with its parents / *WT*: *Muts to You* / *SD*: 4 (W 3/30, TH 3/31, F 4/1 to SA 4/2/38).

1939

36. THREE LITTLE SEW AND SEWS ** ½ / Rl. Jan. 6 / Prod. No. 419 / 16m / *ap* Jules White / *d* Del Lord / *st scr* Ewart Adamson / *ph* Lucien Ballard / *e* Charles Nelson / *C*: Harry Semels (Count Alfred Gehrol), Phyllis Barry (Olga), James C. Morton (Admiral H.S. Taylor), Bud Jamison (Cop) and Vernon Dent (Dignified Man) / *SYN*: The Stooges are three sailors who press naval uniforms, including Admiral Taylor's. Curly poses as Admiral Taylor and Larry and Moe as ship lieutenants, and Count Gehrol, a German spy, invites the trio to his home for a special get-together. The Count makes them steal submarine plans unknowingly, so he can sink the Navy's latest sub. The Count takes the Stooges on his mission, with Curly signalling the Navy flagship to rescue them. Curly saves the day, however, knocking the German spies unconscious with a lead pipe. When Admiral Taylor arrives on board the sub, Curly illustrates how he single-handedly wiped out the Germans, repeating his killer swing by clobbering the pipe on an

aerial bomb, which explodes. As the smoke clears, the Stooges are seen dressed as angels. Curly glances back, remarking "Step on it. Look who's following us!" The Stooges turn around, see the Admiral (also in wings) flying away into the heavens. / *WT*: *Three Goofy Gobs* and *Submarine Behave!* / *SD*: 4 (T 3/22 to F 3/25/38) / *FN*: Stock shot of submarine landing on the ocean floor from *Devil's Playground* (1937, Columbia).

37. WE WANT OUR MUMMY *** / Rl. Feb. 24 / Prod. No. 443 / 17m / *ap* Jules White / *d* Del Lord / *st scr* Searle Kramer and Elwood Ullman / *ph* No credit / *e* No credit / *C*: Bud Jamison (Prof. Wilson), James C. Morton (Prof. Crowe), Dick Curtis (Jackson), Robert Williams (Prof. Tuttle), Ted Lorch (Kidnapper) and Eddie Laughton (Jake, the Taxi Driver) / *SYN*: Professor Tuttle has disappeared. He is the only man in the world who knows the exact location of the King Rutentuten mummy. To solve this mystery, Professor Wilson, an Egyptologist at the Museum of Ancient History, summons three top investigators: Sherlock Bones (Larry), Charlie Chin (Moe) and Philo Pants (Curly). Once in Egypt, the Stooges search aimlessly through an underground tomb, finding that a gang of desperadoes are holding Professor Tuttle in another cavern. The crooks' main interest is to unearth precious jewels hidden in the Rutentuten mummy. In order to circumvent this plot, Moe applies his previous experience as a tailor, dressing up Curly as a makeshift King Rutentuten. When the gang's leader searches through Curly's mummy attire for the diamonds, he finds an old newspaper and reads it aloud: "Yanks Win World Series! Can you beat that!" Blowing his disguise, Curly says, "Ya. And I won five bucks!" A short chase ensues, with Jackson and his gang falling into an open pit that the Stooges covered earlier with an Egyptian rug. With the case now solved, Professor Tuttle reveals that the mummy they found wasn't Rutentuten, but rather his wife, Queen Hotsitotsie. It turns out that the real King is a midget! / *SD*: 4 (T 11/1 to F 11/4/38) / *FN*: The "Yanks Win World Series" gag and Curly's brief scene with a mummy alligator were not in the film's final draft screenplay. "Rutentuten" is spelling in film script.

38. A-DUCKING THEY DID GO *** / Rl. Apr. 7 / Prod. No. 444 / 16½m / *ap* Jules White / *d* Del Lord / *st scr* Andrew Bennison / *ph* Lucien Ballard / *e* Charles Nelson / *C*: Lynton Brent (Blackie), Vernon Dent (Man in Office), Bud Jamison (Police Chief), Vic Travers (Member) and Cy Schindell (Fruit Vendor) / *SYN*: Hungry and unemployed, the Stooges steal a watermelon from a fruit vendor and conclude their getaway in the Canvas Back Duck Club, where they win jobs as sales promoters. The Stooges quickly amaze the two crooked bosses by selling memberships to the police chief and the mayor, with the governor next on their list! The day of the hunt, the police chief warns the Stooges that they better produce

ducks or they'll wind up in jail. Decoy ducks seem to hold the guest hunters until the Stooges devise another solution: Curly arrives (a la the Pied Piper) followed by a huge flock of domestic ducks. The hunting goes full blast until an irate farmer arrives, claiming payment for his prize ducks. The police chief and his men start shooting three other ducks, the Stooges, who dive behind a row of bushes and ride off on the backs of three bulls. / *SD*: 4 (T 11/15 to F 11/18/38) / *FN*: Ending was pulled from *A Pain in the Pullman* (6/27/36).

39. YES, WE HAVE NO BONANZA *** / Rl. May 19 / Prod. No. 438 / 16m / *ap* Jules White / *d* Del Lord / *st scr* Elwood Ullman and Searle Kramer / *ph* Lucien Ballard / *e* Charles Nelson / *C*: Dick Curtis (Jack), Lynton Brent (Pete), Vernon Dent (Sheriff), Suzanne Kaaren, Jean Carmen and Lola Jensen (Saloon Girls) / *SYN*: As singing waiters of the Canyon Creek Saloon, the Three Stooges learn that three chorus girls are indebted to their boss, Jack. If the girls don't work for him, Jack will throw their father in jail. Into the saloon staggers Pete, the boss's henchman. He pays for a drink with a $20 gold piece, whereupon the Stooges quit their jobs to become gold prospectors in order to get the girls out of debt. During their search the boys unearth a gold filling missing from Jack's mouth. As the Stooges shovel deeper, they uncover a satchel full of gold, money and bonds. Believing that they are millionaires, the Stooges return to the saloon, decked out in fancy western attire, and ask the girls to quit their jobs and marry them. However, Jack recognizes the satchel as his own buried loot. In the ensuing chase, Jack and Pete crash their automonile right into the Sheriff's office and are captured. / *WT*: *Yes, We Have No Bonanzas* / *SD*: 4 (M 11/28 to TH 12/1/38) / *FN*: On Columbia's Stage 6, a lake set was built for *A-Ducking They Did Go* (4/7/39). This same structure was used in *Yes, We Have No Bonanza*. The tag lines accompanying Curly's remark, "Yes, we have no bonanza," were ad-libbed. Complete two-reeler reused in *The Three Stooges Follies* (11/74).

40. SAVED BY THE BELLE **½ / Rl. June 30 / Prod. No. 430 / 17m / *ap* Charley Chase and Hugh McCollum / *d* Charley Chase / *st* Elwood Ullman and Searle Kramer / *scr* Charley Chase / *ph* Allen G. Siegler / *e* Arthur Seid / *C*: Carmen LaRoux (Rita), Leroy Mason (Singapore Joe) and Gino Corrado (Gen. LeGrande) / *SYN*: Moe, Larry and Curly are traveling salesmen for a winter clothing manufacturer, marketing their wares in Valeska, an earthquake region of the tropical isles. As guests at Singapore Joe's Palace Hotel, the boys are mistaken for masterminding an uprising against President Ward Robey. Arrested on the suspicion of being spies, the Stooges are escorted to General LeGrande's office, where they meet Senorita Rita, who believes the boys are innocent. LeGrande orders the Stooges

thrown in a dungeon and to be executed the next day, despite Rita's futile pleas. On the day of the execution, however, Rita rescues the boys and they help her recover a battle map from General Casino's headquarters for her leader, Joe, the hotel owner. When the boys deliver the chart, however, it turns out to be a rolled-up calendar they picked up by mistake. The Stooges are spared execution again when Rita comes to their rescue with the right map. / SD: 4 (M 12/12 to TH 12/15/38).

41. CALLING ALL CURS *** / Rl. Aug. 25 / Prod. No. 445 / 17½m / ap d Jules White / st Thea Goodan / scr Elwood Ullman and Searle Kramer / ph No credit / e Charles Nelson / C: Lynton Brent (Duke), Cy Schindell (Tony), Beatrice Curtis (Nurse James), Beatrice Blinn (Nurse Thomas), Dorothy Moore, Robin Raymond and Ethelreda Leopold (Nurses) / SYN: The Stooges run a stylish dog hospital and one of their patients is Garcon, a prize pooch to be entered in a dog show by its owner, Mrs. Bedford. Two crooks, Tony and Duke, posing as newspaper reporters, come to the hospital and steal the Bedford dog. Unable to recover the canine in time for delivery to Mrs. Bedford, the Stooges disguise another dog with black mattress stuffing to resemble the real Garcon. At the Bedford home, when the boys introduce their Garcon look-a-like, the maid accidentally sucks off the pup's disguise while vacuuming. The Stooges then frantically enlist the aid of a hunting dog to sniff out the missing pooch. Successful, the Stooges track down the crook's hideout, overpower Duke and Tony, and locate Garcon, only to discover that she had given birth to puppies. / WT: Dog Hospital / SD: 4 (T 12/27 to F 12/30/38).

42. OILY TO BED, OILY TO RISE *** / Rl. Oct. 6 / Prod. No. 449 / 18½m / ap d Jules White / st scr Andrew Bennison and Mauri Grashin / ph Henry Freulich / e Charles Nelson / C: Dick Curtis (Clipper), Richard Fiske (Mr. Johnson, a Farmer), Eddie Laughton (Briggs), Eva McKenzie (Mrs. Martha Jenkins), Vic Travers (Justice of the Peace), Lorna Gray (May), Dorothy Moore (June) and Linda Winters (April) / SYN: The widow Jenkins has just sold her farmhouse to three con men for ten dollars an acre. Meanwhile, Curly has the unusual gift of making any wish come true. His latest wish produces an abandoned automobile, which transports the Stooges to Mrs. Jenkin's house in time for roast chicken, dumplings and apple pie (another one of Curly's wishes). In return for the meal, the Stooges work for their keep and uncover an oil well on the widow's property. When the Stooges inform Mrs. Jenkins of their discovery, Moe realizes that she has been defrauded by land swindlers and heads up the search for the three hoodlums. During their trip back to town, the boys come across three hitch-hiking crooks (the owners of the abandoned car and the land swindlers) and recover the deed after a rip-roaring chase back to Jenkins' farm. Now heroes, Curly makes

One-sheet for *You Nazty Spy* (1940).

one last wish: that the Stooges get married. As if by magic, the widow's daughters— April, May and June—enter and the Stooges get hitched. / SD: 4 (TH 3/16 to SA 3/18, and M 3/20/39) / FN: Remade as *Oil's Well That Ends Well* (12/4/58). (See *Moe Howard & the 3 Stooges*, pp. 95 and 101.)

43. THREE SAPPY PEOPLE *** / Rl. Dec. 1 / Prod. No. 451 / 18m / ap d Jules White / st scr Clyde Bruckman / ph George Meehan / e Charles Nelson / C: Lorna Gray (Sherry Rumsford), Don Beddoe (J. Rumsford Rumsford), Bud Jamison (Williams the Butler), Ann Doran (Countess), Richard Fiske (Guest) and Eddie Laughton (Guest) / SYN: Sherry Rumsford is a thrill addict and her millionaire husband is tired of her stunts. Seeking professional help, he calls the office of psychiatrists Ziller, Zeller and Zoller, accidentally reaching the Three Stooges, who are telephone repairmen working on the office's switchboard. Smelling a fast buck, the Stooges fill in for the vacationing pyschiatrists, reporting immediately to the Rumford mansion in time for Sherry's birthday party. Naturally, the Stooges' table manners don't win any contests, starting a pie-throwing battle, much to the amusement of Mrs. Rumsford. / WT: 3 Sloppy People / SD: 4 (TH 4/6 to SA 4/8, and M 4/10/39).

1940
44. YOU NAZTY SPY **** / Rl. Jan. 19 / Prod. No. 472 / 18m / p d Jules White / st scr Clyde Bruckman and Felix Adler / ph Harry Davis / e Arthur Seid / C: Dick Curtis (Mr.

238

Onay), Don Beddoe (Amscray), Richard Fiske (Ixnay/2nd Delegate), Florine Dickson (Miss Pfiffernuss), Little Billy (Midget Gestapo), John Tyrell (Mr. Bones, Minister of Oomphola), Joe Murphy (Peasant), Lorna Gray (Mattie Herring) and Bert Young (Storm Trooper) / SYN: The kingdom of Moronica is in financial trouble. The King wants peace but the only way the country can thrive economically is to go to war. Three cabinet members decide to oust the King, replacing him with a dictator stupid enough to follow their every command. In another room are three brainless paperhangers: Hailstone (Moe), Pebble (Larry) and Gallstone (Curly). Mr. Amscray, one of the cabinet advisors, appoints Moe as Dictator, Larry as Minister of Propaganda and Curly as Field Marshall. What follows is the burning of "bookmakers," the march on Bolognia, the conquest of Starvania, and the famous Peace Conference of Oomphola, where Moe argues for a corridor through Double Crossia. The Stooges capably display their talent for satire. / WT: Oh, You Nazty Spy! / SD: 4 (W 12/6 to SA 12/9/39) / FN: Moe Howard's and Jules White's favorite two-reeler, as well as one of Larry Fine's.

45. ROCKIN' THROUGH THE ROCKIES **½ / Rl. Mar. 8 / Prod. No. 461 / 17m / p d Jules White / st scr Clyde Bruckman / ph Henry Freulich / e Arthur Seid / C: Linda Winters (Daisy), Dorothy Appleby (Tessie), Lorna Gray (Flossie), Kathryn Sheldon (Nell) and Bert Young (Indian) / SYN: The Stooges are hired as guides by Nell and her three chorus girls, who are crossing the plains for an engagement in San Francisco. At one of their overnight campsites, wild bears steal their food and Chief Growling Bear and his Indian braves surround Nell's wagon, kidnapping Daisy, Tessie and Flossie and prompting the Stooges to come to the rescue. / WT: Nell's Belles / SD: 4 (W 11/8 to SA 11/11/39) / FN: Linda Winters changed her name to Dorothy Comingore in later film productions and went on to play the prestigious role of one of the wives of Citizen Kane (1941).

46. A-PLUMBING WE WILL GO **** / Rl. Apr. 19 / Prod. No. 462 / 18m / p Del Lord and Hugh McCollum / d Del Lord / st scr Elwood Ullman / ph Benjamin Kline / e Arthur Seid / C: Symona Boniface (Party Guest), Bud Jamison (Officer Kelly), Bess Flowers (Mrs. Hadley), Eddie Laughton (Prosecuting Attorney), Monty Collins (Prof. Bilbo), John Tyrell (Judge) and Dudley Dickerson (Cook) / SYN: In order to keep out of jail, the Stooges pose as plumbers trying to fix leaky pipes in Mrs. Hadley's mansion during a swank party. While Larry searches vainly for a water shut-off valve, Moe and Curly get busy in the basement, where Curly deduces that the pipes are clogged with electrical wiring! Consequently, Moe and Curly remove the wiring from the pipes, hooking them up to the house's water pipes. The house becomes so bugged as a result that household appliances

shower blasts of water rather than volts of electricity. When Mrs. Hadley (the Niagara Falls lady) calls the police, the Stooges take flight while a traveling magician, Professor Bilbo, is outside entertaining Hadley's guests. In an attempt to make his female assistant disappear, Bilbo shuts and then reopens the door, producing a rushing stream of girls, the Stooges, six policemen, and a squad of motorcycle cops! / SD: 4 (W 12/13 to F 12/15, and M 12/18/39) / FN: Curly Howard's favorite film. Reworked with stock footage as Vagabond Loafers (10/6/49), Scheming Schemers (10/4/56), and Pick a Peck of Plumbers (7/23/44), an El Brendel-Shemp Howard comedy. (See Moe Howard & the 3 Stooges, p. 107.)

One-sheet for From Nurse to Worse (1940).

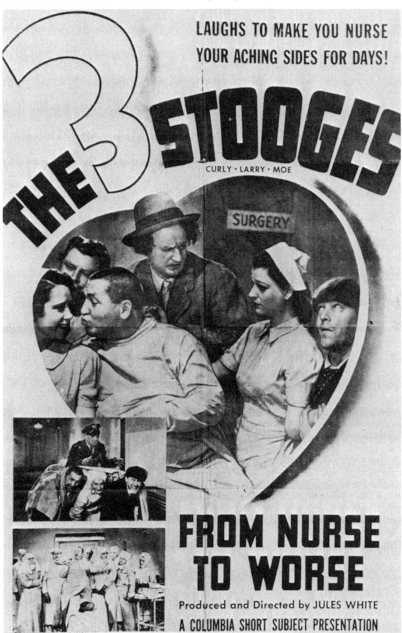

47. NUTTY BUT NICE *** / Rl. June 14 / Prod. No. 465 / 18m / p d Jules White / st scr Clyde Bruckman and Felix Adler / ph John Stumar / e Mel Thorsen / C: Vernon Dent (Dr. Lyman), Eddie Garcia (Mr. Williams, the Girl's Father), John Tyrell (Dr. Walters) and Al Seymour (Butch) / SYN: As singing waiters, the Stooges overhear two doctors reviewing the fate of a little girl who cries pitiably for her missing father. Moe, Larry and Curly rush to the hospital to make the child laugh. All that can save her, the doctors say, is the return of her daddy. The Stooges obtain a description of the man (he's 5'10", bald and likes to yodel) and begin their search. While investigating through the city, the Stooges suddenly hear someone

yodeling from an apartment building; they race inside to rescue the girl's father from his kidnappers.

48. HOW HIGH IS UP? *** / Rl. July 26 / Prod. No. 458 / 16m / *p* Del Lord and Hugh McCollum / *d* Del Lord / *st scr* Elwood Ullman / *ph* Allen G. Siegler / *e* Arthur Seid / *C*: Bruce Bennett (Joe, the Foreman), Vernon Dent (Blake, the Building's Owner) and Edmund Cobb (Worker) / *SYN*: The Stooges are Minute Menders who travel from city to city performing all kinds of odd-jobs. While passing a construction site, however, the boys try drumming up business by punching holes in the workmen's lunch pails, taking flight when the workers detect the leaks in their food boxes. In their haste to escape, the Stooges take refuge in a line of workers seeking employment, and are accidentally hired as riveters to work on the new steel building's 97th floor. When the building owner notices the wild mess the boys are creating on the structure, the Stooges jump off the building, land safely in a truck below and roar off to safety. / *FN*: Footage reused in *Stop! Look! and Laugh!* (7/60).

49. FROM NURSE TO WORSE **** / Rl. Aug. 23 / Prod. No. 468 / *p d* Jules White / *st* Charles L. Kimball / *scr* Clyde Bruckman / *ph* Benjamin Kline / *e* Mel Thorsen / *C*: Vernon Dent (Dr. D. Lerious), Dorothy Appleby (Nurse), Babe Kane (Nurse), John Tyrell (Anesthesiast), Al Seymour (Cop), Joe Palma (Assistant Surgeon), Poppie Wilde (Assistant Surgeon), Charlie Phillips (Assistant Surgeon), Blanche Payson (Nurse), Johnny Kascier (Attendant) and Dudley Dickerson (Assistant) / *SYN*: The Stooges are paperhangers refurbishing the house of their friend, Jerry, who convinces them to act mentally ill in order to collect health insurance. Following his advice, Moe and Larry put Curly on a leash and take him to see Doctor D. Lerious, the company physician. Curly imitates a dog so ferociously that the doctor declares that only a brain operation can save him. The Stooges refuse the idea of Curly getting this cheap haircut and escape momentarily. Later, they are recaptured by Dr. D. Lerious, who prepares to operate on Curly. In the excitement that follows, the ether cone is applied to the wrong nose during Curly's operation, making the unconscious patient the doctor instead of Curly. The trio make their escape on a hospital gurney, complete with sail, speeding out of the hospital and knocking an innocent bicycle rider into a tub of cement. As the man starts emerging from the gooey mess, the boys recognize that he is Jerry and shove him back into the cement. / *FN*: Stock shot of paperhanging routine from *You Nazty Spy* (1/19/40). "Charlie, the Man with the Goofy Limp" gag borrowed from *Uncivil Warriors* (4/6/35) and is later used in *Hold That Lion* (7/17/47).

50. NO CENSUS, NO FEELING *** / Rl. Oct. 4 / Prod. No. 474 / *p* Del Lord and

Hugh McCollum / *d* Del Lord / *st scr* Harry Edwards and Elwood Ullman / *ph* Lucien Ballard / *e* Arthur Seid / *C*: Symona Boniface (Mrs. Bedford), Elinor Vandivere (Bit Woman), Vernon Dent, Bruce Bennett and Max Davidson (Bit Men) / *SYN*: Census takers Moe, Larry and Curly crash an affluent women's bridge party, with Moe and Larry joining the group of players. In the meantime, Curly is mixing punch in the kitchen, adding alum instead of sugar by mistake. The Stooges are shown the door when the women, with their alum-puckered lips, are humiliated since they can't speak. In search of new customers, the Stooges start taking the census of a crowd at a local football game, disguised as football players. The Stooges' plan backfires, however, when Curly steals an ice cream wagon, forcing the boys to escape from an angry mob of football players./ *FN*: The Stooges are also census-takers in *Don't Throw That Knife* (5/3/51).

51. COOKOO CAVALIERS **½ (Not *Cuckoo*) / Rl. Nov. 15 / Prod. No. 455 / 17m / *p d* Jules White / *st scr* Ewart Adamson / *ph* Henry Freulich / *e* Arthur Seid / *C*: Dorothy Appleby (Rosita), Jack O'Shea (Pedro Ruiz) and Bob O'Connor (Manuel) / *SYN*: In an opening segment similar to Laurel and Hardy's *Towed in a Hole*, the Stooges are fish vendors working out of San Diego. When their business begins floundering, a Mexican real estate agent sells them a beauty salon instead of a beer saloon, south of the border. Although the mix-up disappoints them, the Stooges cheer up when they realize that all of their customers will be women! Their first customers are four pretty ladies who need their hair dyed for a new stage revue that is playing in town. Larry, Moe and Curly find the job is a cinch...well, almost. The girls emerge hairless, nailless and eyebrow-less; another woman's face is encased in cement instead of a mud pack! / *WT*: *Beauty a la Mud* / *FN*: Curly's wiggling ears achieved through invisible threads (a gag Stan Laurel used many times). Several publications have erroneously published photographs of the three bald-headed women in this film as a scene from *Loco Boy Makes Good*.

52. BOOBS IN ARMS ***½ / Rl. Dec. 27 / Prod. No. 486 / 18m / *p d* Jules White / *st scr* Felix Adler / *ph* John Stumar / *e* Mel Thorsen / *C*: Richard Fiske (Sgt. Hugh Dare), Evelyn Young (Mrs. Dare) and Phil Van Zandt (Soldier) / *SYN*: The Stooges are door-to-door greeting-card salesmen (peddling such popular selections as: "Happy Birthday Mother. Happy Birthday, Ma. Hi Mommie-Mommie, and hot-cha-cha-cha!"), who wind up escaping from a jealous husband right into what appears to be a breadline. Instead, the boys end up enlisting in the Army and the jealous husband, Mr. Dare, turns up as their sergeant. Dare presses the Stooges into service on a real battlefront, ordering them to fire a new type of shell at the enemy: laughing gas. Curly fires the shell alright, exploding it right in front of the

Stooges, who laugh uncontrollably as the enemy captures them. This culminates in a wild melee that breaks loose and Moe, Larry and Curly render the enemy unconscious. The celebration of their heroics, however, ends with them riding a speeding artillery shell out into the heavens beyond. / *WT*: *All This and Bullets Too* / *FN*: A partial reworking of Laurel and Hardy's *The Fixer Uppers*. Footage used in *Dizzy Pilots* (9/24/43). Columbia's costume department was given strict orders to design Army uniforms to *resemble* the regulation style rather than exact renditions.

1941

53. SO LONG, MR. CHUMPS *** / Rl. Feb. 7 / Prod. No. 484 / 17m / *p d* Jules White / *st scr* Clyde Bruckman and Felix Adler / *ph* Barney McGill / *e* Mel Thorsen / *C*: Vernon Dent (Detective), Robert Williams (B.O. Davis), Dorothy Appleby (Pomeroy's Girl Friend), Bert Young (Cop #2), Eddie Laughton (Pomeroy) and Bruce Bennett (Bit Man) / *SYN*: Street cleaners Larry, Moe and Curly find some bonds belonging to B.O. Davis, an ailing millionaire. When they return the bonds, Davis offers the boys $5,000 in return for tracking down an honest man with executive ability to take over his position. Eventually their search leads to a sobbing young woman who claims that her sweetheart, Percy Pomeroy, is an honest man in prison by mistake. In order to release Pomeroy, the Stooges force the police to arrest them for robbing the First National Bank, which, coincidentally, was just robbed. Sent to prison, the trio meet Pomeroy (Number 41144), their honest man, who is freed when police detectives round up the real criminal, Lone Wolf Louie. The Stooges, however, continue serving their sentence on the rock pile. / *FN*: Footage used in *Beer Barrel Polecats* (1/10/46). The idea of getting arrested purposefully was also used in *Three Smart Saps* (7/30/42) and in *The Noose Hangs High*, a 1948 feature with Abbott and Costello. Omitted from the final script was one scene where a street policeman notices the Stooges and Pomeroy's girl crying. A double-talk routine develops as to why each person is crying.

54. DUTIFUL BUT DUMB **½ / Rl. Mar. 21 / Rl. 485 / 17m / *p* Del Lord and Hugh McCollum / *d* Del Lord / *st scr* Elwood Ullman / *ph* Benjamin Kline / *e* Arthur Seid / *C*: Vernon Dent (Wilson, the Magazine Editor), Bud Jamison (Vulgarian Sgt.), James C. Morton (Captain), Bruce Bennett (Percival), Chester Conklin (Waiter) and Fred Kelsey (Colonel) / *SYN*: Moe, Larry and Curly—photographers Click, Clack and Cluck for Whack Magazine ("If It's a Good Picture, It's Out of Whack!")—are sent to Vulgaria to snap pictures of an invisible ray machine, the country's top-secret invention. Inside Vulgaria, however, where cameras are forbidden under the penalty of death, police arrest the Stooges and line them up for execution. But before meeting their maker the trio make one last request: a final smoke. Their request granted, Curly produces a jumbo-size cigar that takes several days to finish. While the soldiers are sleeping, the Stooges escape and break into the Colonel's office, mistaking the invisible ray machine for a new camera. Then, disguised as Vulgarian soldiers, the Stooges take refuge in the local commissary, where Curly pits his wits against an alive bowl of oyster stew. / FN: Almost every comedian has performed the oyster gag: Lou Costello in *Keep 'Em Flying* (1941) and *The Wistful Widow of Wagon Gap* (1948), both features, and in the 14th episode of Abbott and Costello's TV series, entitled "Hungry." The Stooges repeated the gag in *Income Tax Sappy* (2/4/54), *Shivering Sherlocks* (1/8/48) and *Of Cash and Hash* (2/3/55), using clams in the last two. The gag received

Lobby card for *I'll Never Heil Again* (1941).

one of its first showings in the Billy Bevan comedy, *Wandering Willies* (1926), directed by Del Lord.

55. ALL THE WORLD'S A STOOGE * ½** / Rl. May 16 / Prod. No. 487 / 16m / p Del Lord and Hugh McCollum / d Del Lord / st scr John Grey / ph Benjamin Kline / e Arthur Seid / C: Lelah Tyler (Lotta Bullion), Emory Parnell (Ajax Bullion), Bud Jamison (Grady, the Cop), Symona Boniface (Matron), Olaf Hytten (Barters, the Butler), Richard Fiske (Dentist), Johnny Tyrell (Building Superintendent), Gwen Seager, Poppie Wilde and Ethelreda Leopold (Guests) / SYN: Following a zany escapade as window washers-turned-dentists, the Stooges are abducted by millionaire Ajax Bullion, who dresses them as children and presents them to his wife as three refugees: Johnnie (Moe), Frankie (Curly) and Mabel

(Larry). The next day, Mrs. Bullion throws an expensive party to introduce her newly adopted offspring to her many upper-class friends. Curly makes a big impression when he enters the party smelling like a brick of limburger cheese (he rubbed some on his chest to clear up his cold). In fact, the Stooges are so cute that their cuteness even irritates Mr. Bullion, who chases them out of the house, wielding an axe. / FN: A millionaire wanting three children was later reprised in *Quiz Whizz* (2/13/58).

56. I'LL NEVER HEIL AGAIN * ½** / Rl. July 11 / Prod. No. 500 / 18m / p d Jules White / st scr Felix Adler and Clyde Bruckman / ph L.W. O'Connell / e Jerome Thoms / C: Mary Ainslee (Gilda, the King's Daughter), Johnny Kascier (Napoleon), Vernon Dent (Umpchay), Bud Jamison (Amscray),

Duncan Renaldo (Envoy/Devil), Don Barclay (Bawlin/Devil), Jack Lipson (Chizzilini) and Bert Young (Guard) / SYN: Amscray, Ixnay and Umpchay regret their appointment of Moe Hailstone as dictator of Moronica and pledge to put King Herman 6⅞ back in power. They hire Gilda, the King's daughter, to spy on Hailstone and plant an eight-ball loaded with gunpowder on the dictator's pool table. Successful in her mission, Gilda convinces Hailstone (Moe), Pebble (Larry) and Gallstone (Curly) that their axis partners are plotting to overthrow them. The Stooges call for an important meeting with the Axis Powers and the conference turns out to be an earthshaking experience when the ministers and the Stooges play catch around the room with a model globe, arguing over who gets ownership. In the midst of this unfriendly game, Curly picks up the loaded eight-ball and

throws it at one of his henchmen, blowing up the conference room. When the smoke clears, Gilda is seen reporting her victory to the King, while the Stooges' heads are seen mounted as trophies on a wall. / FN: A sequel to *You Nazty Spy* (1/19/40).

57. AN ACHE IN EVERY STAKE **** / Rl. Aug. 22 / Prod. No. 488 / 18m / Del Lord and Hugh McCollum / d Del Lord / st scr Lloyd A. French / ph Philip Tannura / e Burton Kramer / C: Vernon Dent (Poindexter Lawrence), Bud Jamison (Baker), Gino Corrado (French Chef), Bess Flowers (Mrs. Lawrence) and Symona Boniface (Party Guest) / SYN: Reminiscent of Laurel and Hardy's *The Music Box.* The Stooges' exploits as three clumsy ice delivery men cause Mrs. Lawrence's cook and maid to quit prior to her husband's big birthday party. The Stooges, however, help Mrs. Lawrence prepare for her husband's party, not realizing that Mr. Lawrence was the same man they injured earlier while delivering ice. While in the process of cooking the main entree, Larry pulls a cake out of the oven, deflating it with a pin. In order to rectify his blunder, he re-inflates the cake with a gas hose from the oven. When Mr. Lawrence blows out the candles on the cake, however, the cake explodes, plastering his face with frosting./ FN: Partially reworked later as *Listen, Judge* (3/6/52). Curly's spring-pants gag was also reprised in *Have Rocket Will Travel* (1959) and was done earlier in *Hoi Polloi* (8/29/35). The sequence of carrying ice upstairs and tangling with a man was also in *Ice Cold Cocos* (1926), with Billy Bevan, as directed by Del Lord.

58. IN THE SWEET PIE AND PIE * /** Rl. Oct. 16 / Prod. No. 482 / 17m / p d Jules White / st Ewart Adamson / scr Clyde Bruckman / ph George Meehan / e Jerome Thoms / C: Dorothy Appleby (Tiska), Mary Ainslee (Taska), Ethelreda Leopold (Baska), John Tyrell (Radio Announcer), Symona Boniface (Mrs. Gotrocks), Vernon Dent (Party Guest), Eddie Laughton (Williams, the Butler) and Bert Young (Guard) / SYN: Tiska, Taska and Baska, three beautiful sisters, must be married by midnight to collect a ten-million-dollar legacy. At the advice of their attorney, the girls marry Larry, Moe and Curly, three convicts facing a public hanging for the Mushroom Murders. The ladies can collect, however, only after the boys are executed. When the real killer, Mickey Finn, confesses to the murders, the Stooges are freed from prison and find that their aristocratic wives are not too pleased. The Stooges try to become gentlemen by taking up dancing lessons. Then, at one of the great social digs of the year, the Stooges' wives conclude after a pie-throwing melee that their attorney is the cause of all their troubles, and decide to remain married. / WT: Well, I'll Be Hanged / FN: Footage reused in *Beer Barrel Polecats* (1/10/46). Dance-lesson sequence was from *Hoi Polloi* (8/29/35). Gag of Larry shaving while society matron is applying her makeup is adapted from *Hoi Polloi* as well./ PS: Larry Fine once recalled that the most grueling scenes in this film as well as others were those involving pies. As Fine relates: "Sometimes we would run out of pies, so the prop man would sweep up the pie goop off of the floor, complete with nails, splinters, and tacks. Another problem was pretending you didn't know a pie was coming your way. To solve this, Jules would tell me, 'Now Larry, Moe's going to smack you with a pie on the count of three.' Then Jules would tell Moe, 'Hit Larry on the count of *two*!' So when it came time to counting, I never got to three, because Moe crowned me with a pie!" (See *Moe Howard & the 3 Stooges*, p. 82, last paragraph.)

59. SOME MORE OF SAMOA **½ / Rl. Dec. 4 / Prod. No. 511 / 17m / *p* Del Lord and Hugh McCollum / *st scr* Harry Edwards and Ellwood Ullman / *ph* L.W. O'Connell / *e* Burton Kramer / *C:* Louise Carver (Nurse) and Monty Collins (Explorer) / *SYN:* An ailing millionaire, Mr. Winthrop, hires tree surgeons Howard, Fine and Howard to track down a mate for his persimmon tree so it will be able to bear fruit. The millionaire sends the Stooges to the Isle of Rhum Boogie to complete their quest. But Curly is appointed the cannibals' new chief. The old chief offers the Stooges a persimmon tree and their freedom, providing one of them will marry his sister. Uninterested in the chief's ugly sister, the Stooges take flight with the tree, paddling off in their sinking canoe. / *FN:* Idol gag was later reused in *Hula La La* (11/1/51). In the Stooges' office, Curly's sudden growth (caused by an injection of the Vitamin P.D.Q) was accomplished by dressing him in longer trousers and raising him on a jack through the floor.

1942
60. LOCO BOY MAKES GOOD ***½ / Rl. Jan. 8 / Prod. No. 510 / 17m / *p d* Jules White / *st scr* Felix Adler and Clyde Bruckman / *ph* John Stumar / *e* Jerome Thoms / *C:* Dorothy Appleby (Miss Stompandale), Vernon Dent (Man), Bud Jamison (Baldo the Magician), Robert Williams (Bit Man), Eddie Laughton (Drunk) and John Tyrell (Waldo Finchell) / *SYN:* The Stooges help the widow owner of the Happy Haven Hotel raise money to pay off her note by remodeling the hotel into the Kokonutz Grove, a ritzy nightclub. On opening night, the boys provide the entertainment as "Nill, Null and Void, Three Hams Who Lay Their Own Eggs," singing "She Was Bread in Old Kentucky but She's Just a Crumb Up Here." In attendance is Waldo Finchell, a well-known columnist, whose rave review of the Stooges' show saves the hotel from debt. / *WT: Poor But Dishonest* / *FN:* The segment of Curly unrolling linoleum (instead of carpeting or wallpaper) is an old standard. The "Driving Nails" routine was later redone in *The Three Stooges in Orbit* (1962). The song, "She Was Bread in Old Kentucky," does not appear in the final draft script. Instead, Curly was supposed to mime *Yankee Doodle* like a seal playing several harmonicas. On March 7,

1946, comedian Harold Lloyd sued writers Clyde Bruckman and Felix Adler, director Jules White and Columbia Pictures for Bruckman's use of Lloyd's magician's coat sequence from *Movie Crazy* (1932) in *Loco Boy Makes Good*. Lloyd sought $500,000 in damages.

61. CACTUS MAKES PERFECT ***½ / Rl. Feb. 26 / Prod. No. 513 / 17m / *p* Del Lord and Hugh McCollum / *d* Del Lord / *st scr* Elwood Ullman and Monty Collins / *ph* Benjamin Kline / *e* Burton Kramer / *C:* Monty Collins (Mother Stooge), Vernon Dent (Red) and Ernie Adams (Stumpy) / *SYN:* Curly receives a letter from the Inventors' Association saying that his gold collar button retriever "is incomprehensible and utterly impractical." The Stooges misinterpret the letter to imply that they're a success, and head west to strike gold with Curly's invention (a weird-looking bow-and-arrow combination). During their journey, the trio buys the phoney deed to the Lost Mine from another prospector. The mine supposedly contains 187,000 tons of gold worth $35 an ounce. Two down-on-their-luck prospectors, Red and Stumpy, try swindling the Stooges out of their claim, but the trio wins out.

62 WHAT'S THE MATADOR **½ / Rl. Apr. 23 / Prod. No. 519 / 16½m / *p d* Jules White / *st* Jack White / *scr* Jack White and Saul Ward *ph* L.W. O'Connell / *e* Jerome Thoms / *C:* Suzanne Kaaren (Senora Delores Sanchez), Harry Burns (Jose), Dorothy Appleby (Gorgeous Girl), Eddie Laughton (Shamus O'Brien), Don Zelaya (Sleeping Mexican) and Bert Young (Bull Ring Attendant) / *SYN:* A jealous husband, Jose, gets even with the Stooges for allegedly having a love affair with his wife, Delores. While performing their comedy bullfight act at a local bullfight arena, Jose arranges a real bull to be substituted for the fake one containing Moe and Larry. When matador Curly notices the real bull, he takes evasive action and runs head first into the animal, knocking it unconscious, much to the delight of the crowd, who chant "Olé Americano!" Curly is crowned the matador of the century! / *WT: Run, Bull, Run* / *FN:* Reworked, with some stock footage, as *Sappy Bullfighters* (6/4/59). Scenes also used in *Stop! Look! and Laugh!* (7/60). Originally, when the bull spots the Stooges bowing to the crowd, he was supposed to zero in on their derrieres, uttering, "Eenie, Meenie, Minnie, Moe!"

63. MATRI-PHONY **½ / Rl. July 2 / Prod. No. 527 / 17m / *p* Del Lord and Hugh McCollum / *d* Harry Edwards / *st scr* Elwood Ullman and Monty Collins / *ph* George Meehan / *e* Paul Borofsky / *C:* Vernon Dent (Octopus Grabus) and Marjorie Deanne (Diana) / *SYN:* Moehicus, Larrycus, and Curlycue are potters in ancient Erysipelas during the reign of the rash emperor, Octopus Grabus. When Grabus, seeking a bride, orders all beautiful redheads to report to the palace immediately, one of them, Diana, takes refuge with the

Stooges. It is Diana who Grabus is intent on marrying. When Octopus calls on Diana, Curly disguises himself as the luscious redhead, wooing Octopus (in the previous draft screenplay, Larry was to take Diana's place). The near-sighted emperor warms up to Curly, chasing him around the room and, finally, catching and unmasking him / *FN:* The gag of acting as a puppeteer from behind a curtain for an unconscious victim was reused with Shemp in two Stooge comedies, *Fright Night* (3/6/47) and its remake, *Fling in the Ring* (1/6/55). An earlier screenplay version of *Matri-Phony* had Diana and the Stooges making their final escape up a snake charmer's rope.

64. THREE SMART SAPS *** / Rl. July 30 / Prod. No. 532 / 16½m / *p d* Jules White / *st scr* Clyde Bruckman / *ph* Benjamin Kline / *e* Jerome Thoms / *C:* Julie Duncan (Bella), Julie Gibson (Della), Ruth Skinner (Stella), Bud Jamison (Mr. Hugh, the Tailor), John Tyrell (Mr. Stevens), Sally Cairns (Dancing Partner), Eddie Laughton (Guard), Vic Travers (Justice of the Peace), Frank Coleman (Cop) and Frank Terry (Man on the Street) / *SYN:* It's the Three Stooges' wedding day! Their fiancees, Stella, Della and Bella, refuse to commence with the ceremony because their father, the warden of the city jail, is a prisoner in one of his own cells. The Stooges promise the girls they'll save their father so that the marriage can go as planned. A short time later, at the county jail, the Stooges uncover their future father-in-law and learn that Walker, the new warden, is a crook who is operating the jail as a members-only casino (the members are gangsters). In order to free Walker, the Stooges sneak into the casino and take candid pictures as evidence. Since formal attire is required, Moe clobbers a guest and steals his suit, while Curly finds one with loose stitching. The stiching falls apart when Curly takes to dancing with one of the female members. In the middle of several dance numbers, Curly sidles over to a curtain for repairs (Larry is behind the drape, with a sewing kit). Curly's last pass before the curtain becomes painful when Larry pokes him with a sewing needle, right in the trousers! On the floor in pain, Curly is helped up by his dance partner, who accidentally rips off his suit. With the necessary pictorial evidence in hand, Moe and Larry escort Curly (in his underwear) out of the party. Their future father-in-law is released when the Stooges' photographic evidence undermines the members-only club. / *WT: Father's In Jail Again* / *FN:* The premise of the Stooges getting pinched to help someone else also appears in *The Noose Hangs High* (1948) with Abbott and Costello, and in *So Long Mr. Chumps* (2/7/41), starring the Stooges. The "Are You Dancing?" gag was originally done in *Hoi Polloi* (8/29/35). Curly's loosely hemmed trousers' gag was borrowed from Harold Lloyd's *The Freshman* (1925). / *PS:* Three Smart Saps marked screen actress Julie Gibson's first film with the Stooges. She relates her impressions of working with Curly: "I don't think we ex-

The crew reassures Curly as he hangs 20 feet in
the air during production of *They Stooge to Conga*
(1943).

changed *one* word. He was just absolutely
quiet. Moe and Larry were a lot of fun, more
than Curly. Larry would do a soft-shoe and
tell funny stories. Moe was smart and cute,
kind of a smart ass, but fun. I was afraid to
even say 'hello' to Curly. He was fine when
he was with Moe and Larry; but seemed
deathly afraid of women. The scene I hated
the most was when I had to kiss him. I think
I closed my eyes because he was like a piece
of wood."

65. EVEN AS I.O.U. **½ / Rl. Sept. 18 /
Prod. No. 507 / 15½m / *p* Del Lord and
Hugh McCollum / *d* Del Lord / *st scr* Felix
Adler / *ph* L.W. O'Connell / *e* Paul Borofsky
/ *C*: Ruth Skinner (Mrs. Blake), Stanley
Blystone (Joe), Wheaton Chambers (Bud),
Vernon Dent (Driver of Car), Bud Jamison
(Cop), Billy Bletcher (Voice of Seabascuit),
Heinie Conklin and Jack Gardner (Bit Men)
/ *SYN*: Bookmakers Moe, Larry and Curly
try raising the necessary money to pull an
evicted woman and her child out of debt by
betting the girl's piggy bank money on a
winning filly. Two race track con-artists,
however, fast-talk the Stooges out of their
winnings, trading the cash in for a broken-
down mare named Seabascuit (the horse

talks because one of the thugs is a ventriloquist). To remedy the horse's poor physical
condition, Curly grabs a pipe and tries
blowing a vitamin down the thoroughbred's
throat; but he swallows the pill by mistake.
Within seconds, Curly starts acting and
sounding like a horse and, when his condition worsens, Moe and Larry rush him to
the hospital where he gives birth to a colt
that really talks! / *FN*: The "Press, Press,
Pull" routine first appeared in *Three Little
Beers* (11/28/35) while Curly's bit involving
blowing a vitamin through a pipe was reprised in *Scrambled Brains* (7/7/51) and
Hoofs and Goofs (1/31/57). Selling old dope
sheets is reused in *Las Vegas*, the 22nd TV
episode of *The Abbott and Costello Show*
(1952-3).

66. SOCK-A-BYE BABY **½ / Rl. Nov. 13 /
Prod. No. 539 / 18m / *p d* Jules White / *st scr*
Clyde Bruckman / *ph* Benjamin Kline / *e*
Jerome Thoms / *C*: Julie Gibson (Mrs. Col-
lins), Clarence Straight (Sam Collins), Bud
Jamison (Pete, the Cop) and Baby Joyce
Gardner (Jimmy) / *SYN*: The Stooges find a
baby on their doorstep left by a policeman's
wife. Delighted Moe, Larry and Curly set
out to fix breakfast for the child, but later

read in the newspaper that police are looking for the kidnapped infant. Thus, when
two officers and the child's mother come
knocking at the Stooges' door, the trio take
the foundling and make a run for it in their
station wagon. The police pursue on motor-
cycles and, following a whirlwind chase,
recover the baby, while the cop and his wife
patch up their differences. Meanwhile, the
Stooges get away disguised as bushes. / *WT*:
Their First Baby. / *FN*: Footage revived in
Stop! Look! and Laugh! (7/60).

1943
67. THEY STOOGE TO CONGA *½ / Rl.
Jan. 1 / Prod. No. 533 / 15½m / *p* Del Lord
and Hugh McCollum / *d* Del Lord / *st scr*
Elwood Ullman and Monty Collins / *ph*
George Meehan / *e* Paul Borofsky / *a* Carl
Anderson / *C*: Vernon Dent (Hans), Dudley
Dickerson (Wilbur the Cook) and Lloyd
Bridges (Phone Caller) / *SYN*: The Stooges
are repairmen fixing a doorbell in a house
where top Nazi and Japanese conspirators
are planning to conquer the world with their
new high-powered submarine. While
searching for the house's electrical wiring
system, the boys overhear the spies' plan to
operate the submarine via remote control.

243

Moe and Larry then disguise themselves as Hitler and Tojo, overtake the conspirators, man the controls, and blow up the submarine. / *PS*: *They Stooge to Conga* is one of the most violent Three Stooges comedies, featuring a spike gag that makes even ardent fans cringe. Moe's eyes and ears are on the receiving end of a spike from Curly's shoe while Curly is scaling a telephone pole. Just who is responsible for the crudeness of its presentation—the writer, the producer, or the director? Screenwriter Elwood Ullman is innocent. In the script, Ullman calls for Curly's spike to dig into Moe's ear *once*, never in the eyeball. In an interview session, writer-producer-director Norman Maurer and Edward Bernds discussed the spike gag. As Maurer said: "In the scene you're talking about, that is strictly cutting. And there's only one man who's going to cut that scene, and that's the producer." Edward Bernds added: "You can't blame the producer for a scene that the director directed, but you can blame him for the way he cuts it." In the case of the scene in question, however, it is believed that both the director and producer were responsible: the director for going farther with the gag then the script

intended, and the producer for not having the taste to cut it out.

68. DIZZY DETECTIVES **** / Rl. Feb. 5 / Prod. No. 529 / 18½m / *p d* Jules White / *st scr* Felix Adler / *ph* Benjamin Kline / *e* Jerome Thoms / *a* Carl Anderson / *C*: John Tyrell (Mr. Dill), Bud Jamison (I. Doolittle), Dick Jensen (Second Crook) and Lynton Brent (Mike, the First Crook) / *SYN*: Mysterious burglaries are the topic of conversation when the Ape Man strikes again. Joe Dill, the head of the Citizens' League, demands that the police inspector, I. Doolittle, track down the gorilla or he'll ask for his resignation. Doolittle has no other choice than to hire three new detectives, the Stooges, to solve the case. Hot on the trail, the boys come upon the animal in a curio shop and have a series of freak adventures. In the course of the spooky night, they capture three crooks (one of them is Joe Dill), who own the trained ape. / *WT*: *Idiots DeLuxe* / *FN*: Carpenter routine was used from *Pardon My Scotch* (8/1/35). Remade with Joe Besser and Jim Hawthorne as *Fraidy Cat* (12/13/51), and later as *Hook a Crook* (11/24/55), also with Besser.

69. SPOOK LOUDER *** / Rl. Apr. 2 / Prod. No. 549 / 16m / *p* Del Lord and Hugh McCollum / *d* Del Lord / *st scr* Clyde Bruckman / *ph* John Stumar / *e* Paul Borofsky / *a* Carl Anderson / *C*: Stanley Blystone (Spy Leader), William Kelly (J. Ogden Dunkfeather), Symona Boniface (Well-Dressed Woman), Ted Lorch (Mr. Graves, Inventor) and Charles Middleton (Butler) / *SYN*: A newspaper reporter calls upon a special investigator to sniff out the inside story behind the breaking up of the great spy ring. As the investigator tells the story, the Stooges are seen in flashback as salesmen peddling the Miracle Massage Reducing Machine. Two unsuccessful sales later, Moe, Larry and Curly pay a visit to the house of an eccentric scientist, who mistakes them for caretakers. When the scientist is called to Washington to demonstrate his new death ray machine, however, he asks the Stooges to sleep overnight so spies won't break in to steal his invention. That night, climaxing a series of eerie events, conspirators invade the premises and pies mysteriously explode out of nowhere, plastering the Stooges. Still in pursuit of the spies, however, Curly finally scares them away

Lobby card for *Crash Goes the Hash* (1944).

when he whips out a bomb. The spirit of another being remains in the house, however, and throws another round of lemon meringue pies at the Stooges. Out of flashback, the question remains, "Who threw those pies?" The investigator turns to the screen answering "Oh, *I* threw the pies!" Chuckling devilishly, he gets clobbered with a pie himself! / *SD*: 4 (F 7/17 to SA 7/18, and M 7/20 to T 7/21/42) / *FN*: A remake of Mack Sennett's *The Great Pie Mystery*, also directed by Del Lord.

70. BACK FROM THE FRONT **½ / Rl. May 28 / Prod. No. 522 / 19m / *p d* Jules White / *st scr* Jack White and Ewart Adamson / *ph* John Stumar / *e* Edwin Bryant / *a* Carl Anderson / *C*: Vernon Dent (Lt. Dungen), Bud Jamison (Petty Officer), Stanley Blystone (German Captain), Heinie Conklin (German Sailor) and George Gray (German Sailor) / *SYN*: Moe, Larry and Curly are Merchant Mariners serving their country. As crew members of the S.S. Dotty, the boys' first mission is cut short when their ship is torpedoed, leaving the Stooges stranded on a raft at sea until they climb aboard a passing German cruiser. Immediately, disguising themselves as German soldiers, the Stooges learn that their old commanding officer, Lt. Dungen, has been supplying top secret information to the Germans. The trio knock out every crew member and pose as Hitler, Goering, and Goebbels before capturing the vessel's commanding officers and Dungen. / *WT*: *A Sailor's Mess* / *FN*: Seasick gag was reused in *Dunked in the Deep* (11/3/49) and in *Commotion on the Ocean* (11/8/56) as stock footage.

71. THREE LITTLE TWIRPS *** / Rl. July 9 / Prod. No. 551/ 15½m / *p* Del Lord and Hugh McCollum / *d* Harry Edwards / *st scr* Monty Collins and Elwood Ullman / *ph* John Stumar / *e* Paul Borofsky / *a* Carl Anderson / *C*: Chester Conklin (Joe, the Circus Attendant), Heinie Conklin (Louie, the Attendant), Stanley Blystone (Herman), Bud Jamison (Detective) and Duke York (Sultan of Abadaba) / *SYN*: The Stooges wreak havoc at a local circus, with Curly hiding in a dressing room only to be mistaken by Effie the Bearded Lady as her blind date. He shaves the girl's beard off, causing her to faint. So when Herman, the circus owner, calls on Effie to come out and perform inside the Big Top, Curly disguises himself as the Bearded Lady, but his bonnet gets knocked off, revealing his true identity, and the chase begins. He meets up with Moe and Larry (wearing a horse costume), and takes refuge among some real mares. The Stooges' disguise soon fails when Joe, the circus attendant, tries serving them as a lion's next meal. Later, the Stooges are arrested, but Herman gives them one last break; the Sultan of Abadaba needs three volunteers as human targets for his spear throwing act. / *FN*: Moe and Larry in a horse costume was reprised in *Horsing Around* (9/12/57).

72. HIGHER THAN A KITE *** / Rl. July

30 / Prod. No. 568 / 17m / *p* Del Lord and Hugh McCollum / *d* Del Lord / *st scr* Elwood Ullman and Monty Collins / *ph* Benjamin Kline / *e* Paul Borofsky / *a* Victor Greene / *C*: Dick Curtis (Kelly) and Vernon Dent (Marshall Boring) / *SYN*: Larry, Moe and Curly travel to England with intentions of joining the R.A.F. as pilots, but wind up as garage mechanics when Curly fails an intelligence test. Of course, the Stooges prove they know very little about cars by ruining the Colonel's automobile (it only had a *little* squeak). When the Colonel threatens to kill them, the trio take refuge in what appears to be a sewer pipe, but turns out to be a blockbuster bomb heading for Germany. The Stooges get a free ride, therefore, when the bomb is dropped on Nazi General Bommel's headquarters. Uninjured by the explosion, Larry hides in the wine cellar, while Moe and Curly disguise themselves as German officers. When Marshall Boring arrives to review Nazi war plans, Larry is discovered when the Marshall requests a bottle of wine (Larry is dressed like a German fraulein). General Bommel falls for Larry, and the boys steal the war plans.

73. I CAN HARDLY WAIT ** / Rl. Aug. 13 / Prod. No. 570 / 16½m / *p d* Jules White / *st scr* Clyde Bruckman / *ph* John Stumar / *e* Charles Hochberg / *a* Victor Greene / *C*: Bud Jamison (Dr. Yank), Adele St. Mara (Receptionist) and Dick Curtis (Dr. Tug) / *SYN*: While consuming a ham bone, Curly develops a terrible toothache, with the pain becoming so intense that he can't sleep. But when he does fall into slumber, he dreams that Moe and Larry rush him to the dentist and that Moe shows him there is nothing to be frightened of as he sits in the dentist's chair. The dentist enters and pulls Moe's tooth by accident. Hence, Curly's dream turns into a nightmare, as he tosses in his sleep, and causes his upper bunk to crash down on the two lower bunks containing Moe and Larry. Tired of this ordeal, Moe socks Curly in the jaw, popping out his tooth. / *WT*: *Nothing But the Tooth* / *FN*: Collapsing bed sequence is from *In the Sweet Pie and Pie* (10/16/41). Pulling teeth gag also in *Leave 'Em Laughing* (1928), with Laurel and Hardy.

74. DIZZY PILOTS **½ / Rl. Sept. 24 / Prod. No. 555 / 17m / *p d* Jules White / *st scr* Clyde Bruckman / *ph* Benjamin Kline / *e* Charles Hochberg / *a* Victor Greene / *C*: Richard Fiske (Sergeant), Judy Malcolm, Sethma Williams (Girls in Hanger) and Harry Semels (Test Flight Bystander) / *SYN*: The Stooges, as the Wrong Brothers, have thirty days to prove to the Army that their new airplane, *The Buzzard*, can revolutionize flying. At last, when the boys are ready to test this new-fangled flying machine, Moe discovers one more snag: the plane is too wide to move out of the hangar. This problem is quickly solved when the Stooges saw a larger opening in the airplane's garage. The trio encounter two additional setbacks: their test flight fails and they are drafted

into the Army. For their sergeant's benefit, the Stooges perform a peculiar marching sequence, disrupt the works and make a menace of their commanding officer. / *WT*: *Pest Pilots* / *FN*: Army scenes are from *Boobs in Arms* (12/7/40). The gag of an oversized aircraft in a small hangar was later revived in *The Three Stooges in Orbit*. (1962).

75. PHONY EXPRESS ** / Rl. Nov. 18 / Prod. No. 569 / 17m / *p* Del Lord and Hugh McCollum / *d* Del Lord / *st scr* Elwood Ullman and Monty Collins / *ph* John Stumar / *e* Paul Borofsky / *a* Victor Greene / *C*: Shirley Patterson (Lola), Chester Conklin (Mr. Higgins), Snub Pollard (Sheriff), Bud Jamison (Red Morgan), Sally Cleaves, Gwen Seager (Dancing Partners), John Merton (Joe, Red's Assistant) and Joel Friedkin (Doc Abdul) / *SYN*: After a mine payroll, Red Morgan and his gang invade the town of Peaceful Gulch. The city's newspaper editor publishes a photograph of the Stooges, wanted for vagrancy, claiming they are really three famous marshalls coming to town. In the meantime, Larry, Moe and Curly are across the border selling patent medicine for their boss, Abdul. When the team's patent medicine sales backfire, it's off to the Peaceful Gulch Saloon, where Red Morgan mistakes them for the marshals. Unfortunately, Morgan soon learns from the saloon's waiter that the Stooges are actually wanted for vagrancy. In the ensuing chase, the boys accidentally render Morgan unconscious, and later they are deputized to guard the bank from Morgan's gang of bank robbers. Naturally, Red and his mob rob the bank, with the Stooges recovering the loot to save the day. / *FN*: Reworked with some stock footage as *Merry Mavericks* (9/6/51).

76. A GEM OF A JAM *** / Rl. Dec. 30 / Prod. 575 / 16½m / *p* Hugh McCollum / *d* Del Lord / *st scr* Del Lord / *ph* John Stumar / *e* Paul Borofsky / *a* Victor Greene / *C*: Bud Jamison (Cop), Fred Kelsey (Cop) and Dudley Dickerson (Watchman) / *SYN*: Janitors Moe, Larry and Curly are mistaken for doctors Hart, Burns and Belcher, when three bank robbers suddenly rush in to the doctor's office and order them to remove a bullet from one of the wounded robbers. With no time to explain, the Stooges start operating and accidentally lose their patient, who slides off the operating table and right out the window into a waiting police car. When the remaining two crooks find a skeleton instead of their partner on the operating table, they chase the Stooges into a room of mannequins and wax models. During the commotion, Curly trips into a tray of plaster and arises as a ghost, scaring everyone except the police, who arrest the crooks.

1944

77. CRASH GOES THE HASH ***½ / Rl. Feb. 5 / Prod. No. 4010 / 17m / *p d* Jules White / *st scr* Felix Adler / *ph* George Meehan / *e* Charles Hochberg / *a* Charles Clague / *C*: Vernon Dent (Fuller Bull), Bud

Jamison (Flint, the Head Butler), Dick Curtis (Prince Shaam), Symona Boniface (Mrs. Van Bustle), Wally Rose, Johnny Kascier, John Tyrell (Three Bruised Reporters), Judy Malcolm (Secretary), Bea Blinn, Ida Mae Johnson, Vic Travers and Elise Grover (Party Guests) / SYN: As delivery men for the Star Pressing Company, the Stooges are accidentally hired as reporters for the *Daily News* and sent to cover the wedding of social beauty Mrs. Van Bustle and Prince Shaam. In order to gain entry into the wedding, the Stooges pose as footmen and butlers, serving the guests a wild array of entrees, including their own bizarre version of "canapes" (dog biscuits smothered in peas) and a walking turkey (brought to life by a parrot inside). Following dinner, however, the trio snap a picture of the Prince, showing him in the act of robbing Mrs. Van Bustle's safe. For solving the case, the Stooges' boss gives them a bonus and Curly receives an added prize—the hand of Mrs. Van Bustle. / FN: Parrot in turkey gag was reprised in *G.I. Wanna Home* (9/5/46), *Three Dark Horses* (10/16/52) and *Listen, Judge* (3/6/52).

78. BUSY BUDDIES **½ / Rl. Mar. 18 / Prod. No. 4001 / 16½m / p Hugh McCollum / d Del Lord / st scr Del Lord and Elwood Ullman / ph George Meehan / e Henry Batista / a Charles Clague / C: Vernon Dent (Gus), Fred Kelsey (Bakery Man), Eddie Laughton (Mr. Gordon) and John Tyrell (Referee) / SYN: In order to pay off a $97 pastry bill as operators of a cheap beanery, Moe and Larry enter Curly as one of the contestants in the County Fair's Cow-Milking Contest, with the top prize $1,000. When Curly experiences difficulty milking a real cow, Moe dons a cow costume featuring a giant milk bottle covered with a glove. His substitution plan works successfully until Curly yanks the glove off the bottle, causing the milk to gush out rapidly, disqualifying the Stooges. / FN: See *Hoofs and Goofs* (1/31/57).

79. THE YOKE'S ON ME * / Rl. May 26 / Prod. No. 571 / 16½m / p d Jules White / st scr Clyde Bruckman / ph Glen Gano / e Charles Hochberg / a Charles Clague / C: Bob McKenzie (Pa), Emmett Lynn (Smithers) and Judy Malcolm (Bit Girl) / SYN: The Stooges become farmers as a last resort when every branch of the armed service turns them down as physical liabilities. So the boys buy a dilapidated farmhouse and survey the grounds to find that no livestock exists, except for an ostrich. Later, the Stooges encounter three Japanese soldiers who have escaped from a local Relocation Center. The soldiers' flight is cut short, however, when the Stooges' ostrich consumes some gun powder, laying an explosive egg. / WT: *Fowled by a Fowl* / FN: This Stooge comedy is blacklisted by some television stations because of its racial content.

80. IDLE ROOMERS **½ / Rl. July 16 / Prod. No. 4013 / 16½m / p Hugh McCollum / d Del Lord / st scr Del Lord and Elwood Ullman / ph Glen Gano / e Henry Batista / a Charles Clague / C: Christine McIntyre (Mrs. Leander), Duke York (Lupe, the Wolf Man), Vernon Dent (Mr. Leander), Joanne Frank (Hazel) and Esther Howard (Elderly Woman) / SYN: Two vaudeville performers arrive at a hotel where the Stooges are bellboys with a trunk containing a Wolf Man who goes wild whenever he hears music. Curly unloads the trunk and turns on the radio, causing the Wolf Man to escape into rooms occupied by other guests. When petrified guests report seeing a hairy burglar in the hotel, the manager orders the Stooges to find him. Their frantic search ends in the elevator, which is occupied by—who else— the Wolf Man.

81. GENTS WITHOUT CENTS *** / Rl. Sept. 22 / Prod. No. 4020 / 19m / p d Jules White / ST scr Felix Adler / ph Benjamin Kline / e Charles Hochberg / a Charles Clague / C: Lindsay, Laverne, and Betty (Themselves), Johnny Tyrell (Manny Weeks), Bob Burns (Man with Hard Hat in Audience) and Lynton Brent (Sketch Lieutenant) / SYN: Following an audition for talent scout Manny Weeks, the Stooges and a trio of dancing girls are hired to replace a shipyard act, the Castor and Earle Revue. The Stooges perform "Niagara Falls" and an Army routine, "At the Front," while the girls provide the dancing. The show closes a triumphant success and the Stooges marry the girls, embarking on a honeymoon for— where else—Niagara Falls! / WT: *Tenderized Hams* / FN: The Niagara Falls sequence was originally filmed for Columbia's 1943 feature, *Good Luck, Mr. Yates*, but was cut out of the final release print at the last minute.

82. NO DOUGH, BOYS *** / Rl. Nov. 24 / Prod. No. 564 / 16½m / p d Jules White / st scr Felix Adler / ph George Meehan / e Charles Hochberg / a Charles Clague / C: Vernon Dent (Hugo), Christine McIntyre (Delia), Brian O'Hara (Waiter/Chef), Kelly Flint (Amelia) and Judy Malcolm (Celia)/ SYN: The Stooges are modeling as Japanese soldiers for a photographer. When their shutter-bug boss is called away, the trio grab lunch at Joe's Beanery, still in costume. The waiter mistakes them for three real escaped Japanese soldiers and summons the police. Before the police can arrest them, however, the Stooges flee and take refuge in a room full of Nazi spies awaiting the arrival of three ju jitsu experts. The Stooges pose as the ju jitsu men until the real guys show up. / WT: *The New World Odor* / FN: Smoking an imaginery pipe gag was also used in *Way Out West* (1937), with Laurel and Hardy.

1945
83. THREE PESTS IN A MESS *** / Rl. Jan. 19 (not Jan. 9) / Prod. No. 4022 / 15m / p Hugh McCollum / d st scr Del Lord / ph Benjamin Kline / e Henry Batista / a Charles Clague / C: Vernon Dent (Mr. Black), Vic Travers (Patent Office Man), Snub Pollard (Watchman), Christine McIntyre (Girl), Brian O'Hara (I. Cheatam) and Heinie Conklin (Devil) / SYN: When Larry, Moe and Curly try selling a Patent Office clerk on their fly-catching machine, a woman from the Cheatam Investment Co. mistakes the Stooges as winners of a sweepstakes ticket worth $100,000. Once she discovers she's goofed, however, her two crooked associates return and chase the Stooges into a sporting goods shop, where a rifle falls on Curly's head. He takes the weapon and accidentally fires it. It hits a mannequin and Curly thinks he's killed a real man. The trio stuff the mannequin into a trash bag and try burying the evidence at Ever Rest Pet Cemetery. A night watchman hears them digging, however, and calls the cemetery owner, Mr. Black, who leaves a costume party, bringing along his two partners who are dressed as a devil and a skeleton. Naturally, Black and his men scare the Stooges out of their shoes and out of the cemetery! / FN: To achieve the gag of Larry sliding underneath the door, the prop man dug a hole and covered it with rubber, then pulled Larry below in a speed shot. The gag of disposing of a mock dead body was also in *Habeas Corpus* (1928), with Laurel and Hardy.

84. BOOBY DUPES **½ / Rl. Mar. 17 / Prod. No. 4006 / 17m / p Hugh McCollum / d st scr Del Lord / ph Glen Gano / e Henry Batista / a Charles Clague / C: Vernon Dent (Captain), Rebel Randall (Captain's Girl), Dorothy Vernon (Woman Customer), Johnny Tyrell (Boat Man), Snub Pollard (Ice Cream Vendor), Wanda Perry, Geene Courtney and Lola Gogan (Bathing Beauties) / SYN: Fish salesmen Moe, Larry and Curly set sail on their first fishing expedition and sink the boat when Curly goes after a fish with an axe. Fortunately, the Stooges yank out a spare boat but find that it has no motor. At this same moment, the boys hear a squadron of airplanes passing overhead. Moe quickly manufacturers a flag (a white sheet with a red-stained circle in the center) on a pole and begins waving it wildly. One of the pilots, however, misinterprets his distress signal for a Japanese flag and starts bombing the Stooges' boat. / FN: A partial reworking of Laurel and Hardy's *Towed in a Hole* (12/31/32).

85. IDIOTS DELUXE *** / Rl. July 20 / Prod. No. 4030 / 17½m / p d Jules White / st scr Elwood Ullman / ph Glen Gano / e Charles Hochberg / a Hilyard Brown / C: Vernon Dent (Judge), Paul Kruger (Cop), Gwen Seager (Mamie), and Eddie Laughton (Bit Man) / SYN: The scene is a courtroom. Moe is accused of assaulting his two brothers-in-law, Larry and Curly, with an axe while on a hunting trip searching for peace and quiet. A zany escapade with a ferocious bear in the wilderness is responsible for triggering the altercation. In the courtroom, Moe mumbles that the trip cost him $300, ruined his car (the bear crashed it into a tree) and gave him a complete nervous breakdown. Sympathetic, the judge finds Moe not guilty and allows him to keep his axe. Thanking the judge, Moe wields the sharp tool at Larry and Curly whom he chases out of the courtoom / WT: *The Mal-*

One-sheet for *Micro-Phonies* (1945). Note that Harry Edwards is incorrectly billed as writer and director.

ady Lingers On / FN: Remade with stock footage as *Guns-A-Poppin'* (6/13/57).

86. IF A BODY MEETS A BODY **½ / Rl. Aug. 30 / Prod. No. 4033 / 18m / *p d* Jules White / *st* Gilbert Pratt / *scr* Jack White / *ph* Benjamin Kline / *e* Charles Hochberg / *a* Charles Clague / *C*: Ted Lorch (Jerkington), Fred Kelsey (Detective Clancy) and Joe Palma (Housekeeper) / *SYN*: Moe and Larry read in the newspaper that the relatives of the late Professor Robert O. Link are searching for Curly Q. Link, the heir to his $3 million estate. When Curly informs Moe and Larry that Link was his uncle, the Stooges leave immediately for the reading of the will at a spooky old mansion. But the will gets stolen. At the mansion, meanwhile, there have been reports of murders and other weird happenings. In their room, the Stooges witness so many strange goings-on themselves that they flee downstairs, knocking over the maid, who turns out to be a man and the thief of the Link will. Curly grabs the document, anxious to know his inheritance, and learns that his uncle has bequeathed him the sum of 67 cents! / *WT*: *Nearly in the Dough* / *FN*: A remake of *Laurel and Hardy Murder Case* (1930). Parrot in the skull gag was also used in *Hot Scots* (7/8/48) and in *Scotched in Scotland* (11/4/54).

87. MICRO-PHONIES *** / Rl. Nov. 15 / Prod. No. 4044 / 17m / *p* Hugh McCollum / *d st scr* Edward Bernds / *ph* Glen Gano / *e* Henry Batista / *a* Charles Clague / *C*: Christine McIntyre (Alice Bixby), Gino Corrado (Signor Spumoni), Symona Boniface (Mrs. Bixby), Sam Flint (Mr. Bixby), Fred Kelsey (Boss Dugan), Chester Conklin (Drunk Pianist), Bess Flowers (Party Guest), Lynton Brent (Don Allen) and Ted Lorch (Masters) / *SYN*: When Curly mimes a girl's recording of "Voices of Spring" at a local radio station, Mrs. Bixby, a wealthy dowager, observes his antics and signs Moe, Larry and Curly to perform on her Krispy Krunchies radio program. Bixby is unaware that the demonstation record was cut by her daughter, Alice. The woman also asks the Stooges to sing at her musical party. That evening the boys are reunited at the party with Signor Spumoni, whom the Stooges antagonized earlier at the radio station. The Stooges are also spotted by Alice Bixby, the real singer of "Voices of Spring." When Moe accidentally smashes the demo recording, Alice offers to sing for the boys behind a curtain. At the conclusion of their song, however, Spumoni exposes their fake set-up as the Stooges make a hasty exit, and Alice is asked to appear on her mother's show instead. / *FN*: Footage reused in *Stop! Look! and Laugh!* (7/60). The flipping cherries into an opera singer's mouth gag (changed to grapes) was also used in *Pardon My Scotch* (8/1/35). Plot was also used in *Hot Sports* (1929), with Monty Collins and directed by Jules White.

1946

88. BEER BARREL POLECATS ** / Rl. Jan. 10 / Prod. No. 4045 / 17m / *p d* Jules White/ *st scr* Gilbert W. Pratt / *ph* George Kelly / *e* Charles Hochberg / *a* Charles Clague / *C*: Robert Williams (Guard), Vernon Dent (Warden), Bruce Bennett (Convict 41144) and Joe Palma (Convict) / *SYN*: The Stooges emerge from their 16th cocktail bar still searching for a cold bottle of beer. Rather than continue their hunt, Curly suggests the Stooges produce their own. Their first customer is a police officer, who throws them in jail. Curly refuses to be deprived of his beer, however, smuggling in a keg under his coat. While he is posing for a prison photograph, the hot lights cause his barrel to explode, sending a torrent of suds in all directions. Now in prison for their misdeed, the Stooges plan their escape (stock footage from *In the Sweet Pie and Pie* [10/16/41]). Later, in the prison recreation room, the boys have a run-in with the warden and are sent to the rock pile. His orders are postponed temporarily, however, when a guard orders them to repaint the prison walls (old footage from *So Long, Mr. Chumps* [(2/7/41]). Instead, the boys paint their prison clothes into guard uniforms and dash for the front gate, only to be captured (new footage). Finally, the Stooges wind up on the rock pile making little ones of big ones (again stock from *So Long, Mr. Chumps*). Then, almost half a century later, the Stooges, sporting long, gray beards, are released from prison. Curly's first request: a nice cold bottle of beer! / *WT*: *Three Duds in*

247

the Suds / *FN*: The extensive amount of stock footage was used because Curly's failing health did not permit him to work a normal three- to four-day shooting schedule.

89. A BIRD IN THE HEAD ** / Rl. Feb. 28 / Prod. No. 4043 / 17m / *p* Hugh McCollum / *d st scr* Edward Bernds / *ph* Burnett Guffey / *e* Henry Batista / *a* Charles Clague / *C*: Vernon Dent (Prof. Panzer), Robert Williams (Mr. Beedle), Frank Lackteen (Nikko) and Art Miles (Igor, the Ape) / *SYN*: Paperhangers Moe, Larry and Curly wreck Mr. Beedle's apartment and lose their jobs. They find work at the home of Professor Panzer, an eccentric scientist. Soon, however, the Stooges learn that the scientist is more eager to have them around as possi-

lyn Johnson (Lulu Belle), Robert Williams (Union Lieutenant), Maury Dexter, Ted Lorch, Al Rosen, Joe Palma, Cy Schindell, and Blackie Whiteford (Union Soldiers) / *SYN*: The Stooges' plans to marry their three Southern belles, Lulu, Mary and Ringa, are disrupted by the Civil War. Moe and Larry join the Union Army, while Curly becomes a Confederate soldier. The mix up results in Moe and Larry posing as Curly's prisoners and vice versa. / *WT*: *Three Southern Dumbbells* / *FN*: Stock shot of Union Lieutenant on horseback and squadron of soldiers marching is from *Mooching Through Georgia* (8/11/39) with Buster Keaton. A new rendition of "Dixie" replaced "Three Blind Mice" as the Stooges standard theme song over the opening titles.

that the audience response was only fair and that it was poorest of his previews. Bernds also related that Stooges' comedies were usually previewed at one of three theaters: The Alexander in Glendale (now the Mann Alexander), The Tower in Compton, and the California Theater in Huntington Park.

92. MONKEY BUSINESSMEN *** / Rl. June 20 / Prod. No. 4058 / 17½m / *p* Hugh McCollum / *d st scr* Edward Bernds / *ph* Philip Tannura / *e* Paul Borofsky / *a* Charles Clague / *C*: Kenneth MacDonald (Dr. Mallard), Fred Kelsey (Smiling Sam McGinn), Snub Pollard (Mr. Gramble), Jean Donahue (Nurse Shapely), Cy Schindell (Clarence), Rocky Woods (Roland) and Wade Crosby (George) / *SYN*: The Stooges are electricians who manage to wreck the first place in which they work. Fired, Curly suggests they go somewhere else for a nice, long rest, and they check in at Dr. Mallard's Rest Home and Clinic (whose owner is soaking his patients for every nickel). When the Stooges discover that the clinic is operated by gangsters, they take flight, colliding with Mr. Grimble, a man in a wheelchair, landing on his bandaged foot. Suddenly, the man pronounces his foot cured and begins speeding after Moe, Larry and Curly, later paying them $1,000 for fixing his bad foot. Elated, the Stooges begin planning how to spend it. Curly has one sugeestion: taking a vacation for a nice, long rest! / *SD*: 4 (W 1/30 to SA 2/2/46) / *WT*: *Sanitarium Stooge* / *FN*: Two special effects in the film were achieved as follows: a smoke tube was hidden in Larry's hand when he feels Curly's burning forehead, and compressed air pipes were used to blow Moe's hair upwards. Unlike the finished film, in the first draft script of *Monkey Businessmen*, the Stooges are janitors who end up repairing the electricity at the gymnasium of *Simone's Body Beautiful*, where their motto is: "Trade in Your Old Curves for New Ones. Whistles Guaranteed or Your Money Back." A remake of *Mutiny on the Body* (1938), with Smith and Dale.

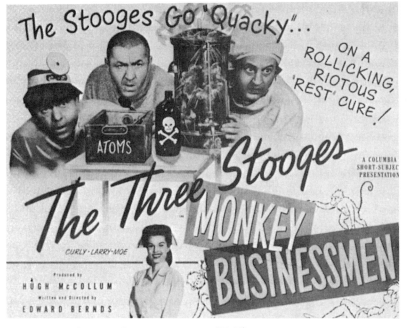

Lobby card for *Monkey Businessmen* (1946).

ble material for a daring experiment. It seems he is trying to transfer the brain of a man to his pet ape, Igor, and naturally Curly's brain is just the right size: tiny. Realizing the Professor's plan, the trio fight their way out, aided by a machine gun and the ape who has, understandably, developed a strong affinity for Curly. / *SD*: 5 (M 4/9 50 F 4/13/45) Filmed on Stage 19 / *PS*: For the most part, Stooges two-reelers took three to four days to film. But *A Bird in the Head* went a fifth day because of the death of President Roosevelt, director Edward Bernds said. Columbia Studios was shut down and everybody went home, returning the next day to finish up.

90. UNCIVIL WARBIRDS *** / Rl. Mar. 29 / Prod. No. 4050 / 17m / *p d* Jules White / *st* Clyde Bruckman / *scr* Jules White / *ph* Philip Tannura / *e* Charles Hochberg / *a* Charles Clague / *C*: Faye Williams (Mary Belle), Eleanor Counts (Ringa Belle), Mari-

91. THREE TROUBLEDOERS *** / Rl. Apr. 25 / Prod. No. 4046 / 17m / *p* Hugh McCollum / *d* Edward Bernds / *st scr* Jack White / *ph* George Kelly / *e* Henry Batista / *a* Charles Clague / *C*: Christine McIntyre (Nell), Dick Curtis (Badlands Blackie), Ethan Laidlaw (Henchman), Blackie Whiteford (Henchman), Hank Bell (Sheriff), Budd Fine (Townsman), Steve Clarke (Townsman) and Joe Garcia (Waiter) / *SYN*: The boys enter Dead Man's Gulch to learn that the last six sheriffs were killed by Badlands Blackie and his gang. Soon the Stooges meet a young girl named Nell at a local blacksmith shop. She tells them her father is being held captive and won't be released unless she marries Blackie. So Curly becomes sheriff and rescues Nell's father. / *SD*: 4 (Known dates F 5/11 and SA 5/12/45) Shot at Providencia Ranch and Stage X on Columbia Ranch. / *PS*: *Three Troubledoers* was previewed in Compton, California, on January 11, 1946. Director Edward Bernds recalled

93. THREE LOAN WOLVES ** / Rl. July 4 / Prod. No. 4053 / 16½m / *p d* Jules White / *st scr* Felix Adler / *ad* Tommy Flood / *ph* George Kelly / *e* Edwin Bryant / *a* Charles Clague / *C*: Beverly Warren (Molly), Harold Brauer (Butch McGee), Wally Rose (1st Henchman), Joe Palma (2nd Henchman), Danny Craig (Curly's Stand-In), Eli Schmuckler (Larry's Stand-In), Dave Levitt (Moe's Stand-In) and Jackie Jackson (Baby Grown-Up) / *SYN*: The boys are pawn brokers whose first customers are Butch McGee, president of the Gashouse Protective Association, and his girl friend, Molly. When the gang skips town, Molly leaves her sister's baby and a phoney diamond with Larry at the hock shop. Moe and Curly return from lunch to help Larry entertain the infant. *WT*: *In Hock*.

94. G.I. WANNA HOME **½ / Rl. Sept. 5 / Prod. No. 4063 / 15½m / *p d* Jules White / *st scr* Felix Adler / *ph* George Kelley / *e* Edwin Bryant / *a* Charles Clague / *C*: Judy Malcolm

(Tessie), Ethelreda Leopold (Jessie), Doris Houck (Bessie), Symona Boniface (Landlady) and Al Thompson (Hobo) / SYN: The Stooges are now ex-GI's confronted with all the trials and tribulations of discharged veterans. Their biggest problem is finding a home for their three lovemates, Jessie, Tessie, and Bessie, who have been dispossessed. The Stooges and their future wives finally make their new home in a vacant lot, until a tractor comes along to plow it under. Then they convert a one-room apartment into a midget-sized bungalow where the six retire after being married. / FN: Film title has been mistakenly listed as G.I. Wanna Go Home. Parrot in turkey gag also in Crash Goes the Hash (2/5/44), Three Dark Horses (10/16/52) and Listen, Judge (3/6/52).

95. RHYTHM AND WEEP **½ / Rl. Oct. 3 / Prod. No. 4057 / 17½m / p d Jules White / st scr Felix Adler / ph Philip Tannura / e Edwin Bryant / a Charles Clague / C: Jack Norton (Mr. Boyce), Gloria Patrice (Wilda), Ruth Godfrey (Tilda) and Nita Bieber (Hilda) / SYN: The Stooges, having lost numerous acting jobs, decide to commit suicide by jumping from the roof of a 60-story skyscraper, along with three other young actresses in the same sad predicament. At the last moment, however, the Stooges and the girls hear some wonderful piano music and discover an eccentric millionaire, Mr. Boyce, who's casting a new Broadway musical. He offers the boys and girls parts in his new show, which they accept, with the Stooges rehearsing an army medical exam sketch. Boyce is so impressed that he prepares to double their salaries and give them star billing. His generous offer is cut short, however, when two attendants drive up and haul Boyce back to Dr. Dippy's Retreat Home. / WT: Acting Up.

96. THREE LITTLE PIRATES *** / Rl. Dec. 5 / Prod. No. 4067 / 17½m p Hugh McCollum / d Edward Bernds / st scr Clyde Bruckman / ph Philip Tannura / e Paul Borofsky / a Charles Clague / C: Christine McIntyre (Rita Yolanda), Vernon Dent (Gov. Enchilada), Dorothy DeHaven (Chiquita), Jack Parker (Soldier), Larry McGrath (Soldier), Robert Stevens (Black Louie), Ethan Laidlaw (Dirk) and Joe Palma (Jack) / SYN: Three survivors of a strange craft—Garbage Scow #188 N.Y.C.—become shipwrecked on Dead Man's Island and are sent to jail by the Governor, supreme ruler of the island, who orders their execution. However, Rita the overlord's beauteous captive and his unwilling bride-to-be, helps the Stooges escape and tags along. The Stooges appease the Governor, reprising their roles in the "Maharaja" routine. Afterward, the Stooges escape to Black Louie's Pirate Den, hoping for safer quarters, while Chiquita, a palace beauty, informs the Governor of the Stooges' masquerade. A zany knife-throwing contest ensues between the Stooges and Black Louie, with one knife going haywire and cutting through a chandelier, which crashes down on the pirate and his men. / SD: 4 (M

4/15 to TH 4/18/46) / FN: The "Maharaja" routine was first enacted in the Columbia feature, Time Out for Rhythm (6/5/41), and later in The Three Stooges Go Around the World in a Daze (9/63). The knife-throwing act was also repeated in Around the World. According to director Edward Bernds, Moe dictated the entire Maharaja routine to writer Clyde Bruckman, "crazy syllable for crazy syllable," in a writer's conference on April 2, 1946.

1947
97. HALF-WITS' HOLIDAY *** / Rl. Jan. 9 / Prod. No. 4056 / 17½m / p d Jules White / st scr Zion Myers / ph George Kelley / e Edwin Bryant / a Charles Clague / C: Vernon Dent (Prof. Quackenbush), Barbara Slater (Lulu, His Daughter), Ted Lorch (Prof. Sedletz), Emil Sitka (Butler), Symona Boniface (Mrs. Smythe Smythe), Helen Dickson (Mrs. Gotrocks) and Vic Travers (Guest) / SYN: The Stooges as plumbers crash a psychologist's home, finding themselves the subjects of a $1,000 bet. Professor Quackenbush wagers he can turn them into polished gentlemen in 60 days. With the aid of his daughter, Lulu, the Professor attempts to teach the boys proper table manners. Following weeks of hard training, the night finally arrives when the Stooges are unleashed on society. All goes well until the Stooges commence with a pie-throwing melee. / WT: No Gents—No Cents SD: 4 (TH 5/2 to SA 5/4, and M 5/6/46) / FN: A remake of Hoi Polloi (8/29/35). Pie fight footage is reused in The Pest Man Wins (12/6/51), Scheming Schemers (10/4/56), and in yet another remake, Pies and Guys (6/12/58) and Stop! Look! and Laugh! (7/60). Moe's wife, Helen, who inspired the original premise for Hoi Polloi, also created the memorable scene in Half-Wits' Holiday, where Moe eludes a pie hanging from the ceiling as Mrs. Smythe Smythe approaches. (See Moe Howard & the 3 Stooges, pp. 145 and 147 for details.) / PS: Half-Wits' Holiday was Curly's last film as a Stooge and actor Emil Sitka's first with the team. Sitka recalls: "When I met Curly, I said, 'My name is Emil Sitka and I'm playing the butler in this picture.' Curly stood up, politely shook my hand, then said seriously, 'Yes, sir. I see.' Then, he sat back down. Now, I don't know if he called me sir because I was dressed like a butler, or if he was trying to be dignified."

Moe, Larry, and Curly also appeared in the following Columbia shorts:

1935
1. SCREEN SNAPSHOTS#6 / Rl. Feb, 22 / 10m / p Harriet Parsons / d st scr Ralph Staub / ph Ken Murray / C: All-Star / SYN: At Los Angeles' Wrigley Field, Ken Murray catches on film the Stooges' crazy antics in the dugout at the 1935 Hollywood Stars' celebrity baseball game.

1939
2. SCREEN SNAPSHOTS #9 / Rl. May 12 / 10m / p d Ralph Staub / C: All-Star / SYN: The Stooges appear at a horse show in the

San Fernando Valley, along with such horse fanciers as Bill Boyd, Irene Harvey, Robert Taylor, Clark Gable, Carole Lombard, Jean Parker and others. Featured earlier are Bing Crosby, Joe E. Brown, Virginia Bruce, Allan Jones, and Robert Young.

Feature Films:
All Columbia releases unless otherwise noted.
1934
1. THE CAPTAIN HATES THE SEA ** / Rl. Oct. 22 / Prod. No. 16 / 92m / d Lewis Milestone / scr Wallace Smith / e Gene Milford / C: Victor McLaglen (Schulte), Wynne Gibson (Mrs. Jeddock), Alison Skipworth (Mrs. McGruder), John Gilbert (Steve), Helen Vinson (Janet Grayson), Fred Keating (Danny), Walter Connolly (Captain), Tala Birell (Gerta Klargi), Leon Errol (Layton). / SYN: In this Grand Hotel formula movie, the Stooges appear as a crazy group of musicians.

1938
2. START CHEERING *** / Rl. Mar. 3 / Prod. No. 8 / 79m / ap Nat Perrin / d Albert S. Rogell / st Corey Ford / scr Eugene Solow / Richard E. Wormser, and Phillip Rapp / ph Joseph Walker / e Gene Havlick / m Johnny Green / md Morris Stoloff / C: Jimmy Durante (Willie Gumbatz), Walter Connolly (Sam Lewis), Joan Perry (Jean Worthington), Dr. Craig E. Earle (Prof. Quiz), Gertrude Niesen (Gertrude), Raymond Walburn (Dean Worthington), Ernest Truex (Blodgett), Hal LeRoy (Tarzan Biddle), Charles Starrett (Ted Crosley), Virginia Dale (Mabel), Chaz. Chase (Shorty) and Broderick Crawford (Biff Gordon) / SYN: Stooges are firemen called to the scene at Midland College. / WT: College Hero and College Follies of 1938.

1941
3. TIME OUT FOR RHYTHM **½ / Rl. June 5 / Prod. No. 90 / 75m / p Irving Starr / d Sidney Salkow / st Bert Granet / scr Edmund L. Hartmann and Bert Lawrence / ph Franz F. Planer / e Arthur Seid / md Morris Stoloff / C: Rudy Vallee (Daniel Collins), Ann Miller (Kitty Brown), Rosemary Lane (Frances Lewis), Allen Jenkins (Off-Beat Davis), Joan Merrill (Herself), Richard Lane (Mike Armstrong), Stanley Andrews (James Anderson), Brenda and Cobina (Themselves), Six Hits and a Miss (Themselves), and Glen Gray and His Casa Loma Band / SYN: In this musical extravaganza, the Stooges perform the "Maharaja" routine. / WT: Show Business.

1942
4. MY SISTER EILEEN ** / Rl. Sept. 24 / Prod. No. 161 / 96m / p Max Gordon / d Alexander Hall / st Ruth McKenney / scr Joseph Fields and Jerome Chodorov / ph Joseph Walker / e Viola Lawrence md Morris Stoloff / C: Rosalind Russell (Ruth Sherwood), Brian Aherne (Robert Baker), Janet Blair (Eileen Sherwood), George Tobias (Appopolus), Allyn Joslyn (Chic Clark), Eliz-

249

abeth Patterson (Grandma Sherwood), Grant Mitchell (Walter Sherwood), Richard Quine (Frank Lippincott), June Havoc (Effie Shelton), Donald MacBride (Officer Lonigan), Gordon Jones (The Wreck) and Jeff Donnell (Helen Loomis) / SYN: The Stooges are subway builders who dynamite their way up into Rosalind Russell's apartment. / FN: The Stooges were not listed on the original cast call sheet, therefore, they were last minute additions to the film.

1945

5. ROCKIN' IN THE ROCKIES **½ / Rl. Apr. 17 / Prod. No. 3017 / 67m / p Colbert Clark / d Vernon Keays / st Louise Rousseau and Gail Davenport / scr J. Benton Cheney and John Grey / ph Glen Gano / e Paul Borofsky / C: Mary Beth Hughes (June McGuire), Jay Kirby (Rusty), Gladys Blake (Betty), Moe Howard (Shorty), Jerry Howard (Curly), Larry Fine (Larry), Jack Clifford (Sheriff Zeke), Forrest Taylor (Sam Clemens), Tim Ryan (Tom Trove), Vernon Dent (Stanton), the Hoosier Hotshots, the Cappy Barra Boys, and Spade Cooley and His Orchestra (Themselves) / SYN: In this musical-western, the Stooges bring their comical antics up to date as termite exterminators.

1946

6. SWING PARADE OF 1946 *** / Rl. Mar. 16 by Monogram / Prod. No. 4517 / 74m / p Lindsley Parsons and Harry A. Romm / d Phil Karlson / st Edmund Kelso / scr Tim Ryan / ph Harry Neumann / e Richard Currier / a Ernest R. Hickson / md Edward Kay / C: Gale Storm (Carol), Phil Regan (Danny), Connee Boswell (Herself), Ed Brophy (Moose), Mary Treen (Marie), John Eldridge (Bascomb), Russell Hicks (Warren), Windy Cook (Windy), Jack Boyle, Will Osborne, and Louis Jordan and His Orchestra (Themselves) / SYN: Waiters Moe, Larry

and Curly and their boss (Ed Brophy) aide an aspiring singer (Gail Storm) in saving a posh nightclub from being closed.

Larry, Moe and Curly also appeared in four additional films: *Stop! Look! And Laugh!* (7/60, Columbia), a feature consisting of clips from Stooges comedies blended with new footage of ventriloquist Paul Winchell and his dummies; *The Three Stooges Follies* (11/74, Columbia), containing several unedited shorts; and *Ken Murray's Shooting Stars* (7/79), with Murray's clip of the Stooges from *Screen Snapshots #6* (2/22/35) and Jack Haley, Jr.'s *Hollywood: The Gift of Laughter* (5/16/82, ABC-TV), featuring scenes from *The Big Idea* (5/12/34) and *Three Little Beers* (11/28/35).

THE THREE STOOGES (Larry, Moe, and Shemp)
Columbia Shorts
1947

98. FRIGHT NIGHT *** / Rl. Mar. 6 / Prod. No. 4071 / 17m / p Hugh Mc Collum / d Edward Bernds / st scr Clyde Bruckman / ph Philip Tannura / e Paul Borofksy / a Charles Clague / C: Harold Brauer (Big Mike), Dick Wessel (Chopper Kane), Cy Schindell (Moose), Claire Carleton (Kitty Davis), Sammy Stein (Gorilla's Trainer), Tommy Kingston (Chuck), Dave Harper (1st Cop) and Stanley Blystone (2nd Cop) / SYN: Larry, Moe and Shemp are Chopper Kane's managers and receive warning from Big Mike, a gangster, that their boxer better lose or else! To decondition Chopper, the boys overfeed him on cream puffs and make him spend time with Kitty, his girl friend. The night of the match, Chopper learns that Kitty has dumped him for Gorilla Watson and that his opponent has a broken fist, thus being unable to fight. The Stooges think this puts them in the clear when all the bets are called off. But an irate Big Mike decides to

take them for a ride to a warehouse./ FN: Shemp's first Stooge short and his personal favorite. Remade as *Fling in the Ring* (1/6/55). The gag of acting as a puppeteer for an unconscious victim was also staged in *Matri-Phony* (7/2/42) and *Fling in the Ring* (1/6/55). The first draft screenplay for *Fright Night* was completed by Clyde Bruckman on May 24, 1946, featuring Curly, even though he had suffered a stroke 18 days earlier.

99. OUT WEST *** / Rl. Apr. 24 / Prod. No. 4077 / 17½m / p Hugh McCollum / d Edward Bernds / st scr Clyde Bruckman / ph George Kelley / e Paul Borofsky / a Charles Clague / C: Jack Norman (Doc Barker), Jacques (Jock) O'Mahoney (Johnny, the Arizona Kid), Christine McIntyre (Nell), Vernon Dent (Doctor), Stanley Blystone (Colonel), George Chesebro (Quirt), Frank Ellis (Jake) and Heinie Conklin (Bartender) / SYN: Shemp has an infected vein in his leg, so his doctor orders him to go west, where the Stooges take refuge in the Red Dog Saloon. Here, a pretty girl named Nell informs them that the notorious Doc Barker has murdered her father, locked up the Arizona Kid downstairs in a cell, and taken over ownership of the saloon. The boys succeed in releasing the Arizona Kid and summoning the United States Cavalry, who arrive late, following the Stooges' nabbing of the Barker gang. / FN: The mixing liquids in an old boot gag was also used in *Pardon My Scotch* (8/1/35), *All Gummed Up* (12/18/47), *Bubble Trouble* (10/8/53), and *Pals and Gals* (6/3/54), a remake of *Out West*. The gag of fighting in the dark was reworked in *Who Done It?* (3/3/49), in its remake, *For Crimin' Out Loud* (5/3/56), and in *The Three Stooges Go Around the World in a Daze* (9/63). The U.S. Cavalry riding in late for the rescue was reprised later in *The Outlaws Is Coming!* (1/65). The exchanging cards under the table gag was also used in *Goofs and Saddles* (7/2/37) and in *Pals and Gals* (6/3/54).

100. HOLD THAT LION *** / Rl. July 17/ Prod. No. 4087 / p d Jules White / st scr Felix Adler / ph George Kelley / e Edwin Bryant / a Charles Clague / C: Kenneth MacDonald (Icabod Slipp), Emil Sitka (Poole, the Attorney), Dudley Dickerson (Porter) and Jerry Howard (Train Passenger, with derby) / SYN: While celebrating their girls' birthdays, the Stooges receive news that the estate of their Uncle Ambrose Rose, deceased millionaire junk dealer, is now being held by its executor, Mr. Icabod Slipp. Slipp turns out to be con artist, however, giving the Stooges—what else—the slip. The boys catch up with Slipp on a train which is also carrying a ferocious lion. (Curly Howard is the passenger with the derby and clothespin on his nose.) Justice prevails when the Stooges outwit Slipp, cornering him in a baggage car and recovering their inheritance. / WT: *The Lion and the Louse* / FN: Remade as *Booty and the Beast* (3/5/53), using stock footage and reusing Curly's cameo. Old footage is also used

Opening title for Stooges films with Shemp.

250

THE STOOGES'LL HAVE *you* HANGIN' ON THE ROPES ...WITH LAUGHTER!

The Three Stooges

in FRIGHT NIGHT

SHEMP
LARRY
MOE

with

DICK WESSEL • CLAIRE CARLETON

Directed by EDWARD BERNDS • Produced by HUGH McCOLLUM

A COLUMBIA SHORT-SUBJECT PRESENTATION

Lobby card for *Fright Night* (1947), Shemp's first short with the Stooges.

in *Loose Loot* (4/2/53) and in *Tricky Dicks* (5/7/53). File cabinet gag is also in *Go West* (1940) with the Marx Brothers. "Charlie, the Man with the Goofy Limp" gag is also featured in *Uncivil Warriors* (4/6/35) and in *From Nurse to Worse* (8/23/40). Curly's cameo was not scripted, and it was filmed without the rest of the cast on the set.

101. BRIDELESS GROOM ***½ / Rl. Sept. 11 / Prod. No. 4095 / 16½m/p Hugh Mc-Collum / d Edward Bernds / st scr Clyde Bruckman / ad Carter DeHaven, Jr. / ph Vincent Farrar / e Henry DeMond / a Charles Clague / C: Dee Green (Fanny Dunkelmeir), Christine McIntyre (Lulu Hopkins), Emil Sitka (J.M. Benton, Justice of the Peace), B. Edney (Moe's Stand-In), Harold Breen (Shemp's Stand-In), J. Murphy (Larry's Stand-In), Nancy Saunders and Doris Colleen (Old Girl Friends) / SYN: Shemp is a vocal instructor who receives word that he will inherit half a million dollars if he marries within 48 hours after the reading of his deceased uncle's will. With only seven hours left in which to locate a suitable mate, Shemp tries calling a few former girlfriends and is met with instant rejection. Desperate, Shemp proposes to Fanny Dunkelmier, one of his adoring

pupils, who accepts his offer of marriage immediately. Moe and Larry rush him to the Justice of the Peace, where Shemp gets involved in a melee with all of his old girl friends (they've just learned of his inheritance). Following this elaborate slugfest, however, Shemp gets married right on time and receives his legacy. / WT: *Love and Learn* / FN: In the Justice of the Peace segment, rubber hands were substituted for piano wires, and Moe and Larry wore shin guards under their trousers during the brawl with Shemp's old girl friends. Footage used in *Husbands Beware* (1/5/56). Plot derived from *Seven Chances* (1925), with Buster Keaton, co-written by Clyde Bruckman.

102. SING A SONG OF SIX PANTS ** / Rl. Oct. 30 / Prod. No. 4088/16½m / p d Jules White / st scr Felix Adler / ph Henry Freulich / e Edwin Bryant / a Charles Clague / C: Dee Green (Bit Girl), Harold Brauer (Terry Hargen), Virginia Hunter (Flossie), Vernon Dent (Officer Sharp), Phil Arnold (Little Man), Cy Schindell (Henchman), Johnny Kascier (Henchman) and Bing Connelly (Bit Man) / SYN: The Stooges are in the tailoring and cleaning business, hard-pressed to pay for their equipment, which is

about to be repossessed by a finance company. Over the radio, the boys hear that a large reward is being offered for the capture of Terry Hargen, a notorious bank robber. Hargen himself slips into their shop and masquerades as a mannequin, eluding the police. When the Stooges try interesting a customer in a pair of pants, they remove Hargen's trousers and find a bank safe combination in a pocket. Embarrassed, Hargen slips out of the store and later returns with his henchman to recover the combination. The Stooges save the day, however, securing Hargen in their pressing machine until the police arrive. / WT: *Where the Vest Begins* / FN: Remade as *Rip, Sew and Stitch* (9/3/53), using stock footage.

103. ALL GUMMED UP ** / Rl. Dec. 18 / Prod. No. 4104 / 18m / p d Jules White / st scr Felix Adler / ph Allen Siegler / e Edwin Bryant / a Charles Glague / C: Christine McIntyre (Cerina Flint), Emil Sitka (Amos Flint) and Al Thompson (Customer) / SYN: With the threat of losing their lease to operate a drug store, the Stooges produce a serum that makes old people young again, trying it first on Cerina, the landlord's wife. Within minutes she changes into a sprightly, beautiful young blonde. When Amos Flint,

Lobby card for *Shivering Sherlocks* (1948).

her husband, returns to the store, he flips over his wife's new shapely figure, offering the Stooges ownership of the store in exchange for making him young too. The serum, however, transforms him into an infant by mistake. / WT: *Sweet Vita-Mine* / Remade as *Bubble Trouble* (10/8/53), using stock footage. The gag of mixing liquids in on old boot returns, and can also be seen in *Pardon My Scotch* (8/1/35), *Out West* (4/24/47), *Bubble Trouble* (10/8/53), and *Pals and Gals* (6/3/54).

1948
104. SHIVERING SHERLOCKS *** / Rl. Jan. 8 / Prod. No. 4103 / 17m / *p* Hugh McCollum / *d* Del Lord / *st scr* Del Lord and Elwood Ullman / *ad* Bill O'Connor / *ph* Allen Siegler / *e* Henry DeMond / *a* Charles Clague / *C:* Christine McIntyre (Gladys Harmon), Kenneth MacDonald (Lefty Loomis), Frank Lackteen (Red Watkins), Duke York (Angel), Harold Breen (Moe's Stand-In), Joe Murphy (Shemp's Stand-In), B. Edney (Larry's Stand-In), Vernon Dent (Capt. Mullins) and Stanley Blystone (Customer) / *SYN:* Larry, Moe and Shemp are mistaken for three armored car robbers. Captain Mullins gives the boys a lie detector test, but finds no reason to hold them. He releases them under protective custody to Gladys Harmon, owner of a small cafe, where the Stooges work .When Gladys is informed that she inherited some money and a spooky old mansion the Stooges escort her to check out the mansion, where the real armored car bandits and their hideous hatchet man, Angel, are hiding. When the mob abducts Gladys, the Stooges come to the rescue with style. / *SD:* (Known dates T 3/25 and W 3/26/47). Shot at the Columbia Ranch on Stage X. / *FN:* Reworked as *Of Cash and Hash* (2/3/55). Restaurant gags

(e.g., preparing chicken soup) borrowed from *Playing the Ponies* (10/15/37). Clam soup gag is a revision of the timeworn oyster stew gag. Plot and other smilar gags are found in *Taxi Spooks* (1928) with Jack Cooper, directed by Del Lord and written by Lord and Ewart Adamson.

105. PARDON MY CLUTCH **½ / Rl. Feb. 26 / Prod. No. 4093 / 15m / *p* Hugh McCollum / *d* Edward Bernds / *st scr* Clyde Bruckman *ph* Allen Siegler / *e* Henry DeMond / *a* Charles Clague / *C:* Matt McHugh (Claude Finkle), Emil Sitka (Escaped Lunatic), Alyn Lockwood (Petunia), Doria Revier (Marigold), Wanda Perry (Narcissus), Stanley Blystone (Dippy, the Attendant) and George Lloyd (Service Station Attendant) / *SYN:* Shemp's nerves are frazzled so the Stooges' friend, Claude sells them his old car and recommends that Shemp go camping. The Stooges, however, never get started because Claude's automobile breaks down. Then, as if things aren't bad enough, an eccentric old man offers the Stooges $1,000 for the car, to be used in a movie he's producing. The glamour of the event sours when two attendants arrive to haul the gentlemen back to the local asylum! *FN:* Remade as *Wham-Bam-Slam* (9/1/55), using stock footage. The changing the flat tire gag and the premise for a delayed departure were borrowed from Laurel and Hardy's *Perfect Day* (1929).

106. SQUAREHEADS OF THE ROUND TABLE ***½ / Rl. Mar. 4 / Prod. No. 4082 18m / *p* Hugh McCollum / *d* Edward Bernds / *st scr* Edward Bernds / *ph* Allen Siegler / *e* Henry DeMond / *a* Harold MacArthur / *C:* Phil Van Zandt (Black Prince), Vernon Dent (King Arthur), Jacques O'Mahoney (Cedric), Christine McIntyre (Elaine), Harold Brauer (Soldier), Joe Garcia (Soldier) and Douglas Coppin (Soldier) / *SYN:* Shemp, Larry, and Moe are troubadours in the days of King Arthur and the Round Table. The boys aide in the elopement of the King's daughter, Elaine, with Cedric the Blacksmith. But the Stooges and Cedric's main nemesis is the Black Prince, who plans on murdering the King, then on marrying Elaine. Moe, Larry, and Shemp prevail, however, exposing the Black Prince and convincing the King to give Cedric permission to marry Elaine. / *FN:* Remade as *Knutzy Knights* (9/2/54), using stock footage.

107. FIDDLER'S THREE *** / Rl. May 6 / Prod. No. 4070 / 17m / *p d* Jules White / *st*

The Hays Office, a movie censorship board, ordered that this musical Ten Commandments scene with Shemp and Moe be struck from the final print of the film *Heavenly Daze* (1948).

scr Felix Adler / ad Jack Corrick / ph Allen Siegler / e Edwin Bryant / a Charles Clague / C: Vernon Dent (King Cole), Phil Van Zandt (Mergatroyd, the Magician), Virginia Hunter (Princess Alicia), Sherry O'Neil (Girl in Box), Joe Palma (Guard), Harold Breen (Shemp's Stand-In), Johnny Kascier (Moe's Stand-In) and Joe Murphy (Larry's Stand-In) / SYN: In the Kingdom of Coleslawvania, the Stooges, as King Cole's fiddlers, ask for permission to marry Princess Alicia's three handmaidens. Their request is granted under the condition that Alicia weds

MacArthur / C: Herbert Evans (The Earl), Christine McIntyre (Lorna Doone), Ted Lorch (Angus) and Charles Knight (McPherson, the Butler) / SYN: The Stooges are aspiring detectives who travel to Scotland Yard, answering advertisements for "yard men," only to find out that yard men are the headquarters' gardeners. When the boys are mistaken for real detectives, however, they call on the Earl of Glenheather Castle, staying overnight to protect his valuables while he's away. The Stooges thwart two servants, Angus and McPherson, from steal-

Travers (Mr. De Peyster), Symona Boniface (Mrs. De Peyster), Moe Howard (Uncle Mortimer), Marti Shelton (Miss Jones, the Blonde Angel) and Judy Malcolm (Switchboard Operator in Heaven) / SYN: Shemp dies and is told by an angel that in order to enter Heaven he must go back to Earth and reform Moe and Larry. His spirit returns to old "terra firma," punishing the boys for trying to sell a businessman on a fountain pen that writes under whipped cream. / WT: Heaven's Above / FN: Reworked as Bedlam in Paradise (4/14/55). / PS: Larry Fine once recalled that when the pen sprung out of the mixer, it actually jabbed into his forehead. Evidently Moe chased director Jules White off the set because he had promised the gag was harmless.

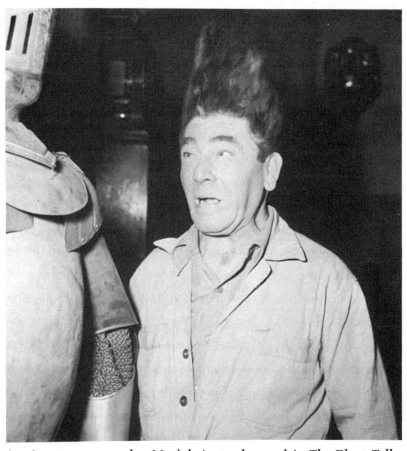

An air-compressor makes Moe's hair stand on end in *The Ghost Talks* (1949).

110. I'M A MONKEY'S UNCLE **½ / Rl. Oct. 7 / Prod. No. 4091 / 15½m / p d Jules White / st scr Zion Myers / ph George Kelly / e Edwin Bryant / a Charles Clague / C: Dee Green (Baggie), Virginia Hunter (Aggie) and Nancy Saunders (Maggie) / SYN: Shemp, Larry and Moe are three Stone Age cavemen who meet three Stone Age women; Aggie, Maggie and Baggie. All goes smoothly until the girls' old boyfriends show up in a blast of dinosaur eggs and lava rocks. FN: Reworked as Stone Age Romeo (6/2/55), using stock footage.

111. MUMMY'S DUMMIES *** / Rl. Nov. 4 / Prod. No. 4105 / 15½m / p Hugh McCollum / d Edward Bernds / st scr Elwood Ullman / ph Allen Siegler / e Henry DeMond / a Charles Clague / C: Dee Green (Fatima), Phil Van Zandt (Futamon), Ralph Dunn (Rhadames), Vernon Dent (King Rootentootin*), Suzanne Ridgeway, Virginia Ellsworth (Pretty Girls) and Wanda Perry (Princess) / SYN: The Stooges are chariot dealers in ancient Egypt who unload a real clunker on King Rootentootin's Chief of the Palace Guards. He seizes the boys and brings them before the King, who spares the Stooges' lives when they cure his bad toothache. Then, when the boys thwart the Prime Minister's plot to steal all of the taxpayers' money, the King offers the Stooges the hand of one of his daughters in marriage. She turns out to be an ugly old dame, with Moe and Larry electing Shemp as the unlucky groom. / FN: *Spelling in film's script.

112. A CRIME ON THEIR HANDS *** / Rl. Dec. 9 / Prod. No. 4111 / 17½m / p Hugh McCollum / d Edward Bernds / st scr Elwood Ullman / ph Henry Freulich / e Henry DeMond / a Clarles Clague / C: Kenneth MacDonald (Dapper), Christine McIntyre (Bee), Charles C. Wilson (J.L. Cameron), Lester Allen (Runty) and Frank Lackteen (Muscles) / SYN: Dapper and his gang have stolen the priceless Punjab Diamond. Runty, one of Dapper's henchmen, defects when Dapper decides on peddling the jewel. Therefore, Runty blows the news of Dapper's plan to the *Daily Gazzette*'s janitors, Moe, Larry and Shemp, mistaking them for reporters. A short time later, the

Prince Galiant first. But Mergatroyd the Magician gets wind of Alicia's wedding plans, and tries overthrowing the King so he can marry the Princess himself (sound familiar?). Mergatroyd then kidnaps Alicia, promising the King he'll make her appear in his magician's box in exchange for the Princess's hand in marriage. When Alicia escapes, however, the Stooges take her place in the box, exposing Mergatroyd and seizing him. / FN: Remade as Musty Musketeers (5/13/54), using stock footage.

108. HOT SCOTS ***½ / Rl. July 8 / Prod. No. 4094 / 17m / p Hugh McCollum / d Edward Bernds / st scr Elwood Ullman / ph Allen Siegler / e Henry DeMond / a Harold

ing the Earl's heirlooms. Later, the Earl and the Stooges celebrate over a glass of his "Breath O'Heather." / WT: Scotland Yard-birds / FN: Reworked as Scotched in Scotland (11/4/54), using stock footage. Scotland yard scenes were reused in Hot Ice (10/6/55). Parrot in the skull gag was also used in If a Body Meets a Body (8/30/45) and in Scotched in Scotland (11/4/54). The moving beds routine was also in Cursed by his Beauty, a 1914 Keystone Comedy.

109. HEAVENLY DAZE *** / Rl. Sept. 2 / Prod. No. 4090 / 16½m / p d Jules White / st scr Zion Myers / ph Allen Siegler / e Edwin Bryant / a Charles Clague / C: Vernon Dent (Lawyer), Sam McDaniel (Spiffingham), Vic

Stooges start investigating the matter further, and wind up in the thick of trouble. Shemp accidentally swallows the diamond, when the Stooges search a room containing Dapper's girlfriend, Bee (the diamond was placed in a bowl of candy, from which Shemp was eating). Dapper and his men return and try operating on Shemp, but the Stooges' pet gorilla intercedes and blows the

One-sheet for *Malice in the Palace* **(1949).**

case wide open. / *FN*: Reworked as *Hot Ice* (10/6/55), using stock footage. Newspaper office footage reused in *Commotion on the Ocean* (11/8/56).

1949

113. **THE GHOST TALKS ** ** / Rl. Feb. 3 / Prod. No. 4108 / 18m / *p d* Jules White / *st scr* Felix Adler / *ph* M.A. Anderson / *e* Edwin Bryant / *a* Charles Clague / *C*: Phil

Arnold (Voice of Tom) and Nancy Saunders (Lady Godiva) / *SYN*: Shemp, Larry and Moe are hired to move furniture out of an ancient castle. While they are lifting a suit of armor, the crumpled old suit comes to life, asking the Stooges to leave him alone. It seems he is the ghost of Sir Tom, a man beheaded for peeping at Lady Godiva. Now, after one thousand years of imprisonment, Tom will meet the spirit of Lady Godiva herself and they will drift off happily ever after. / *WT*: *That's the Spirit* / *FN*: Reworked as *Creeps* (2/2/56), using stock footage.

114. **WHO DONE IT?** **** / Rl. Mar. 3 / Prod. No. 4112 / 16m / *p* Hugh McCollum / *d* Edward Bernds / *st scr* Edward Bernds / *ph* Ira H. Morgan / *e* Henry DeMond / *a* Charles Clague / *C*: Christine McIntyre

(Delores), Kenneth MacDonald (Hackett), Emil Sitka (John Goodrich), Dudley Dickerson (Janitor), Herbert Evans (Nikko), Duke York (Goon), Ralph Dunn (Henchman Servant) and Charles Knight (Crandall) / *SYN*: Detectives Moe, Larry and Shemp ("The Alert Detective Agency") foil the murder plot directed at old man Goodrich, leading them to a zany chase with a gang of crooks and a born-again monster, "The Goon." A hilarious "in-the-dark" fight sequence ensues with the Stooges emerging victorious, producing out of a trap door a very-much-alive old man Goodrich. Shemp becomes the hero by crowning the crooks with his "trusty little shovel." / *SD*: 4 (T 12/9 to F 12/12/47) / *FN*: A reworking of Schilling and Lane's *Pardon My Terror* (9/12/46), originally intended for the Stooges . Remade also as *For Crimin' Out Loud* (5/3/56), using stock footage. The fighting in the dark sequence was also used in *Out West* (4/24/47), in *For Crimin' Out Loud* (5/3/56), and in *The Three Stooges Go Around the World in a Daze* (9/63).

115. **HOCUS POCUS** **½ / Rl. May 5 / Prod. No. 4116 / 16½m / *p d* Jules White / *st scr* Felix Adler / *ph* Vincent Farrar / *e* Edwin Bryant / *a* Robert Peterson / *C*: Mary Ainslee (Mary), Vernon Dent (Insurance Adjustor) and Jimmy Lloyd (Cliff) / *SYN*: As part of a publicity stunt, the Great Svengarlic ("He'll Steal Your Breath Away!") hypnotizes the Stooges to walk on a horizontal flagpole 20 stories above the ground. When a bicyclist knocks the hypnotist unconscious, however, the Stooges break out of their spell and grab onto the pole for dear life. Suddenly, when the pole breaks, the Stooges crash into an insurance office, where their invalid friend, Mary, is receiving a $25,000 check for her injury. The Stooges fall, however, makes Mary jump out of her wheelchair, thus blowing her claim that she is crippled. / *WT*: *Three Blind Mice*/ *FN*: Reworked as *Flagpole Jitters* (4/5/56), using stock footage. Stock shot of flagpole cracking from *The Taming of the Snood* (6/28/40), with Buster Keaton.

116. **FUELIN' AROUND** *** / Rl. July 7 / Prod. No. 4114 / 16½m / *p* Hugh McCollum / *d* Edward Bernds / *st scr* Elwood Ullman / *ph* Vincent Farrar / *e* Henry Batista / *a* Robert Peterson / *C*: Jacques O'Mahoney (Guard), Christine McIntyre (Hazel), Emil Sitka (Prof. Sneed), Vernon Dent (General), Phil Van Zandt (Capt. Rork), Harold Brauer (Leon) and Andre Pola (Cluttz) / *SYN*: The Stooges are hired to recarpet the home of Professor Sneed, a world-famous scientist who has invented a secret super-rocket fuel. While they are working, three spies from the State of Anemia crash into the premises and kidnap the Stooges, mistaking Larry for Professor Sneed. The boys are held captive until the real Professor and his daughter are kidnapped, too. Sneed, his daughter and the Stooges manage to escape with the help of a girl-shy guard. / *FN*: Reworked as *Hot Stuff* (9/6/56), using stock footage.

117. MALICE IN THE PALACE *** / Rl. Sept. 1 / Prod. No. 4119 / 16½m / p d Jules White / st scr Felix Adler / ph Vincent Farrar / e Edwin Bryant / a Charles Clague / C: George Lewis (Ghinna Rumma), Frank Lackteen (Emir of Shmow) and Vernon Dent (Hassan Ben Sobar) / SYN: Two customers of the Cafe Casbahbah ask waiters Moe, Larry and Shemp to recover the King Ruttin' Tuttin diamond from the Emir of Shmow. The Stooges, disguised as Santa Clauses, invade the Shmow's Palace and make off with the gem. / WT: Here We Go Shmow / FN: Reworked as Rumpus in a Harem (6/21/56). The gag of chasing a dog past a customer waiting for franks and beans was also used in Playing the Ponies (10/15/37). Stooges' Santa Claus disguise was lifted (using some old footage) from Wee Wee Monsieur (2/18/38). "Ruttin' Tuttin" is spelling in film's script.

118. VAGABOND LOAFERS *** / Rl. Oct. 6 / Prod. No. 4140 / 16m / p Hugh McCollum / d Edward Bernds / st scr Elwood Ullman / ad F. Briskin / ph Vincent Farrar / e Henry DeMond / a Charles Clague / C: Christine McIntyre (Ethel), Kenneth MacDonald (Allen), Symona Boniface (Mrs. Norfleet), Emil Sitka (Mr. Walter Norfleet), Dudley Dickerson (Henry, the Cook), Herbert Evans (Wilks, the Butler), Johnny Kascier (Moe's Stand-In), Harold Breen (Larry's Stand-In), Charlie Cross (Shemp's Stand-In) and Boyd Stockman (Allen's Double) / SYN: Norfleet Mansion is seriously plagued with leaky pipes. So the butler summons the "Day and Nite Plumbers"—Moe, Larry and Shemp. The Stooges reroute the plumbing and recover Mrs. Norfleet's priceless Van Brocklin painting stolen by a pair of crooks. / SD: (Known dates W 1/26 and TH 1/27/49) / FN: A reworking of A-Plumbing We Will Go (4/19/40). Many stock scenes used later in Scheming Schemers (10/4/56). Shot at the Darmour Studios.

119. DUNKED IN THE DEEP ** / Rl. Nov. 3 / Prod. No. 4137 / 17m / p d Jules White / st scr Felix Adler / ph Vincent Farrar / e Edwin Bryant / a Charles Clague / C: Gene Stutenroth (Bortch) / SYN: Bortch, a seedy-looking foreign spy, must return to his native land and invites his neighbors, the Stooges, to accompany him to Pier Eleven. On board a ship heading for Bortch's homeland, the Stooges discover their friend has a watermelon loaded with microfilm of government documents. The Stooges then proceed to overthrow Bortch and turn him over to the authorities. / FN: Reworked as Commotion on the Ocean (11/8/56). Seasick gag is also seen in Back From the Front (5/28/43) and in Commotion on the Ocean (11/8/56).

1950
120. PUNCHY COWPUNCHERS **** / Rl. Jan. 5 / Prod. No. 4142 / 17m / p Hugh McCollum / d st scr Edward Bernds / ad Sam Nelson / ph Vincent Farrar / e Henry DeMond / a Charles Clague / C: Kenneth MacDonald (Dillon), George Chesebro (Jeff), Bob Cason (Black Jeff), Ted Mapes

(Red), Stanley Price (Lefty), Jacques O'Mahoney (Elmer, the Arizona Kid), Christine McIntyre (Nell) Johnny Kascier (Moe's Stand-In), Charlie Cross (Larry's Stand-In), Harold Breen (Shemp's Stand-In) and Dick Wessel (Sgt. Mullins) / SYN: The Killer Dillons are in town, this time to steal the gold from a nearby saloon. Wise to their plan, Nell, a pretty saloon girl, sends the Arizona Kid to Fort Scott for the U.S. Calvary. There, the Kid asks Colonel Mullins to volunteer three men for a dangerous mission. The Stooges, disguised as desperadoes, are sent to foil the Dillon Gang, which they fail to do until Nell comes to their aid. / SD: (Known dates T 2/8 to W 2/9/49). Shot on the Columbia Ranch and on Stage X.

121. HUGS AND MUGS ** / Rl. Feb. 2 / Prod. No. 4115 / 16m / p d Jules White / st scr Clyde Bruckman / ad Gilbert Kay / ph Vincent Farrar / e Edwin Bryant / a Charles Clague / C: Christine McIntyre (Lily), Nannette Bordeaux (Fifi), Kathleen O'Malley (Ella), Joe Palma (Red), Wally Rose (Bill), Pat Moran (Chuck), Emil Sitka (Clerk), Johnny Kascier (Moe's Stand-In), Charlie Cross (Larry's Stand-In) and Harold Breen (Shemp's Stand-In) / SYN: Three girls—Lily, Fifi and Ella—are released from jail after serving time for shoplifting a pearl necklace.

One-sheet for Dopey Dicks (1950).

Now, one year later, the girls learn that their parcel—containing the necklace—was sold at an auction to Shemp. Lilly, Fifi, Ella, along with Red and his mob, pay the Stooges a visit at their upholstery shop, hoping to retrieve the necklace. / SD: 3 (T 2/15 to TH 2/17/49) Shot at the Darmour Studios.

122. DOPEY DICKS *** / Rl. Mar. 2 / Prod. No. 4131 / 15½m / p Hugh McCollum / d st scr Edward Bernds / ph Vincent Farrar / e Henry DeMond / a Charles Clague / C: Christine McIntyre (Louise), Stanley Price (Prof. Potter) and Phil Van Zandt (Doctor) / SYN: While painting the office of a famous private investigator, Shemp, Larry and Moe discover a note leading them to a woman who is being held captive at a scientist's mansion. The Stooges confront the mad scientist, who needs a human brain for his headless mechanical man. His choice: one of the Stooges. Fortunately, the Stooges manage to escape, along with the girl, hitchhiking a ride in a car driven by the headless monster.

123. LOVE AT FIRST BITE **½ / Rl. May 4 / Prod. No. 4129 / 16m / p d Jules White / st scr Felix Adler / ph Rex Wimpy / e Edwin Bryant / a Charles Clague / C: Christine McIntyre (Katrina), Yvette Reynard (Fifi) and Marie Monteil (Maria) / SYN: In a few hours, the Stooges will be reunited with their fiancees, who are arriving in town on an ocean cruiser. In celebration, the Stooges start drinking toasts to their brides-to-be, winding up drunk. When Shemp passes out, Moe and Larry place him in a tub of cement for a "burial at sea." In order to rectify this situation, once sober, Moe and Larry dynamite Shemp out of the tub and the three of them out of their apartment building. The trio lands on a nearby dock, where their sweethearts await. / WT: New Grooms Sweep Clean / FN: Reworked as Fifi Blows Her Top (4/10/58), using stock footage.

124. SELF-MADE MAIDS **½ / Rl. July 6 / Prod. No. 4141 / 16m / p d Jules White / st scr Felix Adler / ph Vincent Farrar / e Edwin Bryant / a Charles Clague / C: Moella, Larraine and Shempetta (played by Moe, Larry and Shemp) / SYN: As artists, the Stooges commence painting portraits of three beautiful girls: Moella, Larraine and Shempetta. The boys fall in love with the girls and ask for their hands in marriage, pending approval of the girls' father. Their father changes his mind when the Stooges tickle his feet. A year after their marriage, the Stooges' wives give birth to three baby sons: Moe Jr., Larry Jr., and Shemp Jr. / FN All roles were portrayed by the Three Stooges themselves. Moe was also the girl's father.

125. THREE HAMS ON RYE *** / Rl. Sept. 7 / Prod. No. 4107 / 15½m / p d Jules White / st scr Clyde Bruckman / ph Al Zeigler / e Edwin Bryant / a Charles Clague / C: Nanette Bordeaux (Lulabelle), Emil Sitka (B.K. Doaks), Christine McIntyre

(Ginger), Mildred Olsen and Judy Malcolm (Show Girls) / SYN: Barker, a difficult theatre critic, has panned producer B.K. Doaks' last ten shows and Doaks is annoyed. So he asks the Stooges, his three prop men (and part-time bit players), to disguise themselves and stop Barker from sneaking backstage before the premiere performance of The Bride Wore Spurs. A hilarious segment results when the Stooges and cast start coughing up feathers during the show, as a result of eating a cake Moe accidentally infested with a torn potholder. After the show, Barker rushes backstage and commends Doaks for producing a terrifically funny satire. / WT: How Hammy Was My Hamlet / FN: The lettuce washing and clothesline gag was reworked using money in Jail Busters (1955, Allied Artists), featuring the Bowery Boys, and later in a 1965 live-action segment of The New Three Stooges color cartoon series. The coughing up feathers gag was also used in Uncivil Warriors (4/26/35).

126. STUDIO STOOPS *** / Rl. Oct. 5 / Prod. No. 4143 / 16m / p Hugh McCollum / d Edward Bernds / st scr Elwood Ullman / ad Gilbert Kay / ph Vincent Farrar / e Henry DeMond / a Charles Clague / C: Kenneth MacDonald (Dandy Dawson), Charles Jordan (Tiny), Christine McIntyre (Dolly Devore), Vernon Dent (Capt. Casey), Joe Palma (Louie), Stanley Price (Brown), Johnny Kascier (Moe's Stand-In), Harold Breen (Larry's Stand-In) and Charlie Cross (Shemp's Stand-In) / SYN: At B.O. Pictures, Inc., termite exterminators, Moe, Larry and Shemp, turn amateur publicity agents, suggesting to a studio executive that they can make starlet Dolly Devore famous overnight by faking a kidnapping. The kidnapping becomes real, however, when two crooks overhear the plan and abduct Devore for a $10,000 ransom. The Stooges make a successful rescue, without Shemp, who gets caught on the building's 10th floor ledge trapped in a garment bag. / FN: The gag of hanging out a window on an accordion telephone was also used in The Lion's Whiskers (1926), with Billy Bevan, directed by Del Lord.

127. SLAPHAPPY SLEUTHS **½ / Rl. Nov. 9 / Prod. No. 4139 / 16m / p d Jules White / st scr Felix Adler / ph Vincent Farrar / e Edwin Bryant / a Charles Clague / C: Stanley Blystone (Fuller Grime), Emil Sitka (Emil, a Customer), Gene Roth (Crook) and Nanette Bordeaux (Louise) / SYN: The Onion Oil Company is in deep financial trouble. Many of their gasoline stations have been held up by a gang of organized mobsters. To solve the case, the company utilizes three brainy but stupid-looking private detectives posing as gas station attendants. Who else? The Three Stooges. / FN: Painted on eyelids gag was originally used in Restless Knights (2/20/35).

128. A SNITCH IN TIME **½ / Rl. Dec. 7 / Prod. No. 4154 / 16½m / p Hugh McCollum / d Edward Bernds / st scr Elwood Ullman /

ph No credit / e Henry DeMond / a Charles Clague / C: Jean Willes (Gladys Scudder), Henry Kulky (Louie) and John Morton (Steve) / SYN: Furniture shopowners Moe, Larry and Shemp are delivering furniture to their customer, Gladys, when a radio broadcast is interrupted by the news that two well-dressed bandits have robbed $50,000 from a local jewelry store. A $5,000 reward is being offered for information leading to the capture of these men. 'One is six-foot-two, heavily built, and has a scar on his left cheek. Shemp doesn't hear the other mug's description because the bandits themselves enter the room and turn off the radio. It seems they want Gladys' jewelry, too. But Louie and Steve's stealing days come to a bitter end when the police come to the rescue. / FN: The painting a cuckoo clock and revarnishing an antique table gags were borrowed from Tassels in the Air (4/1/38).

1951

129. THREE ARABIAN NUTS *** / Rl. Jan. 4 / Prod. No. 4156 / 16m / p Hugh McCollum / d Edward Bernds / st scr Elwood Ullman / ph No credit / e Henry DeMond / a Charles Clague / C: Vernon Dent (Mr. John Bradley), Phil Van Zandt (Ahmed), Dick Curtis (Hassan) and Wesley Bly (Genii) / SYN: Shemp takes possession of a valuable Aladdin's lamp at a storage company where the Stooges work when a business man junks the item. The lamp produces a real-live genie who grants the Stooges three wishes. But the genie causes more trouble than he's worth when two Arabian spies try to recover the lamp. The Stooges succeed, however, in maintaining ownership of the lamp, with their last wish producing a harem of girls and many treasures. / WT: Genii With the Light Brown Hair / SD: 4 (M 1/9 to TH 1/12/50).

130. BABY SITTERS' JITTERS **½ / Rl. Feb. 1 / Prod. No. 4155 / 16m / p d Jules White / st scr Felix Adler / ph No credit / e Edwin Bryant / a Charles Clague / C: Lynn Davis (Joan Lloyd), David Windsor (Junior), Margie Liszt (Mrs. Crump) and Myron Healey (George Lloyd) / SYN: Behind on their rent, the Stooges turn to babysitting for a child named Junior to earn some money to pay off their debt. Junior's mother leaves the Stooges in charge, while she slips away for the evening. Early the next morning, however, she returns to find Shemp, Larry and Moe sleeping in Junior's crib. But where's Junior? Evidently, the woman's ex-husband kidnapped the baby. So the Stooges take matters into their own hands, attempting to regain the baby from Mr. Lloyd. He refuses and a fight ensues, which is quickly resolved when the young couple decide to give their marriage one more try.

131. DON'T THROW THAT KNIFE *** / Rl. May 3 / Prod. No. 4158 / 16m / p d Jules White / st scr Felix Adler / ph Fayte Browne / e Edwin Bryant / a Charles Clague / C: Dick Curtis (Mr. Wycoff), Jean Willes (Lucy Wycoff, His Wife), Johnny Kascier (Moe's Stand-In), Harold Breen (Shemp's Stand-In) and Charlie Cross (Larry's Stand-In) / SYN: It's April 1st, time to be interviewed by those loco census takers: the Three Stooges! The boys pay their first visit on Mrs. Lucy Wycoff. She answers the Stooges' questions, until her insanely jealous husband, a magician, returns home. It becomes time for the Stooges to hide. When the magician elects to take a nap, he quickly discovers his wife *isn't* his wife (it's Shemp), and that there are two more men in the house! He chases the Stooges from room to room until Mr. Wycoff rehearses his knife-throwing act and egg-throwing machine on the boys as human targets. / WT: *Noncensus Takers* /SD: (Available date: TH 6/22/50) Shot at Columbia Studios on Stage 10. / FN: The gag of a wife faking a headache to fool her jealous husband was reused in *Sappy Bullfighters* (6/4/59). The Stooges are also census takers in *No Census, No Feeling* (10/4/40).

132. SCRAMBLED BRAINS **** / Rl. July 7 / Prod. No. 4157 / *p d* Jules White / *st scr* Felix Adler / *ph* Henry Freulich / *e* Edwin Bryant / *a* Charles Clague / C: Babe London (Nora), Vernon Dent (Nora's Father), Royce Milne (Little Betty May), Emil Sitka (Dr. Gezundhiet), B. Edney (Shemp's Stand-In), Johnny Kascier (Moe's Stand-In) and Joe Murphy (Larry's Stand-In) / SYN: Shemp continues to suffer from hallucinations after being released from the sanitarium. His most constant hallucination is imagining that the hospital's nurse, Nora, is a vivacious blonde rather than fat and ugly. What makes matters worse is Shemp is engaged to marry her! In the process of returning Shemp to the sanitarium for a second time, Moe and Larry confront a fat man in the telephone booth, causing the booth to crash to the ground. Enraged, the man promises to tear Moe and Larry apart if he ever sees them again. Next, Moe and Larry join Shemp and his bride, Nora, on their wedding day. Shemp and Nora get married, even though her father turns out to be the man in the phone booth. He beats up on Moe and Larry, as promised. / WT: *Impatient Patient* / SD: (Available dates W 3/22 and TH 3/23/50) Shot on Stage 10. / FN: The blowing the pill through a pipe gag is also seen in *Even as IOU* (9/18/42), and in *Hoofs and Goofs* (1/31/57). / PS: Although Larry Fine (like Moe Howard) had an affinity for *You Nazty Spy*, Larry later admitted his real favorite was *Scrambled Brains*. It was also one of the few films Larry had in his personal collection.

133. MERRY MAVERICKS **½ / Rl. Sept. 6 / Prod. No. 4161 / 16m / *p* Hugh McCollum / *d* Edward Bernds / *st scr* Edward Bernds / *ph* Allen Siegler / *e* Edwin Bryant / *a* Charles Clague / C: Don Harvey (Red Morgan), Marion Martin (Gladys), Paul Campbell (Duke), Dick Curtis (Pitts), Emil Sitka (Mort, the Jailer) and Slim Gaut (Cowboy Patient) / SYN: In Peaceful Gulch, Morgan and his hombres are back and they've just run the Sheriff out of town. The Stooges are mistaken for three famous marshals and are asked to stop Morgan from stealing money

buried in an old house haunted by the ghost of a headless Indian Chief. Shemp, Larry and Moe soon find out that the Indian Chief, in reality, is one of Morgan's henchmen. Shemp dons the Chief's costume and knocks out the crooks, to save the day. / SD: (T 6/13 to F 6/16/50) FN: A reworking of *Phony Express* (11/18/43), using stock footage. The scene in which the Stooges find handbills showing they're *Wanted for Vagrancy* was photographed during the production of their next film, *The Tooth Will Out*, and was included in that picture's budget. See *The Tooth Will Out* (10/4/ 51).

134. THE TOOTH WILL OUT **½ / Rl. Oct. 4 / Prod. No. 4162 / 16m / *p* Hugh McCollum / *d st scr* Edward Bernds / *ad* Gilbert Kay / *ph* Fayte Browne / *e* Edwin Bryant / *a* Charles Clague / C: Margie Liszt (Miss Beebe), Vernon Dent (Doc Keefer), Emil Sitka (Beggs, the Chef), Johnny Kascier (Moe's Stand-In), Harold Breen (Shemp's Stand-In) and Charlie Cross (Larry's Stand-In) / SYN: The Stooges emerge as graduates from dental school, moving out west to open their first dental office, where they take care of their first customer: an old man. His appointment is cut short when a western outlaw kicks him out; he's evidently in pain, and asks the Stooges to pull his tooth. The Stooges take evasive action—before carrying out this tender operation—as Shemp consults a carpenter's handbook for another opinion! As a result, Shemp pulls the wrong tooth. / WT: *A Yank at the Dentist* / SD: 2 (M 2/19 and T 2/20/50) Shot on Stage X at the Columbia Ranch. / FN: Dentist office gags similar to W.C. Fields' *The Dentist*. /PS: The origin of the film's dental office scenes is unique, as director Edward Bernds explains: "The dentist office sequences were originally filmed for *Merry Mavericks*. The scene ran so long that Mac [Hugh McCollum] was unwilling to cut it. Then he came up with the idea that we had nearly enough footage for another picture. So we took the sequence out of *Merry Mavericks*, shot two extra days, and *The Tooth Will Out* was born."

135. HULA-LA-LA **½ / Rl. Nov. 1 / Prod. No. 4179 / 16m / *p d* Hugh McCollum / *st scr* Edward Bernds / *ph* Henry Freulich / *e* Edwin Bryant / *a* Charles Clague / C: Jean Willes (King's Daughter, Luana), Kenneth MacDonald (Varanu, the Witch Doctor), Emil Sitka (Mr. Baines), Maxine Doviat (Kawana), Lei Aloha (Armed Idol) and Joy Windsor (Bit Girl) / SYN: B.O. Pictures is in deep trouble. Its next film—a South Pacific musical—is being postponed until the natives on the island where this epic is being produced learn how to dance. Studio president, Mr. Baines, asks for the studio's finest dance instructors, Moe, Larry and Shemp, to solve this predicament by teaching the Raribongan natives how to dance. When the boys arrive on the island, however, they meet a witch doctor named Varanu, who wants their heads for his collection and Luana for his bride. The Stooges thwart both plans. / FN: Many-armed idol gag was

first used in *Some More of Samoa* (12/4/41). *Hula La La* marked the directorial debut of Hugh McCollum and was his only film as a director with the Stooges. McCollum replaced director Edward Bernds, who was directing a B-feature for Columbia.

136. THE PEST MAN WINS *** / Rl. Dec. 6 / Prod. No. 4163 / 16m / *p d* Jules White / *st scr* Felix Adler / *ph* Fayte Browne / *e* Edwin Bryant /*a* Charles Clague / C: Margie Liszt (Mrs. Castor), Nanette Bordeaux (Fifi, a French Maid), Emil Sitka (Butler), Vernon Dent (Philander), Helen Dickerson, Symona Boniface (Mrs. Smythe Smythe, in stock footage), Johnny Kascier (Moe's Stand-In), Charlie Cross (Larry's Stand-In) and Harold Breen (Shemp's Stand-In). / SYN: Shemp, Larry and Moe work for the Lightning Pest Control Company. They are called to a society matron's home for an exterminating job, but ruin her lavish party instead. / WT: *Mousers in the Trousers* / SD: (Available dates M 2/12 and T 2/13/51) Shot at Columbia on Stage 10. / FN: A partial remake of *Ants in the Pantry* (2/6/36), using stock footage. Pie fight scenes are from *Half-Wits' Holiday* (1/9/47).

1952

137. A MISSED FORTUNE ***½ / Rl. Jan. 3 / Prod. No. 4159 / 16½m / *p d* Jules White / *st* Searle Kramer / *scr* Jack White / *ph* Fayte Browne / *e* Henry DeMond / *a* Charles Clague / C: Nanette Bordeaux (Fifi), Suzanne Ridgeway, Vivian Mason (Other Two Golddiggers), Vernon Dent (Hotel Mgr.) and Stanley Blystone (Detective) / SYN: The Three Stooges come into big money when Shemp hits the $50,000 radio quiz show jackpot. Before the check arrives, the boys spend their earnings at a swank hotel and order a case of champagne to celebrate. A trio of golddiggers are staying in the next room, and these ladies do everything possible to milk the Stooges out of their winnings. Actually, the Stooges didn't need their help, since the government's tax deductions leave Shemp with only $4.85. / FN: A remake of *Healthy, Wealthy and Dumb* (5/20/38), using stock footage.

138. LISTEN, JUDGE *** / Rl. Mar. 6 / Prod. No. 4180 / 17m / *p* Hugh McCollum / *d* Edward Bernds / *st scr* Elwood Ullman / *ad* C. Hiecke / *ph* Ellis W. Carter / *e* Edwin Bryant / *a* Charles Clague / C: Kitty McHugh (Mrs. Henderson), Vernon Dent (Judge Henderson), Mary Emory (Mrs. Lydia Morton), John Hamilton (Mr. George Hamilton), Gil Perkins (Officer Ryan), Chick Collins (Officer Casey), Emil Sitka (Francois, the French Chef), Johnny Kascier (Moe's Stand-In), Harold Breen (Shemp's Stand-In/Stunt Double), Charlie Cross (Larry's Stand-In) and Teddy Mangean (Larry's Stunt Double) / SYN: The Stooges are repairmen who wind up in court on a vagrancy charge but are released on lack of evidence. The boys are next hired to fix a lady's doorbell, and their unorthodox work habits annoy the chef, butler, and waiter, causing them to quit. With the woman

empty-handed for her husband's birthday party, the Stooges prepare all the food and an explosive birthday cake. The lady's husband gets plastered by the cake after he blows out the candles. He also recognizes the Stooges, since he was the judge who tried them. / SD: 4 (T 11/6 to F 11/9/51) Shot on Stage 10. / FN: A partial reworking of *An Ache in Every Stake* (8/22/41). The premise of them as repairmen was borrowed from *They Stooge to Conga* (1/1/43). The parrot-turkey gag is also seen in *Crash Goes the Hash* (2/5/44), in *G.I. Wanna Home* (9/5/46), and in *Three Dark Horses* (10/16/52).

139. CORNY CASANOVAS **** / Rl. May 1 / Prod. No. 4178 / 16½m / p d Jules White / st scr Felix Adler / ph Henry Freulich / e Aaron Stell / a Charles Clague / C: Connie Cezan (Mabel) / SYN: Moe, Larry and Shemp try proposing to the same girl, Mabel. Each one makes a separate visit, without the others knowing it. When one Stooge arrives, Mabel escorts her recent caller into another room, then greets her next lover. Soon Moe and Larry are disposed of, each of them in different bedrooms. But they eventually get curious and peep out of their rooms and bump into each other. Shemp, meanwhile, is also proposing. The three soon find that each Stooge has been double-crossing the others, and a fight ensues, while Mable escapes. / WT: One Won / FN: Remade as *Rusty Romeos* (10/17/57), using stock footage.

140. HE COOKED HIS GOOSE ** / Rl. July 3 / Prod. No. 4181 / 16m / p d Jules White / st scr Felix Adler / ad Earl Bellamy / ph Fayte Browne / e Aaron Stell / a Charles Clague / C: Mary Ainslee (Belle), Angela Stevens (Millie), Theila Darin (Miss Lapdale, Secretary), Johnny Kascier (Stunt Waiter/Moe's Stand-In), Harold Breen (Shemp's Stand-In) and Charlie Cross (Larry's Stand-In) / SYN: Larry owns a pet shop and the only pets he wants are Moe's wife Belle, and Shemp's fiancee, Milly. / WT: Clam Up / SD: 3 (M 1/7 to W 1/9/52) Shot on Stage 10. / FN: Remade as *Triple Crossed* (10/17/57), using stock footage.

141. GENTS IN A JAM **** / Rl. July 4 / Prod. No. 4183 / 16½m / p Hugh McCollum / d st scr Edward Bernds / ph Fayte Browne e Edwin Bryant / a Charles Clague / C: Emil Sitka (Phineas Bowman), Kitty McHugh (Mrs. Magruder, the Landlady), Mickey Simpson (Mr. Rocky Dugan, the Wrestler) and Dani Sue Nolan (Mrs. Gertie Dugan) / SYN: Shemp's uncle Phineas Bowman (he's worth $6 million) is coming to stay with the Stooges for two weeks. The Stooges promise the landlady that with their Uncle in town they'll be able to pay their back rent. The Stooges get in trouble, however, when the wife of a champion wrestler, Mrs. Dugan, borrows sugar from the trio. When Shemp escorts her to the door after filling her request, he accidentally trips and falls, tearing off her dress. Enter Mr. Dugan: He tears telephone books in half for a living, and spotting his wife with a torn dress, Dugan

One-sheet for *Hula-La-La* (1951).

starts tearing the Stooges apart, all at the same time. When Uncle Phineas tries breaking up the fight, he gets pummeled as well until Mrs. Magruder, the landlady, knocks out Dugan with a vicious left hook. Uncle Phineas rekindles his romance with Mrs. Magruder, an old sweetheart, and marries her. / FN: The hiding the lady in a trunk gag is also used in *Fifi Blows Her Top* (4/10/58) and Laurel and Hardy's *Blockheads* (1938).

142. THREE DARK HORSES **** / Rl. Oct. 16 / Prod. No. 4200 / 16m / p d Jules White / st scr Felix Adler / ad James Nicholson / ph Henry Freulich / e Edwin Bryant / a Cary Odell / C: Kenneth MacDonald (Wm. "Bill" Wick), Ben Welden (Digger), Johnny Kascier (Shemp's Stand-In), Harold Breen (Moe's Stand-In) and D. White (Larry's Stand-In) / SYN: If Hammond Egger is elected President, he'll be able to pull off the biggest "oil grab" of the century. To assure his victory, Egger's campaign managers hire three stupid janitors, Shemp, Larry and Moe, as convention delegates. At the convention, however, the boys learn that their "man" is a crook and throw their support for the other leading candidate, Abel Lamb Stewer. Stewer wins. / WT: Small Delegates at Large / SD: 4 (T 8/26 to F 8/29/52) Shot on Stage 10. / FN: The parrot

in the turkey gag is also seen in *Crash Goes the Hash* (2/5/44) and in *G.I. Wanna Home* (9/5/46), as well as in *Listen Judge* (3/6/52).

143. CUCKOO ON A CHOO CHOO / Rl. Dec. 4 / Prod. No. 4194 / 15½m / p d Jules White / st scr Felix Adler / ph Henry Freulich / e Edwin Bryant / a Charles Clague / C: Patricia Wright (Roberta), Victoria Horne (Lenore) and Reggie Dvorack (Carey, the Bird) / SYN: Larry, Shemp and two girls, Roberta and Lenore, steal a railroad car named *Shmow*, but are discovered by Moe, an ace detective for the Transylvania Railroad Company. The reason for the theft: Larry and Lenore can't get married until Shemp ties the knot with Roberta. It's a family tradition. But Shemp is so drunk that he only cares for his imaginery giant canary, Carey. Without a doubt, the worst Stooge comedy. / WT: *A Train Called Schmow* / PS: Larry Fine liked this film because of his Marlon Brando-type role. When he lived at the Motion Picture Country House, Larry sometimes screened his own print of this film for friends. During one such showing, Larry fell asleep as the film progressed (Larry wasn't the only one!).

1953

144. UP IN DAISY'S PENTHOUSE *** / Rl. Feb. 5 / Prod. No. 4182 / 16½m / p d Jules White / st Clyde Bruckman / scr Jack White / ph Henry Freulich / e Edwin Bryant / a Charles Clague / C: Connie Cezan (Daisy), John Merton (Butch) and Jack Kenny (Chopper) / SYN: Now that the Stooges' mother is getting old, their father is divorcing her and marrying a young blonde moll, Daisy. Mother Stooge asks the boys to stop the marriage. / FN: A remake of *Three Dumb Clucks* (4/17/37), using stock footage.

145. BOOTY AND THE BEAST *** / Rl. Mar. 5 / Prod. No. 4196 / 16½m / p d Jules White / st Felix Adler / scr Jack White / ad Carter DeHaven / ph Fayte Browne / e Edwin Bryant / a Walter Holscher / C: Kenneth MacDonald (Icabod Slipp), Vernon Dent (Watchman) and Curly Howard (Train Passenger in stock footage) / SYN: The Stooges' automobile runs out of gasoline in front of an imposing mansion. The boys notice the owner, Icabod Slipp, trying to budge open the front door and politely offer to help him. The Stooges not only help him break into the house, but also assist him in

blowing open a wall safe. The explosion renders the Stooges unconscious and Slipp, actually a burglar, flees with the bag of loot. When the night watchman catches the Stooges in front of the empty safe, the boys escape and take after Slipp, who is on a train bound for Las Vegas. On board the train, the Stooges succeed in recovering the loot. / WT: *Fun for the Money* / SD: 1 (M 5/19/52) Shot on Stage 10. / FN: Some interior train scenes (including Curly Howard's cameo and a lion in a baggage car) are from *Hold That Lion* (7/7/47).

146. LOOSE LOOT **½ / Rl. Apr. 2 / Prod. No. 4197 / 16m / p d Jules White / st Felix Adler / scr Jack White / ad Carter DeHaven / ph Fayte Browne / e Edwin Bryant / a Walter Holscher / C: Kenneth MacDonald (Icabod Slipp), Tom Kennedy (Joe), Emil Sitka (Attorney Poole in stock footage), Nanette Bordeaux (Fifi), Suzanne Ridgeway (Girl), Johnny Kascier (Moe's Stand-In), Harold Breen (Shemp's Stand-In) and D. White (Larry's Stand-In) / SYN: In order to collect their late Uncle's inheritance, Shemp Larry and Moe are advised to subpoena Icabod Slipp, the executor of the estate. He,

Bud Jamison's face appears on the Hammond Egger poster (here, behind Larry) in *Three Dark Horses* (1952), as a tribute to the long-time character actor who died suddenly before production, September 30, 1944.

of course, gives them the slip! The Stooges corner this conman at the Circle Follies Theatre, assaulting Slipp and his assistants with an arsenal of fruit. They wind up with their inheritance. / WT: *Filthy Lucre* / SD: 2 (T 5/20 to W 5/21/52) Shot on Stage 10. / FN: Scenes with the Stooges' attorney and inside Slipp's office are from *Hold That Lion* (7/7/47).

147. TRICKY DICKS **** / Rl. May 7 / Prod. No. 4199 / 16m / *p d* Jules White / *st*

catch the killer of Slug McGurk. The Stooges promptly start screening two prime suspects: an Italian organ grinder with a fake accent and Gilbraith Q. Tiddlewadder, a frustrated actor. Tiddlewadder (Chopper for short) begins to confess when the real killer enters, admitting to the crime. / WT: *Cop and Bull Story* / SD: 3 (M 7/14 to W 7/16/52) Shot on Stage 10. / FN: The filing cabinet sequence is from *Hold That Lion* (7/7/47).

148. SPOOKS ** / Rl. June 15 (2-D Version

stumble eventually upon a spooky old mansion where Bea is being held captive by Dr. Jeckyl, a mad scientist, Mr. Hyde, his burly assistant, and a rather large gorilla. One of the best scenes concerns the Stooges dodging a low-flying bat whose face resembles Shemp's. / SD: 4 (M 5/11 to TH 5/14/53) Shot at Columbia Sunset Studios, Stage 18. / FN: Filmed and released in 3-D. Script cover was ghost white, incidentally.

149. PARDON MY BACKFIRE **½ / Rl.

Wanda Perry doubling for Virginia Hunter in the role of Princess Alicia in the new footage for *Musty Musketeers*, flanked by Phil Van Zandt and Joe Palma.

scr Felix Adler / *ad* Paul Donnelly / *ph* Wm. E. Whitley / *e* Edwin Bryant / *a* George Brooks / *C*: Benny Rubin (Antonio Zukini Salami Corganzola De Pizza), Connie Cezan (Chick), Ferris Taylor (B.A. Copper, Chief of Detectives), Phil Arnold (Chopper), Murray Alper (Mr. Alpar), Suzanne Ridgeway (Police Woman), Johnny Kascier (Moe's Stand-In), Cy Malis (Shemp's Stand-In) and Hurley Breen (Shemp's Stand-In) / SYN: Police Chief B.A. Copper gives detectives Moe, Larry and Shemp just 24 hours to

Rl. Apr. 15) / Prod. No. 4210 / 16m / *p d* Jules White/ *st scr* Felix Adler / *ad* Eddie Saeta / *ph* Lester H. White / *e* Edwin Bryant / *a* Carl Anderson / *C*: Phil Van Zandt (Dr. Jeckyl), Tom Kennedy (Mr. Hyde), Norma Randall (Bea Bopper), Johnny Kascier (Moe's Stand-In), B. Rose (Shemp's Stand-In) and B. Edney (Larry's Stand-In) / SYN: When George Bopper's daughter, Bea, disappears he hires the Super Sleuth Detective Agency—Moe, Larry and Shemp—to find her. Disguised as pie salesmen, the Stooges

Aug. 15 / Prod. No. 4212 / 16m / *p d* Jules White / *st scr* Felix Adler / *ad* Milton Feldman / *ph* Henry Freulich / *e* Edwin Bryant / *a* Walter Holscher / *C*: Benny Rubin (Charles), Frank Sully (Algernon), Phil Arnold (Shiv), Fred Kelsey (Girl's Father), Ruth Godfrey (Nettie), Angela Stevens (Hettie) and Theila Darin (Betty) SYN: Garage mechanics Moe, Larry and Shemp will lose their brides-to-be, Nettie, Hettie and Betty, to three plumbers if they don't make good soon. Well, the boys succeed beyond their dreams when they apprehend three dangerous criminals at their automobile garage. A reward of $1,500 is awarded to the Stooges for their efforts, and they use the money to marry their sweethearts. / FN: Contrary to previously published reports, *Pardon My Backfire* was also filmed and released in 3-D.

150. RIP, SEW AND STITCH **½ / Rl. Sept. 3 / Prod. No. 4201 / 17m / *p d* Jules White / *st* Felix Adler / *scr* Jack White / *ad* James Nicholson / *ph* Ray Cory / *e* Edwin Bryant / *a* Cary Odell / C: Vernon Dent (Officer Sharp, in stock footage), Phil Arnold (Little Man, in stock footage) and Harold Brauer (T. Hargen, in stock footage) / SYN : Moe, Larry and Shemp run a tailor shop which serves as a temporary hideout for Terry Hargen, an escaped bank robber. / WT: *A Pressing Affair* / SD: 1 (Date not listed) / FN: The same film as *Sing a Song of Six Pants* (10/30/47) using new scenes of the Stooges. One scene was changed to the Stooges rummaging through Hargen's trousers for fifty-dollar bills. This segment segues to two new scenes of the Stooges searching the shop for his whereabouts and receiving reward money for his capture. In the new footage, Jules White cast a double as Terry Hargen, a role which was originally portrayed by Harold Brauer.

151. BUBBLE TROUBLE ** / Rl. Oct. 8 / Prod. No. 4202 / *p d* Jules White / *st* Felix Adler / *scr* Jack White / *ad* James Nicholson / *ph* Ray Cory / *e* Edwin Bryant / *a* Cary Odell / C: Emil Sitka (Amos Flint) and Christine McIntyre (Cerina Flint, in stock footage) / SYN: Unless the Stooges pay back rent, their landlord, Amos Flint, will evict them from their drug store. The trio convince Flint to let them stay when Shemp, Moe and Larry concoct a youth elixir that changes his middle-aged wife back to a volumptuous blonde. But when the landlord consumes the serum, he turns into the world's only talking gorilla. / WT: *Drugstore Dubs* / SD: 1 (M 10/13/52) Shot on Stage 10. / FN: The first half of the film is virtually the same footage from *All Gummed Up* (12/18/47). Later scenes also contain some overlapping of the old with the new. A double for Christine McIntyre is seen in one shot. The gag of mixing liquids in an old boot, which reappears, was used also in *Pardon My Scotch* (8/1/35), *Out West* (4/24/47), *All Gummed Up* (12/18/47), and *Pals and Gals* (6/3/54).

152. GOOF ON THE ROOF *** / Rl. Dec. 3 / Prod. No. 4203 / 16½m / *p d* Jules White / *st scr* Clyde Bruckman / *ad* James Nicholson / *ph* Sam Leavitt / *e* Edwin Bryant / *a* George Brooks / C: Frank Mitchell (Bill) and Maxine Gates (Bride) / SYN: The Stooges receive news from their pal, Bill, that they'll have to move out of his house since he'll be returning with his new bride. Before his homecoming, the boys install Bill's new TV antenna, with disasterous results. So when Bill and his new wife arrive, all hell breaks loose! / SD: 4 (Dates not listed).

1954

153. INCOME TAX SAPPY ** / Rl. Feb. 4 / Prod. No. 4208 / 16½m / *p d* Jules White / *st scr* Felix Adler / *ad* Abner Singer / *ph* Ray Cory / *e* Edwin Bryant / *a* George Brooks / C: Joe Palma, Vernon Dent (Two Confidence Men), Benny Rubin (Mr. Cash), Majorie Liszt (Moe's Wife) and Nanette Bordeaux (Mrs. Cash) / SYN: Moe's wife wants a home so bad that she demands her husband start cheating on his income tax to save money. Her brainstorm works and the Stooges become professional tax advisors (they help their clients cheat). In celebration of their rise to success, the boys stage a lavish dinner party where one of the guests is an FBI agent! / WT: *Tax Saps* / FN: Larry reprises the timeworn oyster stew gag used in *Dutiful But Dumb* (3/21/41) and in other Stooge's comedies.

154. MUSTY MUSKETEERS **½ / Rl. May 13 / Prod. No. 4209 / 16m / *p d* Jules White / *st* Felix Adler / *scr* Jack White / *ad* Irving Moore / *ph* Gert Anderson / *e* Edwin Bryant / *a* Ross Bellah / C: Vernon Dent (King Cole), Phil Van Zandt (Mergatroyd, the Magician), Virginia Hunter (Princess Alicia, in stock footage), Sherry O'Neill (Girl in Box, in stock footage), Joe Palma (Soldier), Wanda Perry (Princess Alicia in new footage) and Heinie Conklin (Guard) / SYN: This film utilizes an earlier premise in which Mergatroyd the Magician blackmails the King into granting him permission to marry his daughter, Alicia. The plan is contingent on Mergatroyd making Alicia, who he has held captive, appear magically by means of a trick box. The Stooges foil his efforts, and Alicia marries Prince Gallant as planned. SD: 1 (Date not listed) / FN: Uses stock footage from *Fiddler's Three* (5/6/48), with the exception of a few new scenes. These scenes include the Stooges riding into Coleslawvania, visiting their girl friends, entangling in a sword fight with Mergatroyd, and the closing reunion with Tilly, Lilly and Milly.

155. PALS AND GALS **½ / Rl. June 3 / Prod. No. 4211 / 17m / *p d* Jules White / *st* Clyde Bruckman / *scr* Jack White / *ad* Irving Moore / *ph* Gert Andersen / *e* Edwin Bryant / *a* Ross Bellah / C : Christine McIntyre (Nell), George Chesebro (Quirt), Norman Willis (Doc Barker in stock footage), Heinie Conklin (Henchman), Vernon Dent (Doctor in stock footage), Jacques O'Mahoney (Johnny, the Arizona Kid, in stock footage), Stanley Blystone (Colonel, in stock footage), Frank Ellis (Jake, in stock footage), Ruth Godfrey (Belle) and Norman Randall (Zell) / SYN: The Stooges return to the Old West, this time rescuing Nell's sisters from the clutches of Doc Barker's gang. / WT: *Cuckoo Westerners* / SD: 1 (Date not listed) / FN: Remake of *Out West* (4/24/47), with only exception being the boys' (not the Arizona kids') freeing of Nell's sisters in new footage. Other script alterations include: Larry winding up in jail, and the trio fleeing from Barker and his gang in a covered wagon

(ulitizing a monkey and meat grinder-machine gun in the scene). Features stock footage from *Goofs and Saddles* (7/2/37). The gag of mixing liquids in an old boot reappears again. Also, the exchanging cards under the table routine appears, which was staged in *Goofs and Saddles* (7/2/37) and in *Out West* (4/24/47).

156. KNUTZY KNIGHTS *** / Rl. Sept. 2 / Prod. No. 4217 / 17½m / *p d* Jules White / *st* Edward Bernds / *scr* Felix Adler / *ad* Irving Moore / *ph* Ray Cory / *e* Edwin Bryant / *a* Carl Anderson / C: Jacques O'Mahoney (Cedric), Christine McIntyre (Princess Elaine), Phil Van Zandt (Black Prince), Vernon Dent (King Arthur), Ruth Godfrey (Lady Title) and Joe Palma (Sir Satchel, in new footage) / SYN: Shemp, Larry and Moe are three troubadours sent to cheer up the broken-hearted Princess Elaine. Her father, the King, has pledged her hand to the Black Prince. But she loves Cedric, the village blacksmith, instead. / SD: 2 (Dates not listed) / FN: A remake of *Squareheads of the Round Table* (3/4/48), using a high volume of stock footage.

157. SHOT IN THE FRONTIER **½ / Rl. Oct. 7 / Prod. No. 4216 / 16m / *p d* Jules White / *st scr* Felix Adler / *ad* Abner Singer / *ph* Ray Cory / *e* Edwin Bryant / *a* George Brooks / C: Emil Sitka (Justice of the Peace), Ruth Godfrey (Bella), Theila Darin (Stella), Vivian Mason (Ella), Kenneth MacDonald (Noonan) and Emmett Lynn (Lem) / SYN: The Stooges become shooting targets for the Noonan Brothers, following the trio's wedding to three voluptuous ladies: Stella, Bella and Ella. This results in a noontime shoot-out between the Noonans and the Stooges (satirizing *High Noon*), complete with an old cowpoke singing and strumming his guitar off key). / WT: *Low Afternoon*.

158. SCOTCHED IN SCOTLAND *** / Rl. Nov. 4 / Prod. No. 4218 / 15½m / *p d* Jules White / *st* Elwood Ullman / *scr* Jack White / *ad* Irving Moore / *ph* Ray Cory / *e* Robert B. Hoover / *a* Carl Anderson / C: Phil Van Zandt (O.U. Gonga, Dean), Christine McIntyre (Lorna), Charles Knight (McPherson, in stock footage), Ted Lorch (Angus, in stock footage), George Pembroke (New Angus) and Herbert Evans (The Earl, in stock footage) / SYN: The Stooges graduate as detectives from the Wide Awake Detective School, with the lowest possible honors. Dean O.U. Gonga arranges for the boys' first case: guarding priceless heirlooms for the Earl, owner of Glenheather Castle in Scotland. WT: *Hassle in the Castle* / SD: 2 (Dates not listed) / FN: A reworking of *Hot Scots* (7/8/48), using stock footage. A double was used for McPherson in new castle scenes. The parrot-skull gag was also in *If a Body Meets a Body* (8/30/45) and in *Hot Scots* (7/8/48).

1955

159. FLING IN THE RING *** / Rl. Jan. 6 / Prod. No. 4223 / 16m / *p d* Jules White / *st*

261

Clyde Bruckman / scr Jack White / ad Eddie Saeta / ph Ray Cory / e Robert B. Hoover / a Edward Ilou / C: Dick Wessel (Chopper Kane, in stock footage), Claire Carleton (Kitty Davis, in stock footage), Frank Sully (New Big Mike), Harold Brauer (Old Big Mike), Cy Schindell (Moose), Tommy Kingston (Chuck), Joe Palma (New Chuck), Johnny Kascier (Moe's Stand-In), Charlie Cross (Larry's Stand-In) and Hurley Breen (Shemp's Stand-In) / SYN: Moe, Larry and Shemp handle Chopper Kane, a heavyweight boxer. Their boss, Big Mike, has bet ten grand on Chopper to lose his next fight, so he expects the Stooges to make sure it happens. / SD: 1 (T 3/27/54) / FN: Remake of *Fright Night* (3/6/47), using a high volume of stock footage. New scenes include a meeting with the new Big Mike (Frank Sully). Watch for the old Big Mike (Harold Brauer) in stock footage. Originally, Jack White's screenplay ended with Moe and Larry speeding off for China in a motorcyle, with Shemp in a sidecar. The gag of acting as a puppeteer for an unconscious victim is also used in *Matri-Phony* (7/2/42) and in *Fright Night* (3/6/47).

160. OF CASH AND HASH *** / Rl. Feb. 3 / Prod. No. 4225 / 16m / p d Jules White / st Del Lord / scr Jack White / ad Eddie Saeta ph Ray Cory / e Robert B. Hoover / a Edward Ilou / C: Kenneth MacDonald (Lefty Loomis, in stock footage), Christine McIntyre (Gladys Harmon), Frank Lackteen (Red Watkins) and Vernon Dent (Capt. Mullins, in stock footage) / SYN: The Stooges are mistaken for three armored car robbers, proving their innocence by capturing the real crooks in an old spooky mansion. / WT: Crook Crackers / SD: 1 (Date not listed) / FN: Stock footage lifted from *Shivering Sherlocks* (1/8/48). Doubles were cast in new scenes as Angel and Lefty. The clam soup gag is also used in *Shivering Sherlocks*.

161. GYPPED IN THE PENTHOUSE ** / Rl. Mar. 10 / Prod. No. 4224 / 16m / p d Jules White / st scr Felix Adler / ad Abner E. Singer / ph Ray Cory / e Henry Batista / a Carl Anderson / C: Jean Willes (Jane), Emil Sitka (Charlie), Al Thompson (Moe's Stand-In), Hurley Breen (Shemp's Stand-in) and Charlie Cross (Larry's Stand-In) / SYN: Larry and Shemp meet inside a woman-haters club to discuss their bygone romances with Jane, an attractive golddigger. After a series of flashbacks, Shemp and Larry are also reunited with Jane's revengeful husband, Moe / WT: Blundering Bachelors / SD: 3 (M 7/19 to W 7/21/54) Shot on Stage 9 at Columbia Studios FN: Jules White is credited with writing the lyrics to the song, "Home on the Farm."

162. BEDLAM IN PARADISE *** / Rl. Apr. 14 / Prod. No. 4228 / 16m / p d Jules White / st Zion Myers / scr Felix Adler / ph Ray Cory / e Paul Borofsky / a Carl Anderson / ad Jerrold Bernstein / C: Moe Howard (Uncle Mortimer), Marti Shelton (Miss Jones, Blonde Angel, in stock footage), Judy Malcolm (Heavenly Switchboard Operator,

in stock footage), Phil Van Zandt (The Devil/ Mr. Heller), Sylvia Lewis (Female Devil/ Helen Blazes), Vernon Dent (Lawyer, in stock footage), Symona Boniface (Mrs. De Peyster, in stock footage), Victor Travers (Mr. De Peyster, in stock footage) and Sam McDaniel (Spiffingham, in stock footage) / SYN: When Shemp dies and goes to heaven, Uncle Mortimer, the Keeper of the Pearly Gates, refuses him entrance into the divine kingdom. The deal: Shemp must reform his partners Moe and Larry, who are involved in a shady deal with the Devil / WT: Gruesome Threesome / SD: 1 (F 7/9/54) / FN: A reworking of *Heavenly Daze* (9/2/48), using stock footage. New scenes include Moe and Larry nursing Shemp before he dies; Shemp's encounter with the Devil; the Devil's meeting on Earth with Moe and Larry, and the ending with Shemp in bed (it was all a dream).

163. STONE AGE ROMEOS *** / Rl. June 2 / Prod. No. 4229 / 16m /p d Jules White / st Zion Myers / scr Felix Adler / ad Jerrold Bernstein / ph Ira Morgan / e Paul Borofsky / a Carl Anderson / C: Emil Sitka (B.Bopper, Curator), Dee Green (Baggie), Nancy Saunders (Maggie), Virginia Hunter (Aggie), Joe Palma, Cy Schindell, Bill Wallace (Cavemen) and Barbara Bartay (Secretary) / SYN: A museum curator will pay the Stooges $25,000 if they return from a scientific expedition with film footage showing that cavemen still exist. Later, the Stooges screen for he curator film footage of cavemen who are actually the Stooges in disguise. / WT: Caved in Cavemen / SD: 1 (TH 8/26/54) FN: Cavemen segments from *I'm a Monkey's Uncle* (10/7/48).

164. WHAM BAM SLAM **½ / Rl. Sept. 1 / Prod. No. 4232 / 16m / p d Jules White / st Clyde Bruckman / scr Felix Adler / ad Willard Sheldon / ph Fred Jackman / e Paul Borofsky / a Cary Odell / C: Matt McHugh (Claude A. Quacker, in stock footage), Alyn Lockwood (Petunia), Doris Revier (Narcissus) and Wanda Perry (Marigold) / SYN: Shemp's nerves are shot so Larry's friend, Claude A Quacker, a self-educated health adviser, suggests the Stooges take him camping. / WT: Enjoying Poor Health / SD: 1 (T 1/18/55) / FN: A reworking of *Pardon My Clutch* (2/26/48), using ample stock footage. New segments: the Stooges eating hotcakes (consuming powder puffs by mistake), a lobster in Shemp's foot bath, and the ending with Shemp being cured by all the excitement.

165. HOT ICE **½ / Rl. Oct. 6 / Prod. No. 4233 / 16½m / p d Jules White / st Elwood Ullman / scr Jack White / ad Willard Sheldon / ph Fred Jackman / e Tony DeMarco / a Cary Odell / C: Kenneth MacDonald (Dapper Dan), Christine McIntyre (Bee, in stock footage), Charles C. Wilson (Inspector McCormick, in stock footage), Lester Allen (Runty), Barbara Bartay (Girl in Cafe), Bud Fine (Thug in Bar) and Blackie Whiteford (Cauliflower-eared Thug) / SYN: Scotland Yard gardeners Moe, Larry and

Shemp turn detectives and recover the Punjab diamond from Dapper Dan. / FN: A reworking of *A Crime on Their Hands* (12/9/48), using stock footage. Scotland Yard scenes (except for reading of memo) are from *Hot Scots* (7/8/48). In new segments, director Jules White cast a double for "Muscles." The Stooges' search through the dresser drawers routine is a revision of their file cabinet gag.

166. BLUNDER BOYS *** / Rl. Nov. 3 / Prod. No. 4222 / 16m / p d Jules White / st scr Felix Adler / ad Willard Sheldom / ph Ray Cory / e Tony DiMarco / a Cary Odell / C: Benny Rubin (The Eel), Angela Stevens (Alma Mater), Kenneth MacDonald (F.B. Eye), Barbara Bartay (Beautician), Bonnie Henjum, Barbara Donaldson, Marjorie Jackson and June Lebow (Turkish Bathers) / SYN: Spoofing TV's *Dragnet*, the Stooges are Halliday (Moe), Tarraday (Larry) and St. Patrick's Day (Shemp). They've just graduated from criminology school, and are now full-fledged detectives. Captain F.B. Eye assigns the boys to their first case: to track down the Eel, a robber who masquerades as a woman. In a wild escapade at the Biltless Hotel, the Eel manages to slip through the grasp of the Stooges, who lose their jobs and become ditch-diggers instead. / WT: Cuckoo Cops / FN: Scenes of Larry on a building ledge were budgeted under *Wham Bam Slam* (9/1/55).

1956

167. HUSBANDS BEWARE ***½ / Rl. Jan. 5 / Prod. No. 4236 / 16m / p d Jules White / st Clyde Bruckman / scr Felix Adler / ad Eddie Saeta / ph Henry Freulich / e Tony DiMarco / a Ross Bellah / C: Emil Sitka (Justice of the Peace), Christine McIntyre (Lulu Hopkins, in stock footage), Maxine Gates (Flora), Lou Leonard (Dora), Dee Green (Fanny Dunkelmeer, in stock footage), Nancy Saunders, Doris Colleen (Old Girl Friends, in stock footage), Johnny Kascier (Moe's Stand-In), Hurley Breen (Shemp's Stand-In) and Charlie Cross (Larry's Stand-In) / SYN: A revised version of the old tale in which Shemp must be married in 48 hours if he is to collect $500,000 inheritance from his deceased uncle's will. Shemp ties the knot with one of his vocal students, Fanny. But the truth emerges later: Moe and Larry wanted Shemp married since they were already henpecked. Shemp reacts to the news by shooting the boys down with a revolver. / WT: Eat, Drink and Be Married / SD: 1 (T 5/17/55) Shot on Stage 2 at Columbia. / FN: A reworking of *Brideless Groom* (9/11/47), using stock footage. New footage is comprised of the Stooges' encounters with Shemp's sisters. In the wedding sequence, a double was used for the Fanny role.

168. CREEPS **½ / Rl. Feb. 2 / Prod. No. 4237 / 16m / p d Jules White / st Felix Adler / scr Jack White / ad Eddie Saeta / ph Henry Freulich / e Harold White / a Ross Bellah / C: Phil Arnold (Voice of Sir Tom) / SYN: The Stooges tell their sons (also the Stooges) a spooky bedtime story on "knights, ghosts and murders" in a haunted castle, where the boys meet some lively antiquated ghosts. / WT: Three Brave Cowards / FN: Haunted castle footage from Ghost Talks (2/3/49), except for the Torture Room scenes.

169. FLAGPOLE JITTERS **½ / Rl. Apr. 5 / Prod. No. 4238 / 16m / p d Jules White / st Felix Adler / scr Jack White / ad Willard Sheldon / ph Irving Lippman / e Harold White / a Cary Odell / C: Vernon Dent (Insurance Adjustor, in stock footage), Beverly Thomas, Barbara Bartay (Chorus Girls), Mary Ainslee (Mary, in stock footage), Bonnie Menjum (Chorus Girl), Don Harvey (Jack), David Bond (Svengarlic), Frank Sully (Jim), Dick Alexander (Fat Cop) and Jimmy Lloyd (Cliff, in stock footage) / SYN: The Stooges try raising money for an operation that will make their invalid neighbor, Mary, walk again. Moe, Larry, and Shemp take on jobs pasting up posters at the Garden Theatre, where they are enlisted as volunteers in a hypnotist's flagpole stunt. The stunt is being staged so Svengarlic's accomplices can rob the Gottrocks Jewelry Company. The Stooges' weight, however, causes the flagpole to snap and they crash inside the jewelry store, foiling the robbery attempt. / SD: 2 (TH 6/30 and F 7/1/55) Shot on Stage 3 at Columbia. / FN: A reworking of Hocus Pocus (5/5/49), using stock footage. New scenes include establishing Svengarlic's crooked motives and the Stooges' encountering three chorus girls. Doubles fill in as Mary and Dick.

170. FOR CRIMIN' OUT LOUD **** / Rl. May 3 / Prod. No. 4239 / 16m / p d Jules White / st Edward Bernds / scr Felix Adler / ad Willard Sheldon / ph Irving Lippman / e Harold White / a Cary Odell / C: Barbara Bartay (Newsgirl), Christine McIntyre (Delores, Goodrich's niece, in stock footage), Emil Sitka (John Goodrich), Duke York (Nikko, the Goon, in stock footage), Charles Knight (Crandall), Kenneth MacDonald (Hackett, in stock footage) and Ralph Dunn (Henchman/Servant) / SYN: The Stooges work for the Miracle Detective Agency ("If We Solve Your Crime, It's A Miracle!") and answer a middle-aged councilman's call to track down some racketeers who have threatened his life. / WT: Nutty Newshounds / FN: Stock footage is used from Who Done It? (3/3/49). The Stooges appear in some new scenes, the most notable being that of them at their detective agency. The fighting in the dark gag is also used in Out West (4/24/47), in Who Done It? (3/3/49) and later in The Three Stooges Go Around the World in a Daze (1963). This was the last film containing new footage of Shemp.

171. RUMPUS IN A HAREM **½ / Rl. June 21 / Prod. No. 4244 / 16m / p d Jules White / st Felix Adler / scr Jack White / ad Willard Sheldon / ph Ray Cory / e Harold White / a Ross Bellah / C: Vernon Dent (Hassan Ben Sobar, in stock footage), George Lewis (Ghinna Rumma), Harriette Tarler (Harem Girl), Diana Darrin, Helen

Jay, Ruth Godfrey White (Stooges' Girls), Suzanne Ridgeway (Harem Girl) and Frank Lackteen (Emir of Shmow) / SYN: The Stooges' girls—Pheba, Sheeba and Heebah—will be sold to the Sultan of Posh Posh unless they each pay a one thousand shillblana virgin tax within three days. In order to raise the money, Moe, Larry and Shemp, waiters at the Cafe Casbahbah, promise two customers to recover the King Rootin' Tootin' diamond from the Emir of Shmow. They'll be handsomely compensated with reward money to pay off their sweethearts' taxes. Disguised as Santa Clauses, the Stooges get the job done. / WT: Diamond Daffy (Scripted Dec. 12, 1955) / FN: A reworking of Malice in the Palace (9/1/49), using stock footage. The first of four films made after Shemp's death, with Joe Palma posing as Shemp in new footage. New scenes: Pheba, Sheeba and Heebah report to Moe and Larry their bad news, Shemp (Joe Palma is conveniently missing) has left a note informing the boys that he couldn't sleep and that their snoring caused him to go and open the restaurant early. Other new scenes include: Moe, Larry and Palma merging for their traditional football huddle in the restaurant and fleeing from a Nubian guard (not the same actor in stock) right into a girls' harem. The gag of disguising as Santa Clauses also appeared in Wee Wee Monsieur (2/18/38) and in Malice in the Palace (9/1/49). Waiter chasing a dog past a customer waiting for franks and beans is also used in Playing the Ponies (10/15/37) and in Malice in the Palace (9/1/49). "Rootin' Tootin'" is spelling in film's script.

172. HOT STUFF ** / Rl. Sept. 6 / Prod. No. 4245 / 16m / p d Jules White / st Elwood Ullman / scr Felix Adler / ad Willard Sheldon / ph Irving Lippman / e Harold White / a Ross Bellah / C: Jacques O'Mahoney (Guard of Cell), Emil Sitka (Prof. Sneed), Christine McIntyre (Hazel, Sneed's Daughter) (all in stock), Evelyn Lovequist (Uranian Female Officer), Connie Cezan (Ava, Uranian Female Officer), Andre Pola (Kronk, Anemia Spy), Vernon Dent (General), Harold Brauer (Guard) (both in stock) and Phil Van Zandt (Capt. Rork) / SYN: Uranian undercover agents, Moe, Larry and Shemp, are seized by Anemian spies mistaking Larry for Professor Sneed, the inventor of a super-rocket fuel, and Moe and Larry for his assistants. The spies transport the trio to the State of Anemia, where they are forced to recreate the famous rocket fuel formula. / WT: They Gassed Wrong (scripted on December 12, 1955) / FN: A reworking of Fuelin' Around (7/7/49), using stock footage. Filmed after Shemp's death. New scenes: The Stooges, wearing beards, enter the Uranian Department of the Inferior. A pretty girl passes by, so Moe orders: "Shemp"—Joe Palma—"follow her, she may be a spy!" Palma utters, "Right," and skips off after her while Moe and Larry engage in a separate scene with two female Uranian officers. Later, in the laboratory, Palma tries to imitate Shemp's famous tagline, "Heep-heep-heep!"

173. SCHEMING SCHEMERS ** / Rl. Oct. 4 / Prod. No. 4246 / 16m / p d Jules White / st Elwood Ullman / scr Jack White / ad Willard Sheldon / ph Ray Cory / e Harold White / a Ross Bellah / C: Christine McIntyre (Ethel, in stock footage), Kenneth MacDonald (Allen), Symona Boniface (Mrs. Norfleet, in stock footage), Emil Sitka (Mr. Walter Norfleet, in stock footage and new), Dudley Dickerson (Henry, the Cook, in stock footage) and Herbert Evans (Wilks, the Butler, in stock footage) / SYN: As plumbers, the Stooges are summoned to the Norfleet mansion to recover a valuable diamond ring which slipped down a wash basin. Instead, the Stooges wreak havoc and start a pie fight. / WT: Pixilated Plumbers (scripted Dec. 29, 1955) / SD: 1 (M 1/16/56)/ FN: A reworking of Vagabond Loafers (10/6/49), using stock footage. Film also incorporates old footage from A-Plumbing We Will Go (4/19/40) and pie-fight material from Half-Wits' Holiday (1/9/47). New segments: Moe and Larry search for the missing ring in a sink and throw pies at Allen (Kenneth MacDonald). Joe Palma is featured as "Shemp" in one shot honking the horn in the trio's jeep. Christine McIntyre is likewise doubled in some scenes.

174. COMMOTION ON THE OCEAN **½ / Rl. Nov. 8 / Prod. No. 4247 / 17m / p d Jules White / st scr Felix Adler / ph Ray Cory / e Harold White / a Ross Bellah / ad Willard Sheldon / C: Charles Wilson (J.L. Cameron, in stock footage), Gene Roth (Bortch), Emil Sitka (Reporter) and Harriette Tarler (Emma Blake) / SYN: When the Stooges learn in a newspaper editor's office that some atomic documents have been stolen, they decide to pose as reporters and investigate the matter. It turns out that their neighbor, Bortch, a seedy-looking foreign spy, has swiped the documents and is planning to return by boat to his native land. The Stooges accompany him and thwart his plan. WT: Salt Water Daffy (scripted December 30, 1955) / SD: 1 (T 1/17/56) FN: A reworking of Dunked in the Deep (11/3/49) with ample stock footage. Newspaper office segment, except for a few shots, is lifted from A Crime on Their Hands (12/9/48). Seasick gag reprised from Back From the Front (5/28/43) and Dunked in the Deep (11/3/49). New footage includes Moe and Larry's search for food (they mistakenly eat a wooden fish, then spew out sawdust a la their Coughing Up Feathers gag, which was first staged in Uncivil Warriors [4/2/35]) and their seizure of Bortch, the foreign spy. The Shemp double, Joe Palma, in his final appearance as a third Stooge of sorts, is featured briefly in the latter scene.

United Artists Feature
1951

1. GOLD RAIDERS ** / Rl. Sept. 14 / Prod. No. 524 / 56m / p Bernard Glasser / d Edward Bernds / st scr Elwood Ullman and Wm. Lively / ph Paul Ivano / e Fred Allen / m Alexandre Starr / C: George O'Brien (George), Sheila Ryan (Laura Mason), Clem Bevans (Doc Mason), Monte Blue (John

Opening title for Stooges films with Joe Besser.

Sawyer), Lyle Talbot (Ed Taggart), John Merton (Clete), Al Baffert (Utah), Hugh Hocker (Sandy), Bill Ward (Red), Fuzzy Knight (Sheriff Wade), Dick Crockett (Blake) and Roy Canada (Slim) / SYN: The Stooges help George O'Brien, an insurance agent, outwit a gang of desperadoes who are after a valuable gold mine shipment / aka The Stooges Go West / SD: 5 (T 12/26 to SA 12/30/50) / PS: Gold Raiders was not exactly director Edward Bernds' favorite, as he explains: "I should have never made that picture. It was an ultra-quickie shot in five days at the unbelieveable cost of $50,000, which, even then, was ridiculously low. I'm afraid the picture shows it!"

THE THREE STOOGES (Larry, Moe and Joe Besser)
Columbia Shorts
1957
175. HOOFS AND GOOFS *** / Rl. Jan. 31 / Prod. No. 4251 / 15½m / p d Jules White / st scr Jack White / ph Gert Andersen / e Harold White / a Paul Palmentola / ad Willard Sheldon / C: Benny Rubin (Mr. Dinklespiel), Harriette Tarler (Dinklespiel's Daughter), Moe Howard (Birdie, the Stooges' sister, in drag) and Tony the Wonder Horse / SYN: The Stooges' sister, Birdie, has been reincarnated as a horse and is about to give birth to a beautiful colt! The scene changes to Joe, sound asleep, mumling, "I'm an uncle! I'm an uncle!" Moe and Larry wake up Joe (he dreamed the whole story), as Birdie, alive and well, comes from the kitchen carrying a casserole. Joe tells her he just dreamed that she was a horse. Far from flattered, Birdie crowns Joe with her casserole WT: Galloping Bride (scripted Mar. 30, 1956) / SD: 3 (dates not listed) / FN: In the final draft screenplay of Hoofs and Goofs, writer Jack White calls for Birdie to whack Joe over the head with a breakaway rolling pin instead of a casserole. The gag of tying a heavy object to an animal's tail is also

enacted in Busy Buddies (3/18/44) and in Abbott and Costello's Ride 'Em Cowboy (1943). Blowing a pill through a pipe gag is borrowed from Even As I.O.U. (9/18/42) and Scrambled Brains (7/7/51) / PS: It has been said that the worst two subjects to direct are children and animals. But according to Joe Besser, Tony the Wonder Horse was no problem: "That horse was wonderful. When Moe, Larry and I were on the set, we fed him carrots."

176. MUSCLE UP A LITTLE CLOSER ** ½ / Rl. Feb. 28 / Prod. No. 4250 / 17m / p d Jules White / st scr Felix Adler / ph Irving Lippman / e Harold White / a Cary Odell / sd Robert Priestley / ad Mitchell Gamson / C: Maxine Gates (Tiny Ray), Ruth Godfrey White (May Trent), Matt Murphy (Elmo Drake) and Harriette Tarler (Mary Brown) / SYN: Tiny, Joe's girlfriend, is upset. Her five-karat diamond engagement ring has been stolen! Moe has a hunch that Elmo Drake, the trucking foreman at the plant where the Stooges and their girls work, stole the ring, since he has a pass key to all the employees' lockers. At work, the Stooges and Tiny confront Elmo in the gymnasium and, after some fancy wrestling, recover the ring so Joe and Tiny can get married. / WT: Builder Uppers /SD: 3 (W 6/27 to F 6/29/56). Shot on Stage 3 at Columbia Studios. / FN: Deleted are some scenes at the Seabiscuit Food Corporation: Joe plays "detective," but Moe searches him, finding a concealed weapon—a salami; and Joe answers a telephone call, unaware that a wad of gum he discarded is stuck to the ear piece.

177. A MERRY MIX-UP *** / Rl. Mar. 28 / Prod. No. 4252 / 16m / p d Jules White / st scr Felix Adler / ph Irving Lippman / e Harold White / a Paul Palmentola / sd Dave Montrose / ad Irving Moore / C: Nanette Bordeaux (May), Jeanne Carmen (Mary), Ruth Godfrey White (Leona), Suzanne

Ridgeway (Jane), Harriette Tarler (Letty), Diana Darrin (Jill) and Frank Sully (Waiter) / SYN: This is the story of nine brothers, three sets of identical triplets born one year apart, who have lost track of each other since the war. The mix-up starts when Moe, Larry and Joe meet the wives of their brothers, Louis, Max and Jack, in a nightclub, much to the consternation of a very confused waiter. The Stooges play all three sets of triplets. / WT: A Merry Marriage Mix-Up / SD: 3 (dates not listed) / FN: A reworking of Our Relations (1936) with Laurel and Hardy. For the ending, screenwriter Felix Adler suggested that the waiter hit himself over the head with a champagne bottle instead of a meat cleaver. / PS: The second to last shot in A Merry Mix-Up was carefully exposed three different times to achieve the effect of Moe, Larry and Joe as the three sets of triplets standing side by side. For each section of film exposed, each Stooge had his own marker on the floor to stand behind. A real merry mix-up developed when Jules White believed Larry was standing behind the wrong marker as compared to the previous exposure. Larry insisted that Jules was wrong and that he was standing in the right spot. Fortunately, Jules listened to Larry, who proved to be right. If Jules hadn't listened, the studio would have had to spend thousands of dollars for a retake.

178. SPACE SHIP SAPPY ** / Rl. Apr. 18 / Prod. No. 4253 / 16m / p d Jules White / st scr Jack White / ph Henry Freulich / e Saul A. Goodkind / a Wm. Flannery / sd Frank A. Tuttle / ad Donald Gold / C: Benny Rubin (Prof. A.K. Rimple), Doreen Woodbury (Professor's Daughter), Lorraine Crawford (Flora), Harriette Tarler (Fauna), Marilyn Hanold (Other Amazon) and Emil Sitka (Liar's Club Emcee) / SYN: Professor Rimple takes three sailors, the Stooges, and his daughter Lisa on an adventurous cruise on a space ship bound for the planet Sunev (that's Venus spelled backwards). Here, the boys flee from three cannibalistic amazon women who want to devour them! As they reach the door to the spaceship, it bursts open, knocking the Professor and Lisa out cold. But there is no cause for alarm. Moe believes he can operate the spaceship. He does until Joe grabs hold of the control lever and breaks it off! As the space ship takes a nose dive, the scene dissolves to the Liar's Club's 27th Annual Convention where an emcee awards the Stooges first prize for being the biggest liars in the world! / WT: Rocket and Roll It / SD: 3 (M 8/27 to W 8/29/56) / FN: Screenwriter Jack White originally planned for the Stooges to go into their Viva! Viva! routine after receiving their award.

179. GUNS A-POPPIN' *** / Rl. June 13 / Prod. No. 1902 / 16½m / p d Jules White / st Jack White and Elwood Ullman / scr Jack White / ph Henry Freulich / e Saul A. Goodkind / a Cary Odell / sd Kay Bobcock / ad Herb Wallerstein / C: Frank Sully (Sheriff), Joe Palma (Mad Bill Hookup, the Ban-

dit) and Vernon Dent (The Judge, in stock footage) / SYN: Moe is accused of assaulting his two brothers-in-law, Larry and Joe, with intent to commit mayhem. But the incident would never have happened if Larry and Joe hadn't taken Moe on a hunting trip to quiet his nerves / WT: Nerveless Wreck / SD: 1 (W 11/28/56). Shot on Stage 34 at the Columbia Ranch / FN: A remake of Idiots DeLuxe (7/20/45), using some stock footage. New subplot: the Stooges' cabin becomes the site of a stand-off between the Sheriff and an escaped bandit, Mad Bill Hookup. The boys eventually capture the crook and a grateful sheriff reveals that they'll receive a $10,000

reward (the same amount Moe owes his creditors!). The news delights the boys so much that they give the Sheriff a big hug while Mad Bill escapes!

180. HORSING AROUND ** / Rl. Sept. 12 / Prod. No. 1901 / 15½m / p d Jules White / st scr Felix Adler / ph Ray Cory / e Wm. Lyon / a Cary Odell / sd Fay Babcock/ ad Herb Wallerstein / C: Emil Sitka (Old Man), Harriette Tarler (Girl) and Tony the Wonder Horse / SYN: Joe learns that the famous circus horse, Schnapps, who is the mate of their reincarnated sister Birdie, is about to be destroyed. The Stooges and Birdie ride

to the fairgrounds and save him. / WT: Just Horsing Around and Just Fooling Around / SD: 3 (M 11/19 to W 11/21/56) Shot on Western and Rock Streets at Columbia Ranch. / FN: A sequel to Hoofs and Goofs (1/31/57). Cow milking sequence reused in Oil's Well That Ends Well (12/4/58). Moe and Larry in a horse costume gag was first seen in Three Little Twerps (7/9/43).

181. RUSTY ROMEOS ***½ / Rl. Oct. 17 / Prod. No. 1904 / 16½m / p d Jules White / st Felix Adler / scr Jack White / ph Henry Freulich / e Saul A. Goodkind / a Cary Odell / sd Tom Oliphant / ad Sam Nelson / C: Connie "Cezan" Geason (Mabel) / SYN: The Stooges are about to propose marriage to the same girl but don't know it. / WT: Sappy Lovers / SD: 2 (T 2/12 to W 2/13/57). Shot on Stage 9 at Columbia Studios. / FN: A remake of Corny Casanovas (5/1/52), with ample old footage. New scenes: the Stooges have pancakes ("Flipper's Fluffy Fablongent Flapjacks") for breakfast, and when Mabel prepares to walk out on the boys, Joe suddenly returns with an automatic B-B gun loaded with tacks and uses Mabel's derriere for target practice! Watch for Shemp's portrait in the stock footage of Mabel's apartment.

182. OUTER SPACE JITTERS ** / Rl. Dec. 5 / Prod. No. 1909 / 16½m / p d Jules White / st scr Jack White / ph William Bradford / e Harold White / a Walter Holscher / sd Sidney Clifford / ad Max Stein / C: Emil Sitka (Prof. Jones), Gene Roth (Grand Zilch of Zunev), Phil Van Zandt (High Mucky Muck), Joe Palma (Army Officer), Dan Blocker (The Goon), Harriette Tarler, Diana Darrin and Arline Hunter (Three Beautiful Girls) / SYN: The Stooges and Professor Jones are sent to the Planet Zunev to learn about its lifestyle, finding it inhabited by three beautiful girls charged with high voltage (they love to eat empty clam shells and drink battery acid!) and a brawny-looking zombie called The Goon. When the Stooges discover they're next in line to become zombies, they grab the Professor and escape. The last scene dissolves to them in their apartment finishing this spooky bedtime story for their children (the Stooges), before going out for dinner. But instead of leaving through the front door, the boys jump out the window; the baby sitter's a vampire! / WT: Outer Space Daze / SD: 2 (dates not listed).

1958
183. QUIZ WHIZZ **½ / Rl. Feb. 13 / Prod. No. 1907 / 15½m / p d Jules White / st scr Searle Kramer / ph Irving Lippman / e Wm. Lyon / a John McCormick / sd Sidney Clifford / ad Jerrold Bernstein / C: Milton Frome (G.Y. Prince), Bill Brauer (R.O. Broad), Gene Roth (Montgomery M. Montgomery), Greta Thyssen (Lisa, His Secretary) and Emil Sitka (J.J. Figbee, Tax Collector) / SYN: Joe wins a big TV jackpot, but then allows two swindlers, G.Y. Prince and R.O. Broad, to invest his earnings in a losing proposition: "Consolidated Fujiama

Columbia Pictures goofed when they inadvertently billed Moe as Shemp on this one-sheet for A Merry Mix-Up (1957).

TRIPLE-HEADER OF HILARITY!

three times wackier than ever

THE THREE STOOGES
A MERRY MIX-UP

SHEMP · LARRY
JOE

with
FRANK SULLY
DIANA DARRIN
RUTH GODFREY WHITE
JEANNE CARMEN
SUZANNE RIDGEWAY
HARRIETTE TARLER
NANETTE BORDEAUX

265

California Smog Bags," filled with smog! When the Stooges confront the crooks in their office, they find themselves adopted by a lonesome old eccentric millionaire and his female accomplice who just happen to be "hit men" for Prince and Broad! Fortunately, the Stooges manage to battle off all parties involved, recover the check for Joe's TV winnings and divvy up the money, tearing the check into thirds! / SD: 2 (TH 5/2 and F 5/3/57) Shot on Stage 7 at Columbia Studios.

184. FIFI BLOWS HER TOP **½ / Rl. Apr. 10 / Prod. No. 1903 / 16½m / p d Jules White / st scr Felix Adler / ph Henry Freulich / e Saul A. Goodkind / a Cary Odell / sd Tom Oliphant / ad Sam Nelson / C: Vanda Dupre (Fifi), Christine McIntyre (Katrina, in stock footage), Yvette Reynard (Maria, in stock footage), Harriette Tarler (Waitress), Wanda D'Ottoni, Suzanne Ridgeway (Girls in Restaurant) and Phil Van Zandt (Mort, Fifi's Husband) / SYN: Joe is depressed. Today would have been the anniversary of the day he met his darling Fifi, but Moe and Larry tell him to forget her. Later, however, the boys take turns reminiscing how they each met their sweethearts overseas. Storytime over, a knock comes at the door and in enters Joe's old girlfriend, Fifi, who now lives across the hall with Mort, her husband. Soon the husband pays the Stooges a visit and they hide Fifi in a trunk while Mort tells them he has another girl lined up and plans to divorce his wife. Furious, Fifi emerges from the trunk, bashes a chair over Mort's head, and reunites with Joe. / WT: Rancid Romance / SD: 2 (T 2/12 and W 2/13/57) / FN: A reworking of Love at First Bite (5/4/50) with some old footage. The gag of hiding a lady in a trunk is also used in Gents in a Jam (7/4/52) and Blockheads (1938), with Laurel and Hardy.

185. PIES AND GUYS *** / Rl. June 12 / Prod. No. 1908 / 16½m / p d Jules White / st Zion Myers / scr Jack White / ph Irving Lippman / e Harold White / a John McCormack / sd Sidney Clifford / ad Jerrold Bernstein / C: Gene Roth (Prof. Frankenberg), Milton Frome (Prof. Quackenbush), Greta Thyssen (Lulu, Quackenbush's Daughter), Helen Dickson (Mrs. Gotrocks, in new and old footage), John Kascier (Party Guest), Harriette Tarler (Countess), Symona Boniface (Mrs. Smythe Smythe, in stock footage) and Emil Sitka (Butler, in new and old footage) / SYN: Professor Quackenbush wagers $1,000 that he can turn three plumbers, Moe, Larry and Joe, into polished gentlemen in 60 days. With the aid of his daughter, Lulu, the Professor attempts the impossible: to teach the boys the proper way of eating. After weeks of hard effort, the night finally arrives when the Stooges are presented to society. Old habits soon emerge, however, when the boys commence with a pie-throwing melee. WT: Easy Come, Easy Go / SD: 2 (M 5/6 and T 5/7/57). Shot on Stage 7 at Columbia Studios. / FN: A scene-for-scene remake of Half-Wits' Holiday (1/9/47), with pie-fight stock footage.

186. SWEET AND HOT *** / Rl. Sept. 4 /

Prod. No. 1910 / 17m / p d Jules White / st Jerome S. Gottler / scr Jerome S. Gottler and Jack White / ph Irving Lippman / e Edwin Bryant / a Adam Gosse / sd Sidney Clifford / ad Mitchell Gamson / C: Muriel Landers (Tiny) / SYN: Joe's sister, Tiny, has an extreme case of "ochlophobia" (she's afraid to sing in front of people), so Larry and Joe take her to see Doctor Hugo Gansamacher (Moe), a German psychiatrist. Gansamacher, or Doc for short, puts Tiny under hypnosis and she recalls that when she was a child, her father (again Moe) pressured her into singing for her two Uncles (Joe and Larry). Once cured, however, Tiny's wish to become a singer is realized when she performs in a nightclub act with Joe and Larry./ SD: 2 (TH 8/22 and F 8/23/57) / FN: Muriel Landers singing "The Heat Is On" (until the chorus) is stock footage from Tricky Chicks (10/57), her own two-reel comedy for Columbia.

187. FLYING SAUCER DAFFY *** / Rl Oct. 9 / Prod. No. 1906 / 17m / p d Jules White / st Warren Wilson / scr Jack White / ph Fred Jackman / e Saul A. Goodkind / a Cary Odell / sd Milton Stumph / ad Jerrold Bernstein / C: Gail Bonny (Moe and Larry's Mother), Emil Sitka (Mr. Barton, President of Facts and Figures magazine), Harriette Tarler, Bek Nelson and Diana Darrin (Girls at Party) / SYN: Joe submits a bogus photograph of a flying saucer to Facts and Figures magazine, winning $50,000. With his prize money, Moe and Larry buy a mansion, elect Joe their one and only house servant, and stage a lavish party. Their celebration is disrupted when Mr. Barton, the magazine's president, storms in and informs them that their so-called flying saucer photograph turned out to be a dirty paper plate with a

gob of potato salad and jelly stains on it. Moe and Larry are hauled off to jail and Joe is thrown out of the house by his Aunt. While camping in the forest, however, Joe meets two authentic Martian women who let him take a picture of their space ship. Jubliant, Joe returns home and offers Moe and Larry, who are out on bail, his new photograph in order to prove their innocence. The boys refuse his offer, so Joe submits the picture himself and wins a big photographic contest, becoming a hero. While he receives a ticker-tape parade for his efforts, Moe and Larry, in strait-jackets, serve time in prison! / WT: Pardon My Flying Saucer / SD: 2 (TH 12/19 to F 12/20/57) / FN: Joe Bessers favorite film. Shot of dirty dishes in sink is from He Flew the Shrew (1/11/51), a Wally Vernon-Eddie Quillan comedy. Footage of "real" flying saucer lifted from Earth vs. The Flying Saucers (1956).

188. OIL'S WELL THAT ENDS WELL *** / Rl. Dec. 4 / Prod. No. 1911 / 16m / p d Jules White / st scr Felix Adler / ph Irving Lippman / e Edwin Bryant / a Adam Gosse / sd Sidney Clifford / ad Mitchell Gamson / C: The Three Stooges (Themselves) / SYN: The Stooges leave for Red Dog Canyon in search of uranium, in order to pay for their father's operation, and find an oil gusher instead./ SD: 2 (M 8/26 to T 8/27/57). Shot on Stage 3 at Columbia Studios and on the Rock and Water Pump Sets at Columbia Ranch. / FN: A partial reworking of Oily to Bed, Oily to Rise (10/6/39), with some stock footage. Cow milking sequence lifted from Horsing Around (9/12/57).

1959
189. TRIPLE CROSSED ** / Rl. Feb. 2 /

The girl to Joe Besser's left, Connie Cezan, doubled for Mary Ainslee in new footage for Triple Crossed. Angela Stevens stands at Joe's right (1959).

266

Prod. No. 1913 / 16m / *p d* Jules White/ *st scr* Warren Wilson / *ph* Fred Jackman / *e* Saul A. Goodkind / *a* Cary Odell/ *sd* Milton Stumph / *ad* Jerrold Bernstein / *C:* Diana Darrin (Miss Lapdale, in stock footage), Angela Stevens (Millie, Joe's girl), Mary Ainslee (Belle, Moe's wife, in stock footage) and Connie "Cezan" Geason (Bell's Double, in new footage) / *SYN:* Larry owns a pet shop and the only two "pets" he really wants are Moe's wife, Belle, and Joe's fiancee, Millie. / *WT: Chiseling Chiseler* / *SD:* 1 (W 12/18/57) / *FN:* A remake of *He Cooked His Goose* (7/3/52), with much old footage. When Moe fires his gun up the chimney, listen for Shemp's yell!

190. SAPPY BULLFIGHTERS ** / Rl. June 4 / Prod. No. 1912 / 15½m / *p d* Jules White / *st scr* Jack White / *ph* Irving Lippman *e* Harold White / *a* Walter Holscher / *sd* Sidney Clifford / *ad* Max Stein / *C:* Greta Thyssen (Greta), George Lewis (Jose), Joe Palma (Bull Ring Attendant) and Pepe the Dog. / *SYN:* Moe, Larry and Joe perform their comedy bullfight act while stranded in Mexico, and run afoul of a beautiful blonde's jealous husband. / *WT: That's Bully* / *SD:* 2 (July, 1957) *FN:* A remake of *What's the Matador* (4/23/42), with ample stock footage. Wife faking headache bit is also staged in *Don't Throw That Knife* (5/3/51).

Moe, Larry and Joe Besser also starred in *The Three Stooges Fun-O-Rama* (1959, Columbia), a feature-length program of unedited shorts.

THE THREE STOOGES (Larry, Moe and Joe DeRita)
Miscellaneous Shorts
1963
1. THE THREE STOOGES SCRAPBOOK *½ / Rl. Sept. by Columbia / Color / Prod. No. 4651 / 8m / *p* Norman Maurer / *d* Sidney Miller / *st scr* Elwood Ullman / *ph* Hal McAlpin / *e* Chuck Gladden / *sd* Frank Lombardo / *ad* Harry Slott / *s* Glen Glenn / *m* Paul Dunlap and George Dunning / *l* Stanley Styne / *C:* (Live-action) Don Lamond (Announcer/Stage Manager), Norman Maurer (TV Cameraman), Edward Innes and Albert Grazier (Bit Men) / *SYN:* A one-reel version of the Stooges unsold 1960 color TV pilot in which the boys, in live-action, introduce *The Spain Mutiny*, a cartoon featuring them in animated form. The pilot's remaining live footage is utilized throughout *The Three Stooges in Orbit* (8/62) / *FN:* Photographs printed in *Moe Howard and the 3 Stooges* on pgs. 176 and 185 (top) are erroneously marked. They are instead from *Scrapbook*.

1968
2. STAR SPANGLED SALESMAN **½ / Rl. Feb. 9 by the United States Treasury Department (U.S. Savings Bond Division) / Color / 17m / *p d* Norman Maurer / *st scr* Bruce Howard / *ph* Emil Oster / *e* Harold F. Kress and Tom Patchett / *ad* Wingate Smith / Song: "Follow the Eagle" by John J. Coyle / *C:* Carl Reiner (Host), Carol Burnett (Miss

Poster for *Three Stooges Fun-O-Rama* (1959).

Grebs), Milton Berle (Studio President), Howard Morris (Himself), John Banner (Chef), Werner Klemperer (Chef's Boss), Rafer Johnson, Tim Conway (Telephone Repairman), Harry Morgan (TV Cop) and Jack Webb (Security Man) / *SYN:* Milton Berle hires Howard Morris to conduct a payroll savings plan drive at Columbia Studios. Morris's second customers are three lighting technicians, the Stooges, on their lunch break.

Feature Films
Unless otherwise indicated, films are released by Columbia Pictures.
1959
1. HAVE ROCKET, WILL TRAVEL ** / Rl. Aug. / Prod. No. 8556 / 76m / *p* Harry Romm / *d* David Lowell Rich / *st scr* Raphael Hayes / *ph* Ray Cory / *e* Danny B. Landres / *a* John T. McCormack / *sd* Darrell Silvera / *m* Mischa Bakaleinikoff / *Title Song:* George Duning and Stanley Styne / *s* Harold Lewis / *C:* Jerome Cowan (J.P. Morse), Anna-Lisa (Dr. Ingrid Naarveg), Bob Colbert (Dr. Ted Benson), Marjorie Bennett (Mrs. Huntingford), Don Lamond (Newspaperman/Narrator), Nadine Ducas (French Girl), Robert J. Stevenson (Voice of the Thing) and Dal McKennon (Voice of the Unicorn) / *SYN:* The Stooges, handymen in a space laboratory, accidentally launch themselves in a rocket while trying to help Dr. Ingrid Naarveg (Anna-Lisa), a beautiful scientist. On the planet Venus, they encounter a fiery monster, a talking unicorn, a Thinking Machine and robots made in their own images. Right here, the boys decide it's time to return home! Back on Earth, they're hailed as heroes—the first men to traverse space./ *WT: Race For The Moon* / *FN:* Spring on trousers gag also used in *Hoi

Polloi (8/29/35), *An Ache in Every Stake* (8/22/41) and Ben Turpin's *Asleep at the Switch* (1923). In addition, Joe DeRita follows in the footsteps of his Stooge predecessors by getting trapped in a maze of pipe a la *A-Plumbing We Will Go* (4/19/40), *Vagabond Loafers* (10/6/49) and *Scheming Schemers* (10/4/56).

1961
2. SNOW WHITE AND THE THREE STOOGES **½ / Rl. July by 20th Century-Fox / DeLuxe Color and CinemaScope / Prod. No. 887 / 107m / *p* Charles Wick / *d* Walter Lang / *scr* Charles Wick (st) and Elwood Ullman / *ph* Leon Shamroy / *e* Jack W. Holmes / *a* Jack Martin Smith / *sd* Walter M. Scott and Paul S Fox / *m* Lynn Murray / *ad* Eli Dunn / *s* Arthur Kirbach and Frank W. Moran / *C:* Carol Heiss (Snow White), Edson Stroll (Prince Charming), Patricia Medina (Queen), Guy Rolfe (Oga), Michael David (Rolf), Buddy Baer (Hordred), Edgar Barrier (King Augustus), Peter Coe (Captain), Lisa Mitchell (Linda), Chuck Lacey (Frederick), Owen McGivney (Physician), Gloria Doggett, Leon McNabb (Specialty Skaters), Blossom Rock (Servant), Leslie Farrell (Snow White, Age 4), Craig Cooke (Young Prince), Burt Mustin (Farmer), Richard Collier (Turnkey), Herbie Faye (Head Cook) and Edward Innes (2nd Cook) / *SYN:* The Queen of Fortunia, fearful that her stepdaughter will someday become queen, orders her to be slain, as well as the prince of neighboring Bravuria, to whom Snow White was betrothed when a child. Her orders, however, are not carried out. Instead, the prince is adopted and raised by the Stooges, strolling minstrels, and Snow White is spared through an act of kindness. The Stooges are not aware that their ward is

a prince until they are called upon to entertain at the palace after a chance meeting in the house of the Seven Dwarfs, where Snow White has taken refuge. When the queen learns that Snow White is not dead and that the prince is also alive, she orders them seized, which sets off a fast and furious chase, with duels and fights, until the queen is vanquished and the lovers reunited.

1962

3. THE THREE STOOGES MEET HERCULES **½ / Rl. Jan. Prod. No. 8617 / 89m / p Norman Maurer / d Edward Bernds / st Norman Maurer / scr Edwood Ullman / ph Charles S. Welborn / e Edwin Bryant / a Don Ament / sd Wm. Calvert / m Paul Dunlap / s James Flaster / ad Herb Wallerstein / C: Vicki Trickett (Diane Quigley), Quinn Redeker (Schuyler Davis), George N. Neise (Ralph Dimsal/Odius), Samson Burke (Hercules), Mike McKeever (Ajax, the Cyclops), Marlin McKeever (Argo, the Cyclops), Emil Sitka (Shepherd/Refreshment Man), Hal Smith (Theseus), John Cliff (Ulysses), Lewis Charles (Achilles), Barbara Hines (Anita), Terry Huntingdon (Hecuba), Diana Piper (Helen), Gregg Martell (Simon), Gene Roth (Captain), Edward Foster (Freddie), Cecil Elliott (Matron), Rusty Wescoatt (Philo) and Don Lamond (Narrator) / SYN: Larry, Moe and Curly-Joe are friends of Schuyler Davis, a young scientist, and his girl friend Diane. They help Schuyler make a time machine which carries them all back to ancient Ithaca, ruled over by King Odius. The king promptly takes a liking to Diane, and ships Schuyler and the Stooges off to the galleys to get them out of the way. In the galleys, Schuyler works so hard he soon becomes a muscleman. When he and his pals escape, the Stooges begin promoting him as "Hercules" in local gladiatorial combats. Then the real Hercules appears and things look bad for the Stooges. But finally they persuade Hercules to help them in a palace coup against Odius. Diane is rescued, and all happily return to the 20th century./WT: Hercules and The Three Stooges / SD: 13 (T 6/6 to F 6/9, M 6/12 to F 6/16, T 6/20 to TH 6/22, and M 6/19 to TH 6/22/61). Filmed on Stages 15 and 18 at Columbia Sunset Studios and at Columbia Ranch (Rock Set Carmen Street, Skid Row Street and Tank Set) / FN: Larry Fine's favorite Stooge feature. Hercules contains an interesting blend of stock shots: fireworks sequence and crowd reactions from You Can't Take It With You (1938, Columbia); battle between armies, eclipse scene and den of lions from Slaves of Babylon (1953, Columbia); heralds trumpeting atop a stone parapet, galley scenes and galley slaves rowing, waterfront of small seaport and townspeople storming palace gates from Salome (1953, Columbia); charging bull from What's the Matador? (4/23/42); and tall chimney exploding from Half-Shot Shooters (4/30/36). The gag of knocking a cell bar upwards is reprised from Out West (4/24/47). Worldwide gross: $2 million. / PS: One scene in Hercules depicts the Stooges running, then jumping into a moving chariot. It was during this scene, on the first take, that Larry Fine lost his grip and fell

Curly in *A-Plumbing We Will Go (1940)*.

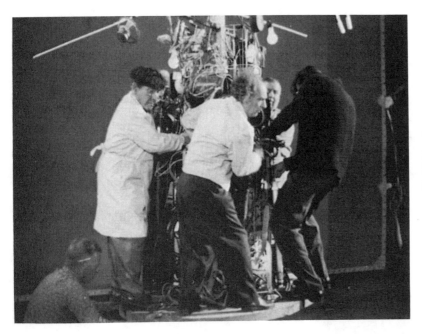

The Stooges preparing for a process shot in their time machine from *The Three Stooges Meet Hercules* (1962).

Joe DeRita recreates Curly's classic scene from *A-Plumbing We Will Go* (1940) in *Have Rocket, Will Travel* (1959).

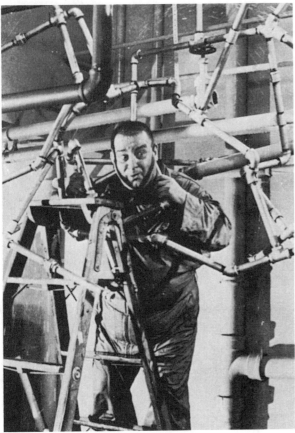

MORE FUN THAN A ROMAN CIRCUS!

One-sheet for *The Three Stooges Meet Hercules* (1962).

269

Storyboard of Cyclops sequence from *The Three Stooges Meet Hercules* (1962).

272

out, taking Curly-Joe with him. Joe landed on top of Larry and knocked him unconscious. Larry was rushed to the hospital where a series of tests revealed that he had diabetes; a disease which he had for the rest of his life. Director Edward Bernds revealed that actor Samson Burke, "Hercules," unlike most men of his stature, was a little uncomfortable with his role: "He was a thorough amateur! Scene after scene, his eyes would seek me out for direction! Eventually, it got so bad that I had to hide from his view. Samson was a bit on the timid side. I would say Moe was braver in doing all the physical stuff than this mighty mass of muscle."

4. THE THREE STOOGES IN ORBIT **½ / Rl. Aug. / Prod. No. 8666 / 87m / p Norman Maurer / d Edward Bernds / s Norman Maurer / scr Elwood Ullman / ph William F. Whitley / e Edwin Bryant / a Don Ament / sd Richard Mansfield / ad Eddie Saeta / m Paul Dunlap / s William Bernds / C: Carol Christensen (Carol), Edson Stroll (Capt. Tom Andrews), Emil Sitka (Prof. Danforth), George N. Neise (Ogg), Rayford Barnes (Zogg), Norman Leavitt (Williams), Nestor Paiva (Chairman), Peter Dawson (Gen. Bixby), Peter Brocco (Dr. Appleby), Don Lamond (Col. Smithers), Thomas Glynn (George Galveston), Marjorie Eaton (Mrs. McGinnis, the Landlady, in stock footage), Maurice Manson (Mr. Lansing), Jean Charney (WAF Sergeant), Duane Ament (Personnel Clerk), Bill Dyer (Col. Lane), Roy Engel (Welby), Jane Wald (Bathing Girl), Cheerio Meredith (Tooth Paste Old Maid) and Rusty Wescoatt (Cook) / SYN: The Three Stooges rent a room in a gloomy old castle owned by eccentric Professor Danforth (Emil Sitka) and his lovely daughter Carol (Carol Christensen). A Martian spy, posing as a servant, is interested in the Professor's newly-invented combination submarine-helicopter-tank. Tom Andrews (Edson Stroll), an Air Force captain who arrives to test the machine, is more interested in Carol. The Stooges soon turn the whole demonstration into a complete shambles. Later, Martian spies capture the machine and go winging through space with Moe, Larry and Joe clinging to its side. Our three heroes finally manage to destroy the all-purpose military weapon and its out-of-space passengers before making their own hilarious escape. / WT: The Three Stooges Meet the Martians / SD: 11 (F 4/6 to F 4/27/62, day-to-day breakdown not available) / FN: The following scenes are used in In Orbit as stock footage from The Three Stooges Scrapbook, an unsold 1960 color TV pilot: apartment eviction for home cooking; searching for a new residence; retiring for the night in Danforth's mansion, then meeting a Martian spy (the Butler); and a montage of the Stooges, in pajamas, thumbing a ride, traveling in a boat, taking off in a helicopter and parachuting into the studio in time for their TV show. Segments depicting the Martians' reign of terror (i.e. buildings exploding and people fleeing) are lifted from Earth vs. The Flying Saucers (1956).

Worldwide gross: $1.5 million. / PS: In Orbit was born out of The Three Stooges Scrapbook, an unsold TV pilot, as producer Norman Maurer recalls: "I approached the Columbia executives with the half-hour Scrapbook film (a $30,000 investment), and an expanded story outline, and they bought it." Needless to say, the studio saved some production costs on the deal.

1963

5. THE THREE STOOGES GO AROUND THE WORLD IN A DAZE **½ / Rl. Sept. / Prod. No. 8705 / 94m / p d st Norman Maurer / scr Elwood Ullman / ph Irving Lippman / e Edwin Bryant / a Don Ament / sd James M. Grove / ad Eddie Saeta / m Paul Dunlap / s William Bernds / C: Jay Sheffield (Phileas Fogg the 3rd), Joan Freeman (Amelia), Walter Burke (Filch), Peter Forster (Vickers Cavendish), Maurice Dallimore (Crotchet), Richard Devon (Maharajah), Anthony Eustrel (Kandu), Iau Kea (Itchi Kitchi), Phil Arnold (Referee), Bob Kino (Charlie Okuma), Murray Alper (Gus), Jack Greening (McPherson), Don Lamond (Bill), Emil Sitka (Butler), Jeffrey Maurer (Timmy), Ramsey Hill (Gatesby), Colin Campbell (Willoughby), Michael St. Clair (1st Mate), Ron Whelan (Harry), Audrey Betz (Woman), Kei Chung (Chinese Guard), John Sheffield (Peters), Mark Harris (Tremble), Aki Aelong (Chinese Non Com), Tom Symonds (Bowers), Clarice Zadagian

One-sheet for *The Three Stooges in Orbit* (1962).

273

Columbia Studios and on Columbia Ranch (Stages 30, 33 and 34, Large Tank, Water Tank, Carmen Street and Firehouse) / *FN:* Wonder why this Stooge picture had so many working titles? Well, there's a simple explanation. United Artists, producers of the 1956 film classic, *Around the World in Eighty Days*, objected to Normandy Productions' original title even though the Jules Verne story was public domain. Eventually, after many title changes, both parties agreed upon *The Three Stooges Go Around the World in a Daze*. The "Maharaja" routine was first enacted by the Stooges in *Time Out for Rhythm* (6/5/41) and later in *Three Little Pirates* (12/5/46). The gag of fighting in the dark is reprised from *Out West* (4/24/47) and also appears in *Who Done It?* (3/3/49) and its remake, *For Crimin' Out Loud* (5/3/56). Curly-Joe becoming fighting mad when he hears "Weasel" is revived from *Punch*

Ogg and Zogg meet see and saw on the set of *The Three Stooges in Orbit* (1962).

(Harem Dancer), Gerald Jann (Chinese General), Laurie Main (Carruthers), Magda Harout (Hand Maiden), George Sabbagh (Specialty), Kanan Awni (Specialty), Joe Wong (Chinese "Joe"), Harold Fong (Chinese "Larry") and Guy Lee (Chinese "Moe") / *SYN:* To win a bet from scoundrel Vickers Cavendish (Peter Forster), Phileas Fogg the 3rd (Jay Sheffield) attempts to duplicate his great-grandfather's famous trip around the world in 80 days, with the added proviso that he will neither pay for, nor work for, his transportation. His three servants, Larry, Moe and Curly-Joe, go along as accomplished chiselers. Cavendish, meanwhile, loots the Regent Street Bank with the help of his own henchmen and then sets out to throw the blame on Fogg, thus ensuring Fogg's defeat. Fogg and the Stooges stow away on a freighter bound for Calcutta, where they rescue Amelia Carter (Joan Freeman) from a pair of thugs. They continue their journey through India to China, Tokyo and San Francisco, circumventing Cavendish and Scotland Yard. Their adventures in Asia and America are hectic and hilarious, but they continue to abide by the terms of the bet. Returning to London with but 30 seconds to spare, Phileas wins the bet and the lovely Amelia, while Cavendish and his henchmen are arrested with the help of the Stooges. /*WT:* The Three Stooges Go Around the World on Eighty Cents, The Three Stooges Go 'Round the Globe on Eighty Cents, The Three Stooges Circle the World on Eighty Cents, The Three Stooges Circle The Globe on Eighty Cents, Around the World on Eighty Cents, The Three Stooges Circle the World on Ninety-Nine Cents, The Three Stooges Go Around the World on Seventy-Nine Cents, The Three Stooges Go Around the World on $1.98, The Three Stooges Meet Phileas Fogg and Merry Go Round the World / *SD:* 13 (TH 5/9 to F 5/10, M 5/13 to F 5/17, M 5/20 to F 5/24, and M 5/27/63). Shot on Stages 12, 12A and 14 at

Norman Maurer's original conception for the film *The Three Stooges Go Around the World in a Daze.*

274

Belgian title card for *The Three Stooges Go Around the World in a Daze* **(1963).**

Drunks (7/13/34). Worldwide gross: $ 1 million. Joe DeRita's favorite Stooges film.

6. IT'S A MAD, MAD, MAD, MAD WORLD ** / Rl. Nov. by United Artists Color / Prod. No. 113 / 162m (originally 195m of laffs) / *p d* Stanley Kramer / *st scr* William and Tania Rose / *ph* Ernest Laszlo / *e* Fred Knudtson / *m* Ernest Gold / *s* John Keene / C: Spencer Tracy (Capt. C.G. Culpeper), Milton Berle (J. Russell Finch), Sid Caesar (Melville Crump), Buddy Hackett (Benjy Benjamin), Ethel Merman (Mrs. Marcus), Dick Shawn (Sylvester Marcus), Mickey Rooney (Ding Bell) and a Cast of Thousands / SYN: A blockbuster comedy featuring the Stooges in a five-second cameo as firemen.

7. FOUR FOR TEXAS **½ / R. Dec. by Warner Bros. / Technicolor / Prod. No. 470 / 124m (also given as 115) / *exp* Howard W. Koch / *ap* Walter Blake / *p d* Robert Aldrich / *st scr* Teddi Sherman and Robert Aldrich *ph* Ernest Laszlo / *e* Michael Luciano / *a* Wm Glasgow / *sd* Raphael Bretton / *ad* Tom Connors and Dave Salven / *m* Nelson Riddle / *s* Jack Solomon / C: Frank Sinatra (Zack Thomas), Dean Martin (Joe Jarrett), Anita Ekberg (Elya Carlson), Ursula Andress (Maxine Richter), Charles Bronson (Matson), Victor Buono (Harvey Burden), Mike Mazurki (Chad) and others / SYN: The Stooges deliver a painting in the "Insulting the State of Texas" routine. / WT: *Two for Texas.*

1965

8. THE OUTLAWS IS COMING! *** / Rl. Jan. / Prod. No. 8731 / 89m / *p d s* Norman Maurer / *scr* Elwood Ullman / *p* Irving Lippman / *e* Aaron Nibley / *a* Robert Peterson / *sd* James W. Crowe / *ad* Donald Gold / *m* Paul Dunlap / *s* James Z. Flaster / C: Adam West (Kenneth Cabot), Nancy Kovack (Annie Oakley), Mort Mills (Trigger Mortis), Don Lamond (Roden), Rex Holman (Sunstroke Kid), Emil Sitka (Abernathy/Medicine Man/Colonel), Henry Gibson (Charlie Horse), Murray Alper (Chief Battlehorse), Tiny Brauer (Bartender), Sidney Marion (Hammond), Jeffrey Alan (Maurer) (Kid), Marilyn Fox (1st Girl), Audrey Betz (Fat Squaw), Lloyd Kino (Japanese Moe), Paul Frees (Narrator) and Special Guests: Joe Bolton (Rob Dalton), Bill Camfield (Wyatt Earp), Hal Fryar (Johnny Ringo), Johnny Ginger (Billy the Kid), Wayne Mack (Jesse James), Ed T. McDonnell (Bat Materson), Bruce Sedley (Cole Younger), Paul Shannon (Wild Bill Hickok) and Sally Starr (Belle Starr) / SYN: When he sends his editor, Kenneth Cabot (Adam West), out into the Great Plains of the West to stop the slaughter of American buffalo, a Boston newspaper publisher uses the occasion to get three troublesome printers, the Stooges, out of his hair. In no time at all, the editor and his pals are targets of every gunslinger west of the Mississippi but, aided by the celebrated trick shot artiste, Annie Oakley (Nancy Kovack), they expose the schemes of a dastardly frontier gang-boss, and persuade the notorious gunslingers to mend their ways / WT: *The Three Stooges Meet the Gunslingers* / SD: 11 (W 5/6 to F 5/8, M 5/11 to F 5/15, M 5/18 to F 5/22, and M 5/25/64). Filmed on the Columbia Ranch (Stages 30, 32 and 33, Glenmoore Cattle Ranch, Western Street, and Boston Street) and on the 66,000 acre Bar-B-Buffalo Ranch near Gillette, Wyoming. / FN: Worldwide gross: $1 million. Moe Howard's and Norman Maurer's favorite Stooges feature. Film's title inspired by Universal's promotion campaign for Hitchcock's *The Birds* ("The Birds' Is Coming!"). The U.S. Cavalry riding in late for the rescue was revived from *Out West* (4/24/47). / PS: Writer-producer-director Norman Maurer remembered a time when selling a script was easy: "I was riding an elevator in Columbia's New York office when Leo Jaffe, the company's chairman of the board, saw the cover artwork on my script outline for *Three Stooges Meet the Gunslingers* (*The Outlaws is Coming*!). He looked at it and said, 'That's funny! Let's make the picture.' " Incidentally, the special guest stars who portray the gunslingers were hosts of Stooges TV programs across the country.

Television Films

1960

1. THE THREE STOOGES SCRAPBOOK **½ / Never Br. / Color / 30m / *p* Norman Maurer / *d* Sidney Miller / *st scr* Elwood Ullman / *ph* Hal McAlpin / *e* Chuck Gladden / *sd* Frank Lombardo / *ad* Harry Slott / *s* Glen Glenn / *m* Paul Dunlap and George Dunning / *l* Stanley Styne / C: (Live-action) Emil Sitka (Prof. Doyle), Marjorie Eaton (Mrs. McGinnis), Don Lamond (Announcer/Stage Manager), Norman Maurer (TV Cameraman), Edward Innes and Albert Grazier (Bit Men) / SYN: The Stooges are hosts of their own weekly live-action and animated TV series. They introduce themselves in a cartoon, *The Spain Mutiny*. / Eps: *Home Cooking* / FN: A majority of the live footage was reused in *The Three Stooges In Orbit* (6/62), and a one-reel version of *Scrapbook* was released to theaters by Columbia in September 1963.

1965

2. THE NEW THREE STOOGES / Synd. in Oct. by Heritage / Color / 30m / *exp* Norman Maurer (live-action) and Dick Brown (animation) / *ap* David Detiege / *d* Edward Bernds (live-action), Eddie Reh-

berg, Sam Cornell and Dave Detiege (animation) / *st* Edward Bernds (live-action), Jack Miller, Sam Cornell, Art Diamond, Warren Tufts, Cecil Beard, Barbara Chain, Jack Kinney, Nick George, Pat Kearin, Homer Brightman, Lee Orgel and Dave Detiege (animation) / *ph* Jerry Smith and Ed Gillette / *e* Wm. J. Faris / *m* Paul Horn / *SYN:* Thirty-nine half-hour shows comprised of 156 five-and-one-half-minute cartoons for which the Stooges supply the voices and appear in 40 live-action wraparounds re-used throughout the series / *LIVE-ACTION WRAPAROUNDS:* #1 *Soldiers:* The Stooges celebrate the anniversary of their induction into the Army with their old Sergeant (Harold Brauer). This live segment is used in cartoon number one only. #2 *Lost:* Larry, Moe and Joe believe they're lost in the woods until they spot a group of teenagers whom they mistake for cannibals. #3 *Campers:* The Stooges embark on a carefully planned camping trip and forget one thing: a horse. #4 *Bakers:* The boys work in a bakery for Mr. Hossenfefler (Emil Sitka) and wind up in a pie fight. #5 *Orangutan:* Moe orders Joe to feed an orangutan and later returns finding both Joe *and* Larry in the animal's cage. #6 *Flat Tire:* The Stooges repair a flat tire only to learn that Joe forgot to buy gasoline. #7 *Fan Belt:* Curly-Joe's suspenders come in handy when the fan belt on the Stooges' car breaks. #8 *Fishermen:* Moe asks Joe to fetch the fishing gear on the pier and Joe returns with a large *gear* from the boys' boat instead. #9 *Dentists:* Larry is the unwilling patient, Moe is the dentist and Joe is the nurse. #10 *Janitors:* The Stooges attempt to clean a deserted mansion inhabited by a ghostly knight. #11 *Artists:* Larry, Moe and Joe create three paintings only an escaped lunatic (Emil Sitka) would buy. #12 *Decorators:* When a wealthy homeowner (Peggy Brown) hires the Stooges to redecorate her house, Moe promises her that when she returns she won't recognize the place. # 13 *Golfers:* The Stooges invade the golf course much to the dismay of its owner (Emil Sitka). Gags revived from *Three Little Beers* (11/28/35). #14 *Hunters:* Moe lectures the boys on the fine art of hunting while a real-live lion lurks behind him. #15 *Weighing In:* The boys encounter a fortune-telling weight machine that predicts their futures. #16 *Telegram:* Curly-Joe receives a telegram, intended for Curly *John,* proclaiming him sole heir to his Uncle Dudley's estate. #17 *Buried Treasure:* The Stooges dig up a chest without treasure and find oil instead. #18 *Outdoor Breakfast:* Moe is unable to speak after he consumes a mouthful of pancakes smothered in glue as prepared by Chefs Joe and Larry. #19 *Setting Up Camp:* Larry and Joe learn that erecting a tent is not that easy. #20 *Rare Bird:* The Stooges want to snap a picture of a rare bird but Joe forgets to remove the lens cap. #21 *Caretakers:* Larry and Joe clean out the elephant cage while Moe plays checkers with a chimpanzee. #22 *Seasick Joe:* The wild surf becomes too much for Joe's stomach and the Stooges' boat hasn't even left the pier. Emil Sitka co-stars

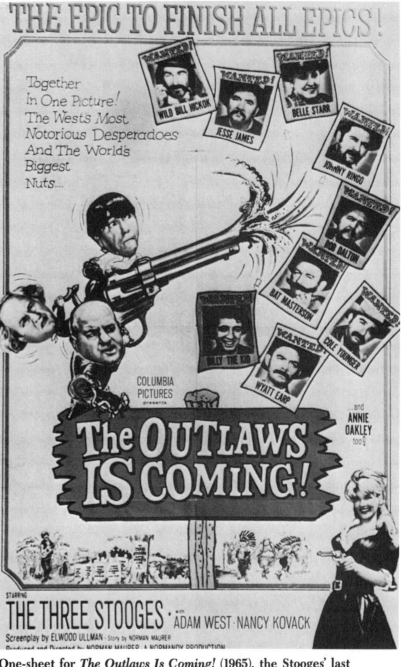

One-sheet for *The Outlaws Is Coming!* (1965), the Stooges' last released feature.

as the Ship Captain. #23 *Electricians:* The Stooges are electricians from the Live Wire Company called to fix a buzzer in a secretary's office. Gags borrowed from *They Stooge to Conga* (1/1/43) and *Monkey Businessmen* (6/20/46). #24 *Salesmen:* Selling ice cream proves successful until Joe begins devouring the profits (*C:* Jeff Maurer, Cary, Tina and Eileen Brown). #25 *Barbers:* An over-protective mother (Peggy Brown) asks the Stooges to be careful when cutting her little boy's *long* hair. Her request, however, develops split ends when a representative of the Barber's Union (Emil Sitka) challenges

the boys' license. #26 *Prospectors:* The boys search for uranium and instead find an old prospector (Emil Sitka) who tells them a story about "The Gunfight at the KO Corral." #27 *Sweepstakes Ticket:* The Stooges possess the winning sweepstakes ticket until, in all the excitement, Moe accidentally tosses the ticket stub out the window. #28 *Sunbathers:* The Stooges offer a female beachgoer (Peggy Brown) their suntan lotion ("Liquid Cement!") and soon find a lifeguard (Emil Sitka) chasing after them. #29 *Inheritance:* Joe inherits a house from his grandfather which is occupied by a headless ghost

276

(voice of Emil Sitka) who mumbles, "I want to get a *head!*" #30 *Melodrama*: The boys stage an old-fashioned melodrama, with Moe as the villain, for a group of youngsters (C: Jeff Maurer and the Brown children). #31 *Waiters*: Larry, Moe and Joe are waiters who give their customers, especially a businessman and his wife (Emil Sitka and Peggy Brown), "super service!" Reprised is the Stooges' *Insulting the State of Texas* routine. #32 *Athletes*: The Stooges take instructions on physical fitness from a record album (C: Jeff Maurer). #33 *Doctors*: Surgeons Howard, Fine and DeRita encounter two patients (both Emil Sitka), one of whose broken leg is in traction. #34 *Shipmates*: The boys decide to rent their boat out to customers and Mr. Guffy (Emil Sitka) is the first to get hooked. #35 *High Voltage*: The Stooges' TV set is on the blink so Larry tries to fix it and gets the shock of his life. #36 *Pilots*: An escaped lunatic (Emil Sitka) asks Larry, Moe and Joe to let him ride on one of their motorbikes. They do and he does, right into the ocean. #37 *Turkey Stuffers*: Larry, Moe and Joe take a hand at stuffing a turkey in an unconventional way (C: Emil Sitka). #38 *Piemakers*: A fly disrupts the Stooges' piemaking efforts, causing Moe to lose his temper. #39 *The Sharpshooter*: Joe as "Eagle-Eye, the Sharpshooter" takes dead aim at a raisin on the forehead of Larry, "Fearless Frizzle-Top." (C: Jeff Maurer and the Brown children). #40 *Magicians*: The Stooges stage all sorts of magic tricks for youngsters, including making themselves disappear (C: Jeff Maurer and the Brown children). / CARTOONS (Four per show. Titles precede live-action wraparounds in parenthesis): #1 *That Little Old Bombmaker* (Soldiers), #2 *Woodsmen Bear That Tree* (Lost), #3 *Let's Shoot the Player Piano Player* (Campers), #4 *Dentist the Menace* (Bakers), #5 *Safari So Good* (Orangutan), #6 *Think or Thwim* (Flat Tire), #7 *There Auto Be a Law* (Fan Belt), #8 *That Old Shell Game* (Fishermen), #9 *Hold That Line* (Dentists), #10 *Flycycle Built For Two* (Janitors), #11 *Dizzy Doodlers* (Artists), #12 *The Classical Clinker* (Decorators), #13 *Movie Scars* (Golfers), #14 *A Bull for Andamo* (Hunters), #15 *The Tree Nuts* (Weighing In), #16 *The Horn Dude* (Telegram), #17 *Thru Rain, Sleet and Snow* (Buried Treasure), #18 *Goldriggers of '49* (Outdoor Breakfast), #19 *Ready Jet Set, Go* (Setting Up Camp), #20 *Behind the 8 Ball Express* (Rare Bird), #21 *Stop Dragon Around* (Caretakers), #22 *To Kill a Clockingbird* (Golfers), #23 *Who's Lion* (Flat Tire), #25 *Wash My Line* (Seasick Joe), #26 *Little Cheese Chaser* (Fan Belt), #27 *The Big Windbag* (Weighing In), #28 *Baby Sitters* (Outdoor Breakfast), #29 *Clarence of Arabia* (Electricians), #30 *Three Jacks and a Beanstalk* (Salesmen), #31 *That Was the Wreck That Was* (Barbers), #32 *The Three Astronutz* (Prospectors), #33 *Peter Panic* (Sweepstakes Ticket), #34 *When You Wish Upon a Fish* (Seasick Joe), #35 *A Little Past Noon* (Sunbathers), #36 *Hair of a Bear* (Inheritance), #37 *3 Lumps in a Lamp* (Melodrama), #38 *Who's for Dessert?* (Waiters), #39 *Watts My Lion* (Athletes), #40 *Which is Witch?* (Buried Treasure), #41 *Suture Self* (Doctors), #42 *The Yolks on You* (Artists), #43 *Tally Moe With Larry and Joe* (Inheritance), #44 *The First in Lion* (Artists), #45 *The Transylvania Railroad* (Shipmates), #46 *What's Mew Pussycat?* (High Voltage), #47 *It's a Bad, Bad, Bad, Bad World* (Pilots), #48 *Bridge on the River Cry* (Decorators), #49 *Hot Shots* (Janitors), #50 *Mel's Angels* (Sharpshooter), #51 *Bee My Honey* (Turkey Stuffers), #52 *That Dirty Bird* (Rare Bird), #53 *Stone Age Stooges* (Caretakers), #54 *Smoke Gets in Your Skies* (Piemakers), #55 *Queen Quong* (Lost), #56 *Campsite Fright* (Buried Treasure), #57 *Goldibear and the 3 Stooges* (Electricians), #58 *The Lyin' Tamer* (Setting Up Camp), #59 *The Pen Game* (Sharpshooter), #60 *It's a Small World* (Melodrama), #61 *Late for Launch* (Doctors), #62 *Forgot in Space* (Buried Treasure), #63 *The Noisy Silent Movie* (Waiters), #64 *Get Out of Town By Sundown Brown* (Salesmen), # 65 *Table Tennis Tussle* (Athletes), #66 *Phony Express* (Prospectors), #67 *Best Test Pilots* (Pilots), #68 *Litter Bear* (Barbers), #69 *A Fishy Tale* (Fishermen), #70 *The Unhaunted House* (Magicians), #71 *Aloha Ha Ha* (Hunters), #72 *The Rise and the Fall of the Roman Umpire* (Piemakers), #73 *Deadbeat Street* (Dentists), #74 *Cotton Pickin' Chicken* (Sweepstakes Ticket), #75 *Larry and the Pirates* (Shipmates), #76 *Tree is a Crowd* (Outdoor Breakfast), #77 *Feud for Thought* (Electricians), #78 *Bat and Brawl* (Piemakers), #79 *Knight Without End* (Telegram), #80 *Up a Tree* (Campers), #81 *Turnabout Is Bearplay* (Magicians), #82 *Pow Wow Row* (Lost), #83 *Flat Heads* (Beachgoers), #84 *No News Is Good News* (High Voltage), #85 *Bully For You, Curly* (Turkey Stuffers), #86 *Tee for Three* (Bakers), #87 *Goofy Gondoliers* (Fishermen), #88 *Bearfoot Fishermen* (Barbers), #89 *Washout Below* (Waiters), #90 *The 3 Marketeers* (Decorators), #91 *Follo the White Lion* (Orangutan), #92 *One Good Burn Deserves Another* (Golfers), #93 *Curly's Bear* (Hunters), #94 *Land Ho, Ho, Ho* (Seasick Joe), #95 *Surfs You Right* (Sharpshooter), #96 *7 Faces of Timbear* (Melodrama), #97 *Bearfoot Bandit* (Flat Tire), #98 *Nuttin' but the Brave* (Prospectors), #99 *3 Good Knights* (Janitors), #100 *Call of the Wile* (Setting Up Camp), #101 *Snowbrawl* (Caretakers), #102 *Rob n' Good* (Doctors), #103 *There's No Mule Like an Old Mule* (Fan Belt), #104 *Squawk Valley* (Weighing In), #105 *Mummies Boys* (Buried Treasure), #106 *The Plumber's Friend* (Electricians), #107 *Rub-a-Dub-Tub* (Fishermen), #108 *Under the Bad-Bad Tree* (Inheritance), #109 *Hairbrained Barbers* (Barbers), #110 *Waiter Minute* (Pilots), #111 *Souperman* (Pilots), #112 *Abonimable Showman* (Rare Bird), #113 *Curly in Wonderland* (Salesmen), #114 *Boobs in the Woods* (Sweepstakes Ticket), #115 *Chimney Sweeps* (Turkey Stuffers), #116 *The Mad Mail Mission* (Janitors), #117 *Out of Space* (Seasick Joe), #118 *3 Wizards of Odds* (Magicians), #119 *3 for the Road* (Telegram), #120 *Feudin', Fussin', and Hillbully* (Telegram), #121 *Don't Misbehave Indian Brave* (Campers), #122 *You Ain't Lion* (Orangutan), #123 *Muscle on Your Mind* (Weighing In), #124 *Badmen in the Briny* (Shipmates), #125 *Furry Fugitive* (Golfers), #126 *How the West Was Once* (Prospectors), #127 *Bowling Pinheads* (Sharpshooter), #128 *The Mountain Ear* (Dentists), #129 *Norse West Passage* (Buried Treasure), #130 *Lastest Gun in the West* (Athletes), # 131 *Toys Will Be Toys* (Outdoor Breakfast), #132 *First Class Service* (Flat Tire), #133 *Strictly for the Birds* (Rare Bird), #134 *Le' Stoogenaires* (Athletes), #135 *The Bear Who Came Out of the Cold* (Artists), #136 *The Bigger They Are, the Harder They Hit* (Salesmen), #137 *Little Red Riding Wolf* (Buried Treasure), #138 *Bell Hop Flops* (Waiters), #139 *Dig That Golpher* (Piemakers), #140 *Gagster Dragster* (Fan Belt), #141 *Just Plane Crazy* (High Voltage), #142 *From Bad to Verse* (Campers), #143 *Droll Weevil* (Caretakers), #144 *The Littlest Martian* (Melodrama), #145 *The Bear Showoff* (Setting Up Camp), #146 *No Money, No Honey* (Hunters), #147 *Get That Snack Shack Off the Track* (Outdoor Breakfast), #148 *Curly's Birthday-a-Go-Go* (Bakers), #149 *The Men from UCLA* (Beachgoers), #150 *Super Everybody* (Inheritance), #151 *Kangaroo Catchers* (Electricians), #152 *No Smoking Aloud* (Shipmates), #153 *The Chicken Delivery* (Decorators), #154 *Sno Ball* (Buried Treasure), #155 *Rug-a-Bye, Baby* (Doctors) and #156 *Dinopoodi* (Turkey Stuffers) / FN: #113 *Curly in Wonderland* and #1 *That Little Old Bombmaker* are the best cartoons in the series.

1970

3. KOOK'S TOUR ** / Never Br. / Color / Prod. No. 1191 / 60m / *p .d st scr* Norman Maurer / *ph* James T. Flocker and Michael Maurer / *e* Pat Somerset / *s* Audio Effects / Narrator: Moe Howard / C: The Three Stooges (Themselves), Emil Sitka (in a black-and-white scene from *Around the World in a Daze*), and Moose the Dog / SYN: Whack! The Stooges are socked in the jaws, thus leading off a black-and-white montage of slapstick clips from *The Three Stooges Meet Hercules* to *The Outlaws Is Coming!* Then, the boys, now well-groomed, enter in *color* explaining that although they've entertained audiences for 50 years, they've never seen anything except the inside of their dressing rooms. So they decide to retire from show business, purchase a self-contained camper and a trailer boat and take off on their first camping trip. But as the title implies, no matter how hard the Stooges try acting *normal*, their journey will always prove to be a KOOK'S tour...especially for Larry! The poor guy just can't catch a fish! His bad luck is only compounded when Moe, who warned Larry, "If you don't hook 'em, you don't eat 'em!," catches his limit every time as does Joe and even Moose the Dog! Thus, fishing trip after fishing trip, Larry comes up empty-handed and on one occasion must settle for a gourmet dinner: corn flakes and milk! As the days wear on, however, Moe and Joe begin feeling sorry for their pal and decide to

accompany him to Lake Pend Oreille, the best site for trout fishing in all of Idaho. But their kind gesture backfires when the day comes to a close and poor Larry has struck out again! Frustrated, Larry tosses his hat decorated with lures into the lake and, ironically, his hat proves to be a better fisherman than he as it hooks enough trout for Moe, Joe and Moose! / *SD*: 23 (M 9/8 to SA 9/14, M 9/15 to W 9/17, F 9/19 to F 9/26, S 11/30 to F 12/5 and S 12/7/69) / *Locations*: Snake River, Jackson Lake and Lodge, Old Faithful Geyser and Inn, Castle and Sawmill Geysers, Yellowstone National Park and Lake, Bridge Bay Marina, Grand Canyon, Jack Lott's Ranch, Henry's Lake, Stanley Springs Lodge, Fishing Bridge at Big Springs, Massacre Rocks at Snake River outside American Falls, Redfish Lake and Marina, Lowman Highway on Idaho State

Moe Howard in an early solo appearance from *Jailbirds of Paradise* (1934). Behind the counter is Dorothy Appleby.

21 before Lowman, Idaho, Lucky Peak near Boise, Lake Pend Oreille and Priest Lake in Idaho, Angeles National Forest, Charlton Flats Picnic Area on Angeles Crest Highway, Lake Piru, Moe Howard's Home and Los Angeles International Airport / *FN*: "Moose" was actually producer Norman Maurer's labrador retriever and a former character in *The Little Stooges* comic book series. Moose died in 1980. Norman Maurer doubled for Moe in the long shots of him steering the Stooges' boat and also filled in for Larry, after his stroke, in a close-up of his hands crumbling corn flakes into a bowl. Larry's picture-taking contraption, a la Rube Goldberg, was designed and assembled by Jeff Maurer. In 1975, a one-hour version of *Kook's Tour* received minor distribution in Super 8 color-sound from Niles Film Products, Inc. This version, however, is now a collector's item.

Larry, Moe and Joe DeRita were also seen

in commercials for *Hot Shot Insecticide*, *Chunky Chocolates*, *Simoniz Car Wax* (all 1960), *Metropolitan Life* (1967/Color), *Dickie Slacks* (1969/Color), and *Coca-Cola* (1976/Color/in a film clip from *The Three Stooges in Orbit* [1962]).

THE STOOGES ALONE

The following is a listing of the solo film achievements of Moe, Curly and Shemp Howard, Joe Besser, Joe DeRita and Ted Healy. Larry Fine never appeared as a single in motion pictures. Except where noted, all films are black-and-white, and roles, where available, follow cast listings.

MOE HOWARD

As a child actor, Moe Howard, using his real name of Harry Moses Horwitz, made his screen debut in *We Must Do Our Best*

(1909, Vitagraph), starring Kenneth Casey and directed by Van Dyke Brooks. Soon thereafter, he co-starred in countless other Vitagraph films before joining Captain Billy Bryant's stock company in 1914. Unfortunately, no more information is available about Moe's early screen roles prior to those listed below:

MGM Shorts
1934
1. JAILBIRDS OF PARADISE / MGM Musical Revue Series / Rl. Mar. 10 / Technicolor / 18m / *d st scr* Al Boasberg / *C*: Dorothy Appleby, Shirley Ross, The Dodge Twins, Jerry Howard and the MGM Dancing Girls / "Escaped Convict" / *WT: Stars and Stripes, Reformers* and *Reformania* / *SD*: 3 (TH 12/28 to SA 12/30/33).

Feature Films
1958
1. SPACE MASTER X-7 / Rl. July by 20th

Century-Fox / 71m / *d* Edward Bernds / *scr* George Worthing Yates and Daniel Mainwaring / *C*: Bill Williams and Lyn Thomas / "Cab Driver" who endeavors to describe to police the fugitive woman.

1966
2. DON'T WORRY WE'LL THINK OF A TITLE / Rl. June by United Artists / 83m / *d* Harmon Jones / *scr* John Hart and Morey Amsterdam / *C*: Morey Amsterdam, Rose Marie, Richard Deacon, and many familiar TV faces / "Mr. Raines".

1973
3. DOCTOR DEATH: SEEKER OF SOULS / Rl. Oct. by Cinerama / 93m / *d* Eddie Saeta / *scr* Sal Ponti / *C*: John Considine, Barry Coe, Cheryl Miller and Leon Askin / "Volunteer in the Audience."

Moe Howard also served as associate producer on the following:
1959
1. SENIOR PROM / Rl. Jan. by Columbia / 82m / *d* David Lowell Rich / *scr* Hal Hackady / *C*: Jill Corey, Paul Hampton, Jimmie Komack, Louis Prima, Ed Sullivan, Mitch Miller, Freddy Martin and others.

As of this writing, according to Herbert S. Nusbaum of the MGM Legal Department, there is no evidence available in the studio's legal archives to support the claim that Moe and Jerome Howard also essayed bit roles in *Broadway to Hollywood*, a 1933 MGM feature. Hence, this claim, as reported in other sources, remains unsubstantiated.

JEROME "CURLY" HOWARD
MGM Shorts
1934
1. ROAST BEEF AND MOVIES / MGM Revue Series / Rl. Feb. 10 / Technicolor / 17m / *d* Samuel Baerwitz / *st* Richy Craig, Jr. / *C*: George Givot, Bobby Callahan and the Albertina Rusch Dancers / "One of Three Bogus Movie Producers" / *WT: Wax Museum, Let Us Spray* and *Movie Bugs*.

2. JAILBIRDS OF PARADISE / MGM Musical Revue Series / Rl. Mar. 10 / Technicolor 18m / *d st scr* Al Boasberg / *C*: Dorothy Appleby, Moe Howard, Shirley Ross, The Dodge Twins and the MGM Dancing Girls / "Escaped Convict" / *WT: Stars and Stripes, Reformers* and *Reformania* / *SD*: 3 (TH 12/28 to SA 12/30/33).

Curly Howard was also scheduled to appear in *Operator 13*, a 1934 MGM feature with Gary Cooper, Marion Davies and Ted Healy, but his role was canceled when the Stooges broke up with Healy.

SHEMP HOWARD
Vitaphone Shorts
1933
1. SALT WATER DAFFY / Jack Haley Series / Rl. Sept. 16 / 21m / *d* Ray McCarey / *st* Jack Henley and Glen Lambert / *C*: Jack Haley, Charles Judels and Lionel Stander / *RNA*.

Moe making an appearance as a cab driver in *Space Master X-7* (1958).

2. IN THE DOUGH / Fatty Arbuckle Series / Rl. Sept. 25 / 22m / *d* Ray McCarey / *st* Jack Henley / *C*: Roscoe "Fatty" Arbuckle, Lionel Stander, Marc Marion, Fred Harper and Dan Coleman / *RNA*.

3. CLOSE RELATIONS / Fatty Arbuckle Series / Rl. Sept. 30 / 20m / *d* Ray McCarey / *st* Glen Lambert and Jack Henley / *C*: Roscoe "Fatty" Arbuckle, Charles Judels, Mildred Van Dorn, Harry Shannon and Hugh O'Connell / *RNA*.

4. HERE COMES FLOSSIE / Ben Blue Series / Rl. Dec. 9 / 18m / *d* Ray McCarey / *st* Glen Lambert and Jack Henley / *C*: Ben Blue, Paul Everton, J. Cherry and Jack Barne / *RNA*.

1934
5. HOW'D YA LIKE THAT? / George Givot Series / Rl. Jan. 13 / 18m / *d* Ray McCarey / *st* Jack Henley and Glen Lambert / *C*: George Givot, Charles Judels and Lionel Stander / *RNA*.

6. MUSHROOMS / Harry Gribbon Series / Rl. Feb. 14 / 20m / *d* Ralph Staub / *st* Dolph Singer and Jack Henley / *C*: Harry Gribbon, Loretta Sayres, Cora Witherspoon and Lionel Stander / *RNA*.

7. PUGS AND KISSES / Charles Judels and Lionel Stander Series / Rl. Feb. 17 / 21m / *d* Ray McCarey / *st* Glen Lambert and Jack Henley / *C*: Charles Judels, Lionel Stander, Greta Grandstedt and Tony Hughes / *RNA*.

8. VERY CLOSE VEINS / Ben Blue Series / Rl. Apr. 14 / 20m / *d* Ralph Staub / *st* Jack Henley and Dolph Singer / *C*: Ben Blue, Dorothy Dare, Robert Glecker and Harry T. Morey / *RNA*.

9. CORN ON THE COP / Harry Gribbon and Shemp Howard Series / Rl. Apr. 28 / 20m / *d* Ralph Staub / *st* Jack Henley and Dolph Singer / *C*: Harry Gribbon, Mary Doran and Boyd Davis / "Salesman."

10. I SCREAM / Gus Shy Series / Rl. May 19 / 20m / *d* Ray McCarey / *st* Jack Henley and Eddie Moran / *C*: Gus Shy, Lionel Stander and Curtis Karpe / *RNA*.

11. ART TROUBLE / Harry Gribbon and Shemp Howard Series / Rl. June 23 / 20m / *d* Ralph Staub / *st* Jack Henley and Dolph Singer / *C*: Harry Gribbon, Beatrice Blinn and Leni Stengel / "Art Student."

12. MY MUMMY'S ARMS / Harry Gribbon and Shemp Howard Series / Rl. June 28 / 19m / *d* Ralph Staub / *st* Jack Henley and Justin Herman / *C*: Harry Gribbon, Sheldon Leonard, Russell Hicks and Louise Latimer / *RNA*.

13. DARE DEVIL O'DARE / Ben Blue Series / Rl. Aug. 11 / 19m / *d* Ralph Staub/ *st* Dolph Singer and Jack Henley / *C*: Ben Blue, Vicki Cummings, Joe Vitale and Owen Martin / *RNA*.

14. SMOKED HAMS / Daphne Pollard and Shemp Howard Series / Rl. Oct. 20 / 18m / *d* Lloyd French / *st* Jack Henley and Dolph Singer / *C*: Daphne Pollard / *RNA*.

15. DIZZY AND DAFFY / Dizzy and Daffy Dean Series / Rl. Dec. 15 / 19m / *d* Lloyd French / *st* Dolph Singer and Jack Henley / *C*: Jerome and Paul Dean / "Near-Sighted Baseball Pitcher."

16. A PEACH OF A PAIR / Daphne Pollard and Shemp Howard Series / Rl. Dec. 29 / 20m / *d* Lloyd French / *st* Dolph Singer and Jack Henley / *C*: Daphne Pollard / "Ham Actor."

1935
17. HIS FIRST FLAME / Daphne Pollard and Shemp Howard Series / Rl. Mar. 9 / 19m / *d* Lloyd French / *st* Jack Henley and Dolph Singer / *C*: Daphne Pollard, John Sheehan, Fred Harper and Don McBride / "Inventive Fireman" / *WT: The Fireman's Bride*.

18. WHY PAY RENT? / Roscoe Ates and Shemp Howard Series / Rl. May 4 / 22m / *d* Lloyd French / *st* Dolph Singer and Jack Henley / *C*: Roscoe Ates, Billie Leonard, Ethel Sykes and Ray LeMay / *FN*: A reworking of Keaton's *One Week* (9/7/20).

19. SERVES YOU RIGHT / Shemp Howard Series / Rl. June 15 / 21m / *d* Lloyd French / *st* Jack Henley and Bob McGowan / *C*: Nell O'Day, Don McBride, Eddie Hall, Connie Almy and Fred Harper / "Process Server."

20. ON THE WAGON / Roscoe Ates and

Lobby card for *Smoked Hams*, a 1936 Vitaphone Comedy.

Shemp Howard Series / Rl. Aug. 24 / 21m / *d* Lloyd French / *st* Jack Henley and Burnet Hershey / *C:* Roscoe Ates, Gertrude Mudge, Dorothy Brown, Lillian Pertka and Billie Leonard / "Husband" pestered by his mother-in-law.

21. THE OFFICER'S MESS / Shemp Howard Series / Rl. Oct. 19 / 22m / *d* Lloyd French / *st* Burnet Hershey and Jack Henley / *C:* Charles Kemper, Detmar Poppen and Louise Swuires / "Army Rookie."

1936
22. WHILE THE CAT'S AWAY / Shemp Howard Series / Rl. Jan. 4 / 20m / *d* Lloyd French / *st* Jack Henley and Burnet Hershey / *C:* Johnny Berkes, Anita Garvin and Jean Cleveland / *RNA.*

23. FOR THE LOVE OF PETE / Joe Palooka Series / Rl. Mar. 14 / 21m / *d* Lloyd French / *st* Jack Henley and Burnet Hershey / *C:* Robert Norton, Lucy Parker, Johnny Berkes, Richard Lane, Michael Dennis, Charlie Althoss, Buddy Bueler and Rex / "Knobby Walsh," Joe Palooka's manager.

Shemp tries pleasing a young female co-star in a scene from *Serves You Right*.

One-sheet for *A Hit With a Miss*, a remake of *Punch Drunks*, a 1934 Stooges comedy. Man on the mat is Joe Palma.

24. ABSORBING JUNIOR / Shemp Howard Series / Rl. May 9 / 21m / *d* Lloyd French / *st* Jack Henley and Burnet Hershey / *C:* Johnny Berkes, Gertrude Merdge, Gerrie Worthing, Kenneth Lundy and Arthur and Morton Havel / "Husband" who must outwit his belligerent mother-in-law.

25. HERE'S HOWE / Joe Palooka Series / Rl. June 6 / 21m / *d* Lloyd French / *st* Jack Henley, Burnet Hershey and Robert Mako / *C:* Robert Norton, Leo Webberman and Beverly Phalon / "Knobby Walsh," Joe Palooka's manager.

26. PUNCH AND BEAUTY / Joe Palooka Series / Rl. Aug. 15 / 20m / *d* Lloyd French / *st* Jack Henley, Burnet Hershey and Eddie Forman / *C:* Robert Norton, Beverly Phalon and Johnny Berkes / "Knobby Walsh," Joe Palooka's manager.

27. THE CHOKE'S ON YOU / Joe Palooka Series / Rl. Sept. 12 / 21m / *d* Lloyd French / *st* Jack Henley, Burnet Hershey and Eddie Forman / *C:* Robert Norton, Beverly Phalon and Johnny Berkes / "Knobby Walsh," Joe Palooka's manager.

28. THE BLONDE BOMBER / Joe Palooka Series / Rl. Nov. 28 / 20m / *d* Lloyd French / *st* Jack Henley, A. Dorian Otvos and Eddie Forman / *C:* Robert Norton, Lee Weber, Harry Gribbon, Johnny Berkes and Mary Doran / "Knobby Walsh," Joe Palooka's manager.

1937
29. KICK ME AGAIN / Joe Palooka Series / Rl. Feb. 6 / 21m / *d* Lloyd French / *st* Jack Henley and Eddie Forman / *C:* Robert Norton, Beverly Phalon and Lee Weber / "Knobby Walsh," Joe Palooka's manager.

30. TAKING THE COUNT / Joe Palooka Series / Rl. Apr. 24 / 21m / *d* Lloyd French / *st* Jack Henley and Eddie Forman / *C*: Robert Norton, Beverly Phalon, Charles Kemper, Johnny Berkes, Regina Wallace, John Vosbough and Jack Shutta / "Knobby Walsh," Joe Palooka's manager.

RKO Radio Shorts
1934
1. HENRY THE ACHE / Bert Lahr Series / Rl. Jan. 26 / 19m / *d* Ray McCarey / *st* Burnet Hershey and Bert Granet / *C*: Bert Lahr and Janet Reade / "One of King Henry's Lackeys."

Slingers Series / Rl. Nov. 24 / 18m / *d* Jules White / *st scr* L.A. Sarecky / *C*: Noah Berry, Jr., Paul Hurst, Dorothy Vaughn, Betty Campbell, Dick Curtis, Cy Seymour, Elaine Waters, Julieta Naldi, Bob Ryan and John Kascier / "Fight Manager."

1940
3. MONEY SQUAWKS / Andy Clyde Series / Rl. Apr. 5 / 16m / *d* Jules White / *st scr* Ewart Adamson / *C*: Andy Clyde / "Andy Clyde's Brother-in-Law."

4. BOOBS IN THE WOODS / Andy Clyde Series / Rl. May 31 / 16m / *d* Del Lord / *scr* Harry Edwards (*st*) and Elwood Ullman / *C*:

1944
7. PICK A PECK OF PLUMBERS / All-Star Comedy Series / Rl. July 23 / 17m / *d* Jules White / *st scr* Felix Adler / *C*: El Brendel, Al Thompson, Johnny Tyrell, Kathryn Keyes, Willa Pearl Curtis, Frank "Billy" Mitchell, Bea Blinn, Jean Murray, Judy Malcolm, Brian O'Hara and Joe Palma / "Plumber" / *FN*: A reworking, with some stock footage, of *A-Plumbing We will Go* (4/19/40), with the Three Stooges

8. OPEN SEASON FOR SAPS / Shemp Howard Series / Rl. Oct. 27 / 18m / *d* Jules White / *st scr* Elwood Ullman / *C*: Christine

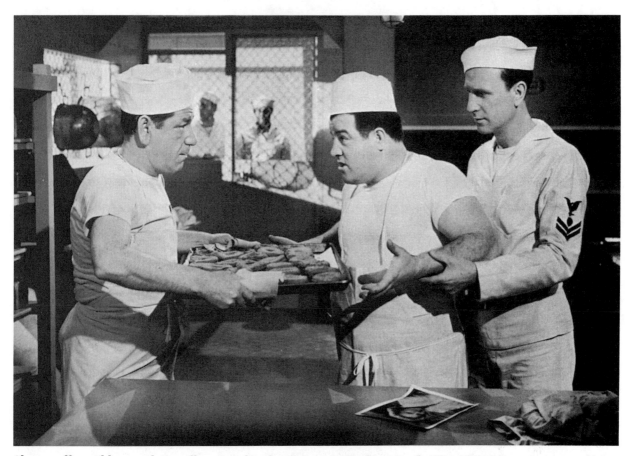

Shemp offers Abbott and Costello some doughnuts in a scene from *In the Navy* (1941).

2. THE KNIFE OF THE PARTY / Shemp Howard and His Stooges / Rl. Feb. 16 / 20m / *d* Leigh Jason / *st* H.O. Kussell and Art Jarrett, Sr. / *C*: Jack Good and Lillian Miles / "Leader of the Stooges."

Columbia Shorts
1938
1. HOME ON THE RAGE / Andy Clyde Series / Rl. Dec. 9 / 17m / *d* Del Lord / *st scr* James W. Horne / *C*: Andy Clyde, Lela Bliss, Gene Morgan and Vernon Dent / "Andy Clyde's Brother-in-Law."

1939
2. THE GLOVE SLINGERS / The Glove

Andy Clyde, Esther Howard, Bud Jamison and Jack Lipson / "Andy Clyde's Brother-in-Law."

5. PLEASED TO MITT YOU / The Glove Slingers Series / Rl. Sept. 6 / 18m / *d* Jules White / *st scr* Ewart Adamson and Clyde Bruckman / *CNA* / "Fight Manager."

1943
6. FARMER FOR THE DAY / Andy Clyde Series / Rl. Aug. 20 / 17½m / *d* Jules White / *st scr* Clyde Bruckman / *C*: Andy Clyde, Betty Blythe, Douglas Leavitt, Adele St. Mara and Bud Jamison / "Andy Clyde's Brother-in-Law."

McIntyre, George Lewis, Early Cantreen, Harry Barris, Jack Lipson and Al Mortino / "Hen-Pecked Husband" / *FN*: A remake of Charley Chase's *The Grand Hooter* (5/7/37).

1945
9. OFF AGAIN, ON AGAIN / Shemp Howard Series / Rl. Feb. 16 / 16m / *d* Jules White / *st* Searle Kramer (*scr*) and Victor Travers / *C*: Christine McIntyre, Russell Trent, Dick Curtis, Grace Lenard, Judy Malcolm, Charles Willey, Frances Haynes, Heinie Conklin and Joe Palma / "Suicidal Husbands."

10. WHERE THE PESTS BEGIN / Shemp

Lobby card for *Crazy Knights* (1944).

Howard Series / Rl. Oct. 4 / 17m / *d* Edward Bernds / *st scr* Edward Bernds and Russell Malmgren / *C*: Rebel Randall, Tom Kennedy, Christine McIntyre and Harry Tenbrook / " 'Helpful' Neighbor."

11. A HIT WITH A MISS / Shemp Howard Series / Rl. Dec. 13 / 16m / *d* Jules White / *st* Jerry Howard, Larry Fine and Moe Howard /*scr* Jack White *C*: Bob Williams, Wally Rose, Joe Palma, Heinie Conklin, Marilyn Johnson, Charles Rogers, Blackie Whitford, George Gray and Johnny Tyrell / "Prizefighter" / *FN*: A remake of the Three Stooges comedy, *Punch Drunks* (7/13/34).

1946
12. MR. NOISY / Shemp Howard Series / Rl. Mar. 22 / 16½m / *d scr* Edward Bernds / *st* John Grey / *C*: Vernon Dent, Walter Soderling, Daniel Kerry, Wally Rose, John Ince, Claire James, Matt Willis, Marilyn Johnson, Don Gordon, Tom Coleman, Brian O'Hara and Fran O'Connor / "Loudmouth Sports Fan" / *FN*: A remake, with some stock footage, of *The Heckler* (2/16/40), with Charley Chase.

13. JIGGERS, MY WIFE / Shemp Howard Series / Rl. Apr. 11 / 18m / *d* Jules White / *st scr* Zion Myers / *C*: Symona Boniface, Early Cantrell, Christine McIntyre, Tom Kennedy and Cy Schindell / "Disobedient Husband."

14. SOCIETY MUGS / Shemp Howard Series / Rl. Sept. 19 / 16m / *d* Edward Bernds / *st scr* Al Giebler / *C*: Tom Kennedy, Etta McDaniel, Charles Williams, Christine McIntyre, Gene Stutenroth (Roth), Rebel Randall, Vernon Dent, Bess Flowers and Helen Benda / "Pest Exterminator" / *FN*: A

reworking of the Stooges' *Termites of 1938* (1/7/38).

1947
15. BRIDE AND GLOOM / Shemp Howard Series / Rl. Mar. 27 / 16m / *d scr* Edward Bernds / *st* John Grey / *C*: Dick Curtis, Jean Donahue (Willis) and Christine McIntyre / "Groom-To-Be" who gets into a marital mix-up / *SD*: 4 (W 2/20 to SA 2/23/47).

Feature Films
    Unless otherwise noted, films are released by Universal Pictures.
1935
1. CONVENTION GIRL / Rl. Oct. 31 by First Division / 62m / *d* Luther Reed / *st scr* George Boyle / *C*: Rose Hobart and Herbert Rawlinson / "Dan."

1937
2. HOLLYWOOD ROUND-UP / Rl. Nov. 16 by Columbia / 63m / *d* Ewing Scott / *st scr* Joseph Hoffman and Monroe Shaff / *C*: Buck Jones and Helen Twelvetrees / "Oscar," an assistant movie director.

3. HEADIN' EAST / Rl. Dec. 23 by Columbia / 63m / *d* Ewing Scott / *st* Joseph Hoffman and Monroe Shaff / *scr* Ethel LaBlanche / *C*: Buck Jones and Ruth Coleman / "Windy."

1940
4. MILLIONAIRES IN PRISON / Rl. July 26 by RKO / 63m / *d* Ray McCarey / *st* Martin Mooney / *scr* Lynn Root and Frank Fenton / *C*: Lee Tracy / "Professor."

5. THE LEATHERPUSHERS / Rl. Sept. 13 / 64m / *d* John Rawlins / *scr* Larry Rhine, Ben Chapman and Maxwell Shane / *C*:

Richard Arlen and Andy Devine / "Slugger."

6. THE BANK DICK / Rl. Nov. 29 / 74m / *d* Edward Cline / *st scr* Mahatma Kane Jeeves (W.C. Fields) / *C*: W.C. Fields / "Joe Guelpe," bartender at the Black Pussy Cat Cafe.

7. GIVE US WINGS / Rl. Dec. 20 / 62m / *d* Charles Lamont / *st* Eliot Gibbons / *scr*: Arthur T. Horman and Robert Lee Johnson / *C*: Billy Halop, Huntz Hall and the Dead End Kids / "Whitey."

1941
8. SIX LESSONS FROM MADAME LA ZONGA/ Rl. Jan. 17 / 62m / *d* John Rawlins / *scr* Stanley Crea Rubin, Marion Orth, Larry Rhine (*st*) and Ben Chapman (*st*) / *C*: Lupe Velez and Leon Errol / "Gabby," a member of a gangster's gang.

9. BUCK PRIVATES / Rl. Jan. 31 / 84m / *d* Arthur Lubin / *scr* Arthur T. Horman / *C*: Bud Abbott, Lou Costello and The Andrews Sisters / "The Chef."

10. MEET THE CHUMP / Rl. Feb. 14 / 60m / *d* Edward F. Cline / *scr* Alex Gottlieb / *C*: Hugh Herbert / "Stinky Fink," a gangster / *WT*: *Who's Crazy Now?* and *Who's Wacky Now?*.

11. MR. DYNAMITE / Rl. Mar. 7 / 63m / *d* John Rawlins / *scr* Stanley Crea Rubin / *C*: Lloyd Nolan, Irene Harvey and J. Carrol Naish / "Abdullah," a bit role.

12. TOO MANY BLONDES / Rl. May 23 / 60m / *d* Thornton Freeland / *scr* Maxwell Shane and Louis S. Kaye / *C*: Rudy Vallee, Helen Parrish and Lon Chaney, Jr. / "Limp-Brained Hotel Manager."

13. IN THE NAVY / Rl. May 30 / 85m / *d* Arthur Lubin / *scr* Arthur T. Horman (*st*) and John Grant / *C*: Bud Abbott, Lou Costello, Dick Powell and The Andrews Sisters / "Dizzy," a not-too-bright sailor.

14. TIGHT SHOES / Rl. June 13 / 75m / *d* Albert S. Rogell / *st* Damon Runyan / *scr* Leonard Spigelgass and Art Arthur / *C*: John Howard and Binnie Barnes / "Okay," Swifty's (Broderick Crawford) confidante and bodyguard.

15. SAN ANTONIO ROSE / Rl. June 20 / 63m / *d* Charles Lamont / *st* Jack Lait, Jr. / *scr* Hugh Wedlock, Jr., Howard Snyder and Paul Gerard Smith / *C*: Jane Frazee and Robert Paige / "Benny the Bounce," Jigsaw's (Lon Chaney, Jr.) partner and shadow.

16. HIT THE ROAD / Rl. June 27 / 61m / *d* Joe May / *scr* Robert Lee Johnson (*st*) and Brenda Weisberg / *C*: Billy Halop, Huntz Hall and the Dead End Kids / "Dingbat," Creeper's sidekick who hears and sees but never speaks.

17. HOLD THAT GHOST / Rl. Aug. 8 / 86m / *d* Arthur Lubin / *scr* Robert Lees (*st*), Fred

Rinaldo (*st*) and John Grant / *C*: Bud Abbott, Lou Costello, Richard Carlson, Evelyn Ankers and Joan Davis / "Wise-Cracking Soda Jerk" / *WT: Oh, Charlie.*

18. HELLZAPOPPIN' / Rl. Dec. 26 / 84m / *d* H.C. Potter / *scr* Nat Perrin (*st*) and Warren Wilson / *C*: Ole Olsen, Chic Johnson, Martha Raye and an array of Universal contract players / "Louie," an awfully dumb movie projectionist / *FN*: Fred Sanborn appears in a bit role as a stooge.

19. THE INVISIBLE WOMAN / Rl. Dec. 27 / 73m / *d* A. Edward Sutherland / *st* Kurt Siodmak and Joe May / *scr* Robert Lees, Fred Rinaldo and Gertrude Purcell / *C*: John Barrymore, John Howard and Charles Ruggles / "Hammerhead Frankie."

1942
20. BUTCH MINDS THE BABY / Rl. Mar. 20 / 75m / *d* Albert S. Rogell / *st* Damon Runyan / *scr* Leonard Spigelgass / *C*: Virginia Bruce, Broderick Crawford and Dick Foran / "Squinty Sweeny," a near-sighted henchman.

21. MISSISSIPI GAMBLER / Rl. Apr. 17 / 60m / *d* John Rawlins / *st* Al Martin and Marion Orth / *scr* Al Martin and Roy Chanslor / *C*: Kent Taylor and Frances Langford / "Milton Davis."

22. THE STRANGE CASE OF DR. RX / Rl. Apr. 17 / 66m / *d* William Nigh / *scr* Clarence Upson Young / *C*: Patric Knowles, Anne Gwynne and Lionel Atwill / "Sergeant Sweeney," a police department stuporsleuth / *WT: Dr. RX.*

23. PRIVATE BUCKEROO / Rl. June 12 / 68m / *d* Edward F. Cline / *st* Paul Gerard Smith / *scr* Edmund Kelso and Edward James / *C*: The Andrews Sisters, Dick Foran and Joe Lewis / "Sergeant 'Mugsy' Shavel," a hard-boiled commanding officer / *FN*: Sidney Miller, director of *The Three Stooges Scrapbook* (1960), appears briefly as the "2nd Jeep Driver."

24. PITTSBURGH / Rl. Dec. 11 / 98m / *d* Lewis Seiler / *st* George Owen / *C*: Marlene Dietrich, Randolph Scott and John Wayne / "Shorty" / *FN*: Watch for Bess Flowers in a bit role.

25. ARABIAN NIGHTS / Rl. Dec. 25 / Technicolor / 86m / *d* John Rawlins / *st scr* Michael Hogan / *C*: Jon Hall, Maria Montez, Sabu, Leif Erikson and Billy Gilbert / "Sinbad," one of Scheherazade's associates in a traveling circus.

1943
26. HOW'S ABOUT IT? / Rl. Feb. 5 / 61m / *d* Erle C. Kenton / *scr* Mel Ronson / *C*: The Andrews Sisters, Grace McDonald and Robert Paige / "Alf," a process server who romances Patty Andrews / *WT: Solid Senders.*

27. IT AIN'T HAY / Rl. Mar. 19 / 80m / *d*

Erle C. Kenton / *st* Damon Runyan / *scr* Allen Boretz and John Grant / *C*: Bud Abbott, Lou Costello and Grace McDonald / "Umbrella Sam" / *WT: Hold Your Horses / FN*: A remake of *Princess O'Hara* (1935).

28. KEEP 'EM SLUGGING / Rl. Apr. 2 / 66m / *d* Christy Cabanne / *st* Edward Handler and Robert Gordon / *scr* Brenda Weisberg / *C*: Huntz Hall, Bobby Jordan, Gabe Dell and the Dead End Kids / "Binky."

29. CRAZY HOUSE / Rl. Oct. 8 / 80m / *d* Edward F. Cline / *scr* Robert Lees and Fred Rinaldo / *C*: Ole Olsen, Chic Johnson, Martha O'Driscoll and Patric Knowles / "Mumbo," a wandering character / *FN*: Fred Sanborn plays "Jumbo."

30. STRICTLY IN THE GROOVE / Rl. Nov. 20 / 60m / *d* Vernon Keays / *scr* Kenneth Higgens and Warren Wilson / *C*: Richard Davies, Mary Healy, Leon Errol, Franklin Pangborn and Ozzie Nelson / "Pops," a campus character who becomes manager of the band.

1944
31. THREE OF A KIND / Rl. July 22 by Monogram / 65m / *d* D. Ross Lederman *scr* Earle Snell and Arthur Caesar / *C*: Billy Gilbert, Maxie Rosenbloom, Helen Gilbert and June Lang / "Shemp" / *aka Cooking up Trouble FN*: The first of three films with Billy Gilbert, Shemp Howard and Maxie Rosenbloom.

32. MOONLIGHT AND CACTUS / Rl. Sept. 8 / 60m / *d* Edward F. Cline / *scr* Eugene Conrad and Paul Gerard Smith / *C*: The Andrews Sisters and Leo Carrillo / "Punchy."

33. THE STRANGE AFFAIR / Rl. Oct. 5 by Columbia / 78m / *d* Alfred E. Green / *scr* Oscar Saul, Eve Greene and Jerome Odlum / *C*: Allyn Joslyn, Evelyn Keyes, Marguerite Chapman, Edgar Buchanan and Nina Foch "Laundry Truck Driver."

34. CRAZY KNIGHTS / Rl. Dec. 8 (*aka* Jan. 13, 1945) by Monogram / 63m / *d* William Beaudine / *scr* Tim Ryan / *C*: Billy Gilbert, Maxie Rosenbloom, Tim Ryan and Jayne Hazard / "Shemp" / *WT: Murder in the Family / aka Ghost Crazy / FN*: The second in a series of films starring Gilbert, Howard and Rosenbloom.

1945
35. TROUBLE CHASERS / Rl. June 2 by Monogram / 62m / *d* Lew Landers / *scr* George Plympton and Ande Lamb / *C*: Billy Gilbert, Maxie Rosenbloom and Patsy Moran / "Shemp" / *WT: Here Comes Trouble / FN*: The last film in the Gilbert, Howard and Rosenbloom series.

1946
36. THE GENTLEMAN MISBEHAVES / Rl. Feb. 28 by Columbia / 74m / *d* George Sherman / *st* Robert Wyler and John B. Clymer / *scr* Robert Wyler and Richard

One-sheet for *Dizzy Yardbird*, with Joe Besser.

JOE'S A ONE-MAN ARMY OF LAUGHS AND HOWLS!

JOE BESSER in DIZZY YARDBIRD

DICK WESSEL · EMIL SITKA
Produced and Directed by JULES WHITE
— A COLUMBIA SHORT-SUBJECT PRESENTATION

Weill / C: Robert Stanton, Osa Massen, Hillary Brooke, Frank Sully and Sheldon Leonard / "Marty" / WT: *Lullaby of Broadway*.

37. ONE EXCITING WEEK / Rl. June 8 by Republic / 69m / d William Beaudine / st Dennis Murray / scr Jack Townley and John K. Butler / C: Al Pearce, Pinky Lee and Jerome Cowan / "Marvin" / FN: A reviewer for the *Independent Film Journal* cautioned exhibitors to "keep this one (film) in the sticks."

38. DANGEROUS BUSINESS / Rl. June 20 by Columbia / 59m / d D. Ross Lederman / st Harry J. Essex / scr Hal Smith / C: Forrest Tucker, Gerald Mohr, Lynn Merrick, Gus Schilling and Frank Sully / "Monk."

39. BLONDIE KNOWS BEST / Rl. Oct. 17 by Columbia / 69m / d Abby Berlin / scr Edward Bernds / C: Penny Singleton, Arthur Lake, Larry Simms and Marjorie Kent / "Jim Gray."

1949
40. AFRICA SCREAMS / Rl. May 27 by United Artists / 79m / d Charles Barton / st scr Earl Baldwin / C: Bud Abbott, Lou Costello, Hillary Brooke, Max Baer, Buddy Baer, Joe Besser, Clyde Beatty, Frank Buck and Bobby Barber / "Gunner," a sharpshooter who can't see past his own nose.

Stooges historian Sal Cincotta reports that Shemp also appeared in *Murder Over New York*, a 1940 Charlie Chan feature for 20th Century-Fox.

JOE BESSER
Columbia Shorts
1938
1. CUCKOORANCHO / All-Star Comedy Series / Rl. Mar. 25 / 16½m / d Ben K. Blake / st I.A. Jacoby / CNA / "Wanderer" mistaken by an impoverished hacienda owner for an American millionaire / FN: Filmed in New York.

1949
2. WAITING IN THE LURCH / All-Star Comedy Series / Rl. Sept. 8 / 16m / d Edward Bernds / st scr Elwood Ullman / C: Christine McIntyre, Vernon Dent, Rodney Bell, James Logan, Andre Pola, Charles Hamilton and Joe Palma / "Eric Loudermilk Potts," a groom who almost misses his own wedding because he's addicted to chasing fire engines / WT: *Left in the Lurch*.

1950
3. DIZZY YARDBIRDS / Joe Besser Series / Rl. Mar. 9 / 17m / d Jules White / st scr Felix Adler / C: Dick Wessell, Brian O'Hara, Jessie Arnold, Bill Wallace, Jim Brown, Mick Arnow and Emil Sitka / "Homer," an Army recruit who does everything wrong.

1951
4. FRAIDY CAT / Joe Besser Series / Rl. Dec. 13 / 16m / d scr Jules White / st Felix Adler / C: Jim Hawthorne, Steve Calvert, Tom Kennedy, Joe Palma and Eddie Baker /

"Detective" / WT: *Silly Sleuths* / SD: 4 (M 7/23 to TH 7/26/51) / FN: A remake of the Stooges' *Dizzy Detectives* (2/5/43). Joe Besser was paid $1500 for four days work.

1952
5. AIM, FIRE, SCOOT / Joe Besser Series / Rl. Mar. 13 / 16m / d Jules White / st scr Felix Adler / C: Jim Hawthorne, Angela Stevens, Henry Kulky and Heinie Conklin / "Soldier in the Starvanian Army" / WT:

Joe Besser puckering up to Angela Stevens as comic straightman Jim Hawthorne looks on in a scene from, *Aim, Fire, Scoot* (1951).

Daffy Draftees / SD: 3 (M 10/22 to W 10/24/51).

6. CAUGHT ON THE BOUNCE / Joe Besser Series / Rl. Oct. 9 / 16m / d Jules White / st scr Felix Adler / C: Maxine Gates, Esther Howard and Edward Coch, Jr. / "Trailerhome Owner" who needs $2500 or the mortgage will be foreclosed / WT: *Gullible's Travels$* / SD: 3 (M 4/28 to W 4/30/52).

1953
7. SPIES AND GUYS / Joe Besser Series / Rl. Apr. 9 / 16½m / d Jules White / st scr Felix Adler / C: Angela Stevens and Emil Sitka (in two roles) / "Soldier in the Republic of Yugonutzland Army" / SD: 3 (T 2/3 to TH 2/5/53).

1954
8. THE FIRE CHASER / Joe Besser Series / Rl. Sept. 30 / 16m / d Jules White / st Elwood Ullman / scr Jack White / C: Christine McIntyre, Vernon Dent, Rodney Bell, James Logan, Andre Pola, Charles Hamilton and Joe Palma / "Eric Loudermilk Potts," a man whose fiancee cancels their wedding plans because he has a habit of chasing fire engines / SD: 1 (TH 7/8/54) / FN: A reworking, with stock footage, of *Waiting in the Lurch* (9/8/49).

1955
9. G.I. DOOD IT / Joe Besser Series / Rl. Feb. 17 / 16m / d Jules White / st Felix Adler / scr Jack White / C: Dick Wessell, Emil Sitka and Phil Van Zandt / "Homer," an Army draftee who recovers some stolen documents and is promoted to sergeant / SD: 1 (W 8/25/54) / FN: A reworking, with stock footage, of *Dizzy Yardbirds* (3/9/50).

10. HOOK A CROOK / Joe Besser Series / Rl. Nov. 24 / 18m / d Jules White / st Felix Adler / scr Jack White / C: Jim Hawthorne, Steve Calvert, Tom Kennedy, Joe Palma, Eddie Baker, Dan Blocker, Lela Bliss and Barbara Bartay (both in new footage) / "Detective" / WT: *Daffy Detectives* / FN: A reworking, with stock footage, of *Fraidy Cat* (12/13/51), which is a remake of the Stooges' *Dizzy Detectives* (2/5/43).

1956
11. ARMY DAZE / Joe Besser Series / Rl. Mar. 22 / 16½m / d Jules White / st Felix Adler / scr Jack White / C: Jim Hawthorne, Angela Stevens, Henry Kulky and Heinie Conklin / "Soldier in the Starvanian Army" / WT: *Army Days* and *Whacky in Khaki* / SD: 1 (TH 10/6/55) / FN: A reworking, with stock footage, of *Aim, Fire, Scoot* (3/13/52).

Miscellaneous Shorts
1953
1. A DAY IN THE COUNTRY / Lippert Pictures' 3-D Featurette Series / Rl. Mar. 13 / 3-D Anscocolor / 15m / p Jack Rieger / CNA / Joe narrates the story of two young country boys' daily activities / PS: In an interview, Joe Besser vividly remembered the closing shot in this unusual production: "They show

a close-up of a cow's derriere (in 3-D) over which I say, 'Well folks, this looks like 'The End!'"

Feature Films

1940
1. HOT STEEL / Rl. May 24 by Universal / 64m / *d* Christy Cabanne / *scr* Clarence Upson Young and Maurice Tombragel (*st*) / *C*: Richard Arlen, Andy Devine and Peggy Moran / "Siggie Landers."

1944
2. HEY, ROOKIE! / Rl. Apr. 6 by Columbia / 74m / *d* Charles Barton / *scr* Henry Myers, Edward Eliscu and Jay Gorney / *C*: Ann Miller, Larry Parks and Jack Gilford / "Pudge Pfeiffer" / *FN*: Joe reenacts his famous *Army Drill* routine. A critic for *Daily Variety* wrote "Joe Besser's comic antics will keep audiences titterpated."

1945
3. EADIE WAS A LADY / Rl. Jan. 23 by Columbia / 67m / *d* Arthur Dreifuss / *st scr* Monty Brice / *C*: Ann Miller, Jeff Donnell

and Jimmy Little / "Professor Dingle" / *WT*: *Lady Known As Lou.*

1946
4. TALK ABOUT A LADY / Rl. Mar. 28 by Columbia / 71m / *d* George Sherman / *st* Robert D. Andrew and Barry Trivers / *scr* Richard Weil and Ted Thomas / *C*: Jinx Falkenburg, Forrest Tucker, Trudy Marshall, Richard Lane and Jimmy Little / "Roly Q. Entwhistle," Falkenburg's guardian in her florist shop / *WT*: *Duchess of Broadway.*

1948
5. FEUDIN,' FUSSIN,' AND A-FIGHTIN' / Rl. July by Universal / 78m / *d* George Sherman / *scr* D.D. Beauchamp / *C*: Donald O'Connor, Marjorie Main and Percy Kilbride / "Sharkey Dolan," Sheriff of Rimrock / *WT*: *The Wonderful Race at Rimrock* / *FN*: Stooge villains Kenneth MacDonald and Gene Roth are featured in supporting roles.

1949
6. AFRICA SCREAMS / Rl. May 27 by United Artists / 79m / *d* Charles Barton / *scr*

Earl Baldwin / *C*: Bud Abbott, Lou Costello, Hillary Brooke, Max Baer, Buddy Baer, Shemp Howard, Clyde Beatty, Frank Buck and Bobby Barber / "Harry," the butler.

1950
7. WOMAN IN HIDING / Rl. Jan. by Universal / 92m / *d* Michael Gordon / *scr* Oscar Saul / *C*: Ida Lupino, Howard Duff and Stephen McNally / "Fat Salesman."

8. JOE PALOOKA MEETS HUMPHREY / Rl. Feb. by Monogram / 65m / *d* Jean Yarbrough / *scr* Henry Blanfort / *C*: Leon Errol, Joe Kirkwood, Jerome Cowan and Pamela Blake / "Carlton," the hotel clerk / *WT*: *Joe Palooka in Honeymoon for Five.*

9. OUTSIDE THE WALL / Rl. Mar. by Universal / 80m / *d scr* Crane Wilbur / *C*: Richard Basehart and Marilyn Maxwell / "Chef," in a bit role.

10. THE DESERT HAWK / Rl. Aug. by Universal / Technicolor / 77m / *d* Frederick De Cordova / *scr* Aubrey Weisberg, Jack Pollexfen and Gerald Drayson Adams / *C*: Yvonne De Carlo, Richard Greene, George Macready and Rock Hudson / "Sinbad," Aladdin's (Jackie Gleason) sidekick / *FN*: According to the *Hollywood Citizen-News*, "Joe Besser and Jackie Gleason do beautifully as comic sidekicks."

1953
11. I, THE JURY / Rl. Aug. by United Artists / 3-D / 87m / *d scr* Harry Essex / *st* Mickey Spillane / *C*: Biff Elliott, Preston Foster and Peggie Castle / "Elevator Operator."

12. SINS OF JEZEBEL / Rl. Sept. 4 by Lippert / Anscocolor / 74m / *d* Reginald LeBorg / *scr* Richard Landau / *C*: Paulette Goddard and George Nader / "Yonkel," a chariot man.

1955
13. ABBOTT AND COSTELLO MEET THE KEYSTONE KOPS / Rl. Feb. by Universal / 79m / *d* Charles Lamont / *st* Lee Loeb / *scr* John Grant / *C*: Bud Abbott, Lou Costello, Fred Clark, Lyn Bari and Mack Sennett / "Hunter," a bit role.

14. HEADLINE HUNTERS / Rl. July by Republic / 70m / *d* William Whitney / *scr* Frederic Louis Fox and John K. Butler / *C*: Rod Cameron and Ben Cooper / "The Coroner."

1956
15. TWO GUN LADY / Rl. Oct. 15 by Associated Film Releasing / 75m / *d st* Richard H. Bartlett / *scr* Norman Jolley / *C*: Peggy Castle, William Talman and Marie Windsor / "Town Drunk."

1959
16. THE PLUNDERERS OF PAINTED FLATS / Rl. Jan. 23 by Republic / Naturama / 70m / *d* Albert C. Gannaway / *scr* Phil

Joe Besser mugging with co-star Ann Miller in *Hey, Rookie!* (1944).

Shuken and John Green / C: Corinne Calvert, John Carroll, Skip Homeier and George Macready / "Andy Heather," Ella's (Bea Benadaret) husband.

17. SAY ONE FOR ME / Rl. June by 20th Century-Fox / DeLuxe Color and Cinema-Scope / 119m / d Frank Tashlin / scr Robert O'Brien / C: Bing Crosby, Debbie Reynolds and Ray Walston / "Joe Greb," Robert Wagner's fourth-rate agent.

18. THE WOODCUTTER'S HOUSE / Never rl. / Walt Disney Productions / "The Green Man," a live-action elf surrounded by animated characters, in a one-reel color screen test for a proposed Disney feature a la *Darby O'Gill and the Little People*.

19. THE ROOKIE / Rl. Dec. by 20th Century-Fox / 84m / d George O'Hanlon / scr Tommy Noonan and George O'Hanlon / C: Tommy Noonan, Peter Marshall and Julie Newmar / "Medic" / WT: *The Last Rookie* / FN: Joe Besser is the only saving grace in this wartime comedy starring the short-lived team of Noonan and Marshall.

20. THE STORY OF PAGE ONE / Rl. Dec. by 20th Century-Fox / 123m / d scr Clifford Odets / C: Rita Hayworth and Gig Young / "Gallagher," owner and operator of Gallagher's Bar / WT: *A Question of Morality*.

1960
21. LET'S MAKE LOVE / Rl. Aug. by 20th Century-Fox / DeLuxe Color and Cinema-Scope / 118m / d George Cukor / scr Norman Krasna / C: Marilyn Monroe, Yves Montand and Tony Randall / "Lamont," a heated joke writer / WT: *The Billionaire*.

1961
22. THE SILENT CALL / Rl. July by 20th Century-Fox / CinemaScope / 63m / d John Bushelman / scr Tom Maruzz / C: Roger Mobley, David McLean and Gail Russell / "Art."

23. THE ERRAND BOY / Rl. Dec. by Paramount / 95m / d Jerry Lewis / scr Jerry Lewis and Bill Richmond / C: Jerry Lewis, Brian Donlevy and Kathleen Freeman / "Studio Projectionist."

1962
24. THE HAND OF DEATH / Rl. May by 20th Century-Fox / d Gene Nelson / scr Eugene Ling / C: John Agar and Paula Raymond / "Gas Station Attendant."

1968
25. WITH SIX YOU GET EGGROLL / Rl. Aug. by National General / Color / 99m / d Howard Morris / scr Gwen Bagni (st), Paul Dubov (st), Harvey Bullock and R.S. Allen / C: Doris Day, Brian Keith, George Carlin and Alice Ghostley / "Chicken Delivery Man."

1969
26. THE COMEBACK / Never Rl. / Cong-

don Films / d scr Donald Wolfe / C: Miriam Hopkins, Gale Sondergaard, John Garfield, Jr., and Minta Durfee Arbuckle "Driver of a Sightseeing Bus" / FN: Joe's role was lensed on 12/19/69.

1970
27. WHICH WAY TO THE FRONT? / Rl. July by Warner Bros. / Color / 90m / d Jerry Lewis / scr Gerald Gardner and Dee Caruso / C: Jerry Lewis, Jan Murray, Kaye Ballard, Paul Winchell and Sidney Miller / "CWO Blanchard," the chief warrant officer / FN: Joe essayed his role for the cameras on W 12/31/69.

1976
28. HEY ABBOTT! / Rl. June by ZIV International / Color / 90m / d Jim Gates / scr Stan Oliver / C: Milton Berle, Steve Allen, Phil Silvers and in black-and-white clips, Bud Abbott, Lou Costello, Sidney Fields, Glenn Strange and Hillary Brooke / Joe reveals the story behind the creation of his character "Stinky" for *The Abbott and Costello Show* in this semi-documentary on the famous comedy duo.

Joe Besser served as an uncredited gag writer on the following film:
1960
1. CINDERFELLA / Rl. Dec. by Paramount / Technicolor / 91m / d Frank Tashlin / C: Jerry Lewis, Ed Wynn and Anna Maria Alberghetti.

Joe Besser also co-starred in a MGM feature (a horse story) as a Dog Catcher but the title of the film is unknown.

Television Films
1969
1. THE MONK / Br. Oct. 21 on ABC in Color / 90m / d George McCowan / st Tony Barrett and characters created by Blake Edwards / C: George Maharis, Janet Leigh, Rick Jason, Carl Betz and Jack Albertson / "Fish Peddler" / Eps: *You Can't Judge a Book*.

JOE DeRITA
Columbia Shorts
1946
1. SLAPPILY MARRIED / All-Star Comedy Series / Rl. Nov. 7 / 16½m / d scr Edward Bernds / st Elwood Ullman and Monty Collins / C: Dorothy Granger, Dick Wessel, Christine McIntyre and Florence Auer / A "Dim-Witted Husband" who is superstitious about Friday the Thirteenth.

1947
2. THE GOOD BAD EGG / Joe DeRita Series / Rl. Mar. 20 / 17m / d scr Jules White / st Al Giebler and Elwood Ullman / C: Dorothy Granger, Norm Olestead, James C. Morton, Emil Sitka, Vernon Dent and Symona Boniface / "Inventor" unhappy about his bachelorhood / SD: 4 (TH 9/12 to SA 9/14 and M 9/16/46) / FN: A remake of Andy Clyde's *Knee Action* (10/7/36), with one stock shot (a book cover entitled *William Tell*) from the same film.

3. WEDLOCK DEADLOCK / Joe DeRita Series / Rl. Dec. 18 / 16m / d Edward Bernds / st Clyde Bruckman / scr Elwood Ullman / C: Christine McIntyre, Charles Williams, Dorothy Granger, Esther Howard and

Joe Besser in his first dramatic role with Robert Wagner in *Say One for Me* (1959).

William Newell / "Eddy," a man whose honeymoon is cut short when his relatives drop in.

1948
4. JITTER BUGHOUSE / Joe DeRita Series / Rl. Apr. 29 / 18m / *d* Jules White / *st scr* Felix Adler / *C*: Christine McIntyre, Emil Sitka, Patsy Moran and the Nov-Elites / "Looney Patient."

Feature Films
1944
1. THE DOUGHGIRLS / Rl. Nov. 25 by Warner Bros. / 102m / *d* James V. Kern / *st* Joseph A. Fields / *scr* James V. Kern and Sam Hellman / *C*: Ann Sheridan, Alexis Smith, Jack Carson, Jane Wyman, Charles Ruggles and Eve Arden / "The Stranger," a man who hasn't slept for two weeks while awaiting a Washington appointment.

1945
2. THE SAILOR TAKES A WIFE / Rl. Dec. 28 by MGM / 91m / *d* Richard Whorf / *scr* Chester Erskin (*st*), Anne Morrison Chapin and Whitfield Cook / *C* : Robert Walker and June Allyson / "Waiter."

1946
3. PEOPLE ARE FUNNY / Rl. Jan. 1 by Paramount / 92m / *d* Sam White / *scr* Maxwell Shane and David Lang (*st*) / *C*: Rudy Vallee, Ozzie Nelson, Helen Walker and Frances Langford / "Comic Bit."

1948
4. CORONER CREEK / Rl. July by Columbia / Cinecolor / 93m / *d* Ray Enright / *scr* Kenneth Gamet / *C*: Randolph Scott, Marguerite Chapman, George Macready, Sally Eilers and Edgar Buchanan / "Bit Role." / *WT: Lawless.*

1958
5. THE BRAVADOS / Rl. July by 20th Century-Fox / DeLuxe Color and CinemaScope / 98m / *d* Henry King / *st* Frank O'Rourke / *scr* Phillip Yordan / *C*: Gregory Peck, Joan Collins, Stephen Boyd and Henry Silva / "Mr. Simms," the hangman / *FN*: A critic for the *Los Angeles Examiner* wrote "on the brighter side-in casting-there is a character in the supporting cast, superbly played by Joe DeRita, who simply must give the first class creeps even the creeps!"

TED HEALY
MGM Short
1933
1. STOP, SADIE, STOP / Never rl. / 12m / *st* Harry Sauber / *C*: Cliff Edwards (Ukelele Ike) / *WT: Singing in the Rain* and *Artist's Studio* / *SD*: 1 (TH 6/8/33) / *FN*: The MGM Legal Archives reports that one print of *Stop, Sadie, Stop* was shipped to New York on July 7, 1933, for a preview but was never returned to the studio. Strangely enough, although the film was never released, a review did appear in *The Motion Picture Herald* (7/22/33): "The first four or five min-

Joe DeRita with co-stars Florence Auer and Christine McIntyre in a scene from *Slappily Married* (1946).

utes of Ted Healy and Cliff Edwards satirically burlesquing *Rain* and *Sadie Thompson* provides a riot of laughter, then the picture shifts into what looks like a pick-up from *Hollywood Revue*, a muchly repeated 'In the Rain, Ready for Love' chorus-boy-girl dance number. The early fun is forgotten in the welter of singing and dancing that affords nothing in the way of novel entertainment."

Feature Films
Unless otherwise noted, films are released by Metro-Goldwyn-Mayer.

1933
1. STAGE MOTHER / Rl. Sept. 29 / 87m / *d* Charles R. Brabin / *scr* John Meehan and Bradford Ropes / *C*: Alice Brady, Maureen O'Sullivan and Franchot Tone / "Ralph Martin."

2. BOMBSHELL / Rl. Oct. 13 / 97m / *d* Victor Fleming / *scr* John Lee Mahin and Jules Furthman / *C*: Jean Harlow, Franchot Tone and Pat O'Brien / "Junior Burns," the lame-brain brother / *aka Blonde Bombshell.*

1934
3. LAZY RIVER / Rl. Mar. 16 / 77m / *d* George B. Seitz / *scr* Lucien Hubbard / *C*: Jean Parker and Robert Young / "Gabby," one of Bill's (Robert Young) stooges.

4. OPERATOR 13 / Rl. June 15 / 86m / *d* Richard Boleslavsky / *st* Robert W. Chambers / *scr* Harvey Thew, Zelda Sears and Eva Greene / *C*: Gary Cooper and Marion Davies / "Doc Hitchcock."

5. PARIS INTERLUDE / Rl. July 27 / 73m / *d* Edwin L. Marin / *scr* Wells Root / *C*: Madge Evans and Robert Young / "Jimmy," the bartender's helper.

6. DEATH ON A DIAMOND / Rl. Sept. 14 / 72m / d Edward Sedgewick / st Cortland Fitzsimmons / scr Harvey Thew, Joseph Sherman and Ralph Spence / C: Robert Young, Madge Evans and Nat Pendleton / "Terry the Umpire" / FN: Healy's role in *Death on a Diamond* garnered him many impressive reviews, including this one from *Daily Variety*: "With Ted Healy and Nat Pendleton, as an umpire and a catcher respectively, they stage a baseball Flagg-Quirt affair, battling all through the film and constantly getting laughs. The picture's strength is practically confined to them. Towards the finish, Healy, never anything but a comic, gets a chance to spread out with a high pressure 'He wuz my pal' crying scene when Pendleton dies. And Healy makes good."

7. THE BAND PLAYS ON / Rl. Dec. 21 / 88m / d Russell Mack / scr Bernard Schubert, Ralph Spence and Harvey Gates / C: Robert Young, Betty Furness, Leo Carrillo and Stuart Erwin / "Joe," a side-street mug / WT: *Backfield*.

1935
8. THE WINNING TICKET / Rl. Feb. 8 / 70m / d Charles F. Riesner / st Robert Pirosh and George Seaton / scr Ralph Spence and Richard Slayer / C: Leo Carrillo and Louise Fazenda / "Eddie," Joe Tomasello's ne'er-do-well hick brother-in-law.

9. THE CASINO MURDER CASE / Rl. Mar. 13 / 85m / d Edward L. Marin / scr Florence Ryerson and Edgar Allen Woolf / C: Paul Lukas, Rosalind Russell and Allison Skipworth / "Sergeant Heath" / FN: Part of the "Philo Vance" series.

10. RECKLESS / Rl. Apr. 19 / 99m / d Victor Fleming / st Oliver Jeffries / scr P.J. Wolfson / C: Jean Harlow and William Powell / "Smiley."

11. MURDER IN THE FLEET / Rl. May 24 / 70m / d scr Edward Sedgewick / C: Robert Taylor and Jean Parker / "Mac O'Neill."

12. MAD LOVE / Rl. July 12 / 83m / d Karl Freund / scr Guy Endore, P.J. Wolfson and John L. Balderston / C: Peter Lorre, Frances Drake and Colin Clive / "Mr. MacDonald," an American newspaper correspondent.

13. HERE COMES THE BAND / Rl. Aug. 30 / 85m / d Paul Sloane / st scr Paul Sloane, Ralph Spence and Victor Mansfield / C: Ted Lewis and Virginia Bruce / "Happy," a member of an Army band / FN: Former Healy stooge Fred Sanborn is cast in a bit role as a comedian.

14. IT'S IN THE AIR / Rl. Oct. 11 / 82m / d Charles F. Riesner / st scr Bryon Morgan and Lew Lipton / C: Jack Benny, Una Merkel and Nat Pendleton / "Chip McGurk" / WT: *Let Freedom Ring* / FN: Stooge imper-

sonator "Skins" Miller from Universal's *Gift of Gab* also appears in a bit role.

1936
15. SPEED / Rl. May 8 / 72m / d Edwin L. Marin / st Milton Krims and Larry Bachman / scr Michael Fessier / C: James Stewart and Wendy Barrie / "Gadget."

16. SAN FRANCISCO / Rl. June 26 / 117m / d W.S. Van Dyke / st Robert Hopkins / scr Anita Loos / C: Clark Gable, Jeanette MacDonald and Spencer Tracy / "Matt" / FN: Healy's stooge replacements James Brewster, Samuel Glasser (Sam Wolfe) and John Pearson appear in bit roles as waiters while Stooge impersonator "Skins" Miller is seen as a "Man on a Stretcher."

17. SING, BABY, SING / Rl. Aug. 21 by 20th Century-Fox / 87m / d Sidney Lanfield / scr Milton Sperling (st), Jack Yellen and Harry Tugend / C: Alice Faye, Adolphe Menjou, Patsy Kelly and the Ritz Brothers / "Al Craven," an agent's assistant.

18. THE LONGEST NIGHT / Rl. Oct. 2 / 51m / d Errol Taggart / st Cortland Fitzsimmons / scr Robert Andrews / C: Robert Young and Florence Rice / "Sergeant."

19. MAD HOLIDAY / Rl. Nov. 13 / 71m / d George B. Seitz / st Joseph Stanley / scr Florence Ryerson and Edgar Allan Woolf / C: Edmund Lowe and Zasu Pitts / "Clarence Hogan," Lowe's Hollywood agent / WT: *The Cock-Eyed Cruise, The White Dragon*, and *Murder in the Chinese Theater*.

1937
20. MAN OF THE PEOPLE / Rl. Jan. 29 / 81m / d Edward L. Marin / st scr Frank Dolan / C: Joseph Calleia and Florence Rice / "Joe," the glut.

21. GOOD OLD SOAK / Rl. Apr. 23 / 67m / d J. Walter Ruben / st Don Marquis / scr A.E. Thomas / C: Wallace Berry and Una Merkel / "Al Simmons," a bootlegger / WT: *The Old Soak*.

22. VARSITY SHOW / Rl. Sept. 4 by Warner Bros. / 80m / d William Keighley / st Warren Duff and Sig Herzig / scr Jerry Wald, Richard Macauley, Dick Whiting and Johnny Mercer / C: Dick Powell, Rosemary and Priscilla Lane / "Williams Williams," a hard-boiled stage manager.

1938
23. LOVE IS A HEADACHE / Rl. Jan. 14 / 73m / d Richard Thorpe / scr Marion Parsonnet, Harry Ruskin, William R. Lippman, Lou Heifetz and Herbert Klein / C: Gladys George, Franchot Tone and Mickey Rooney / "Jimmy Slattery," a publicity promoter.

24. HOLLYWOOD HOTEL / Rl. Jan. 15 by Warner Bros. / 109m / d Busby Berkeley / scr Jerry Wald (st), Maurice Leo (st) and

Richard Macauley / C: Dick Powell, Rosemary and Lola Lane, Hugh Herbert and Glenda Farrell / "Fuzzy."

Ted Healy also reportedly appeared in *Wise Guys Prefer Brunettes* (1926, Hal Roach).

ADDENDA
Moe Howard:
GIVE ME A JOB (1933). Now considered Moe's first film appearance since *Soup to Nuts* with Ted Healy. A musical/dialogue public service film performed in rhyme to promote President Roosevelt's NRA

Larry Fine:
STAGE MOTHER (1933. MGM feature. Until now it was thought he never made any solo appearance in a commercially released film

Shemp Howard:
SO YOU WON'T T-T-T-TALK (1934). Vitaphone short.
NOT GUILTY ENOUGH (1938). Columbia short.
ANOTHER THIN MAN (1939) MGM feature.
MURDER OVER NEW YORK (1940). 20th Century-Fox. Since reporting this, we have now gotten official confirmation to his appearance.
ROAD SHOW (1941). Hal Roach/United Artists feature.
CRACKED NUTS (1941). Universal feature.

Joe Besser:
Also made an appearance in an episode of TV's "Peter Gunn."

Joe DeRita:
HIGH SCHOOL HERO (1946). Monogram feature from The Teen Agers film series. Played "Tiny," proprietor of ice cream emporium.

Ted Healy:
WISE GUYS PREFER BRUNETTES (1926). Hal Roach short.
LA FIESTA SANTA BARBARA (1935) MGM short. Directed by Stan Laurel.

The Three Stooges:
HOLLYWOOD ON PARADE (1932). Spotlite Video, division of Republic Pictures. Features Healy and Stooges in cameo.

Two more *Screen Snapshots* appearances:
Screen Snapshots (Series #6). Released January 31, 1936. Appear at benefit for Sid Grauman's Chinese Theater.
Screen Snapshots (Series #7). Released February 28, 1936. Seen Clowning around with Victor McLaglen in an out-take from *The Captain Hates the Sea*, a 1934 Columbia feature in which the four of them appear.